Romania

WORLD BIBLIOGRAPHICAL SERIES

General Editors:
Robert G. Neville (Executive Editor)
John J. Horton

Robert A. Myers   Hans H. Wellisch
Ian Wallace   Ralph Lee Woodward, Jr.

John J. Horton is Deputy Librarian of the University of Bradford and was formerly Chairman of its Academic Board of Studies in Social Sciences. He has maintained a longstanding interest in the discipline of area studies and its associated bibliographical problems, with special reference to European Studies. In particular he has published in the field of Icelandic and of Yugoslav studies, including the two relevant volumes in the World Bibliographical Series.

Robert A. Myers is Associate Professor of Anthropology in the Division of Social Sciences and Director of Study Abroad Programs at Alfred University, Alfred, New York. He has studied post-colonial island nations of the Caribbean and has spent two years in Nigeria on a Fulbright Lectureship. His interests include international public health, historical anthropology and developing societies. In addition to *Amerindians of the Lesser Antilles: a bibliography* (1981), *A Resource Guide to Dominica, 1493-1986* (1987) and numerous articles, he has compiled the World Bibliographical Series volumes on *Dominica* (1987), *Nigeria* (1989) and *Ghana* (1991).

Ian Wallace is Professor of German at the University of Bath. A graduate of Oxford in French and German, he also studied in Tübingen, Heidelberg and Lausanne before taking teaching posts at universities in the USA, Scotland and England. He specializes in contemporary German affairs, especially literature and culture, on which he has published numerous articles and books. In 1979 he founded the journal *GDR Monitor*, which he continues to edit under its new title *German Monitor*.

Hans H. Wellisch is Professor emeritus at the College of Library and Information Services, University of Maryland. He was President of the American Society of Indexers and was a member of the International Federation for Documentation. He is the author of numerous articles and several books on indexing and abstracting, and has published *The Conversion of Scripts and Indexing and Abstracting: an International Bibliography*, and *Indexing from A to Z*. He also contributes frequently to *Journal of the American Society for Information Science*, *The Indexer* and other professional journals.

Ralph Lee Woodward, Jr. is Professor of History at Tulane University, New Orleans. He is the author of *Central America, a Nation Divided*, 2nd ed. (1985), as well as several monographs and more than seventy scholarly articles on modern Latin America. He has also compiled volumes in the World Bibliographical Series on *Belize* (1980), *El Salvador* (1988), *Guatemala* (Rev. Ed.) (1992) and *Nicaragua* (Rev. Ed.) (1994). Dr. Woodward edited the Central American section of the *Research Guide to Central America and the Caribbean* (1985) and is currently associate editor of Scribner's *Encyclopedia of Latin American History*.

VOLUME 59

Romania

Revised Edition

Peter Siani-Davies
and
Mary Siani-Davies

Compilers

CLIO PRESS
OXFORD, ENGLAND · SANTA BARBARA, CALIFORNIA
DENVER, COLORADO

British Library Cataloguing in Publication Data

Siani-Davies, Peter
Romania – Rev. Ed. – (World bibliographical series; v. 59)
1. Romania – Bibliography
I. Title   II. Siani-Davies, Mary
016.9′498

ISBN 1–85109–244–7

ABC-CLIO Ltd.,
Old Clarendon Ironworks,
35A Great Clarendon Street,
Oxford OX2 6AT, England.

ABC-CLIO Inc.,
130 Cremona Drive,
Santa Barbara,
CA 93117, USA.

Designed by Bernard Crossland.
Typeset by Columns Design Ltd., Reading, England.
Printed in Great Britain by print in black, Midsomer Norton.

THE WORLD BIBLIOGRAPHICAL SERIES

This series, which is principally designed for the English speaker, will eventually cover every country (and some of the world's principal regions and cities), each in a separate volume comprising annotated entries on works dealing with its history, geography, economy and politics; and with its people, their culture, customs, religion and social organization. Attention will also be paid to current living conditions – housing, education, newspapers, clothing, etc. – that are all too often ignored in standard bibliographies; and to those particular aspects relevant to individual countries. Each volume seeks to achieve, by use of careful selectivity and critical assessment of the literature, an expression of the country and an appreciation of its nature and national aspirations, to guide the reader towards an understanding of its importance. The keynote of the series is to provide, in a uniform format, an interpretation of each country that will express its culture, its place in the world, and the qualities and background that make it unique. The views expressed in individual volumes, however, are not necessarily those of the publisher.

VOLUMES IN THE SERIES

To our parents

Contents

Contents

Contents

Contents

Introduction

Romania lies in the South-East of Europe. Following the break-up of Yugoslavia and the USSR, the country is now bordered by Hungary, the Ukraine, the Republic of Moldova, Bulgaria and the Federal Republic of Yugoslavia. Romania is one of the larger countries of the region. With a surface area of 238,391 square kilometres it almost equals the United Kingdom in size and its population of 22,810,035 is the seventh highest amongst European countries outside the former Soviet Union.

The geographical position of Romania has played a large part in shaping the dilemmas that have faced the country. Bisected by the Carpathian Mountains, which form a horseshoe within Romania running from the North-East through to the South-West, the country straddles the area between the northern parts of the Balkan Peninsula and the Central European plain. As such it belongs entirely neither to one geographic entity nor to the other, and this physical division is mirrored in the country's history, as the Romanian lands were long split between the Ottoman and Habsburg Empires. Historically, therefore, Romania has faced both east and west and this had led the country to embrace two distinct and not always compatible cultural traditions, both of which have left their mark. From the mid-19th century, those who championed a general westward orientation for Romania gained the ascendancy. However, there always remained an influential strand of intellectual thought within the country which, whilst not totally rejecting the West, argued that western institutions could not be uncritically transferred to a Romanian environment and that, instead, they should be shaped to reflect more indigenous traditions.

After the Second World War, the question of whether Romania should be aligned with east or west was brutally settled by the imposition of communism on the country and its incorporation into the Warsaw Treaty Organization. However, even under communism echoes of the old dilemma could still be felt, as the régime under

Introduction

Nicolae Ceauşescu at first made some attempt to keep avenues to the West open before it finally turned its back on the world and collapsed into autarkic self obsession. The consequences of this were catastrophic for Romania and, now, in the post-communist transition, the country is seeking a new orientation as it struggles to shed the communist past and turn once more towards western structures and institutions.

The many contradictions and ambiguities encompassed in this geography and history have long bathed the Romanian lands with an aura of mystery for those outside the country, providing a space in which the romantic imagination has flourished. It is no coincidence that it was to Transylvania that the Pied Piper was said to have led the children of Hamlyn. For most people this trend towards the fantastic is exemplified by the Dracula myth which, through Bram Stoker's famous novel and through Hollywood, has grown in the popular imagination to frequently overwhelm not only Transylvania but also Romania as a whole. Yet, in the earlier decades of this century, this sense of the extraordinary, which seems to so readily surround the country, was present in a royal soap-opera which at the time scandalized and titillated all of Europe, as the then prince, and future king, Carol II, and his mistress, the Jewish divorcee Madame Lupescu, chose to elope to Paris rather than surrender to his family's demands that they separate. More recently, this trend towards the unreal was further underlined by the extraordinary stories emerging from the last demented years of Ceauşescu's rule and the manner of his savage and abrupt downfall.

The tragedy which was to envelope Romania in the late 1980s only became fully apparent to most of the outside world when the western press began to reveal the true enormity of Ceauşescu's plan of systematization. Under this Orwellian scheme over 5,000 of the country's traditional villages were scheduled to be bulldozed to the ground and their inhabitants forcibly removed to blocks of flats in a network of new agro-towns. Ostensibly, systematization was driven by a desire to rationalize the use of agricultural space and raise the status of rural communities with the aim of both curtailing the flow of young people to the cities and encouraging professional people, especially doctors, to work in the countryside. However, more invidiously, it would also have facilitated social control and eroded the traditional individualism of Romanian peasants.

In fact, only a few villages were actually destroyed and it was within the urban landscape, especially in Bucharest, that Ceauşescu was to do more irreparable damage. Here a large swathe of the city centre was levelled to the ground to allow for the construction of a wide triumphal boulevard and a huge administrative complex, the *Casa Republicii*, which, it is often claimed, is the second largest building in the world after the Pentagon. Such megalomaniac schemes involving so much destruction drew a barrage of criticism from around the world and led to the formation of a number of organizations in the West dedicated to opposing systematization. Activities such as the twinning of western villages with threatened Romanian settlements helped to draw public attention to the wider plight of the Romanian people and forged links which, after the downfall of Ceauşescu, were to provide a springboard for the aid which flooded into the country, much of it from voluntary organizations. After the Revolution, the stories of suffering were all but confirmed by heartbreaking pictures which regularly appeared in the western media of children's homes crammed with gaunt faced 'orphans', some of whom were suffering from AIDS. Such pictures only reinforced the perception that Romania had somehow slipped the bounds of Europe and it was more appropriate to draw parallels between the country's plight and the worst disasters in the Third World.

Systematization was just one aspect of the absurd and distorted world into which Romania plunged in the 1980s. Endemic food shortages, frequent power-cuts, inadequate winter heating and endless queues transformed everyday life into a battle for survival. Only through the trading of favours, bribes and petty theft from the workplace could most foodstuffs and many other scarce goods be secured. In such a world corruption flourished and knowing the 'right people' became the key to survival – a situation encapsulated by the popular paronomasia that the initials PCR stood not for the Romanian Communist Party (Partidul Communist Român) but for connections, acquaintances and relations (*pile, cunoştiinţe şi relaţii*).

Yet, amidst this poverty and suffering Romania was constantly told that it was living through a golden epoch of unparalleled triumphs, as the whole country was bedecked with slogans trumpeting the glories of socialism. Presiding over this earthly utopia and the subjects of an absurd cult in which they were all but deified were Nicolae and Elena Ceauşescu. The cult image was an obvious lie and through it Ceauşescu became not an authentic leader or an example to be imitated but an idol to be obeyed. There was no meaningful relationship between him and society, with the Romanian people remaining mere onlookers or participants dragooned into his spectacles. The result was a false image open to ridicule, which needed, in the end, just one crack in the façade or, as in this case, one glance of consternation during the disruption of the mass meeting Ceauşescu was addressing on 21 December 1989 in Bucharest, for the whole edifice to come tumbling down.

The cult which projected Ceauşescu as supreme leader also marked a real narrowing of the circle of power in Romania. Increasingly the ruling élite became isolated, both at home and abroad, as the Ceauşescus embraced a world view which bore less and less resemblance to reality. When the Revolution of 1989 erupted in Timişoara, the Romanian leader found it easy to persuade himself that the bulk of the population remained loyal and that the demonstrators were, in fact, only a few malcontents incited by foreign enemies. The extent of the country's international isolation was evident from the fact that he believed that the countries behind the unrest were two fellow members of the Warsaw Treaty Organization, Hungary and the Soviet Union. The explosion of popular anger which swept Ceauşescu from power on 22 December 1989 was to show how far this perception differed from reality. Yet, the ruling élite were not the only ones to misread the Revolution. International news reports regularly spoke of over 60,000 dead, when the true figure was just over 1,000. Furthermore, most of these deaths were to occur after the flight of Ceauşescu from Bucharest on 22 December, when *Securitate* agents – said to be orphans raised to be fanatically loyal to the presidential couple – were reported to be fighting a desperate rearguard struggle on the streets of Bucharest against an Army heroically on the side of the people. In reality, the Army had already played a major role in suppressing the demonstrations prior to the fall of Ceauşescu and only after his departure does it seem, alongside the *Securitate*, to have come onto the side of the Revolution. Little credible evidence has been produced to suggest that the deadly assassins really existed and, in fact, virtually all the deaths after 22 December seem to have been the result of mistaken identity, friendly-fire or savage revenge attacks. However, at the time, amidst rumours of massacres of almost unparalleled brutality, Romania, the land of the extraordinary, passed beyond the bounds of normal credibility once again.

History

The Romanians are usually accepted as having entered recorded history at the end of the 6th century BC, when they were known as the *Getae* or *Dacii* (Dacians). Under kings such as Burebista, who was assassinated in 44 BC, the Dacians rose to be strong enough to attract the attention of the Romans. The latter, from AD 43, developed a permanent presence in the Dobrogea on the Black Sea coast, which had long been the site of Greek cities such as Istria. Eventually, under Trajan in AD 101 and 105 Roman armies crossed the Danube and after two fiercely fought wars, in which the last king, Decebalus, committed suicide rather than fall captive, Dacia was made a province of Rome in 106. This victory was marked by two great monuments: Trajan's column in Rome and the

Tropaeum at Adamclissi in the Dobrogea. With the exception of the
Dobrogea, where they continued to rule for several more centuries, the
Romans were to remain in the other Romanian lands for less than 200
years before, under the Emperor Aurelian, in the years 271-75 they
withdrew to two new Dacian provinces south of the Danube.

Despite its brevity, this period of Roman occupation lies at the very
heart of Romanian identity, because the language of the Romanian
people, notwithstanding later borrowings, is still essentially a Latin
tongue and, thus, utterly distinct from that of all near neighbours. How
the Geto-Dacians came to be so thoroughly romanized is still a matter
of intense debate, with the argument clouded by the almost complete
absence of reliable documentary sources until the early Middle Ages.
One school of thought holds that at the time of Aurelian all the Romans
and romanized inhabitants of the province were withdrawn below the
Danube, leaving the Romanian lands to be swept by various invaders
until the Hungarians arrived in the area at the end of the 9th century. In
this scenario, it was not until the Middle Ages, when a romanized
population crossed the Danube from the south, that the Romanians
entered their current lands. As might be expected, this theory has
proved particularly attractive to Hungarian historians, because it
suggests that they are the autochthonous inhabitants of Transylvania.
Other historians, including most Romanians, have tended to counter
this interpretation with an alternative version known as the Dacio-
Roman continuity theory. This holds that the Roman withdrawal was
only partial, involving the legions and administrators but leaving
behind many colonists and other romanized peoples. In the face of
incursions from the East, this population later retreated into the fastness
of the Carpathians mountains, thus, making the Romanians the
autochthonous population (and legitimate occupiers) of the area. The
question of continuity has always been central to Romanian historiography, with the debate becoming particularly impassioned during the
late 1980s following the publication by Hungarian historians of a three-
volume *History of Transylvania* which met a furious riposte from the
Romanian authorities. The question even impinges on the spelling of
the country's name. Those who persist with the spelling 'Rumania',
rather than the 'Romania' adopted by the Romanians themselves,
generally do so because they reject the Dacio-Roman continuity theory
and object to the Roman connotations within the spelling 'Romania'.
The third variant of the name, 'Roumania', once common but now
rarely encountered in English, derives from French influence.

The Danube basin, open to the vast steppes of the East, has always
been vulnerable to invasion, with a succession of peoples at various
times occupying the fertile Romanian lands. For much of modern

Introduction

history the region has been split between the Habsburg, Ottoman and Russian Empires. However, because it was relatively distant from the imperial centres, the same geography that made the Romanian lands vulnerable to occupation also created the space for a number of sovereign entities to survive between these often warring empires. From the Middle Ages there came into existence three autonomous states of Wallachia, Moldavia and Transylvania. The first two, in particular, long existed under the control of a series of native Romanian princes, the best known of whom were Stephen the Great (1457-1504), Michael the Brave (1593-1601), who in 1600 briefly united the three provinces under his rule and, most notorious of all, Vlad Tepeş, a Prince of Wallachia who is frequently associated with Dracula and whose main period of rule was between 1452 and 1462.

After the defeat of the Hungarians at the great battle of Mohács in 1526, Transylvania passed from Hungarian rule to Ottoman vassalage, a status which was quite distinct from Ottoman Hungary or the remaining royal lands. In the 16th century, with the effective ending of Ottoman offensive capabilities, the Transylvanians took advantage of a temporary balance of power between the great empires of the region to carve out real autonomy under a succession of independent princes. Transylvania's signing of the Peace of Westphalia in 1648 is usually seen as signifying a general recognition of its sovereignty. However, this was to be the high point of Transylvania's existence as an autonomous entity because, ironically, it was also this Peace, ending the Thirty Years War, which allowed the Habsburgs to once more turn their attention east, as growing stability within the sprawling Empire allowed for greater bureaucratic control of the periphery. Following the successful repulse of the Turks from the gates of Vienna in 1683, the Austrians advanced into the Principality and seized political control, with Leopold I taking the title of Prince of Transylvania. Although the Transylvanian Diet nominally retained legislative powers and the right to elect the principality's officials, in reality, all important decisions were henceforth made in the Transylvanian Aulic Chancellery founded in Vienna in 1695. Throughout the period of Austrian rule it remained Habsburg policy to treat Transylvania differently from Hungary and this situation remained in force until 1850 when, following the Revolution of 1848, Hungary was incorporated into the unitary administrative system of the Empire and the Hungarian Crown was divided into four separate provinces, including Transylvania. This state of affairs continued until 1867 when, as part of the *Ausgleich*, the Hungarians, who had long cherished Transylvania, were rewarded with its integration into the Magyar state.

xx

To defend their border kingdom the Hungarians introduced a number of colonists into Transylvania, including Székelys and Saxons. The origins of the Székely has long been a source of debate, but it is generally accepted that they constitute an ethnically distinct group closely linked to the Magyars. Certainly, they see their primary identity today as Hungarian. They live in the 'elbow' of the Carpathian Mountains in an area known as the Székelyföld which is centred on the modern Romanian counties of Covasna and Harghita. The Saxon community were first introduced into the area in the 13th century, with their rights being codified in a charter of 1224 by which András II granted them political and religious autonomy within a region of southern Transylvania known as the *Fundus Regius* or *Königsboden*. The Saxons of Transylvania formed a distinct population from the other German settlement of Swabians in the Banat, most of whom arrived in the 18th century and professed Catholicism as opposed to the Protestantism adopted by the Saxons.

A feudal society arose in Transylvania in which power rested in the hands of three *nationes* – Magyars, Székelys and Saxons – but, in reality, the Magyars dominated. The *nationes* maintained an expressly medieval form, comprising only the privileged members of each ethnic group – those who were not nobles or freemen of whatever nationality were excluded. When the idea of the *natio* later became infused with the 19th-century spirit of nationalism, by a semantic trick the concept of nobility, previously equated with *natio*, was transferred to that of the nation. This placed noble values to the fore of the Hungarian community and laid a theoretical base for the exclusion from power of those 'inferiors' outside these three *nationes* in a form of ethnic apartheid. Likewise only the religions of these *nationes*, Catholicism, Lutheranism, Calvinism and Unitarianism, were recognized. The effect of these divisions was to firmly place Romanians of the Orthodox faith, the most numerous but also the poorest inhabitants of the province, on the bottom rung of the ladder with few collective rights and virtually no political voice. This engendered obvious feelings of frustration and bitterness and when, in the late 17th century, the Emperor Leopold, wishing to consolidate the position of the Catholic Church in Transylvania, offered the Orthodox clergy the chance of advancement through the foundation of the Uniate Church, many readily acquiesced.

The Act of Union was signed in 1698 with the constitutional position of the Uniate Church being laid out in the two Leopoldine Diplomas of 1699 and 1701. The Church was Catholic in form but essentially Orthodox in content, except for four key doctrinal points which included recognition of the Pope. Although few of the immediate hopes of the Orthodox clergy were fulfilled, the Uniate church did come to play a key role in fostering Romanian national consciousness within the Habsburg lands. In particular, it spawned the so-called 'Transylvanian School', many of the most prominent members of whom, including Samuel Micu-Clain, Petru Maior, Ion Budai-Deleanu and Gheorghe Şincai, trained as clergy within the Church. They, and their secular successors, propounded a theory of nationality based on the Roman origins of the Romanians and the Latinity of their language. This shaped an identity which gave a noble ancestry to the Romanian intellectuals, who all derived from peasant stock. To their peasant vernacular language, barely able to express the ideas of the Bible let alone the Enlightenment, it offered not only a glorious classical origin steeped in learning but a rich source of new vocabulary. Shaped in the context of the *nationes* it was an ideology for political advancement where social standing was the defining criteria. Later, when the idea of self-determination came to the fore, the sheer numbers of the Romanians became more important and mass mobilization of the peasant population the key to political gain.

Meanwhile Wallachia and Moldavia, from the 15th century, had also fallen under Ottoman suzerainty, although this was at first somewhat intermittent as the ruling princes were prone to swear allegiance to all the neighbouring empires, effectively playing one state off against another. Indeed, even when the Ottomans became dominant, Moldavia and Wallachia were still not fully incorporated into their Empire, retaining instead a discrete status as vassal states. The two Principalities also retained a distinct social structure in which a narrow native boyar élite continued to preside over a poverty-stricken peasantry. Initially this native élite, even under Ottoman rule, continued to supply the princes (*hospodars*) of the two Danubian Principalities, as the provinces were sometimes known. However, in the face of sporadic rebellions, such as that involving the Prince of Moldavia (1710-11) and historian, Dimitrie Cantemir, who openly sided with Peter the Great during a Russo-Turkish War, and the continuing plotting of other *hospodars*, from the mid-18th century, the local princes were supplanted as rulers by Phanariot Greeks.

These were Greeks, or Hellenized Christians, who took their name from the Phanar district of Constantinople, where the Greek Patriarchate had moved following the fall of the city to the Ottoman Turks in 1453. In their capacity as *dragomans* – agents for the Porte in dealings with foreign powers – the Phanariots had amassed considerable wealth and influence. They virtually controlled the Orthodox Patriarchate and, adopting the names of Byzantine princely families, they came to see themselves as successors to the old Imperial tradition.

Their rule in the Danubian Principalities has long been a source of debate. Many historians, often influenced by Mark Philippe Zallones' infamous anti-Phanariot text *Essai sur les Fanariotes* (Marseilles, 1824), in which he roundly condemned their excesses, have portrayed their rule as being utterly rapacious and corrupt. However, others have attempted to present a more balanced picture, stressing that, whilst they may have presided over a period of economic and social stagnation, *hospodars*, of the like of Constantine Mavrocordatos (ruler several times between 1730-1769), did institute important reforms and helped endow institutions such as the Princely Academies of Iaşi and Bucharest, which became the two greatest centres of learning for Christians in the Ottoman Empire.

As Ottoman power began to ebb in Europe and the balance of power shifted, between 1828 and 1834 the Russians occupied the Danubian Principalities. Russian rule was marked by further attempts at reform, especially, during the governorship of Count Pavel Kiselev (1829-34), when a first proto-constitution for the Principalities, the 'Organic Statues', was enunciated. After years of war and unrest, this sought to bring more orderly and predictable rule to the Romanian lands, although, as it was shaped with the aim of strengthening the existing social order and maintaining the privileges of the Boyars, it was far from a revolutionary document. More radical ideas were to come from a different source, as at this time the sons of an increasing number of boyars were turning to France for their education. Their experiences in the West made them aware of the 'backwardness' of their homeland and fired many with a desire to force reform. The new ideas they brought home not only favoured the modern over the traditional but also firmly tilted the cultural orientation of the Danubian Principalities from the Ottoman East towards the West. In 1848, following the pattern seen throughout Europe that year, a group of these young boyars attempted to stage a liberal revolution in Wallachia. The revolution was a dismal failure but it was to give birth to a radical political programme which was slowly to come to fruition over the coming decades.

At the core of this programme was a desire, already espoused by many Romanians, to see the unification of the two Principalities of Wallachia and Moldavia. At first, the omens were not auspicious, but, following the defeat of Russia in the Crimean War, the international environment became more favourable. After a number of disputed elections, in 1859, the same Prince, Alexander Cuza, was chosen to rule in both Principalities, with a joint administration being subsequently established in 1862. Once in office, Cuza instituted a series of major reforms, including the nationalization of the monasteries, but a proposed

Agrarian Law was blocked by parliament. The new Prince responded by suspending the legislature and ruling by decree, but in adopting this course of action he only succeeded in alienating all sides and in 1866 he was toppled by a *coup d'état*. From the turn of the century, another key plank of the Liberal programme, alongside the desire for unification, had been a demand that a foreign prince should rule the country. This was founded on a belief that rivalries within the fractured native élite would always make rule by a native prince unstable – a fact amply demonstrated by the fate of Cuza – and on a long-standing desire to build stronger links with at least one protecting Great Power. Now, after several other candidates had turned down the opportunity of the Romanian throne, Charles (Carol) of Hohenzollern–Sigmaringen was duly installed as Prince of the united principalities but, again, only after the objections of some of the Great Powers had been by-passed by subterfuge, as the new ruler had to travel to his realm incognito on a Danubian steamer across the Austro–Hungarian lands.

The Liberals and the ideas they espoused dominated the political scene in Romania for much of the second half of the 19th century, but there also circulated an influential counter-philosophy founded on the activities of the Junimea intellectual circle which met in Iași. Most of the members of this group were the sons of high boyars, but the most influential, Titu Maiorescu (1840-1917), was the son of a Professor from Craiova. Perturbed by the direction of Romania's development, he and the other Junimists argued that the country should not uncritically adopt foreign (western) forms which had no basis in the native society. In the eyes of the Junimists, without firm foundations such institutions were destined to remain '. . . lifeless creatures, forms without substance, phantoms without bodies, illusions without truth . . .'. The Junimists did not advocate the total rejection of western forms; instead, they argued that to function properly the institutions of the new Romanian state had to be constructed to take into account the country's historical experience and, in particular, its dominant agrarian base. They were not opposed to change but considered that this should be organic and evolutionary rather than revolutionary.

Associated with Junimea there was also a literary circle which included some of the greatest Romanian writers including the national poet, Mihai Eminescu, and the authors and playwrights Ion Luca Caragiale, Ion Creangă and Ion Slavici. Junimea eventually dissolved but the ideas it championed continued to resonate through Romanian history, finding an echo in intellectual movements as diverse as the peasant conservatives who gathered around Nicolae Iorga, the populists and their peasantist successors, and the interwar traditionalists around Nichifor Crainic. It even had more recent, distorted reverberations in the works of the protochronists who legitimized Nicolae Ceaușescu's drive for autarky.

In 1878, at the Congress of Berlin, following the Russo-Turkish war, in which the Romanian Army, commanded by Carol, had fought alongside the Russians in the protracted siege of Plevna, the united Principalities were finally freed from Ottoman suzerainty and recognized as an independent state. In the trading of territory at this time the new state gained northern Dobrogea and the Danube Delta but lost southern Bessarabia, which had again been part of the Romanian lands since 1856, to the Russians. Finally, in 1881, Romania was elevated to the status of a kingdom with Carol being installed as Carol I (1866-1914). Later, success in the Second Balkan War brought the annexation of Southern Dobrogea and following the First World War, which had seen the Romanians straddle the fence of neutrality before eventually coming down on the side of the Allies, the defeat of Austria–Hungary and the collapse of Russia brought the annexation of Transylvania, the Banat, Crișana, Maramureș, Bucovina and Bessarabia. Greater Romania had been established, with the Habsburg lands eventually being officially ceded by the Treaty of Trianon in 1920.

The new Greater Romania was cast in the model of the Allied victors. It was to be a liberal democracy with universal male suffrage. But how was this to function in an overwhelmingly peasant state, where the bulk of the population were completely untutored in democratic procedures? The two main political parties, the National Liberal Party and the National Peasant Party, both won elections in this period, but wild fluctuations in the number of seats held by the parties and the persisting influence of the bureaucracy have led to charges that the system was nothing more than a 'mimic democracy', in which governments were decided before the elections, with the voting only serving to legitimize the choice.

The new state, although ostensibly based on the principle of self-determination, included large minority populations, not only Hungarians and Germans but also Jews. The need, therefore, was to integrate not only the newly conquered territories into the state but also these disparate populations. A period of nation-building followed, largely marked by an intense romanization campaign, in which Romanian nationalism all too readily rose to the fore. To function properly the new state needed an enlarged élite, yet the middle class contained few Romanians, and in the universities a disproportionate number of Jewish students, especially in faculties like medicine, were seen as holding back ethnic Romanians from enrolling. Soon, petty demands that Jewish medical students should only dissect Jewish cadavers and

Introduction

attempts to limit the numbers of Jews attending university, were to spill over into a more general anti-Semitism. Violence and intimidation increased in tandem with the rise of a number of radical right-wing groups. The most prominent of these was the Legion of Archangel Michael founded in 1927 under the charismatic leadership of Corneliu Zelea Codreanu. A military wing, known as the Iron Guard, was established in 1930 and this generally became the common designation used for the whole organization, which exhibited a number of fascist attributes.

After 1930 and the onset of the economic depression, the political scene became even more unstable. Assassinations became relatively common and, amongst others, they claimed the lives of the great historian and man of politics, Nicolae Iorga, and even Codreanu himself. However, amidst this political turmoil and the rise of the radical right, Romania experienced a great cultural flowering during these years which produced figures of such international stature as the sculptor Constantin Brâncuşi and the playwright Eugene Ionescu. Indeed, in some cases the politics of the time and this cultural blooming became linked, as other members of this generation, including the philosophers Emil Cioran and Constantin Noica, and the historian of religions Mircea Eliade, followed the lead of their mentor, the philosopher Nae Ionescu, and dabble in the politics of the radical right.

Eventually, in 1938, the inter-war experiment in democracy was to succumb to Carol II's royal dictatorship, yet, this was to be merely a prelude to worse disasters, as, during the next few years, the country was effectively dismembered by hostile neighbours. Following the Nazi-Soviet pact, which had carved up Eastern Europe into spheres of influence, in June 1940 Stalin unilaterally demanded that Romania cede Bessarabia and Northern Bucovina to the Soviet Union. Under pressure from the Germans, Carol II was forced to concede and these lands passed from Romanian control, so far never to return. In August of the same year, Romania was forced under the Treaty of Craiova to hand Southern Dobrogea back to Bulgaria and, most painfully, a large swathe of northern Transylvania was ceded to Hungary, according to the conditions of the Vienna Diktat (also known by some historians as the Vienna Awards), and under the threat of German military intervention. Faced with this national calamity Carol had little choice but to abdicate in favour of his nineteen-year-old son, Mihai I (Michael I). General Ion Antonescu, a career military officer, was appointed Minster President and under his leadership on 23 November 1940 Romania adhered to the Axis-led Tripartite Pact. At first Antonescu ruled in conjunction with the Iron Guard but, as the Legionary State of 1940-41 collapsed into anarchy, he took dictatorial powers. In June

1941, when Hitler launched his invasion of Russia, Antonescu, without consulting any other members of the government, ordered Romanian troops to cross the River Pruth and join the German advance. Bessarabia and Bucovina were soon recaptured but the Romanian Army continued to move forward well beyond the borders of these lands until they reached the very edge of Stalingrad, where, in the face of the German defeat, they were forced to begin a painful retreat.

The role of Romania in the Second World War is still highly controversial, especially as regards the country's attitude to the persecution of the Jews. Aside from the deaths associated with the Iaşi Pogrom of June 1941, and a number of other isolated events, it seems that most of the Jews left in 'rump Romania' after the partition of the country survived the War. However, in those lands which had been stripped from Romania at the time of the partition, including those areas in the East which were subsequently recaptured, the vast majority of the Jews seem to have perished, with many being shipped to the death camps. The appalling suffering of this time is most poignantly captured in the elegiac verse of Paul Celan, a Jew from Bucovina who did survive the Holocaust – a term which, in its modern usage, is sometimes ascribed to another Jew born in Romania, Elie Weisel.

Under Antonescu the Romanians fought alongside the Germans until 23 August 1944, when in a *coup d'état* organized by the young King Mihai and the leaders of the main political parties, including the Communists – although their role was far less than they later claimed – Antonescu was arrested and Romania overnight deserted Germany in favour of the Allies. Within days of the coup, the Red Army entered Bucharest and for the next half century Romania was to lie firmly behind what Winston Churchill came to dub the Iron Curtain, as initial non-Communist governments gave way, first, to a 'bogus coalition' under Petru Groza and, then, to full Communist control. All opposition was ruthless crushed with most of the old pre-war leadership of the National Liberal Party and the National Peasant Party being incarcerated, and often perishing, in Sighet and other prisons. Finally, in December 1947 the last vestiges of the old order were swept away when, following the forced abdication of King Mihai, Romania was declared a 'People's Republic'.

Communist Romania only knew two effective leaders, Gheorghe Gheorghiu-Dej and Nicolae Ceauşescu. Under their rule the country was irreversibly transformed as it embarked on a process of massive industrialization on the Soviet model. New factories, many in the heavy industry sector, sprouted across what had until then been a largely agrarian land. To man these new factories vast numbers of peasants migrated from the collectivized countryside to the ever-expanding

Introduction

towns and cities, with their new high-rise blocks. The number of urban residents increased from less than a quarter of the population in 1948 to over fifty per cent in 1981, when the figure for the first time exceeded those living in rural areas. Until the late 1970s, Romania enjoyed one of the fastest growth rates in the world and seemed to be on the verge of economic takeoff, but the second oil price shock and the reverberations of the Polish debt crisis, together with Ceauşescu's decision to embark on a crash debt repayment programme, brought the period of growth to a shuddering and apparently terminal halt. The 1980s were a decade of acute crisis for Romania as Ceauşescu squeezed the economy to breaking point to pay off debts. Romania's command economy had always paid little account to questions of supply and demand or to international and domestic market forces. Now, under a régime of stultifying Stalinist orthodoxy, in which all was politically determined by plan, the economy ground to a virtual halt. Ideologically Romania remained locked into a dream of heavy industrialization more suited to the late 19th century than the close of the 20th century and this has proved a difficult legacy to reverse in the painful transition to a market economy.

Prior to 1945, Romania had one of the smallest Communist parties in Eastern Europe and, although membership of the Party grew at a tremendous rate after the War, it remained organizationally weak. To maintain its hold on power it initially relied on the continuing presence of the Red Army in the country and the widespread application of terror on the Soviet model. Thousands were interned and died in forced-labour camps, such as those on the Danube–Black Sea Canal. This grandiose project had been initiated in 1949 but was abandoned in 1953, to be restarted in different circumstances in the 1970s, when it was taken to a successful conclusion. Others were incarcerated in prisons, such as Piteşti, where, in a particularly inhuman régime, the inmates were themselves forced to torture each other. Such practices declined with the death of Gheorghiu-Dej. Under Ceauşescu, although the institutions of terror remained in place, most notably the infamous Department for State Security, better known as the *Securitate*, and the Party ultimately remained answerable to nobody, the mass detentions ceased and the slave labour camps were abandoned. Society remained tightly controlled and censorship continued to exist, but coercion rather than terror became the norm, although any public voicing of opinions contrary to those of the régime still met swift and, sometimes, violent retribution. The result was that by the late 1980s, when the economic crisis made legitimization through material rewards impossible and the charisma of the Ceauşescus had worn totally threadbare, the only effective means of controlling Communist Romania was still fear.

In such a society, in the absence of formal channels of communication – the news each night usually dwelt almost exclusively on the activities of the presidential couple – gossip and rumour tended to reach fantastic proportions. This fact explains, in part, some of the wilder allegations made during the Revolution. In such an atmosphere, mistrust and suspicion naturally predominated. Although the numbers employed by the *Securitate* appear to have been nowhere near the huge figure often quoted, informers were said to be everywhere. Few could be trusted and no conversation could be conducted with a foreigner without constant glances over the shoulder to see who might be listening. This all-encompassing fear is part of the reason why no appreciable dissent surfaced in Romania, except for the brief flowering around the writer Paul Goma in the late 1970s. The indifference shown by much of the western media to conditions inside Romania before the late 1980s, the relative latitude given to intellectuals to publish and the lack of response in a society used to conforming to the dictates of the authorities also help to explain why Romania produced no dissidents of the stature of Vaclav Hável, Lech Wałęsa or even Zheliu Zhelev in neighbouring Bulgaria. This meant that in 1989 no figures of sufficient standing existed to offer an alternative leadership to the clutch of semi-dissident former Communists who did take power. The most prominent of these was Ion Iliescu, a former Central Committee member who had once been tipped as a potential successor to Ceauşescu, before he fell out with the Romanian leader in the early 1970s, although his disgrace was long drawn out and it was not until the 1980s that he finally lost all his Party positions.

The distinct feature of Communist Romania, which separated it from the rest of the Soviet Bloc, was its semi-autonomous foreign policy. Through this the leaders of the country, whilst maintaining Communist orthodoxy at home, sought to present an independent face to the outside world. The roots of this policy are usually traced to the Gheorghiu-Dej era and the rejection of a Soviet-inspired Comecon economic development plan which would have relegated Romania to little more than the bread basket of Eastern Europe. Under Ceauşescu the semi-autonomous stance was further developed, with Romania skilfully using the discord between Moscow and Peking to present itself as an independent voice. This culminated in 1968, when, in his finest hour, the Romanian leader openly denounced the Warsaw Treaty Organization's invasion of Czechoslovakia. Through such behaviour Romania gained political plaudits in the West, as well as invaluable trade agreements, including the much coveted Most-Favoured-Nation trading status with the United States. Ceauşescu was fêted by world leaders. Richard Nixon became the first American President to set foot in

Introduction

communist Eastern Europe when he arrived in Bucharest in 1969, and
the Ceauşescus, when they visited London in 1978, were granted the
exceptional privilege of lodging with the Queen in Buckingham Palace.
Eventually, the semi-autonomous policy was to be rendered null by
Gorbachev's 'new thinking' in foreign policy with its concomitant
opening to the West. Stripped of his status as the 'maverick' of the
Soviet Bloc, Ceauşescu became just another ageing relic of the Stalinist
past as, in an ironic reversal of roles, the Soviet leader became the great
hope of Romanian reformers. In 1988, even the treasured Most-
Favoured-Nation trading status was voluntary renounced to avoid
further Congressional investigation of Romania's appalling human
rights record. As the West turned its attention away from Romania,
Ceauşescu became as isolated abroad as he was at home and the
weakness of his position was laid bear for all to see.

Another factor which distinguished the Ceauşescu régime from most
other Eastern European states was his fervent embrace of nationalism
as a source of legitimization. The cult served not only to establish
Ceauşescu's personal authority in place of the institutional authority of
the Party, but, through the employment of nationalism, it sought to
project the Romanian leader as the very embodiment of his nation,
thereby creating an alternative form of legitimization to compensate for
the weakening of the official ideology of Marxism–Leninism.
Ceauşescu tied the two together in a formulation that held that it was
only through the ideology of Marxism–Leninism and the ending of
class conflict that the true national destiny of Romania could be
achieved.

This renewed stress on Romanian nationalism naturally alienated
many amongst the national minorities and in some cases their
difficulties were exploited for economic gain. The Second World War
had approximately halved the size of both the Jewish and German
populations, the former through the Holocaust and later emigration to
Israel, and the latter through war service and then flight to Germany or
deportations to the USSR. Now, in the Ceauşescu era, both the Israeli
and West German governments began to pay large sums of money to
Romania to allow their co-nationals to leave the country. In particular,
the vast majority of the remainder of the Jewish population was able to
leave under this process and in 1992 there were only 9,107 Jews left in
Romania. More Germans remained, but the changes induced by
Communism had already drastically eroded the traditional bonds that
bound their community together. Thus, despite a late cultural flowering
in the 1970s and 1980s, once the restrictions on movement imposed by
Communism were lifted in 1989, this centuries-old community was to
desert its ancestral homes and return almost *en masse* to Germany.

Today it is estimated that less than 100,000, mostly elderly, Germans remain out of a population that before the Second World War numbered over 600,000. The largest minority population in Romania remains the Hungarians, who, according to the 1992 census, number 1,624,959. During the difficult years of the 1970s and 1980s, the Hungarians felt the growth of assimilatory pressures, and allegations were often made that they, as a community, were facing 'cultural genocide'. As the situation deteriorated inside the country, it naturally came to impinge on the wider question of relations between Romania and neighbouring Hungary. Polemics became particularly intense in the late 1980s, when, for the first time under Communism, the treatment of the Hungarians in Transylvania became a major issue in Hungarian domestic politics, as opposition groups sought to undermine the legitimacy of the ruling Hungarian Socialist Workers' Party by alleging that they had not been sufficiently purposeful in defending their co-nationals in Romania. Publicity about the plight of the Hungarian community helped undermine the Ceauşescu régime abroad. Indeed, it was to be the actions of one Hungarian, namely, Pastor László Tőkés, which sparked the Revolution of 1989, when he refused to comply with a government order demanding that he leave his church and home in Timişoara.

Immediately after the Revolution, it seemed that a new period of co-operation between the Romanian and Hungarian communities would follow. However, the vexed question of minority-language education soon raised its head and this seems to have been the root cause of the subsequent breakdown in relations between the two communities in Transylvania. The renewal of discord created fertile ground for Romanian nationalist groups, such as *Vatra Românească*, and a hardening of attitudes on both sides, eventually, led to inter-ethnic riots in Târgu Mureş in March 1990 which left at least three dead. Subsequently, although the situation in Transylvania has at times been tense, it has generally remained non-violent. Recognizing that strained inter-communal relations in the area would hinder their efforts to join NATO and the EU, both Hungary and Romania have made considerable efforts to improve the atmosphere, and this led in September 1996 to the signing of a historic Romanian-Hungarian reconciliation treaty. Inside Romania, the 1996 elections also brought some signs of greater tolerance, as the main Transylvanian Romanian nationalist party, the Party of Romanian National Unity, did relatively poorly, whilst the chief Hungarian political party, the Democratic Union of Hungarians in Romania, which again attracted virtually the whole of the Hungarian vote, subsequently joined the new government led by the Democratic Convention of Romania.

Introduction

Leaving aside the continuing debate over whether the events of 1989 can best be described as a *coup d'état* or a revolution – the allegation that many of the new leaders of the National Salvation Front, who took power during the Revolution, including Ion Iliescu, were nothing more than a bunch of neo-communists were partly shaped in the hope of removing legitimacy from the ruling régime – in hindsight, it is clear that the events did possess many of the attributes of a revolution. Many of the institutions of the state, including those concerned with law and order, virtually collapsed and there was a degree of mass mobilization, although it seems that only some twenty-five per cent of the adult population actually participated in a revolutionary event defined at the widest extent to include factory meetings. The breakdown of the institutions of the state brought a situation of near anarchy to Romania and the first six months after the Revolution were marked by a desperate struggle by the National Salvation Front to restore a degree of control.

During this period, the new régime was challenged by those who felt excluded from the new order, especially the students, many of whom had been active on the streets, and also the leaders of the old traditional parties that now began to reappear, in particular the National Peasant Party and the National Liberal Party. After the May 1990 election had produced a landslide in the presidential vote for Ion Iliescu, and in the parliamentary vote for the National Salvation Front, this confrontation reached its bloody climax in the infamous descent of the miners of the Jiu Valley into the centre of Bucharest in June 1990. They came to clear a long-running, but peaceful, student demonstration from the central University Square and, in the process, wreaked bloody havoc, beating indiscriminately all those they considered opponents of the régime. Afterwards, they were shamefully thanked for their efforts by President Iliescu.

Subsequently, aside from a return of the miners in September 1991, when they helped oust the Prime Minister, Petre Roman, from office, Romania has remained largely peaceful and remarkably politically stable. The 1992 elections were won by a successor to the National Salvation Front, the Democratic National Salvation Front, and the government installed at this time under Nicolae Văcăriou was to remain in office for its full parliamentary term. Then, in the elections of November 1996, Romania successfully experienced the first peaceful changeover of power since 1937, when the Democratic Convention of Romania, at the heart of which lies the old National Peasant Party, secured power, in alliance with the Union of Social Democrats and the Hungarian Democratic Union of Romania. Even more momentously, Ion Iliescu was replaced as President by a former

Rector of Bucharest University, and erstwhile supporter of the student demonstrators in 1990, Emil Constantinescu.

If the political transition in Romania, after a shaky start, has been surprisingly successful, the progress of economic and social change has often been tortuous and painful. After initial attempts to restructure the economy, the government of the National Salvation Front and its successors, the Democratic National Salvation Front and the Party of Social Democracy in Romania, proved ideologically resistant to hasty change. Eschewing the 'shock therapy' embraced by Poland and other Eastern European states, they favoured a process of slow evolutionary reform. Amongst the arguments advanced to support this policy was that Romanian society, after the years of deprivation under Communism, could not suffer further privations. However, in reality, this policy only prolonged the pain of the transition from Communism to the free-market, as the Romanian economy stagnated, privatization proceeded at a snail's pace and living standards for most of the population plunged. Bloated bureaucracies, on whom the ruling Party for Social Democracy in Romania relied for political support, remained untrimmed, and never far from the surface has been apparently endemic corruption amidst a growing black economy. The new government has promised it will embark on a more radical reform but, as of the time of writing, this has yet to fully materialize.

Fourteen years ago, when Dennis Deletant wrote the preface to the first edition of this book, Romania was entering its darkest hour amidst the final death throes of Communism. Today, despite the many difficulties that still face the country, the future offers more hope than it has for some time. The painful domestic reform process may still have far to go but political freedoms are being consolidated. The last elections were judged by all to be fully 'free and fair' and freedom of speech has produced a diverse and lively media. In the international arena, Romania is both an Associate member of the EU and part of the NATO Partnership for Peace programme. Indeed, after once being considered as having no chance of entering into NATO in the fore-seeable future, Romania only narrowly missed an invitation for first round entry and was considered of sufficient importance to warrant a personal visit from the American President, Bill Clinton, to promise that the door had been left ajar for 1999. Although it is unrealistic to expect Romanian entry into the EU in the near future, the long-term prospects look better, and there can be little doubt that, as the 21st century dawns, Romania has begun to move from the margins of Europe and is well on the way towards taking its rightful place within the European mainstream.

Acknowledgements

This work is not intended to replace the previous volume by Andrea and Dennis Deletant. Instead, it should primarily be seen as an extension of the earlier edition, covering material which has appeared between 1984, when the previous volume was published, and the summer of 1997, when the research for this work was completed. Included in this volume are references to a large number of recent books, chapters from books and articles written in English about Romania, with only a handful of more significant older works being incorporated from the previous edition. Indeed, we were struck by the amount of material we unearthed whilst compiling this volume, and its sheer quantity can be taken as some gauge of the health of Romanian studies in the English-speaking world. We have endeavoured to make the listing of books comprehensive, but for articles and chapters in books we have been more selective. Although we have tried to cover all major works, omissions have no doubt occurred and for these we take full responsibility. With a few very small exceptions – mostly because they were on our bookshelves – all the material was located in the collections of the School of Slavonic and East European Studies (University of London) the British Library of Political and Economic Science at the London School of Economics, University College London, the Institute of Classical Studies (University of London) and the British Library. A number of staff at these institutions have been helpful in locating material and we would like here to acknowledge their assistance, especially, Lesley Pitman at SSEES.

We decided to include in the current volume only a few articles published in Romanian journals, even if they appeared in English. This decision is not intended to be a reflection on their quality or usefulness, but is made solely on practical grounds. It is in part due to the fact that such material is not readily available in many collections outside Romania but it also reflects both the need to save space and the fact that, whilst somebody interested in, for example, Romanian history, would logically consider looking in the *Revue Roumaine d'Histoire* for relevant articles, the same person would not necessarily consider searching in a specialized western journal, which appears to have nothing to do with Romania. Most of the articles listed are, therefore, drawn from journals published in Western Europe or the United States, but to render the volume of maximum use to the reader we have also included in the 'Professional Periodicals' section a list of journals published in Romania which feature articles in English or other major Western European languages.

A number of people have been drawn into assisting with the compilation of this book and, in the process, we hope, enjoyed learning more about Romania than they had perhaps expected. In particular, we would like to thank Dejan Djokić who at a difficult time gave a hand with the compilation of the final manuscript when deadlines loomed. Tudor Nedelcu came to stay in a household working hard on the bibliography – he would probably say that we were totally obsessed by the book – and was then called upon to comment on some of the more obscure margins of Romanian literature. Peter's father, John Davies, also provided comments on a number of travel books on Romania. In Bucharest Brenda Walker enthusiastically discussed the many works by Romanians issued by her publishing house Forest Books and then treated us to a splendid meal. Finally, we would like to mention our editors, Robert Neville and Julia Goddard, who remained ever keen to see this volume completed and whose careful scrutiny, in the case of Julia Goddard, has greatly improved the quality of this work.

The Country and
Its People

Older descriptions

1 **Transylvania: its products and its people.**
Charles Boner.   London: Longmans, Green, Reader & Dyer, 1865.
642p. maps.
This lengthy tome provides an excellent description of Transylvania in the mid-19th century. Beginning with a warning, no less pertinent today, that 'Any traveller in Transylvania will discover the difficulty of obtaining correct information on particular questions, owing to the influence of nationality and of political feeling', the author nevertheless presents an informative book replete with careful observations which are often backed by statistical findings. During his travels, which covered the length and breadth of Transylvania, Boner noted details relating to all the main ethnic groups, but is particularly informative about the Saxon community. Aside from containing a number of attractive woodcuts, the book is also complemented by a particularly useful and full index.

2 **The Danube and the Black Sea: memoir on their junction by a
railway between Tchernavoda and a free port of Kustendjie: with
remarks on the navigation of the Danube, the Danubian provinces,
the corn trade, the ancient and present commerce of the Euxine; and
notices of history, antiquities, &c.**
Thomas Forester.   London: Edward Stanford, 1857. 226p. map.
An interesting curiosity, this book is in fact a piece of propaganda on behalf of the then newly established Danube and Black Sea Railway and Kustendjie Harbour Company. It was written with the specific aim of promoting the commercial benefits of a proposed railway from Bucharest to the new port facilities at Constanţa and of countering the negative, popular idea that the Dobrogea region was a pestiferous swamp riven with cholera. In spite of these ulterior motives the book nevertheless contains much valuable information on the burgeoning wheat trade of the time amidst

1

more fanciful passages which proclaim the tourist potential of the area and suggest that it offers openings for English emigrants. The experiences of one of these early railway builders on the line from Cernovoda to Constanţa, the construction of which began in 1858, is recounted in Henry C. Barkley, *Between the Danube and the Black Sea, or five years in Bulgaria* (London: John Murray, 1876. 313p.).

3 **The land beyond the forest: facts, figures, and fancies from Transylvania.**
Emily Gerard. Edinburgh, London: William Blackwood & Sons, 1888. 2 vols. 1,340p., 2,370p. map.

A classic description of life in 19th-century Transylvania by an expatriate Scotswoman married to an officer in the Austro-Hungarian Army. Written after two years stationed in the region during the early 1880s, this two-volume work offers a spirited and highly informative account of the country and, particularly, the Saxon and Romanian communities. Consciously avoiding the travelogue format, the author instead devotes chapters to different subjects, including the character of the disparate ethnic communities, folk customs, superstitions, peasant life and even an outbreak of arson and murder in Sibiu in 1883.

4 **A Romanian diary, 1915, 1916, 1917.**
Dorothy Kennard. London: Heinemann, 1917. 191p.

Despite the fact that this book is presented as a continuous diary running from October 1915 until June 1917, according to the preface only the period before Romania's entry into the war contains the author's own first-hand account. The remainder, and indeed the vast bulk of this work, was assembled from letters sent by friends who had remained in the country when she was forced to return to England. However, the reader is immediately assured by the author that 'To these latter I have added nothing of my own imaginings and omitted little of the original text'. Since in part it was published to boost Romania's profile during the war, this book is, to a certain extent, propagandist and the true horror of the conflict seldom impinges directly onto its pages. Nevertheless, it is still a lively narrative which captures well the pace of events and offers an interesting glimpse into life in Romania at the time, whether it be under bombing from Zeppelins, treating the wounded in hospital, or fleeing from Bucharest to Iaşi before the advancing enemy armies.

5 **The mirrors of Versailles.**
Elizabeth Kyle. London: Constable, 1939. 345p.

Although a number of years separate the publication of this book from the same author's *Forgotten as a dream* (London: Peter Davies, 1953. 287p.), and despite the fact that they cover apparently dissimilar itineraries, these two books nevertheless both appear to describe the same journey made by this, at the time, popular novelist (real name Agnes Dunlop) through Eastern Europe in the years immediately prior to the Second World War. Both books contain lengthy sections recording the author's experiences in Romania: in *The mirrors of Versailles*, p. 85-184 and in *Forgotten as a dream*, p. 205-82. However, although the same characters appear in both accounts, it is noticeable that the details often vary, sometimes to a striking degree, and it would therefore seem that, whilst the earlier book is largely a piece of reportage, with a note stating that extracts had already appeared in various newspapers, the later book may have been reworked to give it a more zestful hue. Apart from the information they contain about the Saxon community, these books also provide an insight into the intensity of the Romanian-Hungarian dispute over Transylvania at the time and certainly the author is not the first traveller to the area to note: 'I realised now, for the first time, that all the stories about Rumania and the Rumanians fed to me by the Hungarians had actually shaken my nerve'.

6 Romania: the border land of the Christian and the Turk, comprising adventures of travel in Eastern Europe and Western Asia.
James O. Noyes. New York: Rudd & Carleton, 1858. 520p.

A large section (p. 59-239) of this account by an American traveller of his passage through the lower Danubian lands in the middle of the 19th century is concerned with his time in the Danubian Principalities. Often a distillation of information from other sometimes highly prejudiced and even far-fetched sources, the book is nonetheless not without interest.

7 Journal of a residence in the Danubian Principalities, in the winter and autumn of 1853.
Patrick O'Brien. London: Richard Bentley, 1854. 181p.

This slender account of a single winter spent in Wallachia during the Russian military occupation of the Danubian Principalities contains some interesting and often surprising information, such as the author's encounter with English-run meat processing plants at Galați and Calafat. However, the main emphasis throughout is on the military situation and, as it was written on the eve of the Crimean war, the tone is often markedly anti-Russian. At one point the author gives a description of the aftermath of a battle at Oltanița between the Russians and the Turks and of the prolonged skirmishing that followed along the banks of the Danube. Not without traces of humour, the book is most useful for offering an alternative to some of the prevailing views of the time which have often seeped into later histories. Thus, O'Brien cautions: 'It has become a fashion to speak of the Moldo-Wallachians with contempt, to scoff at their institutions, and to depict them as sunk in immorality, profligacy and ignorance. . . . As far as the inhabitants of Moldo-Wallachia are concerned, a more docile, hardworking, and honest people is not to be found. Such things as drunken riot are unknown, and robbery by a Wallachian is far from common'.

8 Three years in Roumania.
J. W. Ozanne. London: Chapman & Hall, 1878. 227p.

The author spent three years in Bucharest from 1870 and his principal aim in writing this book was to produce a balanced account of a country that was little known in England. Although in places his verdicts may be a little harsh, by and large the author amply succeeds in his task as he gives a fascinating description of the country which is rich in detail and enlivened by numerous personal anecdotes. After an account of his journey to Romania and first impressions of Bucharest, he discusses the attributes of each social group, lingering particularly on the peccadilloes of the boyar class before outlining the largely foreign middle-class and the sturdy virtues of the Romanian peasantry. Descriptions follow of the country's geography, economy, institutions of government, religion, customs and beliefs, and history.

9 **Hungary and Transylvania: with remarks on their condition, social, political, and economical.**
John Paget. London: John Murray, 1839. 2 vols. 1,483p. 631p.
The second volume contains an excellent description of Tranylvania in the early 19th century. Written by a British expatriate, who married a Magyar Baroness and managed her estates around Cluj, the work fully covers the remit of its title by describing in great detail the political, economic and social background of the land as the author passes on a lengthy journey down the Danube, to the Banat and, thence, across Transylvania. Enormously influential in its day, this book virtually introduced the area to the British public and was instrumental in presenting Hungary as a progressive centre of reform in Central Europe.

10 **Roumania in light and shadow.**
Ethel Greening Pantazzi. London: Fisher Unwin, 1921. 279p.
Relating the experiences of a Canadian woman who married a Romanian naval officer, this book is arranged like a diary, providing a month-by-month description of the years between 1909 and 1919. The first section, entitled 'light', is a lively and engrossing account of everyday life in Galați before the war. It includes accounts of the author's travels through the Romanian countryside and her involvement in establishing a kindergarten for the children of working women. The second half of the work, 'shadow', tells of her wartime experiences, first of her life in Bucharest under regular aerial bombing and then of her flight before the advancing enemy armies to Iași and later Odessa. Here the author and her husband became entrapped in the turmoil of the Russian Revolution and her account offers a fascinating insight into the effects of this event on the Romanians evacuated to that town and the activities of a group of Romanian Bolsheviks calling themselves the 'Battalion of Death'. Under the leadership of Rakovsky, the revolutionaries triumphed and the author's husband was taken prisoner but eventually both he and his wife safely returned to Romania.

11 **Twenty years in Roumania.**
Maude Parkinson. London: G. Allen & Unwin, 1921. 255p.
Although sometimes rather naive in its outlook, this charming account of the twenty-two years an intrepid Irishwoman spent teaching at a Bucharest school during the late 19th and early 20th centuries carries a surprising amount of descriptive detail. Within a broadly sympathetic narrative, rich with often amusing anecdotal detail, most attention is paid to the activities of Romanian 'society' but the realities of everyday life are also depicted. The trickery and intimidation of election campaigns is well captured, with the apparently common practice of registering the dead to vote occasioning a comment from one observer that 'In my father's lifetime he never had the vote, but now he is dead they are giving him one'.

12 **In the Carpathians.**
Lion Phillimore. London: Constable, 1912. 348p. map.
An entertaining and eminently readable account of the adventures of an Irishwoman and her husband on a three-month summer traverse of the Carpathian Mountains from Zakopane in Poland to Brașov in Romania. The last third of the book is concerned with their passage through Maramureș and the Szekely lands. Fully confirming any continental prejudices regarding the eccentricities of the British, they chose to shun the normal tourist haunts in favour of the byroads, travelling by horse and peasant cart and camping wherever their tents could be pitched. Written in a style that belies its

age, this is, in many ways, a remarkably modern travel book with the author often being concerned as much with her own voyage of inner discovery as with any external pleasures.

13 **The war in Eastern Europe: travels through the Balkans in 1915.**
John Reed, illustrations by Boardman Robinson. London: Phoenix, 1994. 177p. map.
A reprint of the 1916 original (New York: Charles Schribner's & Sons), this is a caustic eye-witness account of the First World War in South-Eastern Europe by an American journalist more famous for his description of the Russian Revolution (*Ten days that shock the world*, New York: International Publishers; Boni & Liveright, 1919. 371p.). In his journey across the region Reed spent some time on the front line in Bucovina, then part of the Austro-Hungarian Empire, before travelling to a Bucharest still wrestling with the question of whether to enter the war and, if so, on which side. Searching for an indication of which way Romania might turn, the author tries to assess the mood of the population but he is forced to conclude that: 'There is no public opinion in Romania. The peasants will fight for whatever their masters decide will give them the greatest country to exploit. ... So one must ask the politicians, and they will reply that Rumania will join the side that satisfies "national aspirations" – as they call cupidity in the Balkans'.

14 **Roumanian journey.**
Sacheverell Sitwell, illustrated from photographs by A. Costa, Richard Wyndham and others, foreword by Patrick Leigh Fermor. Oxford; New York: Oxford University Press, 1992. 120p.
The fruits of a four-week whirlwind tour of the country in the 1930s, this is one of the classics of Romanian travel literature first published in 1938 (London: B. T. Batsford, 120p.). The author poetically evokes a time long past, as he rhapsodizes about the delights of Romanian food, considered at the time one of the premier native cuisines in Europe, and is enthralled by the diversity of peoples, from the self-mutilating Skoptzt coachmen of Bucharest, to the Lipovans of the Danube Delta whose simple monastery at Petropavlosk he describes as the most wonderful 'spectacle of asceticism'. The famous church at Curtea de Argeş is dismissed as 'a florid and sugary example of the Armenian style' but the painted monasteries of Bucovina are hailed as supreme examples of Byzantine art. Rich descriptions of gypsy life are counterpointed with accounts of brief audiences with Queen Marie and King Carol II.

15 **Raggle-taggle: adventures with a fiddle in Hungary and Roumania.**
Walter Starkie. London: John Murray, 1933. 399p. bibliog.
An evocative account of the author's experiences during 1929 when he left his job as a Professor of Spanish at Dublin University and spent the whole summer wandering as a penniless vagabond with the gypsy musicians of Hungary and Romania. Following a wartime encounter, Starkie had become fascinated by their striking music, with its 'strange cadence' and 'florid trills'. In this engaging book he recounts, in his own rather ornate style, scores of frequently amusing but sometimes hair-raising adventures, which shed light not only on a distant age but also on an often marginalized people.

16 **From Carpathian to Pindus: pictures of Roumanian country life.**
Tereza Stratilesco. London: T. Fischer Unwin, 1906. 379p.

According to the author the aim of this work is to show what she considers to be the most genuine and interesting part of the Romanian nation: the peasantry. The bounds of the nation in this case are not just the peasants of Wallachia, Moldovia and Transylvania but also the Aroumin of the Pindus mountains in present-day Greece. A brief historical introduction is followed by chapters detailing all aspects of peasant life, including their ties to the land, their position on the social scale, their relationship with the state, religious practices and social relations. Many of the peasantry's customs and traditions are described and the text contains a number of stories and proverbs as well as snatches of folk songs.

17 **Journal of a voyage up the Mediterranean; principally among the islands of the archipelago and in Asia Minor.**
Charles Swan. London: C. & J. Rivington, 1826. 422p.

The second part of this work (p. 277-422) contains an English translation of the infamous denunciation of the Phanariots by Mark Philippe Zallones, *Essai sur les Fanariotes* (Marseille, 1824. 351p.). The Phanariots were a Greek oligarchy who derived their name from the Phanar quarter of Istanbul, where the Ecumenical Patriarchate had moved in 1600. They ruled the Danubian Principalities for much of the 18th and part of the 19th century and in his book Zallones claimed that they were nothing less than rapacious plunders whose intemperate behaviour had become a byword for treachery and deceit. At one point he melodramatically laments 'Dacians, your misfortunes are not yet terminated! ... You are become the slaves of the Fanariotes – and the most wretched slaves that the annuals of history can present!' Zallones knew the Phanariots well but as a Roman Catholic Greek he was concerned that they might assume control of the nascent Greek state and his writings bear the traces of an unmistakable political agenda.

18 **Untrodden paths in Roumania.**
Mary A. Walker. London: Chapman & Hall, 1888. 355p.

An entertaining and spirited account, enlivened with numerous charming illustrations, of two journeys made by the author in the Romanian lands during the 1880s. The first, lasting for one month in 1884, took her and two female companions from Galați to the monasteries of Moldavia, which involved a difficult raft journey down the Bistrița River to Piatra Neamț. The second, undertaken in 1887, took the author from Bucharest, where, whilst admiring the many new buildings, she lamented the rage for whitewashing 'that is rapidly obliterating the only picturesque feature of the city – the outside painting of the old churches', on an extended tour to Curtea de Argeș, Sinaia and Brașov, and then to the monasteries of Argeș. The work closes with a brief history of Romania. Another account of the 1884 journey can be found in the same author's *Eastern life and scenery, with excursions in Asia Minor, Mytilene, Crete, and Roumania* (London: Chapman & Hall, 1886, vol. 2, p. 209-69).

19 **An account of the principalities of Wallachia and Moldavia with various political observations relating to them.**
William Wilkinson. London: Longman, Hurst, Rees, Orme & Brown, 1820. 294p.

Between 1813 and 1816 the author was British Consul in Bucharest and this volume is a fascinating record of the observations he made during his tenure of office.

Wilkinson's stated aim was 'to make an accurate and satisfactory description' of the country and, in general, he successfully rises to this task. However, at times his judgement would seem to be clouded by his undisguised hostility towards the ruling Greek Phanariot régime, and this is only placed in proper perspective by the last chapter in which he openly advocates the removal of the Principalities from Ottoman rule and their partition between the Russian and Austrian Empires. Thus, although much valuable information is to be found in this book, it should nevertheless be treated as a slightly prejudiced source.

Recent descriptions

20 **Down the Danube: from the Black Forest to the Black Sea.**

Guy Arnold. London: Cassell, 1989. 180p. map.

As the author describes his travels along the length of the Danube, the most substantial part of his book (p. 132-80) covers his passage through Romania. Ceauşescu still ruled at that time but the author, who is a seasoned traveller with experience of conditions throughout the world, paints a more restrained picture than many other writers. Instead of descriptions of brushes with the *Securitate* and appalling living conditions, Arnold's account depicts a gentler, peaceful and almost unfailingly courteous land. The result is a generally sympathetic portrait of the country.

21 **Romania: a country survey.**

Ronald D. Bachman. Washington, DC: US Library of Congress Federal Research Division, 1991. 2nd ed. 356p.

The research for this volume was completed just five months prior to the fall of Ceauşescu in December 1989. Indeed, the very fact that such work was still being carried out by a division of the US Government as late as 1989 is indicative of the unexpectedness of Ceauşescu's fall to many in the West. Originally intended as a reference work for American government employees, this volume was rendered out of date by the events of 1989, which consigned it, like the communist Romania it analysed, to be a piece of history. As a country survey it therefore has only limited use, although the historical introduction, in particular, still has validity.

22 **Balkan hours: travels in the other Europe.**

Richard Bassett. London: John Murray, 1990. 148p. map. bibliog.

The environment for visitors and, especially foreign journalists, was so hostile during the later Ceauşescu years that this reporter from *The Times* was forced to resort to the subterfuge of declaring he was a harpist in order to try and avoid the attentions of the *Securitate* during his visit to Romania. Unfortunately his cover was blown when the head office in London sent a number of telegrams to his hotel demanding copy. The chapter of this book covering Romania, 'Lights out in Bucharest' (p. 129-38), is a graphic evocation of the bleakness of everyday existence amidst the all-pervasive paranoia of the times. The same author's travels in Transylvania are featured in his book, *A guide to Central Europe* (London: Penguin, 1988. 245p.).

23   **In the communist mirror: journeys in Eastern Europe.**
     Lesley Chamberlain.   London; Boston, Massachusetts: Faber, 1990.
     196p. map.

This highly readable account of the author's travels in Eastern Europe during the
twilight years of communism contains two chapters about Romania, 'From the
Danube station' (p. 76-96) and 'A time for reading' (p. 123-47). The first covers a
visit to the Banat during the summer of 1985 and the second deals with time spent in
Bucharest in the winter of 1986. Eschewing the straightforward political reportage
favoured by many other writers, the author presents a book which is as much
autobiography as travelogue. Drawing upon Chamberlain's impressive knowledge of
Eastern European cultures, this is a sensitive and perceptive account of life under the
Ceauşescu régime.

24   **Between the woods and the water. On foot to Constantinople from
     the Hook of Holland: the middle Danube to the Iron Gates.**
     Patrick Leigh Fermor.   London: John Murray, 1986; London: Penguin,
     1987. 253p.

The second part of a planned trilogy describing the author's adventures, when in 1933,
as a young man of eighteen, he set out to travel by foot across Europe, and covering
his journey through Hungary and Romania. Whether staying in splendid country
houses or sleeping rough on the forest floor, the author in his elegant prose beautifully
conjures up a time long past, peopled by often impoverished but still grandly living
Hungarian noblemen, hospitable Romanian shepherds, itinerant Jewish loggers and
gypsies panning for gold. The politics of the increasingly troubled age seldom enter
this Transylvanian idyll and the clouds of war are banished in favour of a series of
erudite excursuses on subjects as diverse as the question of Romanian and Hungarian
ethnic origins, the Uniate Church, the etymology of local words and the Romanian
character as reflected in the folk ballad *miorița*.

25   **Curtain calls: travels in Albania, Romania and Bulgaria.**
     Leslie Gardiner.   London: Duckworth, 1976. 206p.

A mixture of history and anecdotal travelogue, this book, which is the result of fifteen
years of travel in South-Eastern Europe, contains a number of chapters (p. 70-134)
describing the author's visits to Bucharest, Târgu Jiu, Constanţa and the Danube
Delta. In essence, these chapters form an extended essay on the Romanian monarchy,
the history of which the author seems to have been researching at the time, and these
reflections sometimes sit in a rather incongruous juxtaposition with his descriptions of
the socialist reality of the day. Gardiner seldom strayed from his official minders and
tends towards an upbeat picture of life under Ceauşescu. However, he retains a nice
touch of irony throughout, as when he notes in reference to Brancuşi's 'endless
column' in Târgu Jiu: 'the régime has not gone so far as to mount a red star on the
summit of the pillar of heaven'.

26   **Berlin to Bucharest, travels in Eastern Europe.**
     Anton Gill.   London: Grafton, 1990. 328p. map.

The author visited Romania in the late summer of 1988 and in this political travelogue
he provides a good account of Ceauşescu's last years. Aside from his descriptions of
the familiar world of shabby hotels, restaurants that closed by 7.30 in the evening,
prostitutes and the ubiquitous *Securitate,* he also displays a refreshing willingness to

debunk popular travellers' myths, such as that ascribing particular importance to Kent cigarettes as an alternative currency. In fact, any major Western brand was equally acceptable.

27 **Brief spring: a journey through Eastern Europe.**
Iris Gioia, Clifford Thurlow.   Stroud, England: Alan Sutton, 1992.
227p. map.

In the spring of 1990, an odd couple, a recently divorced socialite and a London journalist, decided after a chance meeting in Manhattan to journey through post-communist Eastern Europe. This book, the chronicle of their travels, is divided into alternating passages by the two authors, Gioia's descriptive and Thurlow's more journalistic. In the chapter covering Romania (p. 169-222), they describe their arrival in Bucharest at the height of the 1990 University Square demonstrations and, indeed, the book is dedicated to Stefan Codrescu, a mathematics teacher who died at this time. Thurlow's appreciation of post-communist Romanian politics is rather jaundiced, and the earthquake they experienced on their travels was not of a political nature but brought real loss of life, as it recorded 6.5-7.5 on the Richter scale.

28 **On foot to the Golden Horn, a walk to Istanbul.**
Jason Goodwin.   London: Chatto & Windus, 1993. 278p. map.

Following in the traditions of Patrick Leigh Fermor and Walter Starkie, the author set out with two friends in the early days of post-communist Eastern Europe to walk from Gdansk to Istanbul. The largest section of the book (p. 141-242) is concerned with his journey through Romania but, having been fed a succession of scare stories beforehand and even losing one companion *en route,* through fear of the perils awaiting in Transylvania, the author entered the country burdened with such anxieties that, as he says, 'I shrank from Romania as if it was a storm'. When their worst nightmares were apparently confirmed by the descent of the miners onto a terrorized Bucharest, the author and his companion, understandably, decided to place their faith in letters of recommendation secured in Hungary and take refuge with a succession of Hungarian pastors during their trek across Transylvania. In consequence, his account of the country is heavily biased towards the Hungarian viewpoint and ethnic Romanians appear only rarely within the narrative. Once in 'Romania proper', as Goodwin calls Wallachia and Moldavia, violent food poisoning forced an abandon-ment of the walk in preference to a rather inglorious lift across the Romanian plain to Giurgiu.

29 **Stealing from a deep place, travels in south-eastern Europe.**
Brian Hall.   London: Heinemann, 1988; London: Heinemann Minerva,
1989. 271p. map.

This cycling American seems to have been an object of considerable curiosity when he travelled through Hungary, Romania and Bulgaria in 1982. The first third of this book (p. 3-88) offers an account of his often rather grim experiences in Romania, supplemented with frequent digressions on the country's history and politics. Like many authors, Hall seems to have been filled with an exaggerated dread of Romania by Hungarian tales, but strangely much of the country seems to have made little impact on him, as he assembles the usual cast of shabby hotel rooms, bad food and pestering children demanding chewing gum, leavened with occasional instances of generous hospitality.

30 **In another Europe, a journey to Romania.**
Georgina Harding. London: Hodder & Stoughton, 1990; London: Sceptre, 1991. 157p. map.

The author travelled through Romania and Hungary by bicycle in 1988 when Nicolae Ceauşescu's hold on power still seemed unassailable. Despite official proscriptions to the contrary, she succeeded in staying in private houses and endured the same life of poverty and endemic shortages as her hosts. The result is a fascinating insight into the everyday existence of the Romanian people during these harsh and troubled times. The author's route meandered across the country as she cycled through the Carpathians and the Transylvanian plateau. Visiting towns like the industrial Copşa Mică, permanently enveloped in its cloud of sooty pollution from the chemical works producing carbon black, she finished in a Bucharest reeling from the mass destruction of much of the city centre which was to enable the construction of the monumental folly that was to be the Presidential Palace.

31 **Travels in the Balkans.**
John Higgins, photographs by Anthony Crickmay. London: Barrie & Jenkins, 1972. 144p. map.

Despite the title, this book is in fact largely concerned with Romania and charts three car journeys made by this journalist from *The Times* in 1968 and 1969. In what is now a slightly dated style, the author offers a rare travelogue of Romania in the early Ceauşescu years when the country was just beginning to open its doors to tourism. Fully conforming to the traits expected of his profession by making frequent halts to sample the local *ţuica* and other beverages, and amidst the usual complaints about poor hotels, often inedible food and appalling roads, the author offers a well-informed description of the country, but one from which the Romanians themselves are strangely absent.

32 **Exit into history, a journey through the new Eastern Europe.**
Eva Hoffman. London: Heinemann, 1993. 363p. map.

Following the success of her earlier critically acclaimed volume, *Lost in translation* (London: Minerva, 1991. 280p.), the author, who is of Polish origins, presents here her impressions of the 'new Eastern Europe' taking shape in the wake of the revolutions of 1989. In the lengthy chapter (p. 232-305) covering Romania, she offers a sensitive and often penetrating account of her travels within the country. Bucharest is memorably described as barely clinging 'to the edge of the continent, threatening to fall off into space, some other idea entirely', and she also travelled to Bucovina and in Maramureş, the village of Sapinţa, the scene of some noted post-revolutionary unrest. Hoffman is especially successful in her attempts to understand the country's intellectual life and in her sensitive biographical portraits, particularly that of the sociologist, Pavel Câmpeanu, she manages to give some impression of what the larger social shifts mean for individuals.

33 **Vagabond.**
Jeremy James. London: Pelham, 1991. 215p.

During the summer of 1990 the author set out with a number of companions to ride on horseback across Bulgaria, Romania and Hungary. James clearly has a deep affection for horses and in a country where the horse is still an important mode of transport, he encountered many others with a similar passion. As he threw himself wholeheartedly into the life of the country, he was rewarded with an insight into everyday life not usually gained by travellers. Frequently overwhelmed by the hospitality he encountered on his travels, the author presents in his colloquial and direct writing style an entertaining and warm account of his adventures.

34 **Balkan ghosts: a journey through history.**
   Robert D. Kaplan.   New York: St Martin's Press, 1993; London:
   Papermac, 1994. 307p. maps. bibliog.
Although the author's remit is all the countries of South-Eastern Europe, the longest section of this book (p. 79-189) covers his travels in Romania immediately after the Revolution. From the outset Kaplan betrays his feelings towards his subject through his subheading 'Romania: Latin passion play' and the picture he proceeds to paint is of a seedy Bucharest teeming with prostitutes. It is perhaps significant that he is soon bored by Timișoara, the seat of the Revolution, because nobody says anything outrageous. Throughout reportage of current politics is supported by references to the country's history, and, indeed, implicit in the title is Kaplan's main contention that it is history that determines the present in the Balkans. In a style which is at times slightly portentous, as when he declares 'It appeared that my lightly taken decision to stop at his door for a few minutes had ended a dark era in this artist's life', he offers an entertaining account of his travels from Bucharest, Iași, Cluj and Sibiu to Sfîntu Gheorghe on the Danube Delta, encountering on the way the usual mixture of bad hotels, doubtful food and traditional Romanian hospitality.

35 **Iron Curtain rising: a personal journey through the changing
   landscape of Eastern Europe.**
   Peter Laufer, with a foreward by Rainer Hildebrandt.   San Francisco:
   Mercury House, 1991. 212p. bibliog.
The chapter covering Romania in this post-Cold War travelogue, entitled 'Unreality in Romania' (p. 138-55), records the author's short foray into the country as he crossed from Arad to Timișoara. Throughout travelogue is mixed with potted history, but the tone is portentous. For instance, after a border guard makes a joke about the rock group Guns 'n' Roses, Laufer notes 'After a few days in post-Ceaușescu Romania it becomes understandable how a band that peddles intolerance would be a hit there'. The author of the foreword is the director of the Checkpoint Charlie Museum in Berlin.

36 **Stalin's nose, across the face of Europe.**
   Rory Maclean.   London: Harper Collins, 1992; London: Flamingo,
   1993. 211p. map.
This highly amusing comic travel book offers an exceptionally sharp and well observed picture of Eastern Europe. Although it can be seen as following in the traditions of the Romanian absurd, the only genre which could, perhaps, capture the true ironies of the recent past, its most immediate progenitor would seem to be Rose Macaulay's *The towers of Trebizond* (London: Collins, 1956. 222p.). This time, instead of Aunt Dot and a camel, the companions on this journey are Aunt Zita, a faded Austrian aristocrat who had married a Soviet spy, and a tamworth pig called Winston. In Aunt Zita's trusty Traubant the party set out to travel to Budapest in search of new dentures from a recommended Hungarian dentist, the pig having mislaid the last ones. The pages devoted to Romania detail their madcap adventures

11

around the Moldavian monasteries and include encounters with a writer of pornographic columns for the Western press and a sinister doctor who demands money with menaces. After being 'abducted' in Sighişoara the pig is happily recovered in Copsu Mică, but only after a bribe of cigarettes.

37 **Danube: a sentimental journey from the source to the Black Sea.**
Claudio Magris, translated from the Italian by Patrick Creagh.
London: Collins Harvill, 1990. 416p.

The last sections of this acclaimed study of the great river of Central Europe feature Romania. More a critical companion than a guidebook, the work comprises a series of short but learned expositions that often transcend the geographical bounds of the river to travel deep into Transylvania and to Bucharest. Magris effortlessly draws upon the history and literary traditions of the region to offer a rich evocation of the culture of Romania and the other Danubian lands.

38 **Empire's Edge, travels in South-Eastern Europe, Turkey and Central Asia.**
Scott L. Malcomson.   London; Boston, Massachusetts: Faber, 1994.
256p.

The first section (p. 3-72) of this American journalist's exploration of the nature of identity at the borders of Europe is concerned with Romania. Using a formula which is part historical essay and part political reportage, Malcomson delves into subjects as diverse as the Romanian Revolution, the Roman remains at Sarmizegetusa and the plight of the Jews and anti-Semitism. A series of sharply drawn pen portraits complete the picture in this valiant attempt to understand some of the more subtle nuances of the country.

39 **Transylvania and beyond.**
Dervla Murphy.   London: John Murray, 1992. 239p. map.

The record of two journeys made by this well-known travel writer through Romania in 1990 and 1991. Despite losing all her luggage at the frontier, where it was stolen by uniformed officers, the author courageously continued her journey, sustained to a large degree by the kindness of the Romanian people with whom she shared the poverty and hunger of the cold winter months. Braving blizzards, dogs and even bears, she was eventually forced to change her plans after breaking her ankle and returned from Cluj to London for treatment. Returning in 1991 she resumed her journey by bicycle enduring a multitude of hazards, from wayward aerial crop spraying to appalling roadside pollution. Despite the presence of more private enterprise shops and a general improvement, at least for the 'better-off', she concludes that even after the Revolution most individuals still feel powerless in the face of the authorities.

40 **Walking good: travels to music in Hungary and Romania.**
Peter O'Connor.   London: Weidenfeld, 1971. 112p.

Following in the traditions of Walter Starkie, in the late 1960s O'Connor, another Irishman in love with the fiddle, took to the roads of Eastern Europe, tape recorder in hand, in search of gypsy musicians. However, the music makers he finds are not so much the itinerant troubadours of Starkie's day, but, in keeping with the changes experienced by Romanian society during the intervening years, they are often professional musicians in state ensembles or settled factory workers playing what the author terms 'urban gypsy music'. In a lively and entertaining style, O'Connor describes his adventures as he travelled across the country from Slobozia to Constanța, Pitești and Cojocna near Cluj, discovering not only fiddlers but also gypsy players of other instruments such as the 'cimbalom', a stringed instrument hit by wooden rods, and the 'gourdon', a large tambourine.

41 **Roads that move: a journey through Eastern Europe.**
Walter Perrie. Edinburgh: Mainstream, 1991. 223p.

In the spring of 1990, following the collapse of communism, the author set out to broadly follow the route of Patrick Leigh Fermor's earlier journey across Europe (*Between the woods and the water*, q.v.) but this time by car rather than on foot. A large section of this book (p. 163-223) covers his journey through Romania. Although his account is well written and contains some sharp observations about Romanian life, it is nonetheless pervaded by an overwhelming bleakness, such as when he notes 'Romanian history can be summed up as a long series of catastrophes interrupted by the occasional disaster to relieve the monotony'.

42 **Romania.**
Mark Sanborne. New York: Facts on File, 1996. 166p. maps. bibliog.
(Nations in Transition).

Provides a basic introduction to contemporary Romania with sections on history, government and politics, people, economy, daily life, arts and culture, foreign policy and future prospects.

43 **Lambada country, a ride across Eastern Europe.**
Giles Whittell. London: Chapmans, 1992. 218p. map.

In the wake of the momentous events of 1989, a young cyclist set out to travel across Eastern Europe with the aim of seeing what difference the revolutions had made to the lives of the people of these lands. In a readable, fast moving style interspersed with some light political reportage, the author offers a sensitive and entertaining description of his travels in Romania, which included a numbing crossing of the Carpathians on Ceaușescu's high altitude white elephant, the Trans-Făgărașan highway. The second edition of the book was entitled *Lambada country, by bicycle across Eastern Europe* (London: Phoenix, 1993).

13

Geography and Geology

General

44 **Romania: Eastern Carpathian studies.**
Herbert John Fleure, Reginald Arthur Pelham, with contributions from
Hilda Ormsby and H. J. Howard. London: Le Play Society, 1936. 79p.
maps.
The first half of this slender study contains a number of general chapters on subjects
as diverse as the physical geography, climate, vegetation, economy, peoples and
settlement patterns of Romania. Included in the later section is an interesting map
correlating ethnicity of settlements with altitude in the Szekely areas – Romanian
villages tending to lie on the uplands whilst those of the Hungarians can be found in
the valleys below. The remainder of the volume consists of a detailed description of
the ethnic Romanian village of Corbu near the town of Borsec which includes a
number of photographs, as well as plans of both the village and individual homesteads.

45 **South Carpathian studies: Roumania II.**
Herbert John Fleure, Emyr Estyn Evans et al., with contributions by
Amy R. Burgess, N. Hunter Stein, Margaret Tatton and others, and a
foreword by P. M. Roxby. London: Le Play Society, 1939. 59p. maps.
The fruit of a visit by members of the Le Play Society to the region around Curtea de
Argeş in August 1936. The volume contains sections on the physical geography of the
region, the human geography of the town, including a number of individual house
plans, the provision of educational and medical facilities, local farming practices and
patterns of transhumance as well as a description of the local fair. An interesting later
study of the motivations of the Le Play society in mounting these excursions to
Romania, which includes extracts from this and *Romania: Eastern Carpathian studies*
(q.v.), is David Turnock, 'British travellers in Romania: geographical studies carried
out by members of the Le Play Society in the 1930s', *Romanian Civilization*, vol. 2,
no. 1 (Spring 1993), p. 3-14.

46   **Anglo-Romanian geographies: proceedings of the second Liverpool-Bucharest geography colloquium.**
      Edited by Duncan Light, Daniela Dumbrăveanu-Andone.   Liverpool,
      England: Liverpool Hope Press, 1997. 238p. maps.
      A collection of nineteen papers given at the colloquium, most of which are concerned
      with Romania. They include: Vasile Cucu, 'The political map of Romania – the geo-
      historical framework', p. 3-9; Ion Velea, 'The structures and function of Romania's
      rural space', p. 21-30; Melinda Cândea, 'The Carpathian Mountains in the life of
      Romania and its people', p. 31-57; Ion Nicolae, 'Human geography and toponymics in
      Transylvania', p. 49-57; Christian Braghină and Liliana Dumitrache, 'Changes in the
      socio-professional structure of Romania's population in the transition period', p. 77-
      88; Daniela Dumbrăveanu-Andone and Liliana Dumitrache, 'Romania – a gateway to
      Europe', p. 89-98; Silviu Costache, 'Socio-demographic characteristics of Romania's
      Gypsy minority', p. 111-17; David Phinnemore, 'Romania and the European Union –
      prospects for entry', p. 119-30; and Valeria Velcea, 'Environmental hazards in the
      Carpathians', p. 175-80. The eighteen papers from the first seminar, which was held in
      1995, can be found in *The first Romanian-British geographic seminar no. 1/1995*,
      edited by George Erdeli, W. J. Chamber (Bucharest: Editura Universității din
      București, 1996. 191p.).

47   **Simion Mehedinți and modern Romanian geography.**
      Ian M. Matley.   *Professional Geographer*, vol. 37, no. 4 (Nov. 1985),
      p. 452-58.
      Within this article Matley reviews the ideas of Romanian geographer Simion
      Mehedinți and traces their origins – he was influenced by geographers such as the
      German Ratzel. In contrast to the experience of geographers in other Eastern European
      countries, the ideas of Mehedinți continued to find official favour during the
      communist era, allowing him to be rightfully acknowledged as the founder of modern
      Romanian geographical thought. A defence of the Romanian position in Transylvania
      by Mehedinți, originally published in 1940, has recently been republished in English
      translation: *What is Transylvania* (Miami Beach, Florida: Romanian Historical
      Studies, 1986. 124p.).

48   **Romanian geography reunited – the integrative approach**
      demonstrated by the conservation movement.
      David Turnock.   *GeoJournal*, vol. 6, no. 5 (1982), p. 419-31.
      This study marks the fact that by the early 1980s Romanian geography seemed to
      have, at last, come to a more balanced view as regards the relationship between human
      development and the environment. A re-evaluation of geography as a science of
      'relationships between geospheres' seemed to have ended the separation of the human
      and physical branches of the subject in favour of a new emphasis on conservation.
      However, whilst applauding this professional realignment, the author also notes a
      continuing ambivalence towards environmental issues on the part of the authorities
      and this was, unfortunately, to remain the case until the demise of the communist
      régime.

49   **Urban development and urban geography in Romania: the contribution of Vintila Mihailescu.**
David Turnock.   *GeoJournal,* vol. 14, no. 2 (March 1987), p. 181-202.
Vintilă Mihăilescu (1890-1978) was the first geographer to apply the principles of urban studies to Romanian geography. This appraisal of his career also provides an opportunity for the author to analyse the evolving relationship between theories of urban development and urban geography as a whole in Romania.

Physical geography and geology

50   **Geology of Romania.**
B. C. Burchfiel, with contributions by M. Bleahu.   Boulder, Colorado: The Geological Society of America, 1976. 82p. maps. bibliog. (The Geological Society of America, special paper, no. 158).
Dominated by the Carpathians Mountains, which form part of the Alpine orogenic belt, Romania, geologically, can be divided into seven major structural units: the Eastern Carpathians, Southern Carpathians, Apuseni Mountains, Dobrogea, Skythian Platform, Moesian Platform and the Transylvanian Basin. In this general survey of the geology of the country each of these units is addressed in turn before the author concludes with some speculations about the geological history of Romania.

51   **Observations on the behaviour of buildings in the Romanian earthquake of March 4, 1977.**
George Fattal, Emil Simiu, Charles Culver.   Washington, DC: US Department of Commerce, National Bureau of Standards, 1977. 160p. maps. (NBS Special Publications, no. 490).
On 4 March 1977 an earthquake of 7.2 on the Richter scale hit Romania with its epicentre in the Vrancea region, approximately 150 km north-east of the capital. 1,578 people were killed and 200,000 left homeless as widespread damage was recorded in Bucharest, Craiova and a number of other cities. At the request of the Romanian government, the United States dispatched a team of experts from the National Bureau of Standards and other bodies to help determine the safety of damaged buildings. This book is a report on their observations in Bucharest and Craiova. It contains a brief seismic history of the region, including details of the 1940 earthquake and a survey and analysis of earthquake damage in specific buildings organized by building type and age, before concluding with some recommendations.

52 **Romania.**
V. Ianovici, M Borcoş.   In: *Mineral deposits in Europe. Volume 2: Southeast Europe.*   Edited by F. W. Dunning, W. Mykura, D. Slater, non-metallic minerals editor A. J. G. Notholt, production editor A. R. Woolley.   London: The Mineralogical Society, The Institution of Mining and Metallurgy, 1982, p. 55-142.

Romania is relatively well endowed with natural resources and in this detailed and highly specialized study the authors identify the main metallic and non-metallic mineral deposits by geological region. The work is copiously illustrated with geological sections and maps.

53 **Water resource management problems in Romania.**
David Turnock. *GeoJournal*, vol. 3, no. 6 (1979), p. 609-22.

In this study the author discusses some of the water-related environmental problems facing Romania and the various projects being undertaken to try and solve them. Through a case-study of the Danube Delta, Turnock stresses the need for a more sophisticated approach in the planning of development in drainage basins, arguing that new measures are needed to increase provisions for water storage and reduce pollution. Attention is also paid to the question of river navigation and the influence this has on hydroelectricity generation and flood control.

Economic geography

54 **Hydro-electricity in the Romanian Carpathians.**
Serban Dragomirescu, Simina Dragomirescu.   *GeoJournal*, vol. 29, no. 1 (Jan. 1993), p. 31-39.

Although Romania's hydro-electric power system dates as far back as the turn of the century, its greatest period of expansion was during the communist period. In this study the authors discuss the latest developments in the field and their impact on the wider electrification programme. In particular, they focus on the Carpathian Mountains where an integrated rural plan combines electricity generation with provisions for forestry and tourism. They conclude by discussing the potential for the further development of hydroelectric power in the context of the wider changes being experienced by the Romanian economy and a growing recognition of the need to protect the environment.

55 **Comparative analysis of urban and industrial hierarchies of Romanian towns in 1990.**
Ioan Ianos.   *GeoJournal*, vol. 29, no. 1 (Jan. 1993), p. 49-56.

The author compares changes in the relative rankings of towns and cities as regards the size of the centre and the level of industralization. He concludes that in the future some industrial centres may lose ground as heavy industry declines and migration from the countryside slackens due to the privatization of agriculture. In contrast, some county centres are set to gain in importance with the projected switch in resources away from the national administration to the local level.

56 **The human geography of the Western Mountains of Romania.**
Ian M. Matley. *Scottish Geographical Magazine*, vol. 87, no. 2 (Sept. 1971), p. 116-27.

A description of the physical features, settlement and economy of the Western Mountains (Munţii Apuseni) of Romania which addresses the question of whether the mountains should be allowed to become a land of deserted villages and abandoned fields and pastures. The high cost of subsidizing the region, the difficulties involved in creating a modern infrastructure and the continuing lure of better employment opportunities in the nearby Transylvanian cities, such as Cluj, leads the author to regretfully conclude that these lands are probably destined to experience a steady depopulation.

57 **The potential for traditional food and drink products in Eastern Europe: fruit processing – especially brandy ('tuica') distilling – in Romania.**
N. Muica. *GeoJournal*, vol. 38, no. 2 (Feb. 1996), p. 197-206.

Plum trees abound throughout Romania, where they provide the raw material for a powerful local brandy, *ţuica*. In this article the author discusses the way in which the plums are distilled and gives some thought to the export potential of *ţuica* on the international market.

58 **Canal on the Danube Delta.**
T. Sharman. *Geographical Magazine*, vol. 55 (1983), p. 317-21.

The author provides a general report on the progress of the construction of the canal after a visit to the site with an engineer in July 1982. His generally positive report on the scheme is supported by a considerable amount of facts and figures.

59 **The Danube-Black Sea Canal and its impact on Southern Romania.**
David Turnock. *GeoJournal*, vol. 12, no. 2 (Jan. 1986), p. 65-79.

The construction of the Danube-Black Sea canal between 1978 and 1984 was the largest single construction project ever undertaken in Romania with a scale of work greater than that involved with the digging of either the Suez or the Panama Canals. The idea of a canal was first conceived in classical times and an early 18th-century prototype also seems to have existed; however, prior to the current project the last major construction attempt had been the infamous Stalinist forced labour project of 1949-53. Although the building of the canal held great political symbolism for the Ceauşescu régime, as it epitomized the capacities and modernity of communist Romania, the author shows in this paper that it also held an economic rationale. Sustained growth in the Romanian economy, especially along the Danube River, had been sufficient to justify a canal linking these new industrial complexes with the Black Sea to facilitate imports and exports.

60   **An economic geography of Romania.**
     David Turnock.   London: G. Bell & Sons, 1974. 319p. maps. bibliog.
     (Bell's Advanced Economic Geographies).
     In this pioneering work the author provides an exhaustive examination of the physical
     resources of the country, its agriculture and forestry, industry and power supplies, and
     foreign trade. The book is mostly concerned with economic development in the late
     1960s and early 1970s, with the author being careful to frame his discussion not only
     in terms of the economic potential of Romania but also the political realities of the
     day.

Urbanization and systematization

61   **Privatised housing and the development of condominiums in
     Central and Eastern Europe: the case of Poland, Hungary, Slovakia
     and Romania.**
     Christopher Banks, Sheila O'Leary, Carol Rabenhorst.   *Review of
     Urban and Regional Development Studies*, vol. 8, no. 2 (July 1996),
     p. 137-55.
     Compares the process of house privatization after the fall of communism in 1989 in a
     number of Eastern European countries, including Romania. In particular the authors
     compare the legal frameworks put in place to facilitate privatization, the role of local
     government in supporting the development of viable condominium associations, the
     bodies established to manage privatized housing, and the differing provisions for
     financial rehabilitation and capital repair projects. In Poland, Hungary and Slovakia
     privatization was marked by the transfer of property from central to local government
     control but in Romania housing was sold directly by central government to sitting
     tenants. The result was that in a town like Braşov the amount of housing in private
     hands rose from only 29.9 per cent in 1991 to 72 per cent by 1994. In this special
     issue of this journal devoted to Eastern Europe a number of other articles carry
     information about Romania, including József Hegedüs, Iván Tosics, Stephen K. Mayo,
     'Transition of the housing sector in the Eastern European countries', p. 101-36.

62   **Ceauşescu's Bucharest.**
     Darrick Danta.   *Geographical Review*, vol. 83, no. 2 (April 1993),
     p. 170-82.
     The author divides Ceauşescu's transformation of Bucharest into two phases. The first,
     carried out between 1965 and 1980, mainly saw the changes limited to the outer zones
     of the city and was dominated by the increased construction of apartment blocks.
     However, the second phase, which lasted from 1980 until Ceauşescu's downfall in
     1989, was far more dramatic, as it saw the destruction of a large area of the centre of
     Bucharest to allow for the construction of a vast palace and a series of triumphal
     squares and boulevards.

63 **Social engineering in Romania: Ceaușescu's Systematization program, 1965-1989.**
   Dennis Deletant. *Romanian Civilization*, vol. 2, no. 1 (Spring 1993),
   p. 53-74.

In this balanced and objective article the author traces the ideological and historical roots of systematization and the means by which it was applied – a Central Commission for Village Systematization had been established as early as 1965. The scheme seems to have been originally conceived, as was a similar plan by Khruschev in the Soviet Union, as a means of alleviating the twin problems of mass immigration of young people to the cities and the reluctance of professional people, especially doctors, to work in the countryside, by raising the status of rural communities. However, in the 1980s, it emerged that it would have meant the destruction of between 5,000-6,000 villages with, for instance, 125 of the 232 villages in Maramureş destined to disappear. The scale of this potential destruction caused such an international outcry that it led to the formation of organizations such as the Belgian-based 'Operation Villages Roumains' which helped arrange the twinning of threatened Romanian villages with Western communities. Few of the villages were actually destroyed and systematization, as the author notes, really only succeeded in 'imprinting Romania onto the consciousness of Europe', but in the process it also forged important links which were later to provide a springboard for humanitarian aid after the Revolution.

64 **The socialist city: spatial structures and urban policy.**
   Edited by R. A. French, Ian Hamilton. Chichester, England: John
   Wiley, 1979. 541p. maps. bibliog.

Contains two important articles directly concerned with Romania: Gordon Church, 'Bucharest: revolution in townscape art' (p. 493-506); and Steven Sampson, 'Urbanization – planned and unplanned: a case study of Braşov' (p. 507-24). Material on Romania can also be found in two other chapters: Ian Hamilton, 'Urbanization in socialist Eastern Europe' (p. 167-94); and Ian Hamilton and A. D. Burnett, 'Spatial structures in East European cities' (p. 195-262).

65 **The razing of Romania's past.**
   Dinu C. Giurescu. New York; London: World Monument Fund,
   Architecture Design and Technology, 1990. 68p. (International
   Preservation Report).

This volume is a *cri de coeur* to the outside world for help in saving the villages and towns of Romania from wholesale destruction at the hands of Ceaușescu. Giurescu, who was an active opponent of systematization, analyses and documents the Romanian leader's ruthless attempt to homogenize the country's culture and destroy much of its past. The full scale of the vandalism is graphically brought home in the many photographs contained in this volume.

66 **Village systematisation in Romania: historical, economic and ideological background.**
   Gábor Hunya. *Communist Economies*, vol. 1, no. 3 (1989), p. 327-41.

An informed study of systematization in which the author discusses Ceaușescu's plan to reduce the number of villages in the Romanian countryside and places it within the context of similar schemes elsewhere in Eastern Europe. However, the important distinction was that at a time when Hungary and Bulgaria were abandoning such ideas as being totally impractical, Ceauşescu was just starting to embark on his far more grandiose vision. Surveying the policy from an ethnic point of view, the author also suggests that a tendency was evident within systematization to eliminate non-Romanian relics of the past, noting that: 'it is not untypical that some Transylvanian villages are trying hard to produce evidence of their Dacian origins in a desperate effort to survive'.

67 **Return of the vampire.**
Anthony Lambert. *Geographical Magazine*, vol. 61, no. 2 (Feb. 1989), p. 16-20.
A study of Ceauşescu's grandiose, but fatally flawed, scheme to raze thousands of Romania's 13,000 villages by the year 2000 and transfer their inhabitants to new agro-industrial complexes, a process which would have affected almost half the Romanian population. The plan was to be carried out in the name of equalizing differences between town and village. After sketching the history of peasant resistance to state sponsored agricultural change in Romania, the author concludes that such a plan was totally unfeasible as the drab lifestyle of the new industrial settlements with their uniform blocks of flats would have been highly unsuitable for peasants accustomed to the independent or semi-independent life of the village.

68 **Romania: an introduction.**
Stuart Lowe. In: *The reform of housing in Eastern Europe and the Soviet Union.* Edited by Bengt Turner, József Hegedüs, Iván Tosics. London; New York: Routledge, 1992, p. 218-19.
A brief survey of Romanian housing policy under communism which places it within the context of general political developments. It is supplemented by a statistical appendix by Ştefan Grecianu, 'The housing sector in Romania: appendix', p. 220-22.

69 **Turning the Romanian peasant into a new socialist man: an assessment of rural development policy in Romania.**
Per Ronnås. *Soviet Studies*, vol. 41, no. 4 (Oct. 1989), p. 543-59.
This is a detailed survey of the ideological, political and economic aims of systematization and the overall feasibility and effects of the project. The author argues that 'strict adherence to a traditional Marxist-Leninist development strategy and supremacy of ideological considerations over pragmatism make it highly unlikely that the program will attain its objective of narrowing the rural-urban divide'.

70 **Urbanization in Romania: a geography of social and economic change since independence.**
Per Ronnås. Stockholm: Economic Research Institute Stockholm School of Economics, 1984. 398p. maps. bibliog.
Based on the author's doctoral thesis, this study ranges far wider than the title would suggest, as Ronnås offers a broad survey of socio-economic change in Romania from the mid-19th century until the early 1980s. A review of the historical background is followed by chapters on population growth and ethnic structure, economic development, industrial change, urban development and, finally, cultural change. The

text is supported by a wealth of useful statistical information. An earlier article in which the same author examines the implications for urbanization of central planning and the means available for policy implementation is 'Centrally planned urbanization: the case of Romania', *Geografiska Annaler, Series B — Human Geography*, vol. 64B, no. 2 (1982), p. 143-51.

71 **Towards a market-orientated housing sector in Eastern Europe: developments in Bulgaria, Czechoslovakia, Hungary, Poland, Romania and Yugoslavia.**
    Jeffery P. Telgarsky, Raymond J. Struyk. Washington, DC: Urban Institute Press, 1991. 258p. bibliog.

A single chapter of this volume (p. 205-20) looks at the serious housing problems confronting post-communist Romania. These in part stem from the lack of investment under Ceauşescu when Romania had the smallest proportion of national income devoted to housing of all the Eastern European countries. This led to persistent shortages with over 500,000 people living in single workers' hostels in 1984. In recent years, problems have also arisen over the quality of construction. Somewhat surprisingly, although most building inevitably occurred within the socialist state sector, between 1979-85 many tenants were able to purchase their flats under favourable terms, with the result that a large percentage of housing prior to 1989 was already in private hands.

72 **City profile: Bucharest.**
    David Turnock. *Cities*, vol. 7, no. 2 (May 1990), p. 107-18.

The author offers a historical review of the development of Bucharest from the first record of the city in 1459 until the end of the Ceauşescu régime, but with the chief focus on the communist period. Turnock argues that, although the remodelling under Ceauşescu was unique in its intensity and trauma, it must also be seen as part of a longer-term cycle of urban development. The article is supplemented by a number of maps, statistical tables and illustrations as the author offers a broad description of industry, housing and planning in the Romanian capital.

73 **Housing policy in Romania.**
    David Turnock. In: *Housing policies in Eastern Europe and the Soviet Union.* Edited by J. A. A. Sillince. London: Routledge, 1990, p. 135-69.

This well-documented survey of housing policy in socialist Romania investigates regional trends and the organization of housing and allocation mechanisms. The author's findings are supported by a number of case-studies drawn from the cities of Cluj and Iaşi as well as from rural areas. He concludes by noting that, whilst generally under socialism the housing programme kept pace with population growth, the economic problems of the 1980s brought house construction to a virtual standstill.

74 **The planning of rural settlement in Romania.**
    David Turnock. *Geographical Journal*, vol. 157, no. 3 (Nov. 1991), p. 251-64.

A sharp and informed critique of Ceauşescu's rural resettlement programme. Although rural depopulation is a problem across Eastern Europe, Romania was distinguished by the radical nature and the sheer brutality of the proposed solution. This was in the form of systematization, a scheme by which Ceauşescu sought to consolidate rural settlements into agro-industrial centres so as to ensure better access to local services and employment. In fact, systematization was calculated to increase the power of the state and in the process erode the traditional individualism of Romanian peasants. A long-term solution of the problem of depopulation will depend on encouraging local initiative and on the willingness of young people to return to village life.

75 **Romanian villages: rural planning under communism.**
David Turnock. *Rural History*, vol. 2, no. 1 (April 1991), p. 81-112.
This is a detailed and meticulous study of Ceauşescu's 'Bulldozer-politik' of the 1980s. Following the model of the Soviet *agrogorod*, the Romanian leader set about 'modernising' the country by constructing 550 new towns. However, rather than an urbanizing this should be seen as a 'counter-urbanizing' strategy, since at the heart of this policy of building secondary centres was a desire to stem migration to the large cities, which Ceauşescu, the son of a peasant, allegedly resented. After the fall of Ceauşescu the scheme was abandoned, and so the author concludes by discussing possible alternative strategies which are more in keeping with the people's needs and which would not involve such high economic and social costs.

Maps and atlases

76 **Atlasul Republicii Socialiste România.** (Atlas of the Socialist Republic of Romania.)
Bucharest: Editura Academiei Republicii Socialiste România, 1974-79.
5 fascicles (1 – 1974, 2 – 1975, 3 – 1976, 4 – 1977 and 5 – 1979).
A comprehensive and informative atlas of Romania with seventy-six maps and various sections covering the physical, economic and social geography of the country. There is useful information on geology, climate, rivers, soil and vegetation, history and toponymy, population, settlements, industry, agriculture and transport.

77 **Atlas of Eastern Europe in the twentieth century.**
Richard Crampton, Ben Crampton. London; New York: Routledge, 1996. 297p.
This atlas is particularly useful for tracing the fluid boundaries of Romania and the rest of Eastern Europe during the 20th century, with each map being accompanied by an explanatory text and statistics, where appropriate. The maps are all in black-and-white, which, given the complexity of many of the territorial rearrangements they show, does not always permit the clearest of cartography. Some of the maps cover individual countries whilst others are thematic, showing topics such as industrialization, agricultural collectivization and Stalinization. The atlas serves as a useful accompaniment to Richard Crampton, *Eastern Europe in the twentieth century and after* (London; New York: Routledge, 1997. 2nd ed. 526p.), an excellent general introduction which places the history of Romania firmly within a regional context.

78 **România: atlas turistic rutier.** (Romania: tourist road atlas.)
Vasile Dragomir, Petru Bulugu, Grigore Toma, Gheorghe Ciobanu.
Bucharest: Flomarco, 1993. 255p.

This road atlas, the most detailed available, covers not only the whole of present-day
Romania but also the former Romanian lands now incorporated into the Republic of
Moldova and the Ukraine. The topographical detail in the latter is limited to the bare
essentials in order to clearly distinguish them from Romania proper. The 105 pages of
road maps at a scale of 1:300,000 are supplemented by 57 pages of detailed town
plans covering all the main centres. There is also a comprehensive index of place-
names. Places of tourist interest are clearly indicated throughout and the key is written
in six languages: Romanian, English, French, Italian, German and Russian.

79 **Romania—Moldavia.**
Euromap. Stuttgart, Germany: Geocenter, 1994/95.

This road map covers both Romania and the neighbouring Republic of Moldavia at a
scale of 1:800,000. The map is clear and easy to read and shows resorts and other
places of interest. The key is in English, German and a number of East European
languages, including Romanian. In one corner of the map there is a small street map of
Bucharest and on the reverse an index of place-names.

80 **Atlas Geologic.** (Geological Atlas.)
Bucharest: Geological Institute, Socialist Republic of Romania,
1971-75.

A series of thirteen maps with accompanying bilingual booklets written in Romanian
and French. Each map and booklet covers a different geological or geographical topic.
The series includes a general geological map (no. 1), the geological structure of
Romanian in different ages (nos. 2-7), mineral deposits (nos. 8-9), hydrological
structure (no. 10), soils (nos. 11-12) and zones of vegetation (no. 13).

81 **Historical atlas of East Central Europe.**
Paul Robert Magocsi, cartographic design by Geoffrey J. Matthews.
Seattle, Washington; London: University of Washington Press, 1993.
218p. (A History of East Central Europe, no. 1).

This atlas accompanies the generally excellent series produced by the University of
Washington Press, 'A History of East Central Europe'. The maps, which are produced
in full colour, graphically chart the ebb and flow of the various empires of the region
in a mostly clear and easy to read form. Beginning from 400 AD, they cover not only
territorial divisions but also topics such as ethno-linguistic distribution, industrial
development and population movements. Each of the maps is accompanied by an
explanatory text which frequently takes the form of a potted history of the country
represented.

82 **Rumania-Bulgaria.**
Bern, Switzerland: Kümmerly & Frey, 1994/95.

This road map covers Romania and neighbouring Bulgaria at a scale of 1:1,000,000.
The map is easy to read, although the small scale means that occasionally details are
lost. Places of interest and holiday centres are clearly shown and the key is in the
major West European languages, including English.

Tourism

83 **The use of traditional symbols for recasting the present: a case study of tourism in Rumania.**
Anca Giurchescu. *Dance Studies*, vol. 14 (1990), p. 47-63.
Drawing on a range of examples from dance, music and literature, the author explores the fashion in which traditional models are manipulated for tourist consumption in Romania.

84 **The changing geography of Romanian tourism.**
Duncan Light, Daniela Andone. *Geography*, vol. 81, no. 3 (July 1996), p. 312-33.
The authors argue that Romania's tourism is undergoing a period of transition parallel to the changes in the country as a whole. Under communism the tourist trade was dominated by visitors from East Germany, Poland or Czechoslovakia, but now these are rarely to be seen. Instead, they are slowly being replaced by small numbers of Western tourists drawn by the outstanding natural beauty of Romania. To increase their numbers further and make the country an attractive holiday destination, the Romanians must both overcome the negative image of themselves and their country that is frequently encountered in the West as well as urgently improve accommodation facilities and the general tourist infrastructure.

85 **The impact of tourism and conservation on agriculture in the mountains of Valcea county, Romania.**
Gheorghe Ploaie. *GeoJournal*, vol. 38, no. 2 (Feb. 1996), p. 219-27.
The county of Vâlcea (Oltenia) extends from the Carpathian Mountains across the Subcarpathians and the verdant expanses of the Piedmont zone. It already boasts a well-developed tourist industry with a number of national parks, spas and nature reserves. In this paper the author examines the potential for a long-term growth in tourism in the region following the introduction of a market economy. Amongst the factors which he suggests may affect this process are the impact of a planned motorway linking Bucharest to Sibiu, a direct railway line from Bucharest to Râmnicu Vâlcea, the designation of more natural parks and other attractions, as well as an increase in hotel accommodation.

Travel Guides

86 **Hippocrene companion guide to Romania.**
Lydle Brinkle. New York: Hippocrene, 1992. 211p. maps.

This basic guide is divided into three sections. Following an introduction which features essays on the geographical setting, people, history and folklore of Romania, there are a number of chapters describing the different regions of the country. Focusing almost entirely on urban centres to the detriment of outstanding rural areas, such as Marmureş, these take the form of a brief historical introduction to each town followed by a list of local 'sights', hotels and restaurants complete with relevant addresses but with few instructions as to how they may actually be reached. This section of the book also contains a chapter on health resorts, spas, drugs and treatments. The last chapter, entitled 'Practical information', seems to be unjustifiably dated given the year of publication. For instance, the author states that a minimum daily currency exchange of $10 per day is still in force, when, in fact, it was abolished after the Revolution, and in the list of Romanian Embassies the country is still conspicuously and erroneously referred to as a Socialist Republic. The tourist would also be left somewhat unprepared by the often unrealistic advice within these pages: certainly not all visitors to an average Romanian restaurant in 1992 would have agreed that modern 'Romanian cuisine is varied and has achieved considerable prestige throughout Europe'. Rather eccentrically the closing section on Romanian menu terms merely contains recipes for meat balls and stuffed cabbage leaves.

87 **Hiking guide to Romania.**
Tim Burford. Chalfont St. Peter, England: Bradt, 1993. 325p. maps.

Romania contains some of the most beautiful landscape in Europe and walking is a perfect way to explore its varied charms. The Carpathian Mountains contain vast tracts of almost virgin forest, dotted with isolated monasteries seemingly locked in a medieval time-warp and a rich diversity of wildlife including bears, boars and wolves. Romanians are rightfully proud of these natural beauties and all the more popular areas are criss-crossed by networks of carefully marked trails. Despite its title, this book aspires to be a fairly complete guidebook to the country with the first third devoted to background information on everything from geology to housing and television. As is inevitable given the rapid changes in the country since the Revolution, some of this information, especially as regards prices, is already out of date. The remainder of the book provides details of walks through various mountain ranges from the popular Bucegi above Sinaia to less well known areas, each chapter being accompanied by a sketch map. The author seems to have walked his routes and his directions are usually comprehensive but, nonetheless, given the difficulty of finding large-scale maps in Romania, the aspiring hiker would be wise to take the precaution of brushing up his Romanian so he can ask for directions before departing to the more inaccessible areas.

88 **Where to go in Romania.**
Harold Dennis-Jones.   London: Settle Press; New York: Hippocrene, 1994. rev. ed. 135p. maps.

This enthusiastic guide to what is a very beautiful and fascinating country is aimed at all travellers but, by virtue of the road-based itineraries, it may perhaps be of most use to the motorist. The author has travelled extensively throughout Romania during the past twenty-five years and the breadth of his experience is evident in the comprehensive nature of this guidebook. The book seems to target those who wish the bare essence of what to see without the clutter of information found in many guidebooks. However, this can sometimes make the resultant descriptions a little 'thin' and, consequently, visitors might be left struggling to interpret a location once they arrive. Likewise, although the potential difficulties sometimes encountered by tourists are mentioned, they are perhaps too readily glossed over and certainly the section on travelling in Romania (p. 12) should be read closely. The book is divided into sections, each encompassing a self-contained tourist area: Bucharest, where the author rightly laments the dilapidated state of many fine buildings; the Black Sea and Danube Delta; Moldavia; and Maramureş. It closes with a brief history and other background information, practical advice, which unfortunately due to rapidly changing circumstances is already a little outdated, and, finally, a brief essential vocabulary. There is no index.

89 **Romania: resorts and spas.**
Dan Ghinea.   Bucharest: Editura Enciclopedică, 1993. 220p.

Arranged alphabetically by location, this book is primarily a practical and informative guide to the 35 towns and 103 villages in Romania which aspire to be medicinal spas. However, it also includes details of a number of other popular cultural and recreational resorts. The spas are mostly located along the Carpathian Mountains or on the Black Sea and in each case, alongside the practical information required by any tourist, the author gives details of the therapeutic properties of the waters and their chemical composition as well as listing the diseases for which they are known as a cure.

90 **The Danube: a river guide.**
Rod Heikell.   St Ives, England: Imray, Laurie, Norie & Wilson, 1991. 199p. maps. bibliog.

Essentially a practical guide – the author calls it a 'working' book – this work is the result of two journeys made by the author down the Danube; one, in 1985, by various modes of transport; and the other, in 1987, by boat alone. After a brief introduction, which includes sections on ferries and problems of navigation, the book is divided according to the countries the river crosses. The river is displayed as a continuous chart running throughout the pages with points of interest being marked and described beside the appropriate place on the map. All distances are marked by kilometres from its source. The chapter on Romania (p. 139-63) covers both banks of the river, when they lie inside the country, but only the left bank when it forms the boundary with Yugoslavia and Bulgaria. An appendix lists harbours, pontoons and anchorages.

91   Rumania.
Nagel's Encyclopedia – Guide.   Geneva; Paris; Munich: Nagel, 1980. 4th ed. 399p. maps.

The volume of this well known series covering Romania offers a comprehensive view of the country, including short essays on such varied subjects as history, literature, science, art, economy, population and traditions. The brief cultural introduction is followed by a number of chapters covering each of the larger cities interspersed with itineraries detailing selected routes between these centres, which are accompanied by descriptions of the various points of interest to be found on the way. Since these itineraries are largely based on the main road network, they would presumably be of most interest to the motorist, but of great benefit to all users are the large number of town plans and the brief historical notes to be found throughout the book. The concluding chapter offers some rather outdated practical information for the traveller.

92   Romania: the rough guide.
Dan Richardson, Tim Burford with additional material by Simon Broughton.   London: Rough Guides, 1995. 368p. maps.

This, the most comprehensive and up-to-date guide available, strikes a judicious balance between the pains and pleasures of travelling in Romania. Any visitor to the country will soon concur with the authors' statement that 'Rather than expect an easy ride, try to accept whatever happens as an adventure – encounters with Gypsies, wild bears, oafish officials and assorted odd characters are likely to be far more interesting than anything purveyed by a tourist board' (although bears, as such, are rather rare). All the areas of the country and 'sights', both major and minor, are covered from Maramureş to the Black Sea. For each town there is a useful sketch map for orientation and a list of hotels and places to eat, although the latter is a fast changing scene in the present economic climate. The text is also supported by information boxes on topics as varied as the *Caritas* pyramid scheme and the philosopher Constantin Noica. The book closes with a potted and rather opinionated history of Romania and some details of the vibrant local culture.

93   Eastern Europe: a Lonely Planet shoestring guide.
David Stanley.   Hawthorn, Victoria; Oakland, California; London; Paris: Lonely Planet, 1995. 3rd ed. 914p. maps.

One of the longer sections (p. 649-764) of this popular, but rather bulky, guidebook is concerned with Romania. As usual with this series the book is distinguished by its excellent town plans and its opinionated, but highly practical, pages of advice. In particular, the author strikes a judicious balance on security and other questions, not disguising difficulties but also taking care not to overstate them. Most of the main sights in Romania are covered in the guide – the author's personal favourite seems to be the town of Sighişoara in Transylvania – alongside up-to-date information on hotels, restaurants and travel connections. It is easy to concur with the author that 'Romania is the most exciting, best-value destination for the adventurous budget traveller in the whole of Eastern Europe'.

Flora and Fauna

94 **Bibliographia ornithologica Romaniae: bibliografia romana și
straina asupra pasarilor din Romania.** (Romanian and foreign
bibliography about birds from Romania.)
Ion Cătuneanu, Sergiu Pascovschi, Matei Tălpeanu, Felicia Theiss.
Bucharest: Comitetul de stat pentru cultură și artă: direcția Muzeelor,
1971. 321p. map.
This useful book lists 3,465 works written about Romanian birds prior to 1971.
Despite the title, the vast majority are drawn from domestic literature as few foreign
ornithologists seem to have ventured to Romania. An introduction in Romanian and
French is followed by the bibliographical listing and the book concludes with a series
of indexes arranged both by author and by historical province so that articles may be
found relating to a specific geographical area.

95 **Where to watch birds in Eastern Europe.**
Gerard Gorman.   London; Auckland; Melbourne; Singapore; Toronto:
Hamlyn, in association with Birdlife International, 1994. 214p. maps.
Despite the ravages of industrialization Romania still remains rich in wildlife. As the
author writes, the country 'has some of the best birds and some of the least-known
bird areas in Europe . . . arguably Europe's greatest wetland, stunning mountain
scenery and innumerable "adventures" in store'. After a brief introduction, the chapter
covering Romania (p. 132-67) provides a useful listing of bird-watching sites.
Understandably, these are largely concentrated in the Dobrogea and the outstanding
Danube Delta but also included are fish-ponds, mountain gorges and nature reserves
from many other areas of the country. Each site is introduced by a brief description,
followed by a month-by-month calendar of birds and details about access, often
accompanied by a handy large-scale sketch map to help orientation.

96   **Important bird areas in Europe.**
      R. F. A. Gremmett, T. A. Jones. Norwich, England: Page Bros, 1989.
      888p. maps. bibliog. (International Council for Bird Preservation,
      European Continental Section. Technical Publication, no. 9).

The objectives of this volume are threefold: to protect birds from direct persecution; to
help conserve sites by encouraging the establishment of protected areas (national
parks, etc.); and to foster concern for the environment by both regulating economic
activities which modify habitats and landscapes and by controlling pollution. The
book is arranged by country with the chapter on Romania, after a short introduction on
the ornithological characteristics of the country, consisting of a detailed description of
a number of important sites. The criteria for inclusion in the work is the importance of
a site for migratory species, globally threatened species and species with relatively
small world range but with important populations in Europe. The ultimate purpose of
the research is to provide a useful base for planning by European governments.

97   **The composition and conservation of Romania's plant cover.**
      E. Cristina Muica, Ana Popova-Cucu.   *GeoJournal,* vol. 29, no. 1
      (Jan. 1993), p. 9-18.

After describing the great diversity of flora to be found in Romania, the authors of this
paper highlight the threat posed by an acute pollution problem. They suggest that
change can only occur through changes in human behaviour and greater protection of
vegetation by national parks and nature reserves.

98   **A note on the present status of geese in Rumania.**
      D. Munteanu, P. Weber, J. Szabó, M. Gogu-Bogdan, M. Marinov.
      Ardea, vol. 79, no. 2 (1991), p. 165-66.

Drawing upon the reports of Romanian and foreign ornithologists, this is a detailed
and meticulous survey of the varieties of geese to be found in Romania. The only
resident breeding species is the Greylag Goose (*Anser Anser*), found throughout
southern Romania along the Danube but also to be seen are the winter visitors, the
White-fronted Goose (*A. Albifrons*) – the most common species in Romania – the
Lesser White-fronted Goose (*A. Erythropus*), the Bean Goose (*A. Fabalis*) and the
Red-breasted goose (*Branta Ruficollis*). All of the latter species leave Romania in
March for their breeding grounds in more northerly climes.

99   **Nature reserves in Romania.**
      Emil Pop, N. Sălăgeanu.   Bucharest: Meridiane, 1965. 175p.

At the time of writing the Romanian national park system covered 75,000 hectares in
130 reserves. Scientific rather than popular in approach, this volume describes the
geology, botany, zoology and cultural history of each reserve. In addition, chapters list
protected plant and animal species and state where they can be found. The book is
profusely illustrated with over 100 photographs.

100 Travel diaries of a naturalist. Volume II. Hawaii, California,
Alaska, Florida, The Bahamas, Iceland, Norway, Spitzbergen,
Greenland, Israel, Romania, Siberia.
Peter Scott.   London; Glasgow; Sydney; Auckland; Toronto;
Johannesburg: Collins, 1985. 288p. maps.
Two chapters of this beautifully illustrated book are dedicated to the author's
adventures in Romania. The first, entitled 'A wild goose chase in Romania', tells of
his encounters with the Red-breasted geese in the Zmeica Peninsula near Constanţa.
The second, 'Further Romanian adventures', which draws upon his diaries from 1971,
1973 and 1977, narrates his return to the Dobrogea area in order to count the geese as
part of a long-term project to monitor their conservation.

101 Factors affecting the feeding distribution of Red-breasted geese
'Branta ruficollis' wintering in Romania.
William J. Sutherland, Nicola J. Crockford.   *Biological Conservation*,
vol. 63, no. 1 (1993), p. 61-65.
The natural habitat of the Dobrogea region in South-East Romania, with its open
expanses, is ideal for the Red-breasted goose, the rarest European species of goose.
Between 23,830 to 33,830 can be found in the region where, the author suggests, they
have benefited not only from the protection afforded by the Danube Delta Biosphere
Reserve – a RAMSAR site – but also from agricultural policies which favoured the
extension of winter wheat planting.

102 Dictionary of weeds of Eastern Europe: their common names and
importance in Latin, Albanian, Bulgarian, Czech, German,
English, Greek, Hungarian, Polish, Romanian, Russian,
Serbo-Croatian and Slovak.
Gareth Williams, Károly Hunyadi.   Amsterdam; Oxford; New York;
Tokyo: Elsevier, 1987. 479p.
After the Latin 'Linnean' name of each plant there follows the local name in each
language cited, together with some indication of the importance of the weed on a scale
of 0 (no importance) to 3 (important competitive weed). There is a comprehensive
index for each language.

Prehistory and
Archaeology

103   **Roman lamps from Ulpia Traiana Sarmizegetusa.**
Dorin Alicu, Emil Nemeș.   Oxford: British Archaeological Reports,
1977. 119p. maps. bibliog. (BAR Supplementary Series, no. 18).
The remains of the city of Sarmizegetusa, the capital of Roman Dacia, are located near
the town of Hațeg in the south-west of Transylvania. Founded by Decius Terentius
Scarinus, its first governor, probably between AD 108-110, as Colonia Dacia, the city
later changed its name to Ulpia Traiana Augusta Dacia Sarmizegetusa on the orders of
the Emperor Hadrian in 118 – the last epithet reflecting a new policy of assimilating
local populations. Since 1973 a series of archaeological excavations have revealed
much of the layout of the Roman city and also produced a large number of small finds
which are catalogued in this and other books in the series, including: *Figured
monuments from Ulpia Traiana Sarmizegetusa,* by Dorin Alicu, Consantin Pop,
Volker Wollmann, translated from the Romanian by Nubar Hampartumian (Oxford:
British Archaeological Reports, 1979. 211p. map. bibliog. [International Series,
no. 55]); *Small finds from Ulpia Traiana Sarmizegetusa,* by Dorin Alicu, Sorin Cociș,
Constantin Ilieș, Alina Soroceanu, translated from the Romanian by Adela Paki and
Angela Morariu (Cluj-Napoca, Romania: National History Museum of Transylvania,
1994. 150p. [Sarmizegetusa Monograph, no. 4]); and *Town-planning and population
in Ulpia Traiana Sarmizegetusa,* by Dorin Alicu, Adela Paki (Oxford: Archaeological
and Historical Associates, 1995. 91p. map. [British Archaeological Reports,
International Series, no. 605]).

104   **The archaeology and history of the Carpi from the second to the
fourth century AD.**
Gh. Bichir, translated from the Romanian by Nubar Hampartumian.
Oxford: British Archaeological Reports, 1976. 211p. maps. (BAR
Supplementary Series, no. 16).
The Carpi, sometimes known as the Poienești or Vîrtișcoiu-Poienești culture, are attested
in the ancient sources. They seem to have inhabited the eastern Carpathians and in this
study of their civilization the author states that at the time of writing 226 Carpic sites

had been discovered in central Moldavia: 177 settlements and 49 cemeteries. After reviewing the available evidence, Bichir argues that the Carpi were the most powerful of the Dacian tribes who, by the 3rd century AD, had become the principal enemy of the Romans in the region. It is not clear whether the Carpi derived their name from the Carpathian mountains or vice versa.

105   The brooches in the Pietroasa treasure.
David Brown. *Antiquity,* vol. 46, no. 182 (June 1972), p. 111-16.

A brief study of the brooches from the fabulous Pietroasa hoard which was discovered in 1837 by two peasants. Originally comprising twenty-two gold jewel-encrusted pieces, most of the hoard was broken up within days of being found for its gold content. What remains today was largely reconstructed on the basis of the descriptions of the peasants who had discovered the hoard. However, in this article the author challenges the veracity of some of these reconstructions and suggests that the brooches were not just chest ornaments, as has previously been thought, but were in fact worn on the shoulders to fasten cloaks. On the basis of similar usage elsewhere in Europe he then argues that 'They are the personal jewellery of a man and of one or two women who saw themselves as equivalent to the Roman imperial family. It is hard to see them as anything less than the regalia of a Gothic king'.

106   Treasures from Romania. A special exhibition held at the British Museum, January – March 1971.
Translated from the French by Richard Camber, Lawrence Dethan, Ian Longworth, Kenneth Painter, Leslie Webster.   London: Trustees of the British Museum, 1971. 111p. map. bibliog.

Written by a number of Romanian experts, this small but informative guide provides an introduction to Romanian history from the earliest prehistoric times to the Byzantine period. Each historical period is given a separate chapter with the text being complemented by photographs of the artefacts on exhibition (jewellery, tools, icons, statuettes, vases, etc.). The aim of the authors is to persuade the reader that the Romanians have a rich artistic tradition and that they contributed extensively to the development of European culture.

107   Evolution of the system of defence works in Roman Dacia.
Ioana Bogdan Cătăniciu, translated from the Romanian by Etta Dumitrescu.   Oxford: British Archaeological Reports, 1981. 121p. maps. bibliog. (BAR International Series, no. 116).

Drawing on a large number of excavation reports, the author offers a study of the development of the defences of the Dacian frontier from the first invasion of Trajan in AD 101 to the end of the 3rd century. Her aim in presenting all the topographical elements is to allow the reader to make an assessment of the strategic function of the various defence works.

108   The Danube in prehistory.
V. Gordon Childe.   Oxford: Clarendon Press, 1929. 479p. bibliog.

A classic study which surveys the prehistory of the Danube Basin from Bavaria to the Black Sea. The coverage of the Romanian lands is necessarily limited given the embryonic state of Romanian archaeology at the time. The author examines each culture chronologically, from the Palaeolithic to the Bronze Age, describing the main traits of each as they are revealed by actual finds and their relationship with other groups, especially the Aegean civilizations, before finally assessing data establishing chronology and origins.

109 **The neolithic settlement at Rast (south-west Oltenia, Romania).**
Vladimir Dumitrescu, translated from the Romanian by Nubar Hampartumian. Oxford: British Archaeological Reports, 1980. 133p. maps. (BAR International Series, no. 72).

A specialized report of the excavations conducted between 1943-50 at the Neolithic settlement of Rast in southern Dolj. The findings belong to the Vinča culture and mark the easternmost extremity of its diffusion.

110 **The Cucuteni-Tripolye culture: a study in technology and the origins of complex society.**
Linda Ellis. Oxford: British Archaeological Reports, 1984. 221p. maps. bibliog. (BAR International Series, no. 217).

The Cucuteni-Tripolye culture straddles the divide between the Neolithic and Bronze ages. It takes its name from the sites at Cucuteni in northern Moldavia, which was discovered in 1884, and Tripolye, near Kiev in present-day Ukraine. In this study the author traces the role technology played, particularly in the development of ceramic products, in the transition over a period of nearly 1,000 years from small scattered farming villages to an embryonic ranked society. The introduction of mass production methods was needed to meet increased demand following a rise in population numbers.

111 **Histria: the city of Histria.**
Radu Florescu, Ion Miclea. Bucharest: Editura Sport-Turism, 1989. 99p. maps.

This scholarly bilingual Romanian-English guide covers one of Romania's premier archaeological sites, the Graeco-Roman city of Histria. Sometimes, perhaps a little exaggeratedly, known as the 'Romanian Pompeii', the city was abandoned in the 7th century AD after attacks by the Avars. It remained virtually undisturbed until 1914, when Vasile Pârvan began a series of excavations which were to mark the birth of Romanian scientific archaeology. A detailed history of the city is followed by a description of the site which is augmented by numerous plans, maps and other illustrations.

112 **The fifth-century A.D. treasure from Pietroasa, Romania, in the light of recent research.**
Radu Harhoiu, translated from the Romanian by Nubar Hampartumian. Oxford: British Archaeological Reports, 1977. 57p. map. (BAR Supplementary Series, no. 24).

Amongst the pieces of the Pietroasa treasure are some breathtakingly beautiful finds of the finest craftsmanship, including a perfectly preserved dish decorated with human figures in various postures and a gold cup ornamented with precious and semiprecious stones with handles in the form of panthers set with garnets. Pieces of the treasure belong to different periods and arise from different cultures – some being Germanic, especially Ostrogothic, and others late Roman – but information from literary sources coupled with archaeological analysis suggests that it dates from the first half of the 5th century AD.

113   **The Dacian stones speak.**
      Paul Mackendrick.   Chapel Hill, North Carolina: University of North
      Carolina Press, 1975. 248p. maps. bibliog.
A highly readable, but still scholarly, exploration of the archaeology of the Romanian lands from the Neolithic sculptures of Cernovoda dating from 3,000 BC to the fall of Histria to the Avars. in the 7th century AD. Chapters cover the Greek cities of the Black Sea, the Dacian hill citadels of Transylvania, the Roman invasion and occupation, and religion, arts and crafts.

114   **Archaeology in Romania, the mystery of the Roman occupation.**
      Andrew Mackenzie.   London: Hale, 1986. 183p. map. bibliog.
In addressing this most 'obscure corner of western history', as it was described by R. W. Seton-Watson, this study is a robust response to those who would argue against continuity of settlement in the Romanian lands. Far from being a strictly academic debate, this issue carries important political connotations because the question of continuity has frequently been directly linked to the legitimacy of the Romanian occupation of Transylvania. The argument of the 19th-century German scholar Roesler and many Hungarians after him was that when the Emperor Aurelian abandoned the province of Dacia and withdrew the Roman legions and administration south of the Danube in 271-276, the local population also departed leaving an empty land for the Magyars to occupy when they arrived in 886 – autochtonous status in this case being seen as the basis for a territorial claim to the region. The author reviews the complex historiography surrounding this issue – the outline of which is well summed up in the chapter entitled 'The Great debate' (p. 133-44) – and the latest archaeological evidence before concluding that Roesler was wrong and that there was indeed continuity of settlement.

115   **Funerary monuments in Dacia Superior and Dacia Porolissensis.**
      Lucia Eposu Marinescu, translated from the Romanian by Nubar
      Hampartumian.   Oxford: British Archaeological Reports, 1982. 244p.
      (BAR International Series, no. 128).
In this study the author offers a detailed catalogue of the more than 500 funerary monuments that have been discovered in these two provinces which covered present-day Transylvania and the Banat. In a detailed typology the monuments are arranged according to the categories of stelae, altars, medallions and *aediculae* (funerary buildings). As the author herself states: 'The deep study of the Roman funerary monuments, perhaps the most significant product of provincial art, give answers to such problems as the origins of artisans and the cultural centres of provinces, the spreading of Romanization from the urban milieu to the rural milieu, the element of continuity in the dress and the ornaments of the native population. They allow us to determine the role and the contribution of Dacia to the history of civilization both in the Balkano-Danubian zone and within the Roman world as a whole'. A similar study covering all of Romania is Luca Bianchi, *Le stele funerarie della Dacia: un' espressione di arte romana periferica* (Funerary stelae from Dacia: an expression of provincial Roman art) (Rome: Giorgio Bretschneider, 1985. 315p.).

116 **Tîrpeşti: from prehistory to history in eastern Romania.**
Silvia Marinescu-Bîlcu, translated from the Romanian by Georgeta
Bolomey. Oxford: British Archaeological Reports, 1981. 187p. maps.
bibliog. (BAR International Series, no. 107).

A highly specialized record of excavations at the village of Tîrpeşti in the county of
Neamţ, northern Moldavia. The site was occupied with breaks from the Neolithic
period to the 6th-7th century AD when it was abandoned. First discovered in 1937, it
was subject to systematic excavation from 1959 with most findings coming from the
precucuteni and *cucuteni* cultures of the Neolithic and Chalcolithic periods.

117 **The Middle Paleolithic in Romania.**
Steven B. Mertens. *Current Anthropology*, vol. 37, no. 3 (June 1996),
p. 515-21.

The author surveys the current state of research into the Middle Palaeolithic in
Romania. Several sites have been discovered in the Dobrogea, Moldavia and within
the Carpathian Mountains. Under communism research was sporadic but excavations
and the study of lithic artefacts have revealed something of the structures inhabited by
these early occupants of the Romanian lands as well as their means of subsistence.
This has allowed scientists to form an understanding of the palaeoclimatic and
palaeoenvironmnetal constraints under which Palaeolithic man lived. Radiocarbon
dating has recently suggested that the sites of the region were occupied between
58,000 and 36,000 years ago. These new dates provide a framework for a regional
chronology and should eventually allow the Romanian Palaeolithic to be placed within
a wider Eastern European context.

118 **The Dacian Iron Age: a comment in a European context.**
John Nandris. In: *Festschrift für Richard Pittioni: zum siebzigsten
Geburstag* (Festschrift for Richard Pittioni: on his sixtieth birthday).
Vienna: Franz Deutiche, 1976, p. 723-36. (Archaeologica Austriaca,
no. 13).

The author discusses the urbanization of native European societies north of the limits
of the Roman Empire and specifically the relationship of the *oppidum* form of
settlement of Celtic ('La Tene') societies in western Europe with the corresponding
forms found in the Dacian society of Eastern Europe. He concludes by suggesting that
the urban civilization of Dacia was as complex as those in the West but that it was
distributed in a different way because of local conditions. Indeed, the structures
created at this time remained appropriate for the greater part of Romania throughout
much of the medieval period and beyond.

119 **Villagers of the Maros: a portrait of an early Bronze Age society.**
John M. O'Shea. New York; London: Plenum Press, 1996. 398p.
maps. bibliog. (Interdisciplinary Contributions to Archaeology).

The 'Maros group' were a distinct cultural entity occupying an area between the Tisza
and Maroş rivers in south-eastern Hungary, northern Yugoslavia and western Romania
between 2700 and 1500 BC. Essentially marsh dwellers, they lived on low islands of
dry land. Applying anthropological techniques to archaeology, the author analyses the
densely encoded social information contained in the group's cemeteries to build a
picture of early Bronze Age life in the Carpathian basin.

120 **The late copper age Coţofeni culture of South-East Europe.**
Petre Roman, translated from the Romanian by Nubar Hampartumian.
Oxford: British Archaeological Reports, 1977. 120p. (BAR
International Series, no. 32).

The Coţofeni culture, named after finds made at Bocşa-Colţani in the late 19th century, flourished at the end of the Neolithic and the beginning of the Bronze Age. It covered most of present-day Romania, except for Moldavia and the Dobrogea, as well as north-eastern Serbia and north-western Bulgaria. Traditionally, the Coţofeni culture has been seen as one of nomadic or semi-nomadic shepherds, but the author questions this view and citing evidence which shows a long occupation of some sites, he instead suggests that they adapted particularly well to their environment and that this produced stable settlement patterns.

121 **Limes Scythiae: topographical and stratigraphical research on the late Roman fortification in the lower Danube.**
C. Scorpan. Oxford: British Archaeological Reports, 1980. 238p. maps. bibliog. (BAR International Series, no. 88).

The word *limes* has no clear equivalent in any modern language, but for the Romans it signified a defence in depth as much as length. Using literary sources as well as archaeological and epigraphic evidence, the author provides an account of the defensive system erected by the Romans in the province of Scythia which had two principle lines of fortification; the first along the Danube, and the second parallel a little way behind. In the 4th century AD it comprised twenty-six forts but by the 6th century these had grown to forty. The author was the director of excavations at the Roman fort of Sacidava between 1969-79, and in a further highly specialized article he has evaluated some inscriptions to suggest who was responsible for constructing this fort: 'Cohors I Cilicum at Sacidava and Scythia Minor', *Journal of Roman Studies*, vol. 71 (1981), p. 98-102.

122 **The east Carpathian area of Romania in the V-XI centuries AD.**
Dan Gh. Teodor, translated from the Romanian by Nubar
Hampartumian. Oxford: British Archaeological Reports, 1980. 126p. maps. (BAR International Series, no. 81).

Moldavia has long been the eastern gateway to Romania through which countless invaders have passed over the years on their way to central and south-eastern Europe. However, archaeological work only really began in the area in the 1960s and this study aims to be a synthesis of the results from a number of excavations relating to the 6th-11th centuries, many of which remain unpublished. The author then compares his findings with other areas of Romania to 'demonstrate not only the continuity of the Romanian population in the east-Carpathian areas of Romania but also the unity of culture within Romania as a whole'.

History

General

123 **History of Transylvania.**
Gábor Barta, István Bóna, Bela Köpeczi, László Makkai, Ambrus Miskolczy et al. Budapest: Akadémiai Kiadó, 1994. 806p. maps. bibliog.
This is a single-volume abridged and, in certain places, revised edition of the highly controversial three-volume *Erdély története* (Budapest: Hungarian Academy of Sciences, Institute of History, 1986). Lucidly written and fully documented, it is the definitive Hungarian view on Transylvanian history and as such many of its conclusions have been bitterly contested by Romanian historians. The latter have produced works refuting its contents, such as the volume edited by Ştefan Pascu and Ştefan Ştefănescu, *The dangerous game of falsifying history: studies and articles* (Bucharest: Editura Ştiinţifică şi Enciclopedică, 1987). In keeping with the perspective of the authors, the bulk of the work is concerned with the history of Transylvania prior to its unification with Romania in 1918 with only a sketch of events afterwards. There is a useful detailed chronology and an extensive critical bibliography. Place-names in the text are given in their Hungarian variant, but the German and Romanian equivalents can be found in the index, and on the endpaper map the names for the principal towns are given in all three languages.

124 **Transylvania in the history of the Romanians.**
Cornelia Bodea, Virgil Cândea. Boulder, Colorado: East European Monographs, distributed by Columbia University Press, 1982. 175p. (East European Monographs, no. 117).
Covering the history of Transylvania from antiquity until the 1980s, this book provides a succinct restatement of the Romanian position on the Transylvanian Question by two well-known Romanian historians. The narrative is complemented by a number of interesting appendices containing documents relating to Transylvanian

history. These include a 1785 letter from a French traveller, Jacques-Pierre Brissot; a 1891 report from A. Nicolson, British Consul General in Bucharest; the programme adopted by the Congress of Nationalities held in Budapest in 1895; and the 1918 decision for the union of Transylvania with Romania.

125 **A history of the Romanians.**
Georges Castellan, translated from the French by Nicholas Bradley.
Boulder, Colorado: East European Monographs, distributed by
Columbia University Press, 1989. 268p. map. (East European
Monographs, no. 257).

A succinct and balanced history of the Romanian people from their first origins to the installation of Nicolae Ceaușescu as Romanian Communist Party leader in 1965. Generally, this is a well produced volume, although the translation has occasionally produced some strange quirks such as the renaming of Mihai Viteazul, who is usually rendered as 'Michael the Brave' in English, as 'Michael the Bold'. The absence of an index detracts from the volume's usefulness. The same author has also produced a general history of the Balkans, which naturally contains similar material on Romania: Georges Castellan, *History of the Balkans from Mohammed the Conqueror to Stalin*, translated from the French by Nicholas Bradley (Boulder, Colorado: East European Monographs, distributed by Columbia University Press, 1992. 493p. [East European Monographs, no. 325]).

126 **Occasional papers in Romanian studies.**
Edited by Dennis Deletant. London: School of Slavonic and East
European Studies, University of London, 1995. 70p.

This collection of papers, which were all delivered during a Romanian Studies Day held at the School of Slavonic and East European Studies in January 1995, includes: Ivor Porter, 'The coup of 23 August 1944: personal recollections of an SOE mission', p. 1-6; Maurice Pearton, 'Puzzles about percentages', p. 7-14; Mark Percival, 'British attitudes towards the Romanian historic parties and the monarchy, 1944-47', p. 15-24; Dennis Deletant, 'What was the role of the Romanian Communist Party in the coup of 23 August 1944?', p. 25-37; Peter Siani-Davies, 'The overthrow of Nicolae Ceaușescu', p. 37-49; Elena Zamfirescu, 'Romania's role in post-Cold War Central Europe', p. 49-61; and Charles King, 'Who are the Moldavians?', p. 61-69.

127 **Studies in Romanian history.**
Dennis Deletant, with a preface by Alexandru Duțu. Bucharest:
Editura Enciclopedică, 1991. 332p.

A useful compilation of articles and papers by this prolific author, most of which have previously appeared in other publications. The contents, with the original place of publication, are: 'Genoese, Tatars and Romanians at the mouth of the Danube in the fourteenth century' (see item no. 184); 'Some considerations on the emergence of the principality of Moldavia in the middle of the fourteenth century' (see item no. 186); 'Moldavia between Hungary and Poland, 1347-1412', *Slavonic and East European Review*, vol. 64, no. 2 (April 1986), p. 189-211; 'Slavonic letters in Moldovia, Wallachia and Transylvania from the tenth to the seventeenth centuries', *Slavonic and East European Review*, vol. 58, no. 1 (Jan. 1980), p. 1-21; 'A survey of Romanian presses and printing in the sixteenth century', *Slavonic and East European Review*, vol. 53, no. 131 (April 1975), p. 161-74; 'Romanian presses and printing in the seventeenth century (I, II)', *Slavonic and East European Review,* vol. 60, no. 4 (Oct. 1982) p. 481-99, vol. 61, no. 4 (Oct. 1983), p. 481-511; 'Some aspects of the Byzantine tradition in the Romanian principalities' (see item no. 185); 'A survey of the Gaster books in the School of Slavonic and East European Studies Library', *Solanus,* no. 10 (June 1975), p. 14-23; 'The Sunday legend', *Revue des études sud-est européenes,* vol. 15, no. 3 (1977), p. 431-51; 'Archie Gibson: The Times correspondent in Romania, 1928-40', the first half of which was presented at a conference whereas the second half had already been published as 'Archie Gibson's prayer for peace, Bucharest, 1944', *Slavonic and East European Review,* vol. 64, no. 4 (Oct. 1986), p. 571-74; 'Some considerations on the implementations of the Allied-Romanian armistice agreement of 12 September 1944: a Soviet-Romanian exchange of letters in spring 1946', previously unpublished; 'A shuttlecock of history: Bessarabia', *South Slav Journal,* vol. 10, no. 4 (Winter 1987/88), p. 1-14; 'Language policy and linguistic trends in Soviet Moldavia', *Language planning in the Soviet Union,* edited by Michael Kirkwood (London: Macmillan in association with SSEES, 1989, p. 189-216 [Studies in Russia and East Europe]); and, finally, 'Ethno-history or mytho-history? The case of the chronicler Anonymous', *Historians and the history of Transylvania* (q.v.).

128   **Men of letters, historians and the 'other' – Anglo-Romanian**
      literary relations in the inter-war period.
      Alexandru Duţu.   In: *Sensus communis. Contemporary trends in*
      comparative literature. Panorama de la situation actuelle en
      Littérature Comparée.   Edited by János Riesz, Peter Broerner,
      Bernhard Scholz.   Tübingen, Germany: Gunter Narr Verlag, 1986,
      p. 409-15.

In his preface to Iorga's book on Anglo-Romanian relations, R. W. Seton-Watson wrote that 'the English reader could no longer find excuse for his ignorance of the Latin people on the Danube with the same plausibility as before the First World War'. The publication of a number of books on English history also means that the same, in reverse, could be said about the Romanians and in this brief but incisive account the author explores the meaning of 'other' in terms of the mental images formed through these literary contacts between two disparate peoples, the Romanians and the English.

129   **Romania.**
      Stephen Fischer-Galaţi.   In: *Nationalism in Eastern Europe.*   Edited
      by Peter F. Sugar, Ivo J. Lederer.   Seattle, Washington: University of
      Washington Press, 1994, p. 373-96.

This classic study was first published in 1966 when the subject of nationalism in Eastern Europe was not the focus of attention it is today. Understandably, this makes the work somewhat dated, but a reprinting in 1994 means that it is still widely available and it remains a good historical introduction to the subject for the non-specialist reader.

130 **Twentieth century Rumania.**
Stephen Fischer-Galați. New York: Columbia University Press, 1991.
2nd ed. 247p. bibliog.
This general introduction to 20th-century Romanian history was first published in
1970 but after the fall of communism it was revised by the author and brought up to
date – indeed the final chapter is punningly called 'Fin de Sickle Rumania'.
Inevitably, the style is now a little dated, but it still remains an accessible guide to the
history of this century and particularly the communist period.

131 **Labyrinth of nationalism: complexities of diplomacy. Essays in
honor of Charles and Barbara Jelavich.**
Edited by Richard Frucht. Columbus, Ohio: Slavica Publishers, 1992.
377p. bibliog.
Aside from a useful bibliography of the many works by these two distinguished
Professors of South-Eastern European history, this Festschrift also includes five
articles on Romania: William Oldson, 'Tradition and rite in Transylvania: historic
tensions between East and West', p. 161-79; James Ermatinger, 'Ceauşescu's
nationalism: ancient Dacian translated into modern Romanian', p. 180-89; Richard
Frucht, 'The Romanian dilemma: Russia and the double election of Cuza', p. 275-89;
Fredrick Kellogg, 'A perilous liaison: Russo-Romanian relations in 1877', 290-317;
and Glenn E. Torrey, 'The ending of hostilities on the Romanian front: the armistice
negotiations at Focşani, December 7-9, 1917', p. 318-30.

132 **The Romanians: a history.**
Vlad Georgescu, edited by Matei Calinescu, translated from the
Romanian by Alexandra Bley-Vroman. London; New York: I.B.
Tauris, 1991. 357p. maps. bibliog.
This revised version of the Romanian-language original of 1984 is the most accessible
single-volume, general history of Romania currently available. Tracing the development of the Romanian lands from the earliest signs of human habitation until the
Revolution of 1989, it is both broad in scope and lucidly written. Indeed, its value can
be gauged from the fact that in post-communist Romania it has been widely used as a
text book in higher education. Georgescu had only revised the first five chapters of the
book before his death in 1988, and so the editor has completed this English-language
version of the work by taking chapter six of the Romanian original and adding to it a
chapter entitled 'Romania in the mid-1980s' which reprints an article published by
Georgescu elsewhere ('Romania in the 1980s: the legacy of dynastic socialism' – see
item no. 306). Finally, the book contains an epilogue entitled 'The 1989 Revolution
and the collapse of communism in Romania' which is also a reprint of an earlier
article by Matei Calinescu and Vladimir Tismăneanu, 'The 1989 revolution and
Romania's future', *Problems of Communism,* vol. 40, no. 1-2 (1991), p. 42-59.

133 **Alexandru D. Xenopol and the development of Romanian
historiography.**
Paul A. Hiemstra. New York; London: Garland, 1987. 210p.
Based on a doctoral thesis, this is a scholarly study of one of the founding fathers of
modern Romanian historiography. After an early education in Romania, Xenopol
attended universities in Germany where he gained doctorates in Philosophy and Law.

On his return to his native land he taught at the University in Iaşi and was appointed Professor of Romanian history in 1883. Xenopol espoused a history grounded in German determinism which placed local historical events in the context of wider developments in European and universal history. He was often a controversial figure and his most important work was the first major synthesis of Romanian history, entitled *Istoria Românilor din Dacia Traiană* (The history of the Romanians of Trajan's Dacia). He also played a leading role in rebutting the theories of the German Robert Roesler who controversially argued that the Romanians had not continuously occupied the Romanian lands but had migrated from below the Danube in the early Middle Ages.

134 **The history of international relations in Central and Eastern Europe: study traditions and research perspectives.**
Cluj-Napoca, Romania: Commission of History of International Relations; Babeş-Bolyai University, Cluj-Napoca, Romania, Institute of Central European History, 1995. 241p.
A collection of papers, most of which were given at a conference in Cluj in October 1993, which addressed questions relating to historiography. The contributions include: Peter Siani-Davies, 'British historiography on Romanian international relations', p. 78-117; Keith Hitchins, 'American historians on Romania's international relations', p. 155-77; and Pompilu Teodor, 'Gheorghe Brătianu, an historian of international relations', p. 178-88.

135 **The historiography of the countries of Eastern Europe: Romania.**
Keith Hitchins. *American Historical Review*, vol. 97, no. 4 (Oct. 1992), p. 1,064-83.
Provides an excellent introduction to 20th-century Romanian intellectual history. Stressing the division between the traditionalists, who rejected the wholesale adoption of Western forms and the Europeanists, who emphasized the value of Western progress, the author highlights the main ideologists and movements within each of the trends. Amongst the traditionalists he lists a number of groups including: Titu Maiorescu (1840-1917) and the *Junimists*, Nicolae Iorga (1871-1940) and the *Sămănătorists*, Constantin Stere (1865-1936) and the *Poporanists*, Nae Ionescu (1888-1940) and the followers of Romanian existentialism (*trăirism*) and Virgil Madgearu (1887-1940) and the Peasantists. Amongst the Europeanists the chief figures were Eugen Lovinescu (1881-1943) and Ştefan Zeletin (1882-1934). The superimposition of a Marxist ideology muted the debate between the two camps after 1945, but with the fall of communism in 1989 it has once more been resurrected as Romania again searches for an appropriate model for modernization and development.

136 **Studies on Romanian national consciousness.**
Keith Hitchins. Pelham, New York; Montreal; Paris; Lugoj, Romania; Rome: Nagard, 1983. 258p.
This is a useful compilation of twelve of Hitchins' ground-breaking articles on Translvanian history and particularly the growth of Romanian national consciousness in the 18th and 19th centuries. All the articles have previously appeared in Romanian or Western journals and, with the place of original publication, they include: 'Religion and Rumanian national consciousness in eighteenth-century Transylvania', *Slavonic and East European Review*, vol. 57, no. 2 (April 1979), p. 214-39; 'Samuel Clain and

the Rumanian Enlightenment in Transylvania', *Slavic Review*, vol. 23, no. 4 (Dec. 1964), p. 660-75; 'The sacred cult of nationality: Rumanian intellectuals and the church in Transylvania, 1834-1869', in *Intellectual and social developments in the Habsburg Empire from Maria Theresa to World War I*, edited by Stanley B. Winters and Joseph Held (Boulder, Colorado: East European Quarterly, 1975, p. 131-60); 'Avram Iancu and the European Revolution of 1848', *Transilvania*, vol. 1, no. 5 (Sept. 1972), p. 19-21; 'Andreiu Şaguna and the Rumanians of Transylvania during the decade of Absolutism, 1849-1859', *Südost-Forschungen*, vol. 25 (1966), p. 120-49; 'Andreiu Şaguna and Joseph Rajačić: the Rumanian and Serbian churches in the decade of Absolutism', *Revue des Etudes Sud-est Européennes*, vol. 10, no. 3 (1972), p. 567-79; 'The Rumanians of Transylvania and the Ausgleich, 1865-1869', *Revue Romaine d'Histoire*, vol. 7, no. 2 (1968), p. 197-231; 'Rumanian socialists and the nationality problem in Hungary, 1903-18', *Slavic Review*, vol. 35, no. 1 (March 1976), p. 69-90; and 'The Rumanian socialists and the Hungarian Soviet republic', in *Revolution in perspective. Essays on the Hungarian Soviet Republic*, edited by A. C. Janos and W. B. Slottman (Berkeley, California: University of California Press, 1971, p. 109-44).

137 **History of the Balkans.**
Barbara Jelavich. Cambridge, England: Cambridge University Press, 1983. 2 vols. 1,407p. 2,476p. maps. bibliog. (American Council of Learned Societies. The Social Science Research Council; the Joint Committee on Eastern European Publications, no. 12.).

This two-volume work is the best general text book currently available for the modern history of South-Eastern Europe. Volume one is concerned with the 18th and 19th centuries. Broadly thematic chapters, covering issues such as 'The formation of national governments' and 'The national issue in the Habsburg Empire', not only contain sections specifically relating to the Romanian lands but also firmly place this history within a regional and international context. The second volume covers the 20th century.

138 **A history of Romanian historical writing.**
Frederick Kellogg. Bakersfield, California: Charles Schlaks Jnr, 1990. 132p. map. bibliog.

The author's stated aim in this book is 'to survey the landmarks in historical learning from the birth of Romanian writing . . . down to the present' and in general he has succeeded in this task. The work is divided into six concise chapters. The first three deal with early, modern and contemporary Romanian historical writing and the fourth with foreign views of Romanian history. The two concluding chapters are entitled 'Resources and organization of Romanian historical research' and 'Current needs of Romanian historiography'.

139 **A journey into the past of Transylvania.**
Andrew Mackenzie, with an introductory outline of Romanian history by David Stephenson. London: Hale, 1990. 192p. map. bibliog.

This is a rather pedestrian restatement of the Romanian line on Transylvanian history which relies to a large extent on lengthy quotes from R. W. Seton-Watson's *A history of the Romanians* (q.v.) and other secondary sources.

140 **Themes in modern and contemporary Romanian historiography.**
Paul E. Michelson. In: *East European history: selected papers of the third world congress for Soviet and East European studies.* Edited by S. J. Kirschbaum. Columbus, Ohio: Slavica Publishers, 1988, p. 27-40.
In this informative and useful essay the author gives some thought to the main themes that have preoccupied Romanian historiography. He suggests that these have been national unity and continuity, national destiny and mission, and the problem of which model to follow for national development. In addressing these questions historians have often engaged in violent debate as they have struggled to set the agenda, and, occasionally, Romanian historians, such as Iorga, have transcended the boundary between history and politics so that they have not only written history but also made it.

141 **From ancient Dacia to modern Romania.**
Mircea Muşat, Ion Ardeleanu. Bucharest: Editura Ştiinţifică şi enciclopedică, 1985. 808p.
This massive tome stands out as the best example of the *Weltanschauung* of official Romanian history in the late 1980s with chapters bearing titles such as ' "We want Dacia as it used to be": Romanian socialists in the van of the struggle for national and state unity'. Invaluable as a source for late Ceauşescu historiography, it has less value as a work of pure history and should be avoided by the general reader. The tone of the work is set from the very first paragraph of the narrative, which states that: 'Having been born as a unitary people on the traditional territory of Dacia, the Romanians have uninterruptedly preserved the continuity of their material life, their ethnic-linguistic and cultural spiritual community, in spite of all the great hardships they faced'. The readability of the book is not helped by the tendency of the authors to reproduce large quantities of selective secondary quotations, if they seem to support their argument, and, although the title promises a full survey of Romanian history, it is in fact primarily concerned with the events surrounding the creation of Greater Romania in 1918.

142 **Romanian nationalism and the ideology of integration and mobilization.**
James P. Niessen. In: *Eastern European nationalism in the twentieth century.* Edited by Peter F. Sugar. Washington, DC: The American University Press, 1995, p. 273-304.
The chapter begins with four texts in translation by Nicolae Iorga, dating from 1908, Nichifor Crainic (1938), Nicolae Ceauşescu (1974), and the programme of the Greater Romanian Party of 1991. In the wide-ranging survey that follows, the author then pays particular attention to the contribution of these figures and groups to a nationalism which he suggests has primarily served the needs of territorial and political consolidation. However, whilst the aim of territorial consolidation has largely been achieved, Niessen argues that the task of political integration has consistently eluded the Romanians and this partly explains the continuing appeal of nationalism until this day.

143 **Transylvania : an area of contacts and conflicts.**
Jean Nouzille, translated by Delia Răzdolescu.   Bucharest: Editura
Enciclopedică, 1996. 310p. maps. bibliog.
A general history of Transylvania from the earliest times to the present day. Indeed,
one of the strengths of the book is that it brings the story up-to-date. The author's
stated aim was to raise the minorities' issue, which he contends is badly understood in
the West, and with it the 'tormented and tragic history of Transylvania'. Strangely,
sections of the history are produced in the present tense and the text of this translation
has a rather breathless, journalistic quality. This work was originally published in
French as *La Transylvanie. Terre de contacts et de conflits* (Strasbourg, France: Revue
d'Europe Centrale, 1993).

144 **A concise history of Romania.**
Andrei Oțetea, English edition edited by Andrew Mackenzie.
London: Robert Hale, 1985. 591p. bibliog.
Based on Andrei Oțetea, *The history of the Romanian people,* translated by Eugenia
Farca (Bucharest: Scientific Pub. Hoose (sic), 1970. 637p. bibliog.), this work was
written by a committee of historians and as such it exhibits many of the traits of such
works as at times it subsides into a dry recital of facts. Written during the communist
period – Oțetea was one of the best-known Romanian Marxist historians – it
inevitably reflects the ideology of its time. However, apart from the attached
commentary, which includes a hagiography of Ceaușescu, there is surprisingly little
on the socialist period in general.

145 **Captive clio: Romanian historiography under communist rule.**
Șerban Papacostea.   *European History Quarterly,* vol. 26, no. 2
(April 1996), p. 181-208.
Despite the title, this informative article is actually as much about the travails of
history after the Revolution as it is about its fate under communism. The author is a
distinguished Romanian historian and Director of the Nicolae Iorga Institute of
History in Bucharest. In this balanced narrative he first notes that communism brought
some benefits to the study of history in Romania; however, enormous damage was
also inflicted. Many historians were prevented from publishing, books became
unavailable and events were even fabricated to make history fit the prescribed Marxist
theoretical model. For instance, a fictitious mass Dacian slave revolt was created at the
end of the Roman occupation. The shift from Stalinism to virulent nationalism in the
party brought a concomitant shift in history and the rise of protochronism and with it
thracomania – an exaggerated exaltation of the Thracian ancestors of the Romanians.
The situation has eased considerably since 1989, but the study of history is still
constrained. Books may once again be freely available, with the principal problem
now being cost, but archives are still under tight control, effectively blocking serious
research on the communist period.

146 **A history of Transylvania.**
Ștefan Pascu, translated by D. Robert Ladd.   Detroit, Michigan:
Wayne State University Press, 1982. 317p. maps. bibliog.
An abridgement of the author's *Voievodatul Transilvaniei* (2 vols, Cluj, 1972, 1979),
this is a work of nationalist history set within a Marxist framework. It stresses the

historical primacy and continuity of the Romanian population within Transylvania and the other Romanian lands as they moved towards their eventual unification in 1918, which was considered inevitable by the author.

147　**Historians and the history of Transylvania.**
Edited by László Péter.　Boulder, Colorado: East European Monographs, distributed by Columbia University Press, 1992. 254p. map. (East European Monographs, no. 332).

This collection of articles on the historiography of Transylvania was in part prompted by the feverish debate which surrounded the publication of the three-volume *History of Transylvania* by the Hungarian Academy of Sciences in 1986 (q.v.). Indeed, alongside a survey of the dispute by Norman Stone, 'Bad blood in Transylvania', and a reprint of Martyn Rady's review of the Hungarian work from *Slavonic and East European Review*, vol. 66, no. 3 (July 1988), p. 482-85, a series of appendices also reproduce the original Romanian riposte to the Hungarian publication from Ştefan Pascu, Mircea Muşat and Florin Constantiniu and a restatement of the Hungarian stance made during a debate at the University of Debrecen, Hungary. The remainder of the book forms a creditable attempt to achieve some balance on the issue with a lengthy introduction on the foundations of the Romanian-Hungarian dispute by László Péter (p. 1-51), followed by contributions from authors such as Domokos Kosáry, 'Historians and Transylvania' (p. 53-66) and Dennis Deletant, 'Ethnos and Mythos in the History of Transylvania: the case of the chronicler Anonymous' (p. 67-85).

148　**Transylvania.**
Titus Podea.　Bucharest: Editura Fundaţiei Culturale Române, 1993. 230p.

A parallel English-Romanian text version of a book originally published in 1936, but sadly without the fine photographs which enlivened the original. The overall tone of the work is fully captured in chapter titles such as: 'The age of Magyarisation', 'The struggle against Magyarisation', and 'Move to national unity'. There is a preface by Nicolae Iorga and an afterword by Elisabeta Simion in which she gives a summary of the history of Transylvania during the Second World War. Simion has also added sixty-one explanatory notes to the original text.

149　**Transylvania and again Transylvania: a historical exposé.**
David Prodan.　Cluj-Napoca, Romania: Centre for Transylvanian Studies, The Romanian Cultural Foundation, 1992. 217p. (Bibliotheca Rerum Transsilvaniae).

A lively and spirited rebuttal of the Hungarian position on Transylvanian history by one of Romania's most distinguished historians. Written, according to the author, not in direct response to the three-volume *History of Transylvania*, produced by the Hungarian Academy of Sciences in 1986 (q.v.), which he says he only consulted just prior to publication, this is in fact mostly a revision of an earlier 1944 tract entitled *The theory of immigration* which received only limited distribution at the time.

150 **A concise history of Dobruja.**
Adrian Rădulescu, Ion Bitoleanu.   Bucharest: Editura Ştiinţifică si
Enciclopedică, 1984. 281p.

The Dobrogea is an ancient historical region which lies on the Black Sea shore below
the Danube Delta. Today only part of the area lies within the bounds of Romania,
where it roughly corresponds with the county of Constanţa, but in the interwar period,
as part of Greater Romania, it extended far to the south into an area which now forms
part of modern Bulgaria. Indeed, the summer palace of the Romanian monarchy was at
Balchik which today lies over the border. Its fertile location on the Black Sea has
historically made the Dobrogea a rich and wealthy area but also one prey to invading
armies. The Romans protected it with sophisticated defences and it remained part of
the Roman Empire far longer than other areas of present-day Romania. Reflecting this
fact, half of this volume is concerned with the history of the region prior to the
Ottoman conquest in 1484. Regretfully there is no index.

151 **Romania in turmoil.**
Martyn Rady.   London; New York: I.B. Tauris, 1992. 216p. maps.
bibliog.

The first eight chapters of this book are concerned with the history of Romania prior to
1989, whilst the remainder, just over half of the book, covers the Revolution and its
immediate aftermath. In the first section, the author is primarily concerned with looking
for clues in Romania's turbulent past to understand the events of today. In particular, he
focuses his attention on the superficial adoption of Western forms, what he calls 'the
politics of illusion', and the culture of violence propagated by the Iron Guard. In
searching for an explanation for the Revolution Rady suggests that 'The country's politics
have traditionally lacked mechanisms for achieving peaceful change and for resolving
conflict in an orderly fashion. For most of the nineteenth and twentieth centuries, therefore
Romania laboured under a false constitutionalism which prevented popular
frustrations being mollified through democratic renewal or a change of government.
Thus, resentment was bottled up until it burst out altogether in a flood of bloodletting'.

152 **Romania: foreign sources on the Romanians.**
Bucharest: General Directorate of the State Archives of Romania,
1992. 384p.

An eclectic collection of documents with no real theme other than that they relate to
the history of Romania and the Romanians and that they are drawn from archives and
other sources outside the country. The 133 documents, which are all translated into
English, range from Herodotus' thoughts on the Dacians to telegrams from the Paris
Peace Conference at the end of the Second World War.

153 **A history of the Roumanians: from Roman times to the completion
of unity.**
Robert W. Seton-Watson.   Cambridge, England: Cambridge
University Press, 1934; Hamden, Connecticut: Archon Books.
Reprinted, 1963. 596p. map. bibliog.

This history of the Romanian people still has much to recommend it, even if it is now
inevitably somewhat dated. Written as a 'national history' in the classic Whig manner,
it follows the travails of the Romanian people from their origins to the completion of

national unity in 1918. The vast bulk of the book is concerned with the 19th century and, mirroring the concerns of the historians of the interwar years, it is primarily a diplomatic history of this period, with an inordinate amount of attention being given to the foreign policy of the Great Powers as it affected Romania.

154   **The Balkans since 1453.**
        L. S. Stavrianos.   New York: Holt, Rinehardt & Winston, 1959. 970p.
        maps. bibliog.

The aims of the author in writing this book, probably still the best single-volume of modern South-East European history available, were twofold: firstly, to offer a new synthesis of the monographic material that had appeared in print since the great Balkan histories of the late 19th and early 20th century, such as William Miller, *The Balkans: Roumania, Bulgaria, Servia and Montenegro* (London: Unwin; New York: G. P. Putnam's Sons, 1896. 476p.); secondly, to emphasize the broader relationships between Balkan, general European and world history. In the opinion of Stavrianos: 'The instability and turbulence of Balkan politics in the modern period becomes meaningful when interpreted as a local manifestation of the world-wide problem of the adjustment of backward areas to the western industrial civilization that has enveloped the globe'. Chapters of synthesis are interwoven with those devoted to national history in a narrative that extends until 1947.

155   **A history of Romania.**
        Edited by Kurt W. Treptow.   Boulder, Colorado: East European
        Monographs in collaboration with the Centre for Romanian Studies,
        Iaşi, distributed by Columbia University Press, 1996. 724p. maps.
        bibliog. (East European Monographs, no. 448).

This large tome, the most recent single-volume history of Romania available, is the result of a collective effort between ten American and Romanian historians. Intended to be a synthesis for the general reader, the work divides the history of Romania into five periods stretching from antiquity to the present day. The running narrative is interspersed with boxes which provide useful ancillary biographical and cultural information. Coverage, in general, is comprehensive but despite the size of the volume some issues such as the 1989 Revolution are dealt with only sketchily. There is a useful historical chronology and a particularly full bibliography of works on Romanian history in English and other Western languages.

156   **Transylvanian villagers: political, economic and ethnic change, 1700-1980.** ·
        Katherine Verdery.   Berkeley, California; Los Angeles; London:
        University of California Press, 1983. 431p. bibliog.

Covering a far wider canvas than the title would suggest, this is a masterly study of social, economic and political change in Transylvania, dealing with life under the Habsburg monarchy, Greater Romania and communist Romania. Throughout sections on regional and international change alternate with more detailed studies of life in the village of Aurel Vlaicu (Binţinţi) and of selected families within that community. Within the broader study there is also much useful material on ethnic relations in the region. Later Verdery presented a summary of her findings in 'On the nationality problem in Transylvania until World War I: an overview', *East European Quarterly*, vol. 19, no. 1 (March 1985), p. 15-30.

157 **The Balkans in our time.**
R. L. Wolff. Cambridge, Massachusetts: Harvard University Press, 1974. rev. ed. 647p. maps.

The aim of the author in writing this book was not only to inform the public about the 'explosive Balkan countries' but also to offer a balanced and authoritative text in a field where too often writers have had a predilection to champion the cause of one group at the expense of another. To a great extent Wolff has succeeded in this aim. However, although there is a section on the 19th- and early 20th-century background, the major part of this study is concerned with the post-war Second World War communist take-overs. As might be expected therefore, it fully reflects the Cold War environment in which it was written because in Wolff's opinion: 'After Yalta, Moscow's policies in the Balkan countries offered the West its best opportunity to study Soviet techniques of imperialist expansion'.

158 **Culture and society. Structures, interferences, analogies in the modern Romanian history.**
Edited by Alexandru Zub. Iaşi, Romania: Editura Academiei Republicii Socialiste România, on behalf of the 'A.D. Xenopol' Institute of History and Archaeology of Iaşi for the 16th International Congress of Historical Sciences (Stuttgart, 1985), 1985. 166p.

This collection of papers, which are all concerned with the modern history of the Romanian lands, includes contributions from: Dinu C. Giurescu, 'Landmarks in the building up of European national states: first half of the XIXth century', p. 41-62; Al Zub, 'Critical school in Romanian historiography: genetic model and strategy', p. 113-26; and Valeriu Florin Dobrinescu, 'The strategy of Romania's neutrality at the outbreak of the two World Wars: a comparative study', p. 155-63.

159 **Identitate/alteritate în spaţiul cultural românesc.** (Identity/otherness in the Romanian cultural space.)
Edited by Alexandru Zub on the occasion of the XVIII International Congress of Historical Science, Montreal, 1995. Iaşi, Romania: Editura Universităţii 'Alexandru Ioan Cuza', 1996. 432p.

This collection of twenty-three papers includes four which are written in English alongside those in Romanian, French and German. Matei Călinescu, in '"How can one be what one is?": Cioran and Romania', p. 21-44, returns to Cioran's question 'How can one be a Romanian?' and reviews it in the light of his rare 1937 work, *Romania's transfiguration*, an 'inflammatory' work written during Cioran's flirtation with the Iron Guard. In '"Imaginary Jew" versus "real Jew" in Romanian folklore and mythology', p. 266-92, Andrei Oişteanu, whilst affirming that the Romanians have never espoused an absolute ideological position as regards the Jews, traces various negative stereotypes that have appeared in Romanian popular literature. Cătălin Turliuc, 'Naturalization of the Jews in Romania after the First World War', p. 337-44, offers a brief comment on the naturalization of the Jewish population in the interwar period. Finally, Norman Simms, 'Romanian collective identity: romantic myth or historical reality', p. 384-92, offers a critical analysis of Romanian collective identity myths as espoused by Lucian Blaga and others.

160 **Southeastern European historiography: themes and accents.**
Alexandru Zub. *East European Quarterly*, vol. 24, no. 3 (Sept. 1990),
p. 335-47.
An elegant and thoughtful discussion by one of Romania's foremost historians of
developments in historiography in an area which he characterizes as one of cultural
convergence where differing national cultures have been grafted on to a 'common
cultural substratum of Roman-Byzantine extraction'. This trend is reflected throughout
the historiography of the area which is a blend of local analytical and area synthetic
studies.

Ancient history

161 **The army in the Roman Dobrogea.**
Andrei Aricescu, translated from the Romanian by Nubar
Hampartumian. Oxford: British Archaeological Reports, 1980. 225p.
maps. bibliog. (BAR International Series, no. 86).
Gathering archaeological, epigraphic and literary evidence from a large number of
sources, the author presents a detailed study of the Roman army in the province of
Scythia Minor from the Principate to the time of Diocletian and Constantine. Chapters
deal with the structure of the army (legions, auxiliaries and fleet) and the defences of
the territory which lay between the Danube and the Black Sea. The author covers
many aspects of military life, including the religious practices of the soldiers, but his
chief area of interest lies in the process of Romanization. This is considered in terms
of political and social organization and the diffusion of the Latin language and culture
to the native population.

162 **Daco-Romania.**
Dumitru Berciu, with contributions by Bucur Mitrea, translated from
the French by James Howarth. Geneva; Paris; Munich: Nagel, 1978.
190p. maps. bibliog. (Archaeologia Mundi).
In many ways this work serves as a sequel to the author's earlier volume *Romania
before Burebista* (q.v.) with the emphasis remaining on the continuity of settlement in
the lower Danubian area. In his search for traces of ethno-cultural integration amongst
the peoples of the region, the author stresses how the Geto-Dacians, assimilating
influence from the Greeks, Celts and Romans, succeeded in fashioning a culture which
far outlasted the relatively short Roman occupation of the area. Chapters on
Christianity, the Latin language and the emergence of the first Romanians further
buttress the author's thesis.

163 **Romania before Burebista.**
Dumitru Berciu. London: Thames & Hudson, 1967. 215p. maps.
bibliog. (Ancient Peoples and Places, no. 57).

The stress in this book is on the continuity of Romanian ethnic and cultural development within the Danubian basin. In support of his thesis the author draws upon archaeological findings (skilfully drawn and photographed) from the early Palaeolithic era down to the Dacian civilization of the Iron Age. Burebista, the King of the Dacians, built an empire over the Danube into Thrace but, following his assassination – like that of Caesar – in 44 BC, his kingdom fractured into several separate realms.

164 **Numismatic aspects of the history of the Dacian state: the Roman Republican coinage in Dacia and Geto-Dacian coins of the Roman type.**
Maria Chiţescu. Oxford: British Archaeological Reports, 1981. 367p.
maps. (BAR International Series, no. 12).

An exhaustive study of the more than 20,000 Roman Republican coins found on Romanian soil as well as the less numerous local Geto-Dacian copies. The author catalogues all the 214 hoards discovered prior to 1977 and, whenever it is possible, describes their contents. She challenges the view expressed by Crawford in 'Republican denarii in Romania: the suppression of piracy and the slave-trade' (see item no. 166) that the coins penetrated Dacia in the middle of the 1st century BC and that they were associated with the slave trade. Instead, she argues that they entered the country at the end of the 2nd century or beginning of the 1st century BC. Like Crawford she accepts that trade alone could not have accounted for such quantities, although she notes the presence of contemporary Greek coins which probably did arise from this source. Instead, she suggests that the bulk of the coins were either plunder seized during Geto-Dacian raids, rewards from Greek rulers for Dacian support against the Romans or even payments made by the Romans to the Dacians to buy their quiescence. The chapter on local Geto-Dacian issues leads to some rather tendentious conclusions about Burebista's 'centralised' Dacian state.

165 **The ancient civilization of Romania.**
Emil Condurachi, Constantin Daicoviciu, translated from the French by James Hogarth. London: Barrie & Jenkins, 1971. 250p. maps.
bibliog. (Ancient Civilisations).

A comprehensive survey of 60,000 years in the life of the Romanian lands from the lower and middle Palaeolithic until the 7th century AD. Informative and well illustrated, the book is particularly strong on the immediate prelude to the historical period and that period itself.

166 **Republican denarii in Romania: the suppression of piracy and the slave-trade.**
Michael H. Crawford. *Journal of Roman Studies,* vol. 67 (1977),
p. 117-24.

One of the great mysteries of Dacian history is how enormous quantities of Republican Roman denarii came to be on Romanian soil well before the conquest of Trajan in 106 AD. Approximately 20,000 to 25,000 coins have so far been discovered dating from circa 130-31 BC. Nowhere in adjoining states are such quantities found, except possibly in neighbouring northern Bulgaria. The author argues that Dacia was not a money economy and that the coins could only have functioned in a rough and ready way as a measure of value. Instead, they were probably exchanged as gifts or dowries. In contrast to the traditional Romanian view, as expressed by Chiţescu, *Numismatic aspects of the history of the Dacian state: the Roman Republican coinage in Dacia and Geto-Dacian coins of the Roman type* (q.v.), he argues that the coins only penetrated Dacia in the middle of the 1st century BC. They did not arrive through general trading nor were they a payment for mercenaries, for which there is no evidence. Instead, he suggests that after Pompey's successful war against the pirates had disrupted traditional slave trading patterns, the Romans found alternative sources of supply through the Dacians, buying slaves at the rate of perhaps 30,000 per year.

167 **Dacian trade with the Hellenistic and Roman world.**
Ioan Glodariu, translated from the Romanian by Nubar Hampartumian.
Oxford: British Archaeological Reports, 1976. 275p. map. bibliog.
(BAR Supplementary Series, no. 8).

Covers the period from the 2nd century BC to the Roman conquest of Dacia in 106. The author's aim is to assess the place of Dacia in the exchange of material objects and spiritual values within the classical world. To this end, the book is divided into two parts. The first comprises a short history of research in the field, a general outline of historical events, an analysis of the general state of trade and an appreciation of the consequences of Hellenistic and Roman economic penetration for the Geto-Dacian lands. The second part is made up of a detailed catalogue of the Greek and Roman artefacts from this period which have been found in Romania; these range from amphorae and silver pieces to coins and glass objects.

168 **The defensive system of Roman Dacia.**
Nicolae Gudea. *Britannia,* vol. 10 (1979), p. 63-87.

A study of the Roman military defences of Dacia which were conceived under Trajan and executed under Hadrian. The lines of defence were largely determined by physical geography, but the author suggests there was also a strategic rationale behind the siting of the ninety-six known fortifications which are listed.

169 **Moesia Inferior (Romanian section) and Dacia: Corpus Cultus Equitis Thracii (CCET) IV.**
Nubar Hampartumian. Leiden, the Netherlands: E. J. Brill, 1979.
128p. map. bibliog. (Études Préliminaires aux Religions Orientales dans l'Empire Romain, no. 64).

A scholarly study of the cult of the Thracian horseman in the Romanian lands. The horseman seems to have been a particularly popular deity in the 2nd and 3rd centuries AD, with most of the monuments coming from the Graeco-Roman cities of the Black Sea (Histria, Tomis, Gallatis). The book is divided into two sections. The first comprises an introduction and a brief exposition of the principal characteristics of the cult, whereas the second consists of a detailed and methodical study of all the known monuments. So far, 206 have been discovered, the vast majority of which are figurative. Each monument is carefully described with both the ancient and the modern name of the place of discovery being given as well as details of the material from which it was constructed, its state of preservation, its size and the museum where it is stored.

170 **Trajan's column: a new edition of the Cichorius plates.**
Frank Lepper, Sheppard Frere. Gloucester, England: Alan Sutton,
1988. 339p. maps. bibliog.
The study of Trajan's column has been greatly facilitated by the photo-gravure plates
produced by Cichorius at the beginning of this century. For these he took the casts of
the column made at the insistence of Napoleon III in the 1860s and arranged them
together to produce a continuous running 'scene'. In this excellent study, the authors
aim to make the plates widely available once more in as high quality a reproduction as
is feasible. To further aid understanding of the plates, they also provide a scholarly
introduction and commentary with notes on such subjects as the column and its
setting, chronology, sources about the Dacian wars, the subject matter of the reliefs
and the aftermath of the wars.

171 **Dacia: an outline of the early civilisation of the Carpatho-Danubian
countries.**
Vasile Pârvan. Cambridge, England: Cambridge University Press,
1928. 216p. map. bibliog.
A synthesis of the early history of the Carpatho-Danubian countries from 1100 BC
until the end of the Roman era by one of the founding fathers of Romanian
archaeology. Well documented and profusely illustrated, the work is divided into five
major chapters which each deal with the relationship of the Carpatho-Danubian
peoples with outside groups: the Villanovans (a north Italian people); the Scythians;
the Greeks; the Celts; and finally the Romans. The aim is to show how even in these
earliest times Western and, especially, Roman, influences were felt in the Romanian
lands.

172 **Adamklissi.**
I. A. Richmond. *Papers of the British School of Rome*, vol. 35/22
(1967), p. 29-39.
The impressive circular monument at Adamklissi in the Dobrogea, which is over 100
feet in diameter, was designed as a *tropaeum* or trophy to commemorate the triumph
of Trajan over local enemies in 108 after the main war in Dacia. Encircled with carved
metopes, forty-nine of which are still extant out of the fifty-four that probably
originally existed, it depicts the Roman defeat of their Dacian, German and Samartian
(an Iranian horsepeople) foes. According to the author, these enemies of Lower
Moesia are quite distinct in appearance from the Dacians of Transylvania to be found
on Trajan's column in Rome. Indeed, he suggests that whilst the two monuments are
often compared, they are totally dissimilar because the column in Rome was intended
to glorify Trajan's success, whilst the *tropaeum* at Adamklisi marks the revenge of
earlier defeats and it is therefore no coincidence that it is dedicated to Mars the
Avenger. The definitive study of the *tropaeum* in Romanian has been translated into
German but not English: Florea Bobu Florescu, *Das Siegesdenkmal von Adamklissi,
Tropaeum Traiani* (The victory monument of Adamklissi, Tropaeum Traiani) (Bonn;
Bucharest: Rudolf Habelt & The Academy of the People's Republic of Romania,
1965. 787p. maps. bibliog.).

173   **Trajan's army on Trajan's column.**
       I. A. Richmond.   *Papers of the British School of Rome*, vol. 23
       (1935), p. 1-40.

In this article the author argues that Trajan's column does not present a carefully studied topographical or historical account of the Dacian campaign. The main events might follow a rough chronology, but the minor scenes were selected more in the interest of maintaining the flow of the narrative than for their historical authenticity. Instead, the column is more valuable for what it shows about Roman social conditions and Richmond considers that the prime task of the artist was the 'representation of army life'. Indeed, such is the accuracy of the scenes on the column that he even suggests the preliminary sketches may have been made on the spot in Dacia during the campaigns. To test this hypothesis sixteen typical scenes from the column, illustrating different aspects of military life, are then compared with actual archaeological findings.

174   **Trajan's column and the Dacian Wars.**
       L. Rossi.   London: Thames & Hudson, 1971. 240p. maps. bibliog.

This was the first book in English devoted to the column erected in Rome by the Emperor Trajan to celebrate his conquest of Dacia. Intended for the general reader as well as the scholar, this study includes, besides a photographic record of the column, a detailed commentary which draws upon Romanian archaeological findings to establish the location of some of the incidents depicted on the monument. The author's main interest is in the military aspects of the campaign and this leads him to survey the background politics and geography of the war from both the Roman and Dacian points of view. Comparisons are also made with the 'provincial panels' of the *Tropaeum Traiani* at Adamklissi in the Dobrogea, the other monument constructed to commemorate the campaign. One of the major engineering feats of the Roman invasion was the creation of a road hacked out of the sheer cliffs of the Danube gorge and widened by means of wooden scaffolding. In an earlier article the same author discusses the representation of this achievement, 'The representation on Trajan's column of Trajan's rock-cut road in Upper Moesia: the Emperor's road to glory', *Antiquaries Journal,* vol. 48, no. 1 (1968), p. 41-46.

175   **The captor of Decebalus. A new inscription from Philippi.**
       Michael Speidel.   *Journal of Roman Studies*, vol. 60 (1970),
       p. 142-53.

A line-by-line commentary of an inscription written in Latin which was found in 1965 together with two reliefs in the fields of Grammeni, a village north-west of ancient Philippi in Macedonia. The inscription tells of the life of a much honoured Roman soldier, Ti. Claudius Maximus, whose most celebrated feat seems to have been his near apprehension of the Dacian king, Decebalus, during Trajan's wars. Indeed, the most prominent relief on the monument graphically depicts the incident when at full gallop, sword in hand, the Roman soldier reaches the Dacian king at the very moment he staggers to the ground, having cut his own throat rather than be taken captive. The reliefs are also valuable as a means of establishing the historical accuracy of Trajan's column where similar scenes are depicted.

176 **Danubian papers.**
Ronald Syme, with a foreword by Emil Condurachi. Bucharest:
Bibliothèque d'Études du Sud-Est Européen, 1971. 255p.

This is a compilation of seventeen previously published articles and reviews covering
the Roman presence in South-Eastern Europe, written over thirty years by the
distinguished historian Ronald Syme. Amongst the works concerned with the history
of the Romanian lands, together with their original places of publication, are: 'The
Lower Danube under Trajan', *Journal of Roman Studies*, vol. 49 (1959), p. 26-33;
'Pliny and the Dacian Wars', *Latomus*, vol. 23 (1964), p. 750-59; and 'The colony of
Cornelius Fuscus: an episode in the "Belum Neronis"', *American Journal of
Philology*, vol. 58 (1937), p. 7-18.

177 **Eastern cults in Moesia Inferior and Thracia (5th century B.C. –
4th century A.D.).**
Margarita Tacheva-Hitova.   Leiden, the Netherlands: E. J. Brill, 1983.
306p. maps. bibliog. (Études Préliminaires aux Religions Orientales
dans l'Empire Romain, no. 95).

Although this book is largely concerned with the Roman provinces which covered
present-day Bulgaria, it also includes a large number of findings from what is now
Romanian Dobrogea. Drawing upon many specialist articles which are generally
inaccessible to most readers, since they are scattered throughout Bulgarian periodicals,
the author presents a detailed study of the eastern cults in the region. The various
religions are divided according to their geographic origins: Egyptian, Anatolian/
Balkan, cults of Zeus (Jupiter), Dolichenus, and other eastern gods and cults. In each
section a catalogue of findings is followed by a commentary which covers topics such
as historiography, sources, epigraphy, the ethnic origins and status of dedicators, the
geographical extent of the worship of the cult and its organization.

178 **A study in Geto-Dacian religion: the cult of Zalmoxis.**
Kurt W. Treptow.   *East European Quarterly*, vol. 21, no. 4
(Jan. 1988), p. 501-15.

A critical and challenging examination of Ancient Greek sources relating to the Geto-
Dacian deity Zalmoxis. The author argues that the cult was monotheistic and that it
possessed its own priesthood which interpreted the oracle and functioned in support of
the ruling military élite. The cult disappeared after the Roman invasion.

179 **Cities in Thrace and Dacia in late antiquity (studies and materials).**
Velikov Velizar.   Amsterdam: Adolf M. Hakkert, 1977. 308p. map.
bibliog. (Studies of the Henri Frankfort Foundation, no. 3).

In the middle of the 3rd century AD, during the reign of the Emperor Aurelian,
pressure from hostile tribes forced the Romans to abandon Dacia. Across the Danube
two new provinces of Inner and Littoral Dacia were then carved out of the old Thrace
and Upper and Lower Moesia. The Dacia within the title of this book refers to these
new provinces, which lay inside present-day Bulgaria. However, still under Roman
rule at that time was Romanian Dobrogea, known as Scythia, and details from the
fifteen towns of this province are also included in this work. As well as a listing of the
known Roman towns in the region, chapters offer surveys of historical events, administration, local government, economic development, class and social relations and
the controversial question of ethnic changes in the area in the 4th and 6th centuries.

180   **Romans, Dacians and Sarmatians.**
J. J. Wilkes.   In: *Rome and her northern provinces: papers presented to Sheppard Frere in honour of his retirement from the chair of Archaeology of the Roman Empire, University of Oxford, 1983.* Edited by Brian Hartley, John Wacher.   Gloucester, England: Alan Sutton, 1983, p. 255-89. map.

This is a scholarly study of the often violent interaction between Romans, Dacians and Sarmatians in the 1st century AD. The focus is chiefly on the Sarmatians who, the author argues, posed a greater threat to the Romans than the Dacians at this time. The Sarmatians were an Iranian horsepeople who inhabited the area from the Hungarian plains to the steppes around the Volga. In the Romanian space they were divided into two main groups, the Jazyges of present-day northern Transylvania and Hungary and the Roxolani of Muntenia. For a more lengthy study of the Sarmatians see T. Sulimirski, *The Sarmatians* (London: Thames & Hudson, 1970. 273p. maps. [Ancient People and Places, no. 73]).

181   **The élite in the Lower Danube provinces of the Roman Empire.**
Marek Żyromski.   Mosina, Poland: ALPIM, 1995. 124p. bibliog.

Defining the lower Danube as comprising the two Moesian and Pannonian provinces together with Dacia, the author provides a sociological analysis of the more than 300 high officials who served in the area during the Principate (27 BC to 284 AD). He is primarily concerned with élite formation and the transformation of Roman society, and, to this end, he surveys topics such as the origins of the élite, stages of senatorial advancement and the importance of factors such as the support of the Emperor, 'political marriages' and the patronage system to build a picture of the extent of social mobility. The work concludes with a valuable prosopographical appendix.

500-1750

182   **Exactly where was Dracula captured in 1462?**
Ştefan Andreescu, Raymond T. McNally.   *East European Quarterly*, vol. 23, no. 3 (Sept. 1989), p. 269-81.

Vlad the Impaler of Wallachia (1431-76), better known in the West as Dracula, thought he had reached an agreement, after negotiations with Matthius Corvinus, the Hungarian king, at Braşov, to support his return to Wallachia to regain the throne from his brother, Radu the Handsome, and to continue his campaigns against the Turks. However, when he reached the borders of his kingdom on 26 November 1462, he was seized by Jan Jiškra of Brandeis on the orders of Corvinus and spent the rest of his days in captivity. The authors, drawing on the description provided by the German *meistersinger*, Michel Beheim, and other documentary, archaeological and place-name evidence, identify the precise location of his capture as the castle of Kings's Rock at Podul Dâmboviţa. They suggest that the seizure took place at this point, just within the bounds of Wallachia, so that Corvinus could avoid accusations that he had violated imperial safe conduct and that it was occasioned by a shift in his policies away from fighting the Turks towards hostilities with Emperor Fredrick III of Vienna.

183 **The involvement of Ştefan Bogdan, a pretender to the Moldavian throne, with Henry Lello, the English ambassador to Constantinople between 1601 and 1606.**
Laura Coulter. *Revue Roumaine d'Histoire*, vol. 30, no. 1 (Jan.-June 1991), p. 79-100.

In 1588 Ştefan Bogdan, a claimant to the Moldavian throne, journeyed to England and played effectively upon the principal of the Divine Right of monarchs to rule in order to gain the support of the English Crown for his cause. However, as Coulter shows in this study, which draws heavily on primary sources, once back in Constantinople, he received more equivocal backing from Henry Lello, the English Ambassador, who understood better the intrinsic weakness of Bogdan's position. The Moldavian's scheming threatened to undermine good Polish-Ottoman relations, important to the Porte at a time of conflict with the Habsburgs, and this eventually led to his imprisonment. He finally escaped, but the perceived failure of Lello to adequately support his candidature undermined the English Ambassador's standing and may have contributed to his replacement by Thomas Glover, a more energetic supporter of Bogdan's cause. Bogdan never succeeded to the Moldavian throne and the author concludes that the whole episode was closely linked to a decline in the prestige of the Embassy under Lello. For a further study of the fortune of Bogdan, which examines his relationship with Thomas Glover, see Laura Coulter, 'Ştefan Bogdan and Sir Thomas Glover: 1607-1612', *Revue Roumaine d'Histoire*, vol. 33, no. 3-4 (July-Dec. 1994), p. 215-73.

184 **Genoese, Tatars and Rumanians at the mouth of the Danube in the fourteenth century.**
Dennis Deletant. *Slavonic and East European Review*, vol. 62, no. 4 (Oct. 1984), p. 511-30.

An investigation of the complex interplay between Romanians, Tatars and Genovese at the mouth of the Danube following the return of Michael VIII Paleologus to the Byzantine throne and the displacement of Venetian influence on the river.

185 **Some aspects of the Byzantine tradition in the Rumanian principalities.**
Dennis Deletant. *Slavonic and East European Review*, vol. 59, no. 1 (Jan. 1981), p. 1-14.

The Byzantine Empire unquestionably had an enormous influence on South-Eastern Europe but, as the author notes here, it was not just a case of the 'slavish imitation' of Byzantine forms by local cultures. Although Byzantine liturgical practices and laws were often adopted, they were also adapted to fit local needs, and this makes it difficult to distinguish what is borrowed from what is indigenous. Surveying the full gamut of the Byzantine influence, Deletant also looks at the mid-15th-century diffusion of Byzantine culture in its medieval Slavonic form as well as the later neo-Byzantine culture of the Phanariots.

186 **Some considerations on the emergence of the principality of Moldavia in the middle of the fourteenth century.**
Dennis Deletant. In: *Historians as nation-builders: Central and South-East Europe.* Edited by Dennis Deletant, Harry Hanak. London: Macmillan, 1988, p. 32-50.

The author draws upon recent Romanian scholarship to elucidate some problems relating to the foundation of the medieval Moldavian state. He argues that in its early history, from its origins until the reign of Stephen the Great (1457-1504), the state was largely dependent on its more powerful neighbours, Hungary and Poland. In establishing a chronology for the early voivodes, he suggests that Moldavia owed its emergence to the successful efforts of Louis of Hungary to extend his influence east of the Carpathians. Louis wished to replace Tatar Moldavia with a vassal territory which would allow access to the Danube.

187 **Dimitrie Cantemir: historian of South Eastern European and Oriental civilizations. Extracts from 'The History of the Ottoman Empire'.**
Edited by Alexandru Duțu, Paul Cernovodeanu, with a foreword by Halil Inalcik. Bucharest: Association Internationale d'Études du Sud-Est Européen, 1973. 358p. bibliog.

Dimitrie Cantemir, Prince of Moldavia in 1693 and 1710-11, unwisely sided with the Russians in a war with the Turks in 1711. After the Russians were defeated, he was forced to flee to Moscow, where he became a councillor to Peter the Great, and wrote his celebrated *History of the Ottoman Empire* (1716). Based on his observations during twenty-two years living in Constantinople, this volume enjoyed a fame which soon spread across Europe, with translations appearing in a number of languages, including English by N. Tindal, *The history of the growth and decay of the Ottoman Empire* (London: James, John & Paul Knapton, 1734-35). It is extracts from this original translation that are reprinted in this work, grouped under headings such as court, architecture, beliefs, customs and ideas, literature, music and personalities. The impact of Cantemir's history in England is considered in Hugh Trevor-Roper, 'Dimitrie Cantemir's Ottoman History and its reception in England', *Revue Roumaine d'Histoire*, vol. 24, no. 1-2 (Jan.-June 1985), p. 51-66.

188 **Dracula Prince of many faces: his life and his times.**
Radu R. Florescu, Raymond T. McNally. Boston, Massachusetts; Toronto; London: Little, Brown & Co., 1989. 261p. maps. bibliog.

This volume is the culmination of twenty years research by these two Dracula specialists. The book is divided into two halves. In the first they consider the life of the Romanian Prince, Vlad Țepeș, and try to place it within the broader context of 15th-century European history. In the second section they trace the growth of the Dracula legend. Here the contrast is between his image in the West, where anti-Dracula propaganda tracts were the basis of best-sellers of 15th-century German horror literature, and Romania, where a popular oral culture transformed him into a hero.

189 **Romania and the Ottoman Empire in the 14th-16th centuries.**
Tahsin Gemil.   Bucharest: Editura Academiei Române, 1991. 231p.

The author surveys the progress of Ottoman-Romanian relations from the emergence
of the Principalities of Walachia and Moldavia in the 14th century until the 16th
century. During this period the policies and strategies employed by the Principalities
towards the Ottoman Empire had to adapt to changed circumstances and, especially, to
the growth of Ottoman power. Thus, after an initial period in which they had tried to
resist Ottoman expansion north of the Danube, they later changed to a policy of
accepting Turkish suzerainty in return for a large measure of autonomy in domestic
affairs. The preservation of these privileges, through skilful diplomacy, subsequently
became the chief concern of the leaders of the Principalities.

190 **Hunyadi: legend and reality.**
Joseph Held.   Boulder, Colorado: East European Monographs,
distributed by Columbia University Press, 1985. 264p. (East European
Monographs, no. 178).

A scholarly study of a figure who is claimed by both Romanian and Hungarian
historiography and who is known to Romanians as Iancu of Hunodoara. Hunyadi's
father seems to have derived from Wallchian Orthodox stock who, according to Held,
after moving to Transylvania, probably married a lower Hungarian noblewoman and
was then accepted into the local nobility. A great military leader against the Turks, he
rose to be Voivode of Transylvania between 1441-46 and Governor of Hungary, 1446-
53. In 1456 he died of the plague and was buried in the Catholic Church at Alba Iulia.
This study looks not only at his life but also at aspects of late medieval society in the
region with chapters covering the Church and the people.

191 **Ethnic continuity in the Carpatho-Danubian area.**
Elemér Illyés.   Boulder, Colorado: East European Monographs,
distributed by Columbia University Press, 1988. 439p. maps. bibliog.
(East European Monographs, no. 249).

A lengthy study of the vexed problem of the ethnogenesis of the Romanian people.
The debate hinges on whether the Romanians and their Dacian forefathers
continuously occupied the lands north of the Danube River (the so-called Dacio-
Roman continuity theory) or whether they in fact migrated to the area of present-day
Romania from below the river in the early Middle Ages. The author assesses the
evidence by dividing it into various categories: history, archaeology, linguistic and
geographical names. Although no overall conclusion is reached, the consistent line
adopted throughout is that the idea of continuity is a myth.

192 **Dracula was a woman: in search of the Blood Countess of
Transylvania.**
Raymond T. McNally.   London: Robert Hale, 1983. 254p. maps.
bibliog.

Building on his work on Vlad Țepeș and the Dracula legend, McNally here looks at a
purported female equivalent, the Hungarian Countess Elizabeth Báthory (1560-1614),
another inhabitant of Transylvania, who was said to have bathed in the blood of
freshly slaughtered maidens in order to halt the process of ageing. In the first half of
the book the author narrates the biography of the countess and in the second he looks

at the three taboos which she was said to have broken – vampirism, werewolfism and necrophilia – and the way that they have been treated in literature, theatre and cinema. Drawing both the male and female Draculas together, the author suggests that the creator of *Dracula*, Bram Stoker, became engrossed in the legends surrounding Báthory, which he found in a book by Sabine Baring-Gould, *The book of the Werewolves,* and that these provided a source of inspiration for his own work.

193 **The fifteenth century manuscript of Kritoboulos of Imbros as an historical source for the history of Dracula.**
Raymond T. McNally. *East European Quarterly*, vol. 21, no. 1 (March 1987), p. 1-13.

Offers a critical rereading of an original manuscript preserved in the Tokapî Palace Library in Istanbul which is dedicated to Sultan Mehmed II and presumed to be the work of the Greek historian Kritoboulos of Imbros. The author concludes that the four pages of the manuscript concerned with 'The revolt of the Drakouli, Chief of the Getae' are reasonably accurate and should be taken as a serious historical source. He suggests that the origins of the name Dracula comes from the fact that Vlad's father, Vlad II, was invested with the Order of the Dragon by the Holy Roman Emperor, King Sigismund, at Nürnberg in 1431. Dracula was, therefore, the son of 'he who holds the Order of the Dragon', by virtue of the enclitic ending '-a' common in Romanian surnames.

194 **In search of Dracula: the history of Dracula and vampires.**
Raymond T. McNally, Radu Florescu. Boston, Massachusetts; New York: Houghton Mifflin Co., 1994. 297p. maps. bibliog.

Intended for the general reader, this popular distillation of the authors' research on Dracula is a completely revised and updated version of the earlier ground-breaking study of 1973. Taking into account the great deal of research undertaken in the last decades, it retains the lively but critical spirit of the earlier volume. The book has also appeared under the title: *In search of Dracula: a true story of Dracula and vampire legends* (London: Robson, 1995. 299p. maps. bibliog.).

195 **The beginnings of Slavonic culture in the Rumanian countries.**
Grigore Nandriş. *Slavonic and East European Review*, vol. 24, no. 63 (Jan. 1946), p. 160-71.

Early in the medieval period, the Romanians adopted a number of Slavic cultural forms including the Cyrillic alphabet and the Slavonic liturgy. In this learned article the author discusses the date of these changes, the source of these cultural borrowings, and the circumstances in which they were adopted.

196 **The Byzantine Commonwealth: Eastern Europe, 500-1453.**
Dimitri Obolensky. London: Sphere Books, 1974; Crestwood, New York: St. Vladimir's Seminary Press, 1982. 552p.

An excellent study of the political, economic, cultural and ecclesiastical links forged by the Byzantine Empire with the Romanian principalities and the rest of South-Eastern Europe and Russia during the Middle Ages. There is also a useful collection of articles by the same author on this subject: *The Byzantine inheritance of Eastern Europe* (London: Variorum Reprints, 1982. 300p.).

197 **Stephen the Great, Prince of Moldavia, 1457-1504.**
Şerban Papacostea, translated from the Romanian by Sergiu Celac.
Bucharest: Editura Encicolpedică, 1996. 87p. bibliog.
A succinct yet illuminating account of this famous Romanian king's contribution to
the defence of Christian Europe against the Ottoman Turks during the last quarter of
the 15th century, and of his attempts to assert Moldavia's independence from
vassalage to Poland.

198 **Church and State in Eastern Europe during the fourteenth**
century: why the Romanians remained in the Orthodox area.
Ioan-Aurel Pop. *East European Quarterly*, vol. 29, no. 3 (Fall 1995),
p. 275-84.
Although present-day Romania lies on the Orthodox side of the religious fault line
crossing Europe, with its Latin heritage it could quite easily have belonged to the
Western Church. Within this article the author suggests that the main reason why this
is not so is because of the Papacy's heavy reliance on Hungary to spread Catholicism
which inevitably meant that proselytization became enmeshed with schemes of
political conquest.

199 **East Central Europe in the Middle Ages, 1000-1500.**
Jean W. Sedler.   Seattle, Washington; London: University of
Washington Press, 1994. 556p. maps. bibliog. (A History of East
Central Europe, vol. 3).
Arranged by topic rather than by country, this wide-ranging volume nevertheless
contains a great deal of material relating to the Romanian lands. Chapters deal with
state formation, monarchy, nobles and landlords, laws and justice, religion and the
churches, peasants, towns and townspeople, commerce, the art of war, and ethnicity
and nationalism. An appendix contains a useful chronology, lists of monarchs and a
table of place-name equivalents. A critical review of the Romanian material in this
volume by Kurt W. Treptow can be found in *Romanian Civilisation,* vol. 4, no. 2
(Summer 1995), p. 117-20.

200 **Moldavia in the 11th-14th centuries.**
Victor Spinei, translated from the Romanian by Liliana Teodoreanu
and Ioana Sturza.   Bucharest: The Academy of the Socialist Republic
of Romania and the Academy of Social and Political Sciences of the
Socialist Republic of Romania, 1986. 277p. map. bibliog. (Bibliotheca
Historica Romaniae, Monographs, no. 20).
The time span of this study is set by the fact that the earliest written evidence on the
Romanian population in the region east of the Carpathians dates back to the 11th
century and that the foundation of the Moldavian feudal state was achieved in the 14th
century. In a series of chronologically arranged chapters, the author draws upon a
wide range of archaeological, historical and other evidence to trace the history of the
area during the period and the inhabitants' interaction with foreign peoples, including
the Mongols during their great invasion of 1241-42.

201 **Domination of Eastern Europe: native nobilities and foreign absolutism, 1500-1715.**
Orest Subtelny. Kingston, Canada; Montreal: McGill-Queen's University Press; Gloucester, England: Alan Sutton, 1986. 270p. maps. bibliog.
It is a truism that for much of its history Eastern Europe has been under the dominance of foreign powers. In this book the author looks to the 16th and 17th centuries to try and find out why this should be. Arguing that the process can only be understood through an analysis of those who initially opposed, and later allied with, the conquerors, he surveys the socio-economic and political circumstance of five native élite groups: the Polish, Hungarians, Livonians, Moldavians and Ukranians. As in Western Europe he sees the internal politics of Eastern Europe as dominated by the struggle between monarchical absolutism and noble privilege. However, in contrast to Western Europe, in the East the latter were able to stop the rise of the former, but this ultimately left them vulnerable to foreign incursions.

202 **Documents concerning Rumanian history (1427-1601) collected from British archives.**
Eric D. Tappe. The Hague: Mouton, 1964. 162p.
The main concern of the author in producing this volume of 218 documents relating to the Romanian lands was to provide other historians with easier access to primary sources. Until the year 1582 the documents largely contain second-hand information, but in that year William Harborne was given the status of diplomatic agent by Elizabeth I and in 1588 a commercial agreement was signed between England and Moldavia.

203 **'Countess Dracula': the life and times of Elisabeth Báthory, the Blood Countess.**
Tony Thorne. London: Bloomsbury, 1997. 288p.
In this scholarly but readable work, the author investigates the story of Elizabeth Báthory (1560-1614), an Hungarian aristocrat from Transylvania, who was said to have hideously tortured and murdered over 650 maidens. After a trial in which some of her so-called accomplices were sentenced to death, the Countess was imprisoned in her own castle. Reviewing the historical evidence, the author suggests that much of it is ambiguous and that some of the more fanciful stories, such as that which says that the countess bathed in the blood of the young women to halt the process of ageing, first appeared over a century after her death in the works of a Jesuit priest. Thorne suggests that in harsh and superstitious times Báthory was probably little more than the victim of envious neighbours who coveted her property, and to support this argument he draws upon similar cases where the reputation of a woman was besmirched so as to deprive her of her estate.

204 **Dracula: essays on the life and times of Vlad Ţepeş.**
Edited by Kurt W. Treptow. Boulder, Colorado: East European Monographs, distributed by Columbia University Press, 1991. 336p. bibliog. (East European Monographs, no. 323).
A useful collection of fourteen previously published essays about the historical Vlad Ţepeş and the Dracula legend by Romanian and Western scholars. The contents

include: Matei Cazacu, 'The reign of Dracula in 1448', p. 53-62; P. P. Panaitescu, 'The German stories about Vlad Țepeș', p. 185-96; and Alexandru Duțu, 'Portraits of Vlad Țepeș: literature, pictures and images of the ideal man', p. 239-45. Five appendices provide details of Țepeș' genealogy, a chronology, a historical bibliography and a list of selected primary sources.

1750-1918

205 **A 19th century Greek scholar in Bucharest: Mihail Christaris and his library.**
Roxane D. Argyropoulos. *Balkan Studies*, vol. 30, no. 1 (1989), p. 67-82.
Mihail Christaris, born in Ioannina in 1773, first came to Bucharest to study under the renowned scholar Lambros Photiadis. He was to remain in Bucharest for the next twenty years working as a physician and playing a leading role in the political and cultural life of the city. A prominent member of the local Greco-Dacian society in 1818, he was inducted into the Greek revolutionary group, the *Philiki Etaireia,* becoming a member of the Council of Alexander Ypsilantis. In this study the author considers both Christaris' life and his written work. She considers his *Catechism of the main social duties* (1831) to be 'the most representative work of the neohellenic enlightenment'. Within it, echoing French writers such as Rousseau, Christaris introduced the idea of Social Autonomy and placed human rights within the context of social relations.

206 **Economic prerequisites for the establishment of independent Romania.**
Dan Berindei. *East European Quarterly,* vol. 22, no. 1 (March 1988), p. 23-25.
Within this article the author musters a considerable amount of interesting statistical evidence to support his argument that economic development fuelled political demands for independence.

207 **The emergence of the Romanian National State.**
Gerald J. Bobango. Boulder, Colorado: East European Monographs, distributed by Columbia University Press, 1979. 312p. bibliog. (East European Monographs, no. 58).
The declaration of independence from the Ottoman Empire by the united principalities of Moldavia and Wallachia on 9 May 1877 was merely the climax of a lengthy process which had begun in earnest with the 1829 Treaty of Adrianople. In this scholarly and sympathetic study, the author follows the course of this process from Adrianople through the double election of Alexander Cuza as Prince of both Moldavia and Wallachia in 1859 to his deposition in 1866.

208   **Precursors of the Romanian Academy (1867).**
Cornelia Bodea.   *East European Quarterly*, vol. 22, no. 3 (Fall 1988),
p. 341-50.
The author traces the antecedents of the Romanian Academy to local cultural societies
such as the *Societatea Literară* of Wallachia established in 1821. Indeed, when the
Romanian Academy was originally founded in 1867 with the task of establishing a
standard Romanian orthography and compiling a Romanian dictionary and grammar,
it first bore the name *Societatea Literară*. At its inaugural session it adopted the name
Societatea Academică Româna and with its remit suitably enlarged, the name
'Romanian Academy' was finally adopted in 1879.

209   **R. W. Seton-Watson și românii, 1906-1920 (R. W. Seton-Watson
and the Romanians, 1906-1920).**
Cornelia Bodea, Hugh Seton-Watson.   Bucharest: Editura Științifică și
Enciclopedică, 1988. vol. 1, p. 1-556; vol. 2, p. 557-999.
Through his work as a historian and as a propagandist during the First World War,
when he was the editor of the journal *A new Europe*, R. W. Seton-Watson strove
energetically for the Romanian cause. In consequence, he occupies a special place in
Romanian historiography and these two volumes provide a fitting tribute to his links
with the country. In addition to his correspondence with distinguished Romanians,
they also include other letters about Romania, historical notes and unpublished
material from his personal papers. The correspondence is published in the original
language of writing, usually English, French and German, but the entire critical
apparatus, including the introductions by Bodea and Hugh Seton-Watson (the son of
R. W. Seton-Watson), is presented in both English and Romanian. The lengthy
documentary summaries and detailed footnotes are also written in both languages.
Material from this volume can also be found in the excellent study by Hugh Seton-
Watson and Christopher Seton-Watson, *The making of a new Europe, R. W.
Seton-Watson and the last years of Austria-Hungary* (London: Methuen, 1981. 458p.).

210   **Hungarian exiles and the Romanian national movement,
1849-1867.**
Béla Borsi-Kálmán, translated by Éva Pálmai.   Boulder, Colorado:
Social Science Monographs. Atlantic Research and Publications,
distributed by Columbia University Press, 1991. 333p. (Atlantic
Studies on Society in Change, no. 67; East European Monographs,
no. 331).
After the Revolution of 1848 a number of the defeated Hungarian leaders in exile,
including Lajos Kossuth, opened talks with the Romanians in the hope of securing
their co-operation in an attempt to renew the struggle against the Habsburg authorities.
This is a detailed and scholarly study of the progress of these negotiations from the
excessive expectations of the 1850s to the more sober attempts of 1862-64. The author
looks at the growth of Romanian consciousness on both sides of the Carpathians, the
fruitless plans and negotiations of 1849-63 and the final attempt to reach an agreement
in 1864, on the basis of Hungarian proposals for a Danubian Confederation. This
would have seen a historic Hungary, divided into Hungary and Transylvania, take its
place in a democratic Danubian federation of coequal states. However, the scheme had
no real prospects. The Hungarian émigrés had few resources and the Romanians were
preoccupied with state-building in the newly united principalities.

211 **A turning point in the history of Bessarabia: winter 1917-1918.**
Michael Bruchis. *Nationalities Papers*, vol. 15, no. 2 (Fall 1987),
p. 194-214.

An examination of the differing perceptions of Bessarabian history to be found in Romanian and Soviet historiography. In particular, in an attempt to legitimize their current political positions, the two sides offered drastically opposing interpretations of the events of 1917-18, when the area was annexed to Romania. Having surveyed both the Soviet and Romanian literature, the author gives his unequivocal support to the Romanian view, describing the Soviet-sponsored *History of the Communist Party of Moldavia* as a glaring example of 'wilful distortion and falsification'.

212 **A diplomacy aborted: Italy and Romania go their separate ways in May, 1915. A reassessment.**
H. James Burgwyn. *East European Quarterly*, vol. 21, no. 3
(Sept. 1987), p. 305-18.

Drawing on original Italian sources, this is a detailed study of the abortive negotiations conducted between Italy and Romania during the First World War, which sought to secure their joint entry into the conflict in May 1915 with a concerted attack against Austro-Hungary. The author questions the received view that the Italian Foreign Minister, Sidney Sonnino, missed a chance through his own indifference and left Romania in the lurch. Instead, he suggests that although the overbearing attitude of Sonnino towards the Romanians did not help, the Romanian premier, Ion Brătianu, must also bear responsibility for the failure of the talks, since he was determined to retain Romania's neutrality as long as possible and his policies were shaped, to a large extent, by the fluctuating fortunes of the Russian Army, a factor outside the calculation of the Italians.

213 **The market tradition and peasant rebellion: the case of Romania in 1907.**
Daniel Chirot, Charles Ragin. *American Sociological Review*,
vol. 40, no. 4 (Aug. 1975), p. 428-44.

The authors use two models to analyse the peasant rebellion of 1907. The first of these, usually identified with Wolf, Barrington-Moore, Tilly and Hobsbawm, suggests that such revolts are caused by the introduction of market forces into a strongly traditional society. The second, advocated by Stinchcombe, suggests that rural stratification is more important, with rebellion being most likely in those areas where family tenancies predominate and where there is the greatest inequality in land-holdings. After a brief historical introduction, the authors analyse the intensity of the rebellion using multiple regression technique. They conclude that the most important causes of the revolt were a combination of peasant traditionalism and the penetration of market forces.

214 **István Széchenyi, Miklós Wesselényi, Lajos Kossuth and the problem of Romanian nationalism.**
István Deak. *Austrian History Yearbook*, vol. 12-13, part 1
(1976-77), p. 66-77.

Transylvania lay at the violent epicentre of the Hungarian Revolution of 1848-49 and in this special issue of this journal devoted to the Revolution, under the title

'Nationalist interests and cosmopolitan goals in the Hungarian Revolution of 1848-49', there are a number of articles concerned with the region and its Romanian population. In his article, Deak considers the relationship between the Romanians and the Hungarian revolutionaries. In 'Debunking a myth: the Magyar-Romanian national struggle of 1848-1849' (p. 82-89), Radu R. Florescu calls for a more multi-faceted approach to the conflict, arguing that it is wrong to see it as a simple struggle between the so-called 'historic' nationalities (Magyars, Saxons and Szeklers) and the 'non-historic' nations (Romanians and Slavs). For instance, in the Apuseni Mountains, Romanians fought Hungarians, whilst in the Banat and Maramureş they joined General Józef Bem in the fight against the Habsburgs. Deak is also the author of a comprehensive study of the revolution in English, which again has much material on the Romanian minority, *The lawful revolution: Louis Kossuth and the Hungarians, 1848-1849* (New York: Columbia University Press, 1979. 415p.).

215 **Jewish farmers in the Bucovina.**
Henry Delfiner. *East European Quarterly*, vol. 24, no. 4 (Jan. 1991), p. 529-37.
Following the Russo-Turkish war of 1769-74 Bucovina passed to the Austro-Hungarian Empire. After years of strife, the province was seriously depopulated and during the reign of Joseph II an attempt was made to entice Jewish settlers to the area from Galicia. However, as the author shows in this article, despite considerable blandishments and even threats of expulsion if they did not take up farming, the Jews seem to have been reluctant to abandon their traditional pursuits of leasing and managing large land-holdings as well as selling alcohol, thereby rendering the experiment less than an unalloyed success.

216 **New discoveries – on the basis of original documentary materials – on the life and activity of Bishop Sofronij Vračanski (1739-1813) in Wallachia, his adoptive country (1802-1813) (correctives and clarifications).**
Nicolae Dura. *Bulgarian Historical Review*, vol. 19, no. 1 (1991), p. 29-46.
Sofroni of Vratsa (Vrachanski, 1739-1813), as the author of the first work of modern Bulgarian literature, *Zhitie i stradaniia greshnago Sofroniia* (Life and sufferings of Sofroni the sinner), occupies a central place in Bulgarian history. However, he spent much of his life outside his native land in Wallachia and in this article the author sets out to find the answer to a number of questions relating to his life: when he fled to Romania; when he wrote his famous autobiography; when and where he died; where he was an abbot; and which was the Serban Voda monastery in which he died.

217 **The great Rumanian peasant revolt of 1907: origins of a modern jacquerie.**
Philip Gabriel Eidelberg. Leiden, the Netherlands: Brill, 1974. 259p. bibliog. (Studies of the Institute on East Central Europe, Colombia University).
The Romanian peasant revolt of March 1907 was the last great European *jacquerie* (peasant revolt). Beginning in the north-east of the country, it soon spread across both the Danubian Principalities leaving in its wake a trial of wanton destruction, arson and

murder. Eventually the authorities suppressed the uprising but only at the cost of between 1,000 and 10,000 deaths. In this detailed and scholarly work, the author offers not a narrative of the events, but rather an analysis of the causes of the revolt as he traces its 'social, economic, political and ideological antecedents'. In addition, he aims to offer an agrarian history of the period 1864-1917 and to treat Romanian history in both national and regional terms, in particular, highlighting the dichotomy between northern Moldavia and Wallachia.

218 **The Lower Danube river: in the Southeastern Europe political and economic complex from antiquity to the conference of Belgrade in 1948.**
Spiridon G. Focas, translated from the Romanian by Rozeta J. Metes.
Boulder, Colorado: East European Monographs, distributed by
Columbia University Press, 1987. 697p. bibliog. (East European
Monographs, no. 227).

A monumental study which is largely concerned with the status of the river in international law during the late 19th and early 20th centuries. The author provides an exhaustive analysis of the various treaty provisions and legal statutes following the internationalization of the river in 1856. Largely focused on Romania, with the author drawing on his experience as secretary of the Special Autonomous Administration of the Maritime Danube – the Romanian Administration which in 1938 took over the duties of the former European Commission of the Danube – this study also sheds light on the country's relationship with the Great Powers.

219 **The Courier de Moldavie and Der Kriegsgebote: two views of the French Revolution for Romanians.**
Robert F. Forrest. *East European Quarterly*, vol. 25, no. 1 (Spring 1991), p. 91-99.

The *Courier de Moldavie*, a French-language journal, appeared under the aegis of the occupying Russian commander, Prince Grigori Aleksandrovich Potemkin (1739-91), in Iaşi between February and April 1790. It published regular synopses of the unfolding events in France. Drawn from consular reports and the Western press, these appeared as quickly as twelve days after they had occurred, but the interpretation of the events offered was unremittingly hostile. *Der Kriegsgebote*, printed in Sibiu under various names between 1787-1862 by Martin Hochmeister, presented a more sophisticated analysis of the events which was hostile to both the *ancien régime*, deemed to be unsupportable, but also to the Revolution, seen as being only a harbinger of chaos.

220 **Political ideas and the enlightenment in the Romanian principalities (1750-1831).**
Vlad Georgescu. Boulder, Colorado: East European Quarterly,
distributed by Columbia University Press, 1971. 232p. bibliog. (East
European Monographs, no. 1).

A study of the evolution of political ideas in the Danubian principalities between 1750 and 1831. The first date saw not only the beginning of a major domestic reform programme by the Phanariot princes but also the first direct translation of a work in French into Romanian, whilst the second year was marked by the Organic

Regulations, which constituted an early attempt at a constitution, drawn up by the Russians during their occupation of Wallachia and Moldavia between 1829 and 1834. The author argues this was not only the epoch of the Phanariots in Romania but also the age of the Enlightenment. Concerned with the study of concepts rather than authors, Georgescu looks at how prevailing social and cultural conditions influenced writers and political thinkers. Chapters deal with man and society, the theory and practice of state leadership and the growth of patriotism and the national idea. An article by the same author, summarizing some of these ideas, is 'The Romanian boyars in the eighteenth century: their political ideology', *East European Quarterly*, vol. 7, no. 1 (1973), p. 31-40.

221 **The discreet charm of the little sister: France and Romania.**
Doina Harsanyi, Nicolae Harsanyi. *East European Quarterly*, vol. 28, no. 2 (June 1994), p. 183-92.

From the first cultural contacts made through French Enlightenment authors in Greek translation to the onset of full-blown Francophilia in Wallachia and Moldova during the 19th century, the authors sketch the development of a link which has been of abiding importance to both nations. In particular, they stress the importance of the *Collège de France* and the influence of intellectuals such as Jules Michelet (1798-1874) and Edgar Quinet (1803-75) on the embryonic Romanian student societies and on the awakening of Romanian national aspirations.

222 **Orthodoxy and nationality: Andreiu Şaguna and the Rumanians of Transylvania 1846-1873.**
Keith Hitchins. Cambridge, Massachusetts; London: Harvard University Press, 1977. 325p. bibliog.

An excellent study of the career of Andreiu Şaguna (1809-73), one of the leading lights of the Romanian national movement of Transylvania during the middle years of the 19th century. Born into a family of Vlach merchants, Şaguna entered the church, rising in 1847 to become the Romanian Orthodox Bishop of Transylvania. During the Revolution of 1848, and afterwards, he remained a moderate voice in the Romanian community. Whilst being a fervent advocate of the interests of the Romanians, he remained loyal to the Habsburg monarchy. His church reforms were to culminate in 1864 with the creation of an Orthodox Metropolitanate for Transylvania with Şaguna as the first incumbent. A specialized article by the same author on this subject is 'Andreiu Şaguna and the restoration of the Romanian Orthodox Metropolis in Transylvania, 1846-1868', *Balkan Studies*, vol. 6, no. 1 (1965), p. 1-20.

223 **Religion and Romanian national consciousness in eighteenth-century Transylvania.**
Keith Hitchins. *Slavonic and East European Review*, vol. 57, no. 2 (April 1979), p. 214-39.

In this article the author investigates the growth of national consciousness amongst the Romanian population in 18th-century Transylvania. This is assessed through a study of two events, the Act of Union of 1697, which formed the Uniate Church, and the popular uprising in Southern Transylvania against this new church led by the wandering monk Visarion in 1744. Generally, whilst the new élite based on the Uniate Church was open to the ideas of nationalism, the peasantry remained grounded in a millennialism which saw them mobilized only in defence of traditional beliefs.

224   **The Romanians, 1774-1866.**
Keith Hitchins.   Oxford: Clarendon Press, 1996. 337p. maps. bibliog.
As authoritative as its prequel, Hitchin's *Rumania 1866-1947* (q.v.), this is another
excellent general history of developments in the Romanian lands under both Austro-
Hungarian and Ottoman rule. The time span covers the period from the 1774 Treaty of
Kuchuk Kainardji between the Ottoman Empire and Russia, which established a
precedent for Russian involvement in the Danubian Principalities, until the end of the
reign of Prince Alexandru Cuza under whom Wallachia and Moldavia were united as
the first step towards the foundation of the modern Romanian state. As well as being
an important step in Romanian nation-building, these years also marked the transition
from an agrarian state still largely organized on medieval lines towards a modern
urban orientated society.

225   **Rumania 1866-1947.**
Keith Hitchins.   Oxford: Clarendon Press, 1994. 579p. maps. bibliog.
(Oxford History of Modern Europe).
The definitive study in English of the history of all Romanian lands during the years in
question as, prior to the post-First World War establishment of Greater Romania, the
author covers not just the history of the Danubian Principalities but also the fortunes
of the Romanian population in the Austro-Hungarian Empire. The book is largely
arranged chronologically with a number of chapters on domestic political history,
which also contains much information on Romania's relations with the Great Powers.
However, other chapters offer wide-ranging studies of various aspects of economic,
social and culture history. Essentially, this book is a study in nation-building; it begins
in 1866, the year in which Carol, a prince of the Hohenzollern- Sigmaringen line,
ascended the Romanian throne and a new constitution was adopted which, although it
was later subject to many modifications, nevertheless established the institutional
framework of modern Romania. It finishes in 1947, when the communist take-over
overthrew all previous constitutional arrangements and turned Romania into a
republic.

226   **The Rumanian national movement in Transylvania, 1780-1849.**
Keith Hitchins.   Cambridge, Massachusetts: Harvard University
Press, 1969. 311p. bibliog. (Harvard Historical Monographs, no. 61).
Drawing extensively on Habsburg and Romanian archives, this book is the first
systematic study in English of the growth of national consciousness amongst the
Romanians of Transylvania in the 18th and 19th centuries. Cast outside the three
'recognised' *natio* of the Hungarians, Szekely and Germans, the Romanians were
politically disenfranchized. In addition, their Orthodox Church was not recognized as
one of the 'received' churches. Only with the advent of the Greek-Catholic, or Uniate,
Church did the Romanians gain an institutional base on which to base a national
movement and in this study Hitchins ably charts the growth of this movement, usually
known as the Transylvanian School. Taking their inspiration from Ancient Rome,
these intellectuals, both Uniate and Orthodox, fashioned a glorious past for the
Romanians and used this to argue for political equality in the Transylvania of their
day.

227 **Mihail Kogălniceanu: historian as Foreign Minister.**
Barbara Jelavich. In: *Historians as nation-builders: Central and South-East Europe.* Edited by Dennis Deletant, Harry Hanak.
London: Macmillans, 1988, p. 87-105.

The founder of modern Romanian historiography and the statesman primarily responsible for the major agrarian reform law of 1864, Mihail Kogălniceanu was also Foreign Minister between 1877-78 when Romanian gained its full independence from the Ottoman Empire. In this article the author discusses Kogălniceanu's achievements as a historian and as a Foreign Minister with the aim of demonstrating 'how the ideas of the historian influenced his decisions as a foreign minister and how he attempted to gain his objectives'.

228 **Romania in the First World War: the pre-crisis, 1912-1914.**
Barbara Jelavich. *International History Review*, vol. 14, no. 3 (August 1992), p. 441-51.

Although Romania was an ally of the Central Powers prior to the First World War, by 1914 her relations with Serbia, France and Russia had improved to such an extent that King Carol was forced to declare Romania neutral in the current conflict. According to the author, the volte-face was instrumental in persuading Austria-Hungary to declare war on Serbia in the summer of 1914, before the balance of power could shift further.

229 **Russia and the formation of the Romanian National State 1821-1878.**
Barbara Jelavich. Cambridge, England: Cambridge University Press, 1984. 356p. maps. bibliog.

The stated aim of the author in this work is to examine the role played by Tsarist Russia in the formation of an independent Romanian state and to study the reaction of a Balkan nationality to a neighbouring Great Power which was both a protector and a menace. Jelavich reveals that the Russians played an important role in the Romanian struggle for independence, especially in the first half of the 19th century, when treaties with the Ottoman Empire secured Romania's autonomy. However, the Romanians preferred connections with the West, especially with France, and this led the Russians, who constantly worried that Romania would become a centre for revolutionary activity, to turn to other, more responsive Balkan countries.

230 **Russia's Balkan entanglements, 1806-1914.**
Barbara Jelavich. Cambridge, England: Cambridge University Press, 1991. 291p. map. bibliog.

A well-documented survey of Russian interests in the Balkans from the 1806-12 Russo-Turkish War until the outbreak of the First World War, which contains much material on the Danubian Principalities and Romania. The overriding theme of the work is the significance of Russia's moral commitment to its Balkan co-religionists which sometimes led it to take decisions not entirely based on *realpolitik*.

231 **The establishment of the Balkan national states, 1804-1920.**
Charles Jelavich, Barbara Jelavich.   Seattle, Washington; London:
University of Washington Press, 1977. 358p. maps. bibliog. (History of
East Central Europe, no. 8).

This classic textbook of South-Eastern European history places the formation of the
modern Romanian state within a wider regional context with only one chapter (p. 126-
54) dealing exclusively with Romania. As with all the other books of this series, this
volume is intended to provide an introduction to the subject for the 'scholar who does
not specialise in East Central Europe and the student who is considering such a
specialisation'.

232 **The road to Romanian independence.**
Frederick Kellogg.   West Lafayette, Indiana: Purdue University Press,
1995. 265p. map. bibliog.

Rather than a chronologically arranged, narrative history of the events leading to
Romanian independence, this book is more a collection of essays on topics from the
period 1866-80 which the author felt illustrated the aspirations and concerns of the
Danubian Principalities at that time. Issues covered include: why the Romanians chose
to give the throne of the new state to a foreign prince, seemingly for a mixture of
practical politics and historical precedents; the vexed Jewish Question; railway
building; the quest for commercial accords with the Great Powers; relations with
Balkan neighbours; and the events surrounding the Russo-Turkish War, and the
achievement of independence.

233 **The crucial decade: East Central European society and national
defence, 1859-1870.**
Edited by Béla K. Király.   Boulder, Colorado; Highland Lakes, New
Jersey: Social Science Monographs, Brooklyn College Press,
distributed by Columbia University Press. 1984. 633p. (War and
Society in East Central Europe, no. 14; Brooklyn College Studies on
Society in Change, no. 33; East European Monographs, no. 151).

Amongst the ten essays concerned with Romania in this volume can be found the
following: Barbara Jelavich, 'The effects of the Franco-Sardinian-Austrian War, the
Austro-Prussian War, and the Polish insurrection on Romanian political development',
p. 15-27; Stephen Fischer-Galati, 'The effects of the unification of Romanian on East
Central Europe', p. 28-32; Gerald J. Bobango, 'Foundations of the independence
army: the Romanian military in the unification era', p. 388-96; Radu R. Florescu,
'Cuza, Florescu, and army reform, 1859-66', p. 402-14; and Florin Constantiniu,
'Romania's foreign military relations, 1859-66', p. 415-20.

234 **East Central European society and war in the era of revolutions, 1775-1856.**
Edited by Béla K. Király. New York: Social Science Monographs, Brooklyn College Press, distributed by Columbia University Press, 1984. 651p. (War and Society in East Central Europe, no. 4; Brooklyn College Studies on Society in Change, no. 13; East European Monographs, no. 150).

Amongst the essays concerned with Romania in this volume are: Vlad Georgescu, 'The idea of the national army in Romanian political thought, 1775-1848', p. 47-54; Florin Constantiniu, 'Tudor Vladimirescu's revolutionary army', p. 230-44; and Ioan Talpes, 'Romanian society and armed forces during the first half of the nineteenth century', p. 245-55.

235 **East Central European war leaders: civilian and military.**
Edited by Béla Király, Albert A. Nofi. Boulder, Colorado: Social Science Monographs, distributed by Columbia University Press; Highland Lakes, New Jersey: Atlantic Research and Publications, 1988. 366p. (War and Society in East Central Europe, no. 25; Atlantic Studies on Society in Change, no. 44; East European Monographs, no. 243).

This volume contains two informative items relating specifically to Romania: Glenn E. Torrey, 'Alexandru Marghiloman of Romania: war leader', p. 95-115; and Radu Florescu, 'General Ion Emanoil Florescu: father of the Romanian Army', p. 197-221.

236 **The Phanariots and the Byzantine tradition.**
Cyril Mango. In: *The struggle for Greek independence.* Edited by Richard Clogg. London: Macmillan, 1973, p. 41-66.

Despite the author's avowal that it is only a sketch, this is, nonetheless, an excellent introduction to the Phanariot Greeks who ruled Romania for most of the 18th and part of the 19th century. As the author shows, far from being descended from the great families of Byzantium, as they claimed, most were from humble backgrounds. Other important subjects touched upon include: Phanariot historiography; the source of their wealth; their relations with the Orthodox Church; and the rich literary tradition they inspired. A reproduction of this article can also be found in Cyril Mango, *Byzantium and its image: history and culture of the Byzantine Empire and its heritage* (London: Varorium, 1984. 360p.).

237 **Conflict and crisis: Romanian political development 1861-1871.**
Paul E. Michelson. New York; London: Garland, 1987. 327p. maps. bibliog. (Modern European History).

An excellent study of Romanian political culture as it developed in the Danubian Principalities of Moldavia and Wallachia in the decade after unification. Providing a welcome counterpoint to the diplomatic histories of the period, the author concentrates on domestic political developments within Romania. The four sections cover: the political, social and economic background to the 1860s; the last five years of Cuza's reign leading to his abdication in 1866; the first five years of Carol I's reign and the domestic conflict which almost led to his abdication in 1871; and, lastly, a number of conclusions. Aside from the historic narrative, topics discussed include regionalism, élite formation, the Jewish question and the viability of early constitutional structures.

238 **The temptation of Homo Europaeus.**
Victor Neumann, translated from the Romanian by Dana Miu.
Boulder, Colorado: East European Monographs, distributed by
Columbia University Press, 1993. 269p. (East European Monographs,
no. 384).

In this work of cultural and intellectual history, the author considers the transition from the late medieval to the modern in South-Eastern Europe and, in particular, in the Romanian lands. Examining the cultural interplay between the Austro-Hungarian and Ottoman Empires, he contends that this process was as much one of convergence as divergence. In a rather dense style, Neumann considers, amongst other topics, the religious crisis of conscience, the role of the Jews and the importance of libraries.

239 **A providential anti-semitism: nationalism and polity in nineteenth century Romania.**
William O. Oldson. Philadelphia: American Philosophical Society,
1991. 177p. map. bibliog. (Memoirs of the American Philosophical
Society, no. 193).

Romania has famously been called by Hannah Arendt 'the most anti-semitic country in pre-war Europe'. Yet, despite this record, about half of the country's Jews survived the Second World War, far more than in neighbouring, and, ostensibly, historically far more tolerant, Hungary. Whilst accepting that wartime political considerations and socio-economic traits, such as bribery, may have contributed to this rate of survival, the author also suggests that it is rooted in the very nature of Romanian anti-Semitism which itself represents a *tertium quid*. To understand Romanian anti-Semitism properly he argues that it is necessary to look at the 19th century and the struggle for independence, because only then did there emerge 'the peculiarly Romanian mixture of ethnic bravado and defensiveness that made anti-Semitism an essential part of being a nationalist'. When this was coupled with tensions aroused by a vast influx of Jewish immigrants from Galicia and Russia, it produced an anti-Semitism which came to be seen as a normal attribute of society. To the intelligentsia it was fully justified and being anti-Semitic almost became synonymous with being Romanian, as anti-Semitism as an ideology occupied the political centre stage.

240 **Colonel Nicolae Plesoianu and the national regeneration movement in Wallachia.**
Dan V. Pleshoyano. Boulder, Colorado: East European Monographs,
distributed by Columbia University Press, 1991. 176p. map. (East
European Monographs, no. 310).

Written in a somewhat romantic and idolizing vein by one of his descendants, this is, nevertheless, an interesting biography of Colonel Pleşoianu (1815-59). Based on secondary sources, the book does not pretend to be a history of the 1848 Revolution nor of the movement for the unification of the Romanian Principalities. Rather it is the story of a Romanian patriot who, influenced by the ideals of the French Revolution, played a significant role in the events of 1848. Colonel Pleşoianu devoted his whole life to the struggle for the unification of the two Danubian Principalities which, ironically, materialized just days after his death.

241 **Early American-Romanian relations.**
G. M. Razi. *East European Quarterly*, vol. 21, no. 1 (March 1987), p. 35-65.

Drawing heavily on extracts from reports to the State Department, this study examines American-Romanian relations before the establishment of formal diplomatic relations between the two countries in 1880. Prior to that date American consulates had been operating in Galaţi since 1859 and Bucharest since 1867.

242 **Nationalism and colonization in the Banat of Temesvár, 1718-1778.**
Karl A. Roider. In: *Nation and ideology: essays in honor of Wayne S. Vucinich.* Edited by Ivo Banac, John G. Ackerman, Roman Szporluk. Boulder, Colorado: East European Monographs, distributed by Columbia University Press, 1981, p. 87-100. (East European Monographs, no. 65).

The region of north-west Romania, known as the Banat, passed from the Ottoman to the Austro-Hungarian Empire at the conclusion of the 1716-18 war. The newly regained lands were placed under the administration of a specially created joint Austro-Hungarian Commission in Vienna which saw as its first task the repopulation of the area which had been devastated by war. The new emigrants who arrived were predominately German, and in this article Roider attempts to clarify the motives behind the colonization. Previously, various authors have suggested that it was part of a conscious effort to Germanize, Catholicize or Westernize the area. However, after reviewing the evidence, Roider concludes that the process should best be seen in the light of the contemporary population theories of 18th-century mercantilism which held that people constituted a state's wealth.

243 **Activism and inertia: Ottokar Czernin's mission to Romania, 1913-1916.**
Garry W. Shanafelt. *Austrian History Yearbook*, vol. 19-20, part 1 (1983-84), p. 189-214.

The author shows how during his tenure as Austro-Hungarian ambassador to Romania between 1913 and 1916, Ottokar Czernin frequently advocated a more forceful policy than that desired by Vienna.

244 **Was the peasant uprising a revolution? The meaning of a struggle over the past.**
E. M. Simmonds-Duke. *East European Politics and Societies*, vol. 1, no. 2 (1987), p. 187-224.

Writing under the pseudonym, E. M. Simmonds-Duke, Katherine Verdery traces the differing reactions of Romanian historians to the bicentennial of Horea's uprising of 1784. Those closest to the régime tended to term the events a revolution, whilst those who adopted a more impartial viewpoint tended to see it as an uprising.

245 **Distant lands: the genesis and evolution of Romanian-American relations.**
Ion Gh. Stanciu, Paul Cernovodeanu. Boulder, Colorado: East European Monographs, distributed by Columbia University Press, 1985. 281p. (East European Monographs, no. 195).
A welcome publication in English by two historians who over the years have made an enormous contribution to the study of Romanian relations with the Anglo-Saxon world. In this pioneering study they present the first Romanian impressions of the New World and give a chronological account of contacts between the two countries prior to the establishment of formal diplomatic relations in 1880. Based largely on archival sources, this is a useful work for exploring the first contacts of what are two historically, geographically, socio-economically, politically and religiously different societies.

246 **Symposium l'époque phanariote 21-25 octobre 1970: à la mémoire de Cléobule Tsourkas.**
Thessaloniki: Institute for Balkan Studies, 1974. 481p.
Frustratingly little is known about the Phanariot period in Romanian history. Consequently, the Phanariots remain shadowy figures who all too readily subside into the caricatures of Zallones (cf. Charles Swan, *Journal of a voyage up the Mediterranean; principally among the island of the archipelago and in Asia Minor*, q.v.). This volume goes some way towards lifting this veil with thirty-eight papers from leading Romanian and Greek scholars on the Phanariot epoch and beyond – papers cover the years until the 1830s. Issues raised include education, philhellenism in the Danubian Principalities, the Phanariots and the 1821 revolution as well as the art and architecture of the era. All the papers in this volume are in French.

247 **Indifference and mistrust: Russian-Romanian collaboration in the campaign of 1916.**
Glenn E. Torrey. *Journal of Military History,* vol. 57, no. 2 (1993), p. 279-300.
When Romania finally joined the First World War in 1916, it was as an ally of Russia. However, as the author shows in this study, a mixture of indifference and suspicions between the two countries, especially over Bessarabia, hampered collaboration and contributed to Romanian defeat.

248 **The redemption of an army: the Romanian campaign of 1917.**
Glenn E. Torrey. *War and Society,* vol. 12, no. 2 (Oct. 1994), p. 23-42.
The success of the Russo-Romanian armies in their 1917 campaign against the Central Powers has often been overlooked. In the Romanian theatre of operations the Russians fought significantly better than elsewhere, but the author contends that it was the performance of the Romanian army in the battles of Mărăşeşti and Oituz that really made a difference. For, whereas the offensive of 1917 was to precipitate the disintegration of the Russian Empire, it was to facilitate the building of a Greater Romania.

249   **Romania in the First World War: the years of engagement,
       1916-1918.**
       Glenn E. Torrey.   *International History Review*, vol. 14, no. 3
       (Aug. 1992), p. 462-79.

The sequel to V. N. Vinogradov's article 'Romania in the First World War: the years
of neutrality, 1914-1916' (see item no. 251). It discusses the change in Romanian
policy towards the Allies during the years of belligerency (1916-18) when they sought
their support to build a Greater Romania. In particular, the author considers the often
tactless and uncompromising diplomacy of Ion Brătianu which at times angered his
allied counterparts and even mystified his fellow Romanians.

250   **Romania leaves the war: the decision to sign an armistice,
       December 1917.**
       Glenn E. Torrey.   *East European Quarterly*, vol. 23, no. 3 (Sept.
       1989), p. 283-92.

The purpose of this well-researched study is to examine the decision making process
which led to the Armistice of Focşani of 9 December 1917. This was a prelude to the
ruinous Peace of Bucharest of 7 May 1918 which ended the political career of the
Prime Minister Alexandru Maghiloman. The position of the Romanian Army had been
fatally compromised by the collapse of the Russian forces due to the Revolution. They
were under pressure from the Allies to keep the Eastern Front alive, but with no
material replacement for Russian troops forthcoming the only prospect was of a
disastrous retreat into Southern Russia. The armistice was secured by Ion Brătianu and
although at the time it was heavily criticized by the French Premier, Clemenceau, the
author argues that by preserving the Romanian Army it permitted the occupation of
Transylvania and Bessarabia at the end of the war, thus forcing the Allies to recognize
Greater Romania.

251   **Southeast European maritime commerce and naval policies from
       the mid-eighteenth century to 1914.**
       Edited by Apostolos E. Vacalopoulos, Constantios D. Svolopoulos,
       Béla K. Király.   Boulder, Colorado; Highland Lakes, New Jersey:
       Social Science Monographs, Atlantic Research and Publications,
       Institute for Balkan Studies, Thessaloniki, distributed by Columbia
       University Press. 1988. 410p. (War and Society in East Central Europe,
       no. 23; East European Monographs, no. 266).

The five essays concerned with Romania in this volume are: Richard Charles Frucht,
'War, peace, and internationality: the Danube, 1789-1916', p. 79-98; Emil Palotás,
'The problems of international navigation on the Danube in Austro-Hungarian politics
during the second half of the nineteenth century', p. 99-114; Spiridon G. Focas, 'The
Greeks and navigation on the Lower Danube, 1789-1913', p. 115-30; Virginia
Paskaleva, 'Shipping and trade on the Lower Danube in the eighteenth and nineteenth
centuries', p. 131-52; and Despoina Tsourka-Papastathis, 'The decline of the Greek
"companies" in Transylvania: an aspect of Habsburg economic policies in the Black
Sea and the Mediterranean', p. 213-20.

252 **Romania in the First World War: the years of neutrality, 1914-1916.**
V. N. Vinogradov. *International History Review*, vol. 14, no. 3 (August 1992), p. 452-61.
The author narrates the course of Romania's negotiations, and more specifically those of the Prime Minister, Ion Brătianu, with the Allies prior to Romania's eventual entry into the First World War on their side. Previously Romania's foreign policy was determined by the country's ambitions towards Transylvania, its long-time membership of the Triple Alliance, and the opinion of the Romanian general staff who believed that benevolent neutrality was preferable to active support of the Entente. This article not only offers an analysis of the reasons why Romania stayed neutral for the first part of the war but also discusses the whole issue comparatively in relation to the position of other countries, such as Greece, and the pressures exerted by both sides.

Interwar period, 1918-40

253 **Rumania.**
Zev Barbu.   In: *Fascism in Europe*.   Edited by S. J. Woolf.
London; New York: Methuen, 1968, p. 151-70.
In this study of the Iron Guard the author stresses not only the social status of its supporters but also their psychological characteristics. In another work he also adopts a similar approach: 'Psycho-historical and sociological perspectives on the Iron Guard, the fascist movement of Romania' in *Who were the fascists? Social roots of European fascism*, edited by Stein Ugelvik Larsen, Bernt Hagtvet and Jan Petter Myklbust (Bergen, Norway: Universitetsforlaget, 1980, p. 379-94).

254 **Romania's diplomatic relations with Yugoslavia in the interwar period, 1919-1941.**
Eugene Boia.   New York: East European Monographs, distributed by Columbia University Press, 1993. 501p. (East European Monographs, no. 356).
In the Eastern Europe of the interwar years there was an exception to the general rule of discordant relations between neighbouring states; those of Romania and Yugoslavia which remained friendly throughout most of this period despite the presence of such potentially contentious issues as the Banat. This area had been divided between Romania and the new Kingdom of Serbs, Croats and Slovenes [Yugoslavia] at the time of the dismemberment of the Austro-Hungarian Empire. Faced with revisionist neighbours both states were intent on upholding the Paris Accords and preserving the status quo. However, as the author shows, these good relations could not survive the economic crisis of the 1930s and growing pressures from the Axis powers. New agreements often negated old and with the collapse of both the Little and Balkan Ententes, which lay at the foundation of both Romanian and Yugoslavian foreign policies, the two states were eventually drawn into the Second World War on opposite sides. This chronologically arranged study is comprehensive, even if it is slightly one-sided, as it only draws upon Romanian documents.

255 **From private philanthropy to public institutions: the Rockerfeller Foundation and public health in inter-war Romania.**
Maria Bucur. *Romanian Civilization*, vol. 4, no. 2 (Summer 1995), p. 47-60.
Reviews the involvement of the Rockerfeller Foundation in the creation of public health programmes and institutions in interwar Romania. The author argues that its role went beyond mere financial support and that the 'work of a few devoted individuals helped shape the very notion of state responsibility towards public health and contributed to strengthening the government's commitment – financial and ideological – to state sponsored institutions and programs which the Rockerfeller Foundation helped get off the ground during the inter-war period'.

256 **In praise of wellborn mothers: on the development of eugenicist gender roles in interwar Romania.**
Maria Bucur. *East European Politics and Societies*, vol. 9, no. 1 (Winter 1995), p. 123-42.
This study traces the ideas of a group of Romanian eugenicists during the interwar years who believed it was possible to strengthen and modernize Romania by controlling both the reproductive capabilities of women and their social role as mothers.

257 **Leaders and martyrs: Codreanu, Mosley and José Antonio.**
Stephen M. Cullen. *History*, vol. 71, no. 233 (Oct. 1986), p. 408-30.
Drawing on the original writings of the Romanian Iron Guard leader, Corneliu Codreanu, the author uses the typology of fascism advanced by Stanley G. Payne in his book *Fascism: comparison and definition* (Madison, Wisconsin: University of Wisconsin, 1980. 234p.) to compare the ideology of Codreanu with those of other European fascist leaders, Oswald Mosley and José Antonio Primo de Rivera. He concludes that they all fit Payne's model, despite the fact that Codreanu's anti-programmatic, terroristic, anti-modern and anti-imperial ideology was almost the exact opposite of Mosley's beliefs.

258 **Anglo-French policy in relation to South-East Europe 1936-1939.**
F. W. Deakin. In: *Les relations franco-britanniques de 1935-1939* (Franco-British relations from 1935 to 1939). Paris: Editions du Centre National de la Recherche Scientifique, 1975, p. 63-90.
Much of this study of Anglo-French policy in South-Eastern Europe on the eve of the Second World War is concerned with Romania. Drawing heavily on documents from the British Public Record Office, the author persuasively argues that Great Britain had little interest in the region during the interwar years, as it had no specific treaty obligations and its commercial interests were negligible. French interests were stronger but their commitments were still limited with the Franco-Romanian treaty of 1926 carrying guarantees but no military convention. From 1937 there was an acceleration of German interest in the area linked to the stockpiling of strategic reserves such as oil. This growth in German influence was facilitated by the fragmentation of the Little Entente, a policy of seeking active alliances in the area on the part of Germany and the general passivity of Britain and France.

259 **Romania 1919-1938.**
Mattei Dogan. In: *Competitive elections in developing countries.*
Edited by Myron Weiner, Ergun Ozbundun. Durham, North Carolina:
Duke University Press, 1987, p. 369-89.

The author argues that Romania between the two World Wars can best be charac-
terized as a 'mimic democracy', that is, a democracy where the political process was
reversed since the parliament was not elected by a free ballot but, instead, the party in
power manipulated elections in order to have the necessary majority. Whilst at first
sight such an arrangement would seem to be the very antithesis of a 'real' democracy,
the author cautions against describing a 'mimic' democracy in completely pejorative
terms on account of the fact that it brought Romania a degree of political stability that
was noticeably lacking in neighbouring states.

260 **Count Istvan Bethlen's secret plan for the restoration of the
empire of Transylvania.**
N. F. Dreisziger. *East European Quarterly*, vol. 8, no. 4 (Jan. 1975),
p. 413-23.

Istvan Bethlen, Premier of Hungary between 1921-31, had a special attachment to
Transylvania, the land of his ancestors and the place of his own birth. After his
departure from high office in 1931, he became an influential elder statesmen who held
some influence with the Regent, Admiral Horthy. In this capacity he sought a revision
of the 1920 Trianon Treaty, which had stripped Hungary of many of her former lands,
including Transylvania, in favour of a new 'just partition'. On the outbreak of the
Second World War, Bethlen submitted a policy document to the Hungarian
government arguing that a neutral Hungary had to keep its options open in the coming
conflict. He also presented a plan that suggested any postwar settlement should see a
separate Hungary, Transylvania and Romania bound together within a wider Eastern
European union, with Transylvania under a sort of joint Romanian-Hungarian rule. In
this article the author discusses the origins of this scheme and its feasibility.

261 **Rumania: the war and the army, 1914-1930.**
Catharine Durandin. *War and Society*, vol. 3, no. 2 (1985), p. 45-68.

Although it was to be the springboard for the unification of the Romanian lands, the
First World War also had a number of more baleful influences on Romanian life, as
revealed by the author in this article. In particular, serious deficiencies were revealed
in the Romanian armed forces.

262 **Jew and peasant in interwar Romania.**
Stephen Fischer-Galati. *Nationalities Papers*, vol. 16, no. 2
(Fall 1988), p. 201-08.

The author investigates popular peasant attitudes towards the Jewish minority in
Romania during the first half of the 20th century and suggests that they were not
strongly anti-Semitic.

263 **Nicolae Iorga and fascism.**
Radu Ioanid. *Journal of Contemporary History*, vol. 27, no. 3
(July 1992), p. 467-92.

Drawing largely on the writings of Iorga himself, this article traces the often
contradictory relationship between the historian and Romanian fascism. By nature a
conservative monarchist, with a deep attachment to tradition, Iorga, along with
Alexander Cuza, founded the right-wing Democratic Nationalist Party in 1910.
However, the two later parted company and, whilst Cuza founded the fascist League
of Christian National Defence, Iorga's relationship with fascism was to remain more
ambiguous. A supporter of Mussolini but an opponent of Hitler and Nazism, he was
heavily critical of the actions of the League of Archangel Michael, yet nevertheless
campaigned for the release of its leaders from prison. He was considered by Mircea
Eliade to be a spiritual father of Nae Ionescu, the chief ideologue of the Legion, yet it
was the 'mad assassins' of that movement, as Iorga termed them, who murdered him
in 1940.

264 **The pogrom of Bucharest 21-23 January 1941.**
Radu Ioanid. *Holocaust and Genocide Studies*, vol. 6, no. 4
(Dec. 1991), p. 373-82.

In January 1941 a deterioration in relations between Marshal Antonescu and the Iron
Guard under Horia Sima prompted the latter to stage an armed uprising to try and
impose a 'pure' legionary government. The Guard were fiercely anti-Semitic and in
the ensuing struggle in Bucharest a number of Jews died. Both sides looked to the
Germans for backing, and in this article the author, apart from reviewing the events in
Bucharest, also considers the relationship of the two sides with Germany.

265 **The sword of the Archangel: fascist ideology in Romania.**
Radu Ioanid. Boulder, Colorado: East European Monographs,
distributed by Columbia University Press, 1990. 323p. maps.
(East European Monographs, no. 292).

Beginning with a useful discussion of the subject in both Romanian and Western
historiography, in this study the author covers not just the Legion of Archangel
Michael but also other rightist parties, including the League of Christian National
Defence and the National Christian Party as well as more ephemeral groups such as
the Guard of National Conscience. The bulk of the study, however, as might be
expected, is concerned with the Legion and the characteristics of its ideology, which
the author suggests were anti-communism, nationalism, anti-Semitism and mysticism.
Ioanid also examines the sources of the Legion's support before concluding with a
chapter on the persecution of the Jews during the Second World War.

266 **Cultural politics in Greater Romania: regionalism, nation building
and ethnic struggle, 1918-1930.**
Irina Livezeanu. Ithaca, New York; London: Cornell University
Press, 1995. 340p. maps. bibliog.

Making good use of archive sources, the author explores the means by which the
newly acquired territories of Transylvania, Bucovina and Bessarabia were integrated
into Greater Romania after the First World War. As a large proportion of the educated
élite in the newly acquired lands were from minority groups, a concerted process of

Romanization was unleashed, aimed at raising an element of the ethnic Romanian peasantry to fill their place. The chosen vehicle for this was the education system, but in the process assertive nationalism all too readily gave way to an anti-urban, xenophobic and anti-Semitic ideology which was eventually to bear tragic fruit in the fascism of the Iron Guard.

267 **The French and British attitudes towards the Goga-Cuza government in Romania, December 1937 – February 1938.**
Dov. B. Lungu. *Canadian Slavonic Papers*, vol. 30, no. 3 (Sept. 1988), p. 323-41.

The author shows that, despite the avowed anti-Semitism of Cuza and Goga and their pronounced leaning towards the Axis Powers, Great Britain and France still remained content to give King Carol the benefit of the doubt in internal affairs and failed to dissuade him from asking the National Christian Party to form a government.

268 **Romania and the Great Powers, 1933-1940.**
Dov B. Lungu. Durham, North Carolina; London: Duke University Press, 1989. 294p. maps. bibliog.

Drawing extensively on archival sources, including those of the Romanian Foreign Ministry, this is a detailed study of the often torturous course of Romanian foreign policy in the years immediately preceding the Second World War. Lungu charts the souring of the historic relationship with France and then the attempts to maintain a precarious nonalignment between the Scylla and Charybdis of the Soviet Union and Germany before Romania was, finally, drawn into the clutches of the latter. Two related articles by the same author are 'Nicolae Titulescu and the 1932 crisis concerning the Soviet-Romanian pact of non-aggression', *East European Quarterly*, vol. 18, no. 2 (1984), p. 185-213 and 'The European crisis of March-April 1939: the Romanian dimension', *International History Review*, vol. 7, no. 3 (1985), p. 390-414.

269 **Developmental models and social value choices in the Rumanian 1940's: the case of the *Cercul Literar* in Sibiu.**
Virgil Nemoianu. *International Journal of Rumanian Studies*, vol. 7, no. 1a (1989), p. 53-72.

Argues that contrary to popular belief young Romanian intellectuals in the 1940s caught between Legionism and Leninism did not totally abandon the liberal developmental model. In support of this contention the author points to the activities of the Sibiu literary group, the *Cercul Literar*. The main members of this were I. Negoițescu (1921-) and Radu Stanca (1920-62) but they also included Ștefan Augustin Doinaș (1922-), N. Balotă (1925-) and C. Regman (1919-), whereas Victor Iancu and Lucian Blaga served as the group's mentors. The group never achieved much importance and most were subsequently to suffer persecution and imprisonment under the communists; however, later, to varying degrees, they all entered the system and were able to introduce a differing value system. This, according to the author, is where their long-term significance lies.

270 The historical nationalist thought of Nicolae Iorga.

William O. Oldson. Boulder, Colorado: East European Quarterly, distributed by Columbia University Press, New York, 1973. 135p. (East European Monographs, no. 5).

Nicolae Iorga strides like a colossus across Romanian historiography. The author of a staggering 1,250 books and countless thousands of articles, he also found time for an active career on the nationalist right of politics, rising to the post of Prime Minister between 1931-32. Oldson has no pretences to be a biographer and this book does not set out to chart Iorga's career. Instead, this is a study of the political thought of Iorga with the emphasis being placed on what he understood to be the nature of history and nationalism as well as his conception of the function of a historian of the Romanian people. A shorter article by the same author on this subject is: 'Nicolae Iorga: the Romanian nationalist as historian', *East European Quarterly*, vol. 6, no. 4 (Jan. 1973), p. 473-86.

271 Revolutions and intervention in Hungary and its neighbor states 1918-1919.

Edited by Peter Pastor. Boulder, Colorado: Social Science Monographs, Atlantic Studies on Social Change, distributed by Columbia University Press, 1988. 530p. maps. (Atlantic Studies on Social Change, no. 30; East European Monographs, no. 240; War and Society, no. 20).

Following the collapse of the Austro-Hungarian monarchy at the end of the First World War, Hungary dissolved into a period of chaos out of which eventually emerged Bela Kun's Soviet Republic. The Western powers, alarmed by what they saw as the prospect of the contagion of communism spreading throughout the region, sanctioned the intervention of neighbouring states in Hungary, with Romanian armies fresh from their triumphs in Transylvania eventually occupying Budapest. This volume contains several studies concerning the Romanian intervention in Hungary including: Jean Nouzille, 'The July campaign of the Hungarian Red Army against Romania as seen by France', p. 81-88; Glen E. Torrey, 'General Henri Berthelot and the army of the Danube, 1918-1919', p. 277-92; Stephen Fischer-Galati, 'The impact of the Russian Revolutions of 1917 on Romania', p. 293-300; and Glen E. Torrey, 'The Romanian intervention in Hungary, 1919', p. 301-20.

272 Nicolae Iorga as historian and politician.

Maurice Pearton. In: *Historians as nation-builders: Central and South-East Europe*. Edited by Dennis Deletant, Harry Hanak. London: Macmillans, 1988, p. 157-73.

In this elegant essay on the nature of history, the author explores the link between political consciousness and historical explanations in the life and work of Romania's foremost historian, Nicolae Iorga. Tracing Iorga's career and exploring the milieu in which he lived, Pearton examines his concept of history and the influence of romanticism on his work.

273 The importance of Queen Marie in Romanian history.

Paul D. Quinlan. *Balkan Studies*, vol. 32, no. 1 (1991), p. 35-41.

A sketch of the personality and attainments of Queen Marie of Romania (1875-1938) whom the author calls an 'elusive Queen'. In an effort to find a satisfactory definition of her character, the author turns to the personalities of other powerful female figures in history. He asks whether Hannah Pakula's description of the Queen as 'The last romantic' (see item no. 341) is appropriate and wonders whether the Queen should not be seen as a 20th-century Catherine the Great or even a Romanian de Medici. On reflection, however, he concludes that perhaps closest to the Queen's attributes would be the personality of Theodora, Empress of Byzantium.

274 **Lupescu: Romania's gray eminence.**
Paul D. Quinlan. *East European Quarterly*, vol. 28, no. 1 (Spring 1994), p. 95-104.

Elena Lupescu, born in Bessarabia in 1899 of Jewish parentage, divorcee and 'outgoing, self-confident, hostile, dominant woman' is cast by Quinlan as a conniving *femme fatale* who stole the heart of Prince Carol, a 'weak, irresolute, immature boy'. After attending the funeral of Alexandra, the wife of Edward VII, in London in 1925, the couple eloped to Paris where they lived for five years scandalizing all Europe. In June 1930 Carol agreed to return to Romania to claim his throne with Lupescu allegedly agreeing to remain in exile. However, by August 1930 she had followed the King back to Romania, which prompted the resignation of the Premier, Iuliu Maniu. Arguing that 'the key to understanding Carol and his reign is his relationship with his mistress', Quinlan presents Lupescu as a pre-communist Elena Ceauşescu. She surrounded herself and the King with only trusted acolytes and second-rate opportunists, known as the Camarilla, and her renowned love of extravagance and show made her 'the most hated woman in the country and a symbol of all that was wrong with Romania'. Throughout the tone of this article is unremittingly hostile, with even Lupescu's dislike of the Iron Guard leader Codrescu painted in negative terms. However, she followed Carol faithfully into exile and remained by his side until his death in 1953. She died in 1977 and is buried beside him in Lisbon.

275 **Rumania: political problems of an agrarian state.**
Henry L. Roberts. London: Oxford University Press, 1951. 414p. bibliog.

This book, which was reprinted in 1969 in Hamden, Connecticut by Archon Books, offers an objective political and economical analysis of Romania between 1922 and 1945. As the author served with the American military mission to the country in 1944-45 and thus had first-hand experience of the communist take-over, his narrative on this particular issue, which is supported by primary sources, is especially illuminating.

276 **Romanian nationalism: the legionary movement.**
Alexander E. Ronnett. Chicago: Romanian-American National Congress, 1995. 2nd ed. 251p. bibliog.

The bias of this book is immediately apparent from the dedication which is to 'the memory of all legionary martyrs who so willingly gave their lives for the freedom of the Romanian nation'. This second edition is a greatly expanded and revised version of a book which was first published by Loyola University Press in 1974. The author was first prompted to set pen to paper when the Ceauşescu government refused to allow the daughter of Vasile Postecua, an exiled supporter of the Legion, to visit her dying father in the United States. This issue received some press coverage at the time but few journalists knew anything of the Legionary movement or, if they did, they tended to be unremittingly hostile. The author, who himself is a former legionary, wrote this book to tell the 'truth' about the movement. Despite the fact that it is an unrestrained apologia for the Legion, this volume nevertheless contains some interesting information and personal reminiscences. However, the book should perhaps be consulted in conjunction with the stinging review of the first edition by Sherman D. Spector in *Balkan Studies*, vol. 17, no. 1 (1976), p. 169-70.

277 **The concept of political trading in peacetime. The British Government and trade with South-Eastern Europe, 1938-1939.**
M. J. Rooke. *Revue des Études Sud-Est Européennes*, vol. 22, no. 2 (April/June 1984), p. 171-95.

In the years immediately prior to the Second World War, British policy was frequently contradictory and lacked direction. In this study the author concentrates on economic trade as a political weapon and shows that the British free market was incapable of competing for influence with the state-controlled German economy. Any attempts to buy goods at uneconomic – above world market – prices to gain political leverage were frustrated by the British treasury and the sheer unwillingness of any manufacturers to buy products which were perceived as being of inferior quality to others on the market, as was the case with Romanian grain and Greek tobacco.

278 **East Central Europe between the two world wars.**
Joseph Rothschild. Seattle, Washington; London: University of Washington Press, 1974. 420p. (A History of East Central Europe, no. 9).

The section of this book covering Romania (p. 281-322) provides an excellent introduction to the interwar history of the country. The First World War may have brought into fruition the cherished dream of a Greater Romania but a greatly expanded territory also brought the associated problem of integrating different political, economic and social traditions. In the first part of the section covering Romania, the author reviews these problems, and particularly the minority and peasant questions, before he surveys political developments in the interwar years, which he divides into three distinct periods. During the first of these, 1918-28, the National Liberal Party commanded the political scene; in the second, 1928-30, the National Peasant Party briefly held power; and between 1930 and 1940, there was a 'Carolist decade' in which the King increasingly dominated politics, leading eventually, in 1938, to royal dictatorship.

279 **Prelude to dictatorship in Romania: the National Christian Party in power, December 1937-February 1938.**
Paul A. Schapiro. *Canadian-American Slavic Studies*, vol. 8, no. 1 (Spring 1974), p. 45-88.

A scholarly study of the National Christian Party government of Octavian Goga and Alexandru C. Cuza which includes a detailed analysis of the 1937 elections. To the puzzle of why Carol offered the chance of forming a government to a party which gained less than ten per cent of the vote, the author suggests that it was the only possible option as all the other candidates had invalidated themselves for one reason or another.

280 **Relapse into bondage 1918-1947: the political memoirs of Alexandre Cretzianu, free Romania's last world diplomat.**
Sherman David Spector. *Southeastern Europe*, vol. 11, no. 1 (1984), p. 101-24.

Alexandre Cretzianu (1895-1979), the wartime Romanian Minister to Ankara, fled Romania after the war and, whilst in exile, produced a number of books and articles criticizing the communist régime and lamenting what he saw as the past failures of policy which had allowed the country to fall under Soviet occupation. During his exile Cretzianu also wrote a memoir concerning interwar Romanian foreign policy, but on his death it remained unpublished. It is this work that is reproduced in this and subsequent issues of this journal. Chapter two, 'Titulescu's policy without Titulescu', appears in vol. 12, no. 1, p. 103-24; chapter three, 'The last throes of peace', in vol. 12, no. 2, p. 243-59; and chapters four, 'Royal dictatorship', five, 'The sinking of the Little Entente' and six, 'Crisis with Germany', can be found in vol. 15, no. 1-2, p. 99-136.

281 **Native fascism in the successor states 1918-1945.**
Edited by Peter F. Sugar. Santa Barbara, California: ABC-Clio, 1971. 166p. (Twentieth Century Series, no. 4).

This collection of essays contains two chapters on Romania. The first, by Emanuel Turczynski, 'The background of Romanian fascism' (p. 101-11), places the Romanian right of the interwar period within the wider framework of Romanian nationalism. The second, by Stephen Fischer-Galati, 'Fascism in Romania' (p. 112-21), provides a general study of the Legion of Archangel Michael and looks in particular at its relationship with King Carol II.

282 **The politicisation of history: Marshal Antonescu and Romania.**
Mark Temple. *East European Politics and Societies*, vol. 10, no. 3 (Fall 1996), p. 457-503.

The place in history of the wartime leader Marshal Antonescu has recently been the subject of considerable debate in Romania with a number of disparate groups trying to effect his rehabilitation, claiming that his unfair representation under communism is still being perpetuated in the West. In this paper the author seeks to put the Marshal's career and, particularly his treatment of the 'Jewish Question', into historical perspective. He argues that the quest for rehabilitation is largely being used as a political weapon and that this may be a legacy of the communist past when, in the absence of any meaningful political debate, historical figures were often used to comment on current affairs.

283 **To arm an ally: French arms sales to Romania, 1926-1940.**
Martin Thomas. *Journal of Strategic Studies*, vol. 19, no. 2 (June 1996), p. 231-59.

Covering the period from the signing of a bilateral French-Romanian treaty until the onset of the Second World War, the author illustrates how Romania gradually came to lose faith in French military power. Despite the traditional close ties between the two countries, as France desperately scrambled to rearm herself in the years prior to the War, many Romanian arms orders remained undelivered. Although the author cautions that the significance of this should not be overstated, this failure to deliver weapons, in so much as it was seen as being a litmus-test of French intentions, may have played a role in determining Romania's decision to turn to the Axis Powers.

284 **The shadow of the Swastika: the rise of fascism and anti-Semitism in the Danube basin, 1936-1939.**
Bela Vago. Farnborough, England: Saxon House for the Institute of Jewish Affairs, 1975. 431p.

In the first part of this book the author offers a description of the rise of fascism and anti-Semitism in the states of the Danubian Basin. The section concerned with Romania (p. 19-72) begins with the end of the First World War and the creation of Greater Romania, but the main part of the narrative is concerned with the rapid rise of the Right in the mid-1930s and the attitude of the Iron Guard and the Monarchy to the Jewish Question. The second section contains a selection of documents, many relating to Romania, which are drawn from the British Foreign Office papers deposited at the Public Record Office.

285 **National character and national ideology in interwar Eastern Europe.**
Edited by Katherine Verdery, Ivo Banac. New Haven, Connecticut: Yale Center for International and Area Studies, 1995. 255p.

Contains three essays on interwar Romanian history. In 'National ideology and national character in interwar Romania' (p. 103-34), Katherine Verdery begins by surveying the various attempts by Romanian cultural figures to define the traits which supposedly made the Romanians distinctive as a people or a nation. Religion was considered to be at the heart of any Romanian 'national essence' and this is discussed by Keith Hitchins in 'Orthodoxism: polemics over ethnicity and religion in interwar Romania' (p. 135-56). Finally, the position writers took in the debate, and, particularly, the posture of Vasile Pârvan, Eugen Lovinescu, Garabet Ibrăileanu and Mihail Ralea, is surveyed by Marian Papahagi in 'The "national essence" in interwar Romanian literary life' (p. 157-80).

286 **Nationalist ideology and anti-Semitism: the case of Romanian intellectuals in the 1930s.**
Leon Volovici, translated from the Romanian by Charles Kormos. Oxford; New York; Seoul, Tokyo: Published for the Vidal Sassoon International Center for the Study of Antisemitism, Hebrew University of Jerusalem by Pergamon Press, 1991. 213p. bibliog. (Studies in anti-Semitism).

The author argues that anti-Semitism was the dominant theme in the political and intellectual life of Romania in the 1930s. Romanian intellectuals were divided in their attitudes to the 'Jewish Question' between extremist ideologues, such as Cuza and Codreanu, who preached a solution through elimination of the Jews, and nationalists who supported a 'rational' anti-Semitism. These, who included Nicolae Iorga and Nae Ionescu, argued that there was a Jewish problem, but where the Jews did not compete with ethnic Romanian interests, they could be tolerated and, indeed, those who 'served' Romanian culture and science could even be accepted and respected.

287 **Romanian Cassandra: Ion Antonescu and the struggle for reform,
1916-1941.**
Larry L. Watts.   Boulder, Colorado: East European Monographs,
distributed by Columbia University Press, 1993. 390p. (East European
Monographs, no. 358).

Few figures in Romanian history are more controversial than Marshal Ion Antonescu
(1882-1946), *Conducator* of Romania during the Second World War. The Marshal was
executed by the communist régime in 1946 and damned to universal condemnation
thereafter, but in this well researched biography Watts argues that it is time to re-
evaluate his career – a cause which has been taken up with gusto by many Romanians
since 1989. He was considered to be a 'Cassandra' because many of his prophecies
were never heeded, such as his warnings of the German-Hungarian threat to Romania's
territorial integrity long before the Vienna Awards of 1940. Watts presents a man who
was a determined upholder of constitutional rule, who suppressed the Iron Guard,
purged the government of corruption and tolerated a mild pluralism. Essentially an
idealist, he believed in the 'fundamental goodness of his people'. A searching and
lengthy review of this book can be found in Paul Michelson, 'In search of the 20th
century: Marshal Antonescu and Romanian history – a review essay', *Romanian
Civilization*, vol. 3, no. 2 (Fall-Winter 1994), p. 72-103. Watts has also contributed a
series of articles which provide more details of Antonescu's career, in the same journal:
see, for instance, 'Antonescu and the Great War: a reconsideration of the roles played
by Ion Antonescu, Constantin Prezan, and Alexandru Avrescu', *Romanian Civilization*,
vol. 3, no. 2 (Fall-Winter 1994), p. 3-45; vol. 4, no. 1 (Spring 1995), p. 59-100.

288 **Romania.**
Eugen Webber.   In: *The European right: a historical profile.*   Edited
by Hans Rogger, Eugen Webber.   Berkeley, California: University of
California Press, 1974, p. 501-74.

Although best known for his work on France, this distinguished historian here turns
his attention to the Romanian right and, in an important essay, traces its development
in the interwar period. Most emphasis is naturally placed on Corneliu Zelea Codreanu
and his Legion of the Archangel Michael which sought the moral and spiritual
rejuvenation of Romania through an ideology based on tradition, orthodox mysticism
and anti-Semitism. A further article by the same author on this subject is 'The men of
the Archangel', *Journal of Contemporary History*, vol. 1, no. 1 (1966), p. 101-26.

289 **An eyewitness note: reflections on the Rumanian Iron Guard.**
Zvi Yavetz.   *Journal of Contemporary History*, vol. 26, no. 3-4 (Sept.
1991), p. 597-610.

The author, who was born in Romania and is now a distinguished Professor of Ancient
History at the University of Tel Aviv, offers his personal memories on the rise of the
Legion of Archangel Michael and the Iron Guard in interwar Romania. These thoughts
were partly prompted by the publication of Armin Heinen's book, *Die legion
'Erzengel Michael' in Rumänien: soziale Bewegung und politische organization: ein
Beitrag zum problem des internationalen Faschismus* (The Legion of 'Archangel
Michael' in Romania: social movement and political organization: a contribution to
the problem of international fascism) (Munich: Oldenbourg, 1986. 558p. bibliog.
[Südosteuroäische Arbeiter, no. 83]). Evaluating the results of the Romanian elections
of 1937 and their significance for both the Romanian people and the future of the Iron
Guard, Yavetz argues that they can only be interpreted by referring to a number of
analytical models.

The Second World War

290 **Armata Română în al doilea război mondial: Romanian army in World War II.**
Bucharest: Editura Meridiane, 1995. 215p. maps. bibliog.
Prepared by staff of the National Military Museum, this bilingual Romanian-English text describes the actions of the Romanian army during the Second World War when it fought, first alongside the Axis Powers and then with the Allies against them. This attractive volume is lavishly illustrated with numerous photographs of the war and maps and plans of the various engagements.

291 **Third axis, fourth ally: Romanian armed forces in the European war 1941-1945.**
Mark Axworthy, Cornel Scafeş, Cristian Craciunoiu.   London: Arms and Armour, 1995. 368p. maps. bibliog.
The first six chapters of this study offer a strictly chronological account of the progress of the land war, concentrating on the deployment of forces and the details of various battles, although the author also discusses the readiness and the abilities of the Romanian troops and the calibre of their leadership. The remainder of the book deals with the performance of the Romanian airforce and navy during the war. Throughout the text is supported by an enormous amount of technical detail about the specifications of the armaments available to the combatants.

292 **Prodding the Russian bear: pro-German resistance in Romania, 1944-45.**
Perry Biddiscombe.   *European History Quarterly*, vol. 23, no. 2 (April 1993), p. 193-232.
An interesting article which traces the efforts of the Germans to organize an anti-Russian resistance in Romania during the last months of the Second World War. The Germans parachuted German and Romanian agents into the country thinking they would find ready recruits amongst the indigenous German population (the *Volksdeutsche*), former Iron Guard supporters, and the thousands of German Army stragglers left in the country in the wake of the German retreat. However, most *Volksdeutsche* of military age were already serving in the German Army and erstwhile Iron Guard supporters were already drifting towards other political groupings – the leader of the Iron Guard underground in Romania, Horatiu Comaniciu, at this time declared for the National Peasant Party. Some of the infiltrators, joined by National Peasant Party supporters and disaffected army officers, may have formed the backbone of the later anti-communist, 'white resistance' groups, but, in general, they seem to have achieved little other than to prod the Soviet authorities towards the deportation of the remainder of the *Volksdeutsche* population to the USSR and to exert tighter control over the country as a whole.

293 **A turning point in World War II: 23 August 1944 in Romania.**
Ilie Ceauşescu, Florin Constantiniu, Mihail E. Ionescu. Boulder,
Colorado: East European Monographs, distributed by Columbia
University Press, 1985. 235p. (East European Monographs, no. 191).
The *coup d'état* of 23 August 1944, which deposed Marshal Antonescu and led to
Romania switching from the Axis to the Allied cause in the Second World War, held a
special place in communist Romania, as it constituted one of the chief foundation
myths of the régime. The communists elevated the events to a 'anti-fascist and anti-
imperialist revolution for the social and national liberation of Romania', and in the
process downplayed the role of King Michael and vastly overstated their own
importance. They also presented it as one of the key moments of the Second World
War, investing it with greater significance for the course of the war than such
contemporary events as the liberation of Paris. This volume is the definitive statement
of late Ceauşescu historiography on the coup and its aftermath.

294 **Ploieşti: the great ground-air battle of 1 August 1943.**
James Dugan, Carroll Stewart. London: Cape, 1963. 309p. bibliog.
In August 1943 178 B.24 Liberators of the 9th USAAF took off from Benghazi in
Libya on the long journey to bomb the oil refineries at Ploieşti, Romania. The
operation was meant to be secret but the Luftwaffe managed to break the Allied
forces' code and read their transmissions. This is a graphic account of the air battle
that followed in which fifty-three Liberators were lost (including eight interned in
Turkey), fifty-five damaged, and 310 American airmen killed (about one in five of the
1,620 men who reached the target area). The Luftwaffe lost four aircraft over Ploieşti
and two over Greece. The Romanian air force losses were recorded at only two planes,
and the damage inflicted to Ploieşti was not sufficient to make any impact on the oil
deliveries to the Reich.

295 **German historians and the Romanian National Legionary state
1940-41.**
Rebecca Haynes. *Slavonic and East European Review*, vol. 71, no. 4
(Oct. 1993), p. 676-83.
Drawing largely on the work of German historians, the author suggests a revision is
needed of the traditional view that Germany, after backing the foundation of the
Legionary State, found its radicalism uncongenial and so switched its support to the
more conservative Marshal Antonescu. Instead, she argues that Hitler and the Reich
Foreign Office backed Antonescu in the expectation that after removing the incumbent
leaders he would place himself at the head of the Legionary movement. At the same
time rival elements in the Nazi Party and the SS continued to support the Legion and
its leader, Horia Sima, until the Legionary rebellion was crushed on 21 January 1941.

296 **The Holocaust in Romania: the Iaşi Pogrom of June 1941.**
Radu Ioanid. *Contemporary European History*, vol. 2, no. 2
(July 1993), p. 119-48.
A thoroughly researched account of the worst outbreak of anti-Semitic violence in
Romania, the Iaşi Pogrom of June 1941. The author suggests that the pogrom was a
consequence of a long-term anti-Semitic tradition, official anti-Semitic propaganda,
manipulation by the Romanian Intelligence Service (SSI) and mass panic within Iaşi

occasioned by the outbreak of war and the commencement of Soviet bombing of the city on 24 June 1941. Indeed, the first victims of the pogrom on 26 June were alleged to have been firing rockets to signal to the Russians the location of Romanian Army units. In the days of slaughter that ensued around 6,000 Jews were killed in the city with another 2,600 perishing on two death trains. In June 1948, forty-six of the perpetrators of the pogrom were tried in Bucharest, with many sentenced to forced labour for life.

297 **The military obligation of the Volksdeutsche of Eastern Europe towards the Third Reich.**
Valdis O. Lumans. *East European Quarterly*, vol. 23, no. 3 (Sept. 1989), p. 305-25.

This well researched and informative survey of German policy towards the estimated 7,000,000 ethnic Germans of Eastern Europe during the Second World War concentrates on South-Eastern Europe and, in particular, the Yugoslav lands, but it also covers Romania. Many of Romania's German population served in the Waffen SS during the war. Initially, it was the Germans resettled from the Soviet-occupied areas of Eastern Europe, including Bucovina and Bessarabia, who provided Himmler with 'lucrative opportunities for recruitment', but later virtually all enlistment of Germans from South-Eastern Europe was placed in the hands of the Waffen SS. Officially, the Romanians remained reluctant throughout the war to sanction such recruitment of their own German citizens, protesting that this would mark a loss of sovereignty. To assuage Romanian reservations, a German-Romanian treaty was signed in May 1943 which allowed the recruitment of Germans on the stipulation that the recruits retained Romanian nationality. However, Marshal Antonescu continued to procrastinate over the matter. The reality was that the *Volksdeutsche* of Romania had little choice but to serve in the Waffen SS during the war, but, because Romania never officially surrendered sovereignty over her citizens, the Germans of Romania could not excuse their service on the basis that their state had transferred their military obligations to the Reich. As the author concludes: 'legally their service with the Waffen SS had been on a voluntary basis', and this was to bring harsh consequences at end of the war.

298 **Operation Autonomous: with S.O.E in wartime Romania.**
Ivor Porter. London: Chatto & Windus, 1989. 268p. maps.

The author was part of a three-man SOE (Special Operations Executive) team parachuted into Romania at the end of December 1943. Their mission was to make contact with the National Peasant Party leader, Iuliu Maniu, to persuade him that, if Romania was to switch from the Axis to the Allied side in the war, he would have to be prepared to deal not with the Western powers but with the Russians. In fact, on landing the team were immediately captured by the Romanian security forces and dispatched to Bucharest. There they endured eight months of incarceration but the Romanians protected them from the Germans and instead of advising Maniu, they became a link between Marshal Antonescu and the Allies. In this engaging and lively memoir the author tells of his own experiences during these days and the *coup d'état* of 23 August 1944 which brought about his release.

299   **Clash over Romania. British and American foreign policy towards Romania: 1938-1947.**
Paul D. Quinlan.   Los Angeles: American Romanian Academy of Arts and Sciences, 1977. 173p. bibliog.
Examines British and American policy towards Romania during the Second World War and immediately afterwards. This authoritative study draws upon both published and unpublished documents of the British Foreign Office and the American State Department. While much of the material confirms what was already known, new information is brought to light on the part played by the American administration in an attempt to overthrow the Groza government in August 1945.

300   **From Antonescu to Groza: implicit factors in American-Romanian relations, 1944-1946.**
Larry L. Watts.   *Südost-Forschungen*, vol. 48, no. 1 (1989), p. 141-61.
A study of US relations with Romania during the Second World War and its immediate aftermath. The author argues that US policy towards Romania throughout most of this period was both inattentive and incoherent. This was partly due to a naive belief that considerations appertaining to wartime could be disregarded in peacetime. Thus, a tactical wartime acceptance of Soviet domination in Eastern Europe was to clash with the idealistic peacetime vision encompassed in the Atlantic Charter and the Yalta Declaration. Wider US foreign policy goals, such as winning the war and building a strong foundation for the postwar UN organizations, also tended to dominate over local Eastern European considerations. The author investigates a number of other factors which shaped US policy: the US perception of Romania during the War, when for much of the time it had fought on the side of the Axis powers; the 1942 Anglo-Soviet Treaty of Alliance; the divisive nature of Romanian domestic politics; and the inauguration of the Rădescu government, which led to the Americans adopting a much more proactive policy.

Communist period, 1945-89

301   **Ceauşescu and the miners: István Husszú's story.**
Zolt Csalog.   *New Hungarian Quarterly,* vol. 30, no. 116 (Winter 1989), p. 5-11.
An eye-witness account of the strike by the Jiu Valley miners in 1977 in which they occupied their pits to protest at moves by the régime to curtail social benefits and increase working hours. The authorities responded by opening negotiations with senior Party member, Ilie Verdeţ, but after he had been taken captive by the strikers, Ceauşescu arrived in person to eventually promise, amidst chaotic scenes, that the bulk of the workers' demands would be met. Subsequently, the ringleaders of the strike were rounded up and either imprisoned or sent to distant internal exile. Looking at the strike in retrospect, Husszú admits that the miners were naive and that they failed in their aims.

302 **Ceauşescu and the Securitate: coercion and dissent in Romania 1965-1989.**
Dennis Deletant. London: Hurst, 1995. 424p. map. bibliog.
Far wider in scope than the title would suggest, this volume is in fact the culmination of the author's many years of research into the Ceauşesu régime. Indeed, as he reveals in the deeply personal preface, Deletant's understanding of Romania during these years was shaped not only by his own research but also all too often by the travails of both himself and his wife's Romanian family. His father-in-law had been sent to a labour camp during the Dej era and as his wife came from such a known anti-communist family, the Deletants had to battle for many months in the labyrinths of Romanian bureaucracy to secure permission for her to emigrate to England. Then, as the Ceauşescu régime slipped into its terminal decline, the author was caught in the dilemma of whether to speak openly, which may have placed his wife's family at risk, or to hold his peace. Eventually, encouraged by his father-in-law's vigorous denunciations of the Ceauşescus on the telephone, he spoke out and was declared *persona non grata* by the régime. The chapters in this well-researched book cover such diverse topics as the structure of the *Securitate*, the régime's nationalities policy in Transylvania, the 'Bessarbian Question', compliance and dissent amongst Romanian intellectuals, and systematization.

303 **New light on Gheorghiu-Dej's struggle for dominance in the Romanian Communist Party, 1944-49.**
Dennis Deletant. *Slavonic and East European Review*, vol. 73, no. 4 (Oct. 1995), p. 659-90.
This scholarly article makes use of material newly available since 1989 to investigate early internal power struggles in the Romanian Communist Party. The author contends that these were based more on personality than ideology as in the space of ten years the Party leader, Gheorghe Gheorghiu-Dej, removed three powerful potential rivals from power: Ştefan Foriş, Lucreţiu Pătrăşcanu and Ana Pauker.

304 **Soviet decision-making and the withdrawal of Soviet troops from Romania.**
Donald R. Falls. *East European Quarterly*, vol. 27, no. 4 (Winter 1993), p. 489-502.
The stationing of Soviet troops in Romania had hardly been formalized in April 1957 before on 24 May 1958 it was announced, surprisingly, that they were to be withdrawn. Amongst the reasons advanced at the time for this abrupt volte-face was the fact that as Romania did not border any capitalist states, it was of limited geostrategic importance to the USSR. The Romanians also seemed to have persuaded the Russians that the continuing presence of their troops in the country undermined the legitimacy of the Romanian Communist Party, as it suggested that only their presence sustained the Party in power. In this article the author also looks at a number of other factors which might have had a bearing, including Romanian nationalism, Russian attempts to boost the standing of Emil Bodnăraş – a Romanian-born Soviet agent of Ukrainian-German parentage who was Romanian Minister of Defence at the time of the withdrawal of the Russian troops, economic integration, economic exploitation, the Hungarian Revolution of 1956 as well as the so-called China and North Korea cards.

305 **Downfall: the Ceauşescu's and the Romanian Revolution.**
George Galloway, Bob Wylie. London: Futura, 1991. 308p. bibliog.
In contrast to many of the books that appeared after the downfall of the Ceauşescus,
this volume is mostly concerned with the actual December Revolution and its
aftermath, with coverage of events until June 1990. Intended for the general reader, it
is a fast-moving and engaging account but one which can be faulted for following too
uncritically the version of events advanced by the leaders of the National Salvation
Front. However, the access the authors enjoyed to the leaders of the new régime, such
as Ion Iliescu and General Victor Stănculescu, means that it cannot be ignored as a
source of information on the Revolution.

306 **Romania in the 1980s: the legacy of dynastic socialism.**
Vlad Georgescu. *East European Politics and Societies*, vol. 2, no. 1
(Winter 1988), p. 69-93.
A sobering survey of the sorrowful state to which Romania had plunged by the late
1980s. The author highlights the disastrous mismanagement of the economy, as
Ceauşescu maintained his crash debt repayment programme, the collapse of the
standard of living, the narrowing of rule to only a small despotic élite and the absurd
cult of personality, which only bred 'mini-Ceauşescus' throughout the system. In
contrast to some other authors, Georgescu sees little political continuity between the
1960s and the 1980s in terms of the strategies pursued or the composition of the élite.
Writing a year before the Revolution, the author also presciently notes a clear
psychological change in Romanian society and a growing radicalism of action.

307 **The multiple legacies of history: Romania in the year 1990.**
Trond Gilberg. In: *The Columbia history of Eastern Europe in the
twentieth century.* Edited by Joseph Held. New York: Columbia
University Press, 1992, p. 277-305.
Rather than being a specially written history of Eastern Europe during the present
century, this volume in fact contains a collection of papers from a conference. In his
contribution, Trond Gilberg first outlines some of the main features of Romania's
political culture in the 20th century, such as the prevalence of mutual distrust between
political groupings, the lack of *noblesse oblige*, the experience of authoritarianism and
the presence of endemic corruption. He then traces the way in which these traits were
reflected in the communist system established after 1945 before closing with some
observations on the collapse of communism and the future of Romania as seen from
the perspective of 1990.

308 **Romania's communist take-over: the Rădescu government.**
Dinu C. Giurescu. Boulder, Colorado: East European Monographs,
distributed by Columbia University Press, 1994. 202p. (East European
Monographs, no. 388).
The government of General Nicolae Rădescu, which lasted for only a few short weeks
between 6 December 1944 and 28 February 1945, was to be the last non-communist
administration in Romania for over forty years. It thus occupies a pivotal position in
the post-Second World War communist take-over of Romania and in this scholarly
study, which draws upon Romanian newspapers and Western archive sources,
Giurescu offers a detailed and enlightening study of its troubled months in office. In
particular, he focuses on the growing tensions with the Soviet authorities which were

eventually to lead to Andrei Vishinsky, Soviet Deputy Foreign Minister, issuing an ultimatum to King Michael to replace Rădescu with the more pliable Petru Groza.

309 **Cold War crucible: United States foreign policy and the conflict in Romania, 1943-1953.**
Elizabeth W. Hazard. Boulder, Colorado: East European Monographs, distributed by Columbia University Press, 1996. 258p. bibliog. (East European Monographs, no. 442).

A controversial study of United States policy towards Romania in the aftermath of the Second World War which suggests that it contributed to a polarization of the political situation inside the country, increased Soviet suspicions and eventually led to an escalation of hostilities. The author argues that the Kremlin did not have a clear policy as regards Romania and that it could have tolerated some role for the non-communist parties. However, the politics of confrontation overwhelmed the politics of compromise and American policy makers both in the United States and in Bucharest must share some responsibility for the ensuing crisis.

310 **Communism in Romania 1944-62.**
Ghiţa Ionescu. London: Oxford University Press for the Royal Institute of International Affairs, 1964. 378p. bibliog.

This classic and still largely unsurpassed study covers the Romanian Communist Party from its origins through its take-over of power until the early 1960s. Within a strictly chronological approach, the author, whilst taking into account international events, keeps his focus firmly on internal developments. A Professor at the University of Bucharest, after a diplomatic posting in Ankara during the Second World War, Ionescu remained in the West and became Emeritus Professor of Politics at Manchester University.

311 **Did Ana Pauker prevent a 'Rajk trial' in Romania?**
Robert Levy. *East European Politics and Societies*, vol. 9, no. 1
· (Winter 1995), p. 143-78.

Based on extensive interviews and documentary sources, this article examines the mystery of why an apparently servile Romania did not provide a Titoist show trial despite the urgings of the Soviet Union. Justice Minister, Lucreţiu Pătrăşcanu, had been purged in 1948 but he was not brought to trial until 1954, after the death of Stalin. Subsequently, Gheorghiu-Dej stated that he had been thwarted in his attempt to bring Pătrăşcanu to trial by Ana Pauker, Foreign Minister, and Vasile Luca, Finance Minister, and, indeed, he used this as a justification for their purging. After careful investigation the author concluded that there is some truth in this interpretation of events as Pauker had a personal friendship with the independently minded Pătrăşcanu and that this is at least one case when the so-called 'Moscow Communists' in Romania went against the Soviet line.

312 **The 'right deviation' of Ana Pauker.**
Robert Levy. *Communist and Post-Communist Studies*, vol. 28, no. 2
(June 1995), p. 239-54.

Drawing upon the archives of the Romanian Communist Party, the author shows in this interesting article that the charges of 'right deviation' levelled against Ana Pauker in May 1952 were, in fact, grounded in some truth. Pauker, who has long been viewed as one of the most unyielding of the first communist leaders, held the post of Central Committee Secretary in charge of agriculture as the collectivization of the peasantry began. However, she seems to have seen this as an essentially voluntary process and was absent from the country at the time of the first forcible collectivization drive. When she returned, she seems to have opposed the policy and even tried to halt the campaign. By adopting this line she came into conflict with Gheorghiu-Dej and the other communist leaders as well as the Soviet Union.

313   **The OSS in Romania, 1944-45: an intelligence operation of the early Cold War.**
      Eduard Mark.   *Intelligence and National Security*, vol. 9, no. 2 (April 1994), p. 320-44.

Drawing upon the archives of the US Office of Strategic Services, this article provides an informative and interesting overview of the activities of OSS units in Romania from September 1944 until September 1945. The choice of Romania for the study is particularly apposite because, as the author notes in his introduction, the OSS spent more time in Romania than in any other future communist state except for Yugoslavia. However, unlike Yugoslavia, Romania was to all intents and purposes under occupation by Soviet troops, and this record of OSS activities therefore represents a valuable source for the origins of the Cold War.

314   **The rehabilitation of Nicolae Titulescu.**
      Wim van Meurs.   *Romanian Civilization*, vol. 4, no. 1 (Spring 1995), p. 101-08.

After years of being cast in the wilderness, the great interwar Romanian diplomat Nicolae Titulescu was rehabilitated in Romanian historiography during the period 1966-67, partially as an oblique means of raising the thorny 'Bessarabian Question'. In this article the author traces the response of the Moldavian and Soviet authorities to his rehabilitation. He argues that after the initial knee-jerk response they offered a more measured riposte in which they suggested that Titulescu had been an exception to the general rule that all pre-war Romanian politicians had been aggressively anti-Soviet.

315   **Romania: the entangled revolution.**
      Nestor Ratesh, with a foreword by Edward N. Luttwak.   New York; Westport, Connecticut; London: Praeger with the Center for Strategic and International Studies, Washington, DC, 1991. 179p.
      (The Washington Papers, no. 152).

A particularly objective and balanced account of the Revolution by a former head of Radio Free Europe's Romanian Broadcasting Department. Drawing on all the available evidence, Ratesh probes the many mysteries of the Revolution, such as the identity of the terrorists, whether foreign mercenaries were present, the extent of the pre-Revolutionary conspiracy and the origins of the National Salvation Front, and, of course, whether it was a spontaneous revolution or a *coup d'état*.

316   **Dependence and centralization in Romania 1944 to 1956.**
Tamás Réti.   *East European Politics and Societies*, vol. 3, no. 3
(Fall 1989), p. 465-99.
This is a detailed survey of the political economy of Romania from the Second World
War to the introduction of Stalinist planning. The author highlights changes in
economic policy and the gradual tightening of communist control, emphasizing the
crucial rule played by the Soviet Union as it took a growing share of Romania's trade.

317   **The Great Powers and Rumania, 1944-46: a study of the early
Cold War era.**
Liliana Saiu.   Boulder, Colorado: East European Monographs,
distributed by Columbia University Press, 1992. 290p. bibliog. (East
European Monographs, no. 355).
This is a searching study of the communist take-over of Romania. The author's stated
aim is to discover at what point the country's absorption into the Soviet orbit became
inevitable, whether Great Britain and the US could have adopted another strategy and
which factors affected the policies they did follow. Likewise, she examines what the
chief influences on Soviet policy were and how events in Romania affected the
development of Soviet plans for Eastern Europe as a whole.

318   **The view from Romania.**
Cortland V. R. Schuyler.   In: *Witnesses to the origins of the Cold
War.*   Edited by Thomas T. Hammond.   Seattle, Washington;
London: University of Washington Press, 1982, p. 123-60.
The author was assigned to Bucharest in the autumn of 1944 as the American military
representative on the Allied Control Commission. He remained in this post until 1947.
This valuable account of his mission is compiled from the detailed diaries he kept at
the time. The same editor has also compiled a collection of academic essays on the
take-over, one chapter of which is about Romania: Stephen Fischer-Galati, 'The
communist take-over of Rumania: a function of Soviet power', *The anatomy of
communist take-overs*, edited by Thomas T. Hammond, with a foreword by Cyril E.
Black (New Haven, Connecticut; London: Yale University Press, 1975, p. 310-20).

319   **The darkness crumbles: despatches from the barricades revised
and updated.**
John Simpson.   London: Hutchinson, 1992. 368p.
The well-known foreign affairs editor of the BBC here presents his first-hand account
of events in the communist world in the years 1989-91. As might be expected, a
substantial part of the book is devoted to the overthrow of Nicolae Ceauşescu (p. 221-
94). Although the stories Simpson records are not always accurate – one man's claims
that he was involved in fierce fighting to secure the Central Committee building at the
time of Ceauşescu's departure is patently untrue – this book, nevertheless, contains
much interesting incidental detail. Also useful is the comparative view that Simpson,
from his vast experience around the world, can cast on events, such as when he notes
that rumours similar to those that claimed the *Securitate* had poisoned the water
supply of Timişoara and other major cities had circulated during the Iranian
Revolution.

320 **The tragicomedy of Romanian communism.**
Vladimir Tismaneanu. In: *Crisis and reform in Eastern Europe.*
Edited by Ferenc Fehér, Andrew Arato. New Brunswick, New Jersey;
New York: Transaction, 1991, p. 121-74.
A thoughtful and well-researched survey of the history of the Romanian Communist
Party from its weak roots in the interwar years through its seizure of power to its
enfeebled collapse under Nicolae Ceauşescu. The author traces the persistence of
Romanian Stalinism throughout these years, arguing that the rule of Ceauşescu should
not be seen as an aberration but merely a consequence of the system which produced
him. A version of this article originally appeared under the same name in *East
European Politics and Societies,* vol. 3, no. 2 (Spring 1989), p. 329-76.

321 **Romania.**
Bela Vago. In: *Communist power in Europe 1944-49.* Edited by
Martin McCauley. London: Macmillans in association with the
School of Slavonic and East European Studies, University of London,
1977, p. 111-30.
This brief but useful survey of the communist take-over draws upon primary sources
from the British Public Record Office. Whilst concluding that the take-over was
mainly due to 'Soviet interference, pressure and military presence', the author also
points to a number of secondary causes: the weak leadership of a relatively small
Social Democratic Party; the low standing of many traditional politicians because of
their pre-war record and their readiness to collaborate with the communists; the war-
weariness of the population; and the dedication and determination of the Romanian
Communist Party.

322 **Military occupation and diplomacy: Soviet troops in Romania,
1944-1958.**
Sergiu Verona, with a foreword by J. F. Brown. Durham, North
Carolina: Duke University Press, 1992. 211p. bibliog.
The departure of the Red Army from Romania in the summer of 1958 marked the first
withdrawal of Russian forces from the People's Democracies of Eastern Europe after
the Second World War. At the time American and British diplomats viewed the move
as being largely inconsequential for the balance of power in Europe but Verona argues
that it set an important precedent and that along with several other moves, it signalled
a growing Soviet desire to seek a *rapprochement* with the West. Romania's
geographical position – it had no borders contiguous with the West – coupled with its
tradition of political conformity made withdrawal a low risk strategy and, indeed, the
apparent leeway it gave to Romanian policy makers could be interpreted as an
example of the enlightened nature of Soviet rule in Eastern Europe. However,
particularly in foreign policy, this latitude was seized upon more eagerly by the
Romanians than the Russians had anticipated. The merit of the author's approach to
this contentious question is that it allows the independence of action by the
Romanians to be viewed as both a sham and a genuine attempt to gain legitimacy.
Although the book is based on a meticulous study of American and British records
material, it is undoubtedly hampered by the author's lack of access to Soviet and
Romanian archives.

Biographies and Memoirs

323 The rise and fall of Nicolae and Elena Ceauşescu.
Mark Almond. London: Chapmans, 1992. 296p. bibliog.
A full biography of the Ceauşescus which traces their rise from humble beginnings to the very pinnacle of power. By drawing on examples of policies from Western modernization as well as socialist planning, the author convincingly puts into perspective the megalomaniac vision that prompted the Ceauşescus to raze part of the centre of Bucharest and replace it with a building said to be second only to the Pentagon in size. The author is particularly sharp about the lauding of the Ceauşescus in the West by Western socialists, such as Tony Benn, and the Bishop of Southwark, Mervyn Stockwood. This book builds on an earlier work by Almond which was first published as a pamphlet in 1988 and which graphically charted the human suffering of late 1980s Romania: 'Decline without fall: Romania under Ceauşescu', *Europe in turmoil: the struggle for pluralism*, edited by Gerald Frost (London: Adamantine Press, 1991, p. 279-329).

324 Out of Romania.
Dan Antal. London: Faber & Faber, 1994. 226p.
These are the engaging memoirs of a natural rebel in the absurdist nightmare of the Ceauşescu state, who was born in a cart on a stony track between two villages. Antal's life has since rarely strayed far from the rocky path. In his youth he and a group of friends, the 'Hells Angles', decided to escape to the West by any means possible: being smuggled in lorries, feigning madness, or, in Antal's case, by hot air balloon, although this burnt to a cinder before it left the ground. During his student days he wrote a dissertation on Saul Bellow, just as the American was publishing his novel critical of the Romanian régime, *The Dean's December* (London: Secker & Warburg, 1982. 312p.), which made Bellow a non-person expunged from the historical record and Antal's dissertation politically unacceptable. After university Antal endured a number of years as a poorly paid teacher, but when he finally made an official application to emigrate, he was stripped even of this job. Forced to find temporary employment he eventually ended up dubbing Western movies into Romanian. Often the films were pirated from Western television programmes and, when Antal started to

dub shampoo advertisements with voice-overs telling the audience 'Don't use this Western product, it makes your hair fall out!', he not surprisingly lost this job as well. He was constantly harassed by the *Securitate* until the Revolution, when he suddenly founded himself catapulted into office as president of a large service co-operative in Bacău. Initially the authorities declared his election void, but after protests from the workers and a strike they backed down and accepted his elevation. Antal lasted in the post until September 1990, when his anti-régime views made his position untenable, and he decided to finally make his escape to the West.

325 **Eros, magic and the murder of Professor Culianu.**

Ted Anton.   Evanston, Illinois: Northwestern University Press, 1996. 301p. bibliog.

A strange mixture of detective story and academic biography, this book tells of the life and mysterious death of Ioan Petru Culianu. A brilliant scholar, who followed in the footsteps of his fellow countryman, Mircea Eliade, to a chair in religious history at the University of Chicago, Culianu was murdered in his faculty building on 21 May 1991. He was a fierce critic of the National Salvation Front and Ion Iliescu and much speculation has surrounded the possibility that the Romanian intelligence services may have been behind his murder. However, no real evidence has emerged to tie them to the assassination and, although in this book the author follows a number of leads, he can offer few further clues as to the identity of the killers. The book closes with a useful bibliography of all Culianu's known writings.

326 **Kiss the hand you cannot bite: the rise and fall of the Ceauşescus.**

Edward Behr, with an introduction by Ryszard Kapuściński.   London: Penguin, 1991. 255p.

An informative biography of the Ceauşescus by a veteran journalist and author of books on such diverse subjects as the Algerian War and the last Emperor of China. Using the techniques of investigative journalism, Behr interviews many of those who knew the presidential couple at various stages of their life. The result is a convincing and intimate portrait. As General Ştefan Kostyal, a long-standing member of the Romanian Communist Party who played a minor role in the Revolution, was amongst Behr's interviewees, this book is also a good source for the various plots against Ceauşescu.

327 **The wasted generation: memoirs of the Romanian journey from capitalism to socialism and back.**

Silviu Brucan.   Boulder, Colorado; San Francisco; Oxford: Westview Press, 1993. 227p.

Silviu Brucan has always been something of an enigmatic figure in contemporary Romanian politics. Never entirely at the centre of power, he nevertheless has often seemed to wield considerable influence – after December 1989 it was something of a cliché in the international press to call him the *éminence grise* of the Revolution. Previously Romanian ambassador to both the United States and the United Nations, he is also an academic and author of a number of books, two of which have been translated into English, on Marxist theory: *World socialism at the cross-roads: an insider's view* (New York: Praeger, 1987. 179p.); and *Pluralism and social conflict: a social analysis of the communist world* (New York: Praeger, 1990. 186p.). Eventually, he was to fall from grace and became the main force behind the celebrated 'Letter of

Biographies and Memoirs

the Six' by which he and five other senior former RCP leaders denounced Ceauşescu in March 1989. As a senior member of the RCP, Brucan knew virtually all of the most prominent personalities in the last half-century of Romanian history. His autobiography is thus a revealing and interesting historical source. However, particularly as regards the Revolution of 1989, it would seem that Brucan is writing at least in part to seal his own image for posterity and so this book should perhaps be read in conjunction with the detailed review by Dennis Deletant, 'Myth-making and the Romanian Revolution', *Slavonic and East European Review*, vol. 72, no. 3 (July 1994), p. 483-91.

328 **The hole in the flag: a Romanian exile's story of return and revolution.**
Andrei Codrescu. New York: William Morrow, 1991. 249p.

The author is a poet who, following many years of exile in the USA, returned to Romania after the Revolution of 1989 as a reporter for National Public Radio. The result is an entertaining, deeply personal account of his homecoming which offers an interesting insight into the Romanian psyche and the workings of the international media during the Revolution. After describing his experiences in Bucharest and his hometown of Sibiu immediately following the fighting, the author voices many concerns over the true nature of the Revolution, fears which, he concludes, were fully justified when he made a return visit to the country later in 1990.

329 **The silent escape: three thousand days in Romanian prisons.**
Lena Constante, translated by Franklin Philip, introduction by Gail Kligman. Berkeley, California; Los Angeles; London: University of California Press, 1995. 257p. (Societies and Cultures in East-Central Europe, no. 9).

Lena Constante was an artist and friend of Elena Pătrăşcanu, and the two women tried to establish the first puppet theatre in Bucharest in 1945. Along with her companion, the ethnomusicologist Harry Brauner, she became caught up in the tangled web which was spun around the so-called 'espionage conspiracy' of Elena's husband, the senior communist leader, Lucreţiu Pătrăşcanu. Sentenced to jail in 1949, Constante was to spend a total of twelve years in prison before her release in 1961. This book covers the first eight years of her incarceration, which she spent in solitary confinement, being the only women to endure this ordeal. Written in the form of a diary – the days are recorded in the form: Day 1541 of detention – April 6 1954 – this is not a book of political reflection but rather a practical and emotional record of prison existence, of the nature of interrogations and the rituals of daily life.

330 **In the eye of the Romanian storm. The heroic story of Pastor Laszlo Tokes.**
Felix Corley, John Eibner. Old Tappen, New Jersey: Fleming H. Revell, 1990. 272p.

A compelling biography of László Tőkés, the catalyst of the 1989 Romanian Revolution. In a dramatic tale of personal faith, resilience and courage, the authors present Tőkés' life from his upbringing in Cluj to Timişoara and the outbreak of the Revolution. For Tőkés' own autobiography, see item no. 348.

331 **They stole my parents.**
Lia Cruickshank. Shrewsbury, England: Sylvana Books, 1993. 174p.
This is an extraordinary autobiographical tale of separation, anguish and adventure. Lia, who comes from the small village of Slobozia in Bessarabia, became separated from her mother and father during the Second World War when that province was seized by the Russians and her parents were sent to Siberia. They were not to see each other again for twenty years until finally, after a Ulysses-like quest, they were all reunited in Slobozia.

332 **Journey to freedom.**
Nicholas Dima. Washington, DC: Selous Foundation Press, 1989. 399p. maps.
The engaging autobiography of an author best known for his books on recent Romanian and Bessarabian history. Born in Bucharest in 1936, Dima rejected communism at an early age and in 1956 made a rather naive attempt to escape to the West. Detained by border guards he was incarcerated for a total of five years in some of the most notorious prison and labour camps in Romania, including Jilava and Gherla. On his release he attended Bucharest University before, in 1967, he finally made a successful escape to the West through Yugoslavia.

333 **The quality of witness: a Romanian diary 1937-1944.**
Emil Dorian, selected and edited by Marguerite Dorian, translated by Mara Soceanu Vamos, introduction by Michael Stanislawski.
Philadelphia: Jewish Publication Society of America, 1982. 350p.
The diaries of Emil Dorian, a Romanian-Jewish intellectual and successful writer, who was a doctor by profession, form a valuable historical record of life in Romania during the period 1937-44. In this selection of entries Dorian charts the drift of Romania into the Nazi orbit and the imposition of anti-Semitic legislation. On a more personal level, he also uses the diaries to explore questions relating to his dual identity and the strains placed upon this by the war. Following his death in 1956 the twenty-two notebooks, which formed the diaries, were kept by family friends before they eventually passed to his daughter, Marguerite, who realized their value as a historical document and abridged the first seven for this volume.

334 **Looking for George. Love and death in Romania.**
Helena Drysdale, with a foreword by Tobias Wolff. London: Picador, 1996. 239p. map.
This book tells an unusual, but true, story. Whilst a student in Romania in 1979, the author had met and befriended a young Romanian monk and poet, Gheorghe. Afterwards they had remained in correspondence. In his letters, which were full of lyrical but strong language, Gheorghe had often been sharply critical of the oppressive Ceauşescu régime and as the situation deteriorated in Romania he eventually asked Helena to marry him and help him escape. The letters then abruptly stopped and all communication ceased before Helena could reply. After the revolution of 1989, Helena, who was married by then, returned to Romania in search of Gheorghe, only to find he had died as a political prisoner in a mental hospital. This tale is not just a journey through the cruel labyrinth of Ceauşescu's Romania but also the labyrinths of human feelings and emotions. The original hardback appeared under the title *Looking for Gheorghe* (London: Sinclair-Stevenson, 1995. 239p. map).

101

335 **Autobiography. Volume I, 1907-1937: journey east, journey west.**
Mircea Eliade, translated from the Romanian by Mac Linscott Ricketts.
Chicago; London: The University of Chicago Press, 1981. 335p.

Mircea Eliade, who was born in Bucharest in 1907, was awarded a scholarship after graduating from his hometown University that allowed him to spend four years in India. On his return to Romania in 1931 he completed a PhD on yoga and took up the post of assistant Professor in the Faculty of Letters at the University of Bucharest. In 1940 he was posted as cultural attaché to the Romanian legation in London and then transferred to Lisbon, where he remained until the end of the war. He did not return to communist Romania but took up a post of visiting professor at the Sorbonne and then Professor of the History of Religions at the University of Chicago. He died in 1986. This first volume of his three-volume autobiography was initially published in Romanian in 1966. In a lucid and engaging narrative Eliade describes his formative years as he progressed from a Bucharest school boy to stand on the threshold of international scholarly acclaim. The book also provides a fascinating glimpse of intellectual life in Romania prior to the Second World War.

336 **Five years and two months in the Sighet penitentiary (May 7, 1950 – July 5, 1955).**
Constantin C. Giurescu, with an introduction by Dinu C. Giurescu, edited, with appendices and index by Lia Ioana Ciplea, English translation by Mihai Farcaș and Stephanie Barton-Farcaș. Boulder, Colorado: East European Monographs, distributed by Columbia University Press, 1994. 181p. (East European Monographs, no. 406).

This poignant tale of resistance and survival by one of Romania's leading historians makes harrowing reading. It tells of the barbaric and inhuman treatment meted out to the author and over one hundred other leading political, religious and cultural figures by the communist authorities at the infamous jail of Sighet. Indeed, this book in many ways stands as a memorial to the suffering as it is completed by a long screed of names of those who were imprisoned, many of whom also perished in the jail.

337 **Helen, Queen Mother of Rumania.**
Arthur Gould Lee. London: Faber & Faber, 1956. 296p.

This is an authorized biography of Queen Helen (1896-1982), wife of King Carol II and mother of King Michael. She was the eldest daughter of Constantine, Crown Prince and later King of the Hellenes. Although divorced from Carol when he reigned, she was known as the Queen Mother of Romania because of the support she offered to her son during his period of rule (1940-47). She had a rather turbulent life, with her ex-husband forcing her into exile and allowing her to see her son only one month each year. When Carol abdicated in September 1940, Michael summoned her from Florence to Bucharest. She worked wholeheartedly for the war-wounded and sustained King Michael throughout the war and during the daring *coup d'état* of 23 August 1944. During the three years that ensued she offered pertinent advice to her son in the face of the threats of the Soviet Union and Romanian communists until Michael was forced to abdicate in December 1947. Her years of exile were spent near Florence.

338   **King Carol II: a life of my grandfather.**
Prince Paul of Hohenzollern-Romania.   London: Methuen, 1988.
238p. maps. bibliog.
King Carol II is usually portrayed in an unflattering light. His marriages, an elopement
to Paris and a long-running affair with the Jewish divorcee, Madame Lupescu, made
his life the scandal of Europe during the 1930s and provided a source of inspiration
for romantic authors such as Barbara Cartland, *The scandalous life of King Carol*
(London: Muller, 1957). Politically, he not only undermined his country's fragile
democratic institutions but also presided over the dismemberment of Greater Romania
– a disaster which prompted his abdication in favour of his son by Helen of Greece,
Michael. In this biography his grandson through his earlier marriage – although it was
pronounced invalid by Carol's father, King Ferdinand, and the Romanian Supreme
Court – to a Romanian commoner Ioana Lambrino, attempts, as he sees it, to set the
record straight arguing that his grandfather was a man of 'depth and charm' and a
'shrewd and courageous politician'.

339   **Jagendorf's foundry: a memoir of the Romanian holocaust,
1941-1944.**
Siegfried Jagendorf, with an introduction and commentary by Aron
Hirt-Manheimer.   New York: Harper Collins, 1991. 209p. bibliog.
The extraordinary memoir of a charismatic and resourceful fifty-six-year old Jewish
former executive at Siemens, Schmiel (Siegfried) Jagendorf. Along with countless
other Romanian Jews, Jagendorf was deported from Bucovina in 1941 to the town of
Moghilev-Podolski in Axis-occupied Ukraine. Here he persuaded the Romanian
Prefect to allow the Jewish deportees to repair the broken electrical system of the city
together with its iron works – the foundry (Turnatoria) of the title. Eventually over
15,000 Jews came to be employed in various enterprises in Moghilev with Jagendorf
presiding over them in a complex mixture of dictator and saviour. Unfortunately, the
memoirs did not see the light of day during the author's lifetime but they remain an
eloquent testament to both human cruelty and human resistance.

340   **Red horizons: the extraordinary memoirs of an East European spy
chief.**
Ion Mihai Pacepa.   London: Coronet Books, 1989. 446p.
The arrival of Ion Mihai Pacepa in the West in 1978 was one of the highest level
defections from Eastern Europe during the whole of the Cold War. Pacepa was a
Deputy Minister of the Interior and deputy-head of the Romanian External
Intelligence Service. His departure shook the Ceauşescu régime and led to a
widespread reorganization of the Romanian security services. So great was the amount
of information that Pacepa carried that it reportedly took the CIA three years to fully
debrief him and when this process was finished they then caused further discomfort to
the Ceauşescu régime by sanctioning the release of these pacey and engrossing
memoirs. The publication of *Red horizons* helped to remove any tattered remnants of
credibility still affixed to the Ceauşescu régime in the West as they revealed the
debauched lifestyle of Nicu, Ceauşescu's eldest son, the megalomania of the ruling
couple, particularly of Elena, and an ugly penchant on the part of the Romanian
authorities for international espionage, blackmail and murder. In fact, the 'Red
Horizons' of the title was the code-name given by Ceauşescu to a massive deception
operation, by which he spread the impression that Romania was striving to distance

itself from the USSR in order to gain access to Western science and technology. At its heart the book is therefore about deception but whom is actually deceiving whom in this account is a moot point. Specialists have pointed to the many inaccuracies in Pacepa's descriptions and elements of the book, such as the attacks on Yasser Arafat, suggest nothing less than a CIA smear campaign. Where the truth really lies in the murky world of espionage will probably never be known but it seems likely that although the gist of the story holds some truth, many of the supporting details are more questionable.

341 **The last romantic: a biography of Queen Marie of Roumania.**
Hannah Pakula. London: Weidenfeld & Nicolson; New York: Simon & Schuster, 1985. 510p. bibliog.

The grand-daughter of both Queen Victoria and Tsar Alexander II of Russia and first cousin to Kaiser Wilhelm II, Marie Alexandra Victoria was only nineteen when on 24 December 1892 she married Prince Ferdinand of Hohenzollern-Sigmaringen, the Crown Prince of Romania. Subsequently, the young Marie seems to have totally immersed herself in the cause of her new country, even travelling to Paris and London to lobby heads of state during the Paris Peace Conference. In 1914 her husband had already ascended the crown of the united principalities and on 19 October 1922 they were crowned King and Queen of Greater Romania. The Queen by all accounts was a popular monarch and has always been treated as something of a romantic figure by biographers. This lengthy and detailed work does little to stray from this tradition. Marie also wrote her own autobiographical account of her reign based on the diaries she kept from an early age until the end of the First World War: *The story of my life* (London: Cassell, 1935. 3 vols.).

342 **The playboy king: Carol II of Romania.**
Paul D. Quinlan. Westport, Connecticut; London: Greenwood, 1995. 264p. bibliog. (Contributions to the Study of World History, no. 52).

King Carol II (1893-1953) reigned in Romania between 1930 and 1940. In 1918 he became infatuated with Zizi Lambrino, a commoner, whom he married after smuggling her to Russia. His father, King Ferdinand, and the Supreme Court in Romania pronounced the marriage illegal and kept Carol in confinement in Bistriţa, where he met Helena Tîmpeanu, wife of a cavalry officer, and developed a close relationship. In March 1921, however, he married Princess Helen of Greece and in October of the same year Prince Michael was born. Nevertheless, the marriage was not destined to last, and Carol continued to see Helena Tîmpeanu, who by then was also divorced and bore her maiden name of Lupescu. The notoriety of Carol's affair with Madame Lupescu reached such heights that it filled the gossip columns of many international newspapers. In this book Quinlan attempts to give Carol 'his rightful place in history', arguing that whilst he was undoubtedly a playboy, he was also a more complex character than is often supposed and that his life cannot be divorced from the context of his family, country and epoch.

343   **Mircea Eliade: the Romanian roots, 1907-1945.**
Mac Linscott Ricketts.   Boulder, Colorado: East European
Monographs, distributed by Columbia University Press, 1988. 2 vols.
1,453p. (East European Monographs, no. 248).
This is the definitive biography of the Romanian intellectual, Mircea Eliade, during
his early Romanian years. The author not only narrates the life story of his subject but
also offers a detailed description and analysis of his first Romanian writings.

344   **Dangers, tests and miracles: the remarkable life story of Chief
Rabbi Rosen of Romania as told to Joseph Finklestone.**
Moses Rosen, Joseph Finklestone.   London: Weidenfeld & Nicholson,
1990. 328p.
This is a fascinating memoir of Moses Rosen, the chief Rabbi of Romania for most of
the country's communist period. A controversial figure, he is criticized by his
detractors for excessive collaboration with the Ceauşescu régime, but praised by his
supporters for winning concessions from the authorities which allowed greater
freedom of worship, extended religious education and easier emigration of Jews to
Israel, although the latter has resulted in the virtual disappearance of the Jewish
minority from Romania.

345   **Resisting the storm: Romania, 1940-1947. Memoirs.**
Alexandre Safran, edited and annotated by Jean Ancel.   Jerusalem:
Yad Vashem, 1987. 464p. bibliog.
These are the memoirs of the chief Rabbi of Romania, Alexandre Safran, who
painfully witnessed the physical and spiritual sufferings of the Jews in Romania
during the Second World War and communist take-over. During this time the Jewish
community was more than halved, declining from 800,000 to 300,000.

346   **Woman behind bars in Romania.**
Annie Samuelli.   London: Frank Cass, 1997. 2nd ed. 227p.
This is an emotional and powerful account of the author's experiences during almost
twelve years in prison in Romania. She was detained, together with her sister, at the
time of the mass arrest of all Romanian nationals working for the US and the British
legations. After nine months of torture and interrogation, the sisters were sentenced to
twenty and fifteen years of imprisonment respectively. Released in 1961, upon
payment of a ransom, they were then exiled to the West. This is a revised edition of
The wall between (Washington, DC: Robert B. Luce, 1967. 227p.).

347   **The life and evil times of Nicolae Ceauşescu.**
John Sweeny.   London; Sydney; Auckland; Johannesburg:
Hutchinson, 1991. 243p.
As a feature writer for *The Observer*, the writer was an eye-witness to part of the
Romanian Revolution and this gives a particular immediacy to the few pages in this
book that he devotes to the events after the downfall of Ceauşescu. However, the bulk
of this work is a biography of the late Romanian dictator and as well as written
sources Sweeny draws upon a number of interviews he conducted with those who
knew or worked with the Ceauşescus. In particular, he throws some fascinating light

onto Ceauşescu's medical condition suggesting that his megalomania was, at least in part, a result of poorly treated diabetes. A doctor who examined Ceauşescu reveals that the public image was not just for external consumption when he states that Ceauşescu was 'convinced that he was the greatest Romanian, that fate chose him. He believed in everything he said'.

348 **With God, for the people: the autobiography of László Tőkés.**
László Tőkés, as told to David Porter. London; Sydney; Auckland; Toronto: Hodder & Stoughton, 1990. 226p.

László Tőkés will endure lasting fame as the trigger which sparked the Romanian Revolution, but prior to 1989 he already had an impressive record as a dissident priest within the Hungarian community. In this book he tells his own life story from his early years spent in Cluj, where his father was also a clergyman in the Hungarian Reformed Church, through seminary to his first posting in Braşov and, eventually, to Timişoara. From an early age, Tőkés and a few friends had begun to protest at the treatment of the Hungarian minority in Ceauşescu's Romania, in the face of silence from the upper hierarchy of his church. He was a contributor to the samizdat journal *Ellenpontok* (Counterpoints) and gave an interview broadcast on Hungarian television in early 1989 in which he roundly criticized the policy of the Ceauşescu régime. The 'troublesome priest' had been despatched to Timişoara by the authorities in the mistaken belief that he could do no harm there. However, for a variety of reasons Tőkés again came into conflict with the authorities and when they tried to secure his eviction from his living his parishioners stood firm and mounted an illegal demonstration in his support. This quickly escalated beyond the bounds of the Hungarian community and Tőkés to encompass many thousands of ethnic Romanians and, as a peaceful demonstration turned into scuffles with the security forces, so the Revolution was born.

349 **General Henri Berthelot and Romania: mémoirs et correspondance 1916-1919.**
Edited with a biographical introduction by Glenn E. Torrey. Boulder, Colorado: East European Monographs, distributed by Columbia University Press, 1987. 247p. maps. bibliog. (East European Monographs, no. 219).

These memoirs of the French General, Henri Berthelot, give a fascinating insight into the nature of his two military missions to Romania. During the first (October 1916-May 1918) he was responsible for rebuilding the Romanian army after their defeats, whilst in the second he was placed in command of an anti-Bolshevik force that the Allies hoped to raise in Southern Romania. The memoirs are written as a diary and at the editor's instigation some of Berthelot's correspondence has also been inserted to allow the reader to form a better understanding of his personality.

350 **The snows of yesteryear: portraits of an autobiography.**
Gregor von Rezzori, translated from the German by H. F. Broch de Rothermann. London: Vintage, 1991. 290p.

The author was born into a land-owning family in Bucovina and here he lifts the veil on a world that was to vanish totally in the maelstrom of the 20th century. In a book which displays all the documentary qualities of a memoir and the poignancy of an autobiographical account, as well as the lyricism and the fluidity of fiction, the author describes his Central European childhood before Bucovina fell into the hands of Hitler and Stalin.

Population

351 **Historical demography in Romania: a selected bibliography.**
Ioan Bolovan. *Romanian Civilization,* vol. 2, no. 2 (Fall-Winter 1993), p. 42-50.
This bibliographical study aims to equip the foreign specialist with information – mostly of books published in English, French and German – about Romanian research on historical demography. The works covered include censuses, professional journals, statistical and demographical publications, books and various other studies.

352 **Migration in market and democracy transition: migration intentions and behavior in Romania.**
Dumitru Sandu, Gordon F. De Jong. *Population Research and Policy Review,* vol. 15, no. 5 (Dec. 1996), p. 437-57.
An analysis of the factors which determine internal migration patterns in post-communist Romania. The authors, using early 1990s internal migration surveys, census and population registration data, conclude that choice is largely determined by the economic and political profile of the destination with areas with the highest levels of market liberalization and democratization proving most popular.

353 **Făgăraş: patterns of Central and East European life.**
Sarolta Solcan. Boulder, Colorado: East European Monographs, distributed by Columbia University Press, 1997. 178p. bibliog. (East European Monographs, no. 468).
This is a detailed investigation of the demographic development and economic structure of the Făgăraş region of southern Transylvania during the 17th century. Throughout the findings are complemented by a vast amount of statistical data covering family size, birth patterns, migratory movements and demographic trends. Some comparisons are also made with conditions in other European countries at this time.

Population

354 **Demographic engineering: the case of Romania.**
Frances J. Webb. *The Bloomsbury Geographer*, vol. 13 (1985),
p. 20-27.
Discusses the Romanian government's efforts to control population size. In 1966 a
draconian decree (no. 770) was introduced which severely restricted the rights of
Romanian women to determine whether or not they had children. Abortion became
available only to women of over forty-five years of age, those who already had
families of four or more children, those whose life would be endangered if the
pregnancy was to continue and those whose pregnancies were the result of rape or
incest. In this study the author presents the issue of abortion in terms of a power
struggle between the Romanian state and the individual's right of choice. The law was
modified in 1977 but remained in force essentially unchanged until the fall of
Ceauşescu in 1989.

Anthropology and Ethnography

355 You call this a living? A collection of East European political jokes.
C. Banc, Alan Dundes.   Athens, Georgia; London: University of
Georgia Press, 1990. 184p. bibliog.

Despite the title, this book is in fact a collection of jokes gathered from Romanian oral sources. The authors (one of whom is presumably writing under a pseudonym as his name translates as 'what a joke' in Romanian) see jokes as a communal defence mechanism against the hardship of life under communism. In many of the jokes the ultimate target was the communist party itself, as in the following example: 'Do you known what prizes the communists are now offering for recruiting new party members? If you get one new member, you don't pay dues. Two new members, you can quit the Party. And for three, you get a certificate saying you were never a member'. The jokes are classified according to subject matter with categories covering 'the terror', food shortages, Jews, the leadership, etc. First published as *First prize, fifteen year!* (Madison, New Jersey: Fairleigh Dickinson University Press, 1986), the new title of the study comes from the following joke: 'A man knocks on the door of a ramshackle house on the outskirts of Bucharest and asks the old man who peered through the window – Does the tailor Rabinowitch live here? – No, – Who are you? – Rabinowitch, – And aren't you a tailor? – Yes, I am, – Then, why did you say you didn't live here? – You call this a living?' An earlier article by Alan Dundes on the same subject is 'Laughter behind the Iron Curtain: a sample of Rumanian political jokes', *Ukrainian Quarterly*, vol. 27, no. 1 (1971), p. 50-59.

356 Indigenous anthropologists in socialist Romania.
Sam Beck.   *Dialectical Anthropology*, vol. 10, no. 3-4 (1986),
p. 265-74.

The author discusses the fate of anthropology and the related discipline of sociology in communist Romania. The latter was effectively suppressed for more than twenty years until it revived following a speech by Ceauşescu in December 1965. However, restrictions still existed and, in particular, research on ethnic relations was virtually impossible, unless it conformed with the régime's assertion that they were totally harmonious.

357 **'What courage': Romanian 'our leader' jokes.**
Robert Cochran. *Journal of American Folklore*, vol. 102, no. 405
(1989), p. 259-74.
One of the last remaining mechanisms for ordinary Romanians to protest at their
living conditions under the Ceauşescu régime were jokes. Here the author discusses
the various meanings behind the many Romanian jokes about their President.

358 **The Rumanian folklore calendar and its age categories.**
Emilia Comişel. In: *The performing arts: music and dance.* Edited
by John Blacking, Joann W. Kealiinohomoku. The Hague; Paris;
New York: Mouton, 1979, p. 185-201. (World Anthropology).
This collection of papers from the 9th International Congress of Anthropological and
Ethnographical Sciences held in Chicago in August-September 1973 includes one
study about Romania. In this paper the author groups the ceremonies of the Romanian
folklore calendar according to the four seasons. He argues that although the
ceremonies have lost some of their meaning in the modern world, they still reveal
many of their archaic traits and as such remain an important source of folk values and
a means of understanding the roots of Romanian culture.

359 **The walled-up wife: a casebook.**
Edited by Alan Dundes. Madison, Wisconsin: University of
Wisconsin Press, 1996. 210p.
Contains eighteen studies all concerned with the myth that a female victim had to be
enclosed in a certain building to ensure the successful construction of the edifice. The
myth is especially prevalent in South-Eastern Europe, although it can also be found as
far afield as India. In Romania it is connected with the magnificent church at Curtea de
Argeş and three studies in this volume relate to this: Mircea Eliade, 'Master Manole
and the Monastery of Argeş', p. 71-94 (reprinted from *Zalmoxis: the vanishing God*
(q.v.); Sharon King, 'Beyond the pale: boundaries in the "Monastirea Argesului"',
p. 95-101; and Şerban Anghelescu, 'The wall and the water: marginalia to "Master
Manole"', p. 102-08.

360 **Gender identity and dance style in rural Transylvania.**
Diane C. Freedman. *East European Quarterly*, vol. 23, no. 4
(Jan. 1990), p. 419-30.
A more wide-ranging article than is suggested by the title, this study is concerned with
the status and condition of women in Romanian rural society. The author holds that in
such societies 'Dance is a symbolic system in which gender identity is salient, since it
involves the interaction of men and women during courtship and marriage rituals' and
that the courtship ritual 'reinforces patterns of gender separation and provides a
context for the separation to be mediated'. From the findings of her fieldwork
conducted in the Ţara Oaşului region of Satu Mare, the author examines the
relationship between the sexes and the separation of men and women, the
public/private dichotomy and how roles are expressed through dance. On the darker
side the author also writes of the physical abuse of wives by their husbands and the
conditions of women in Romanian villages in general. Modernization is having an
effect on traditions and dance, and the nationalization of folk tradition has led to a
standardization of routines and a change of dance code.

361 **Wife, widow, woman: roles of an anthropologist in a Transylvanian village.**
Diane C. Freedman. In: *Women in the field: anthropological experiences.* Edited by Peggy Golde. Berkeley, California; London: University of California Press, 1986, p. 333-58.

Accompanied by her husband, the author arrived in Romania to conduct anthropological fieldwork on dance rituals in a Transylvanian village at the height of the Ceauşescu era. Tragically, her work was soon cut short by the death of her husband and in this highly personal account she describes the reaction of the villagers to her change in status from married to single woman. As a widow she was eligible to marry again and the expectation of the villagers was that she would take a new partner, perhaps from amongst the men of the village, after a suitable period of mourning.

362 **Strategies of adaptation: a Hungarian region of Rumania since the political changes of 1989.**
Ágnes Fülemile. In: *Encountering ethnicities: ethnological aspects on ethnicity, identity and migration.* Edited by Teppo Korhonen. Helsinki: Suomalaisen Kirjallisuuden Seura, 1995, p. 98-104. (Studia Fennica Ethnologica, no. 3).

This is a study of the forty Hungarian Protestant villages, known as the 'Kalotaszeg' in Hungarian, which straddle the road between Cluj and Oradea. The author suggests that the various villages display different mentalities and that this affects their response to change. Since 1989 virtually all agriculture in these villages has returned to private hands as farmers have abandoned the co-operatives. In many cases this has meant a revival of archaic farming practices. There have also been some changes in social structure as entrepreneurs have established businesses and in a few cases prospered. The post-communist period has also seen some migration from the towns back to the villages, although overall the prevailing pattern in most villages is of population decline due to a falling birth-rate and a slow migration to Hungary. The author concludes that in general, economic hardship has left the mood in most of the villages one of depression verging on neurosis.

363 **The solitude of collectivism: Romanian villagers to the Revolution and beyond.**
David A. Kideckel. Ithaca, New York; London: Cornell University Press, 1993. 255p. (Anthropology of Contemporary Issues).

Drawing on many years of fieldwork in the Olt Land of southern Transylvania and, in particular, in the commune of Hîrseni, this is a scholarly anthropological study of change in Romanian village life during the years of communism. The author looks at the efforts of villagers to follow their own choices in the face of official directives, examining 'how local life was influenced by and in turn influenced the nature of life in the socialist state, in particular, how individual compromises reinforced political stagnation'. The title reflects a fundamental contradiction of socialism in that it sought to homogenize society and create a new man fired with a collective conscience but only succeeded in creating atomized and apathetic individuals.

364   **The wedding of the dead: ritual poetics and popular culture in Transylvania.**
Gail Kligman.   Berkeley, California; Los Angeles; London: University of California Press, 1988. 410p. maps. bibliog. (Studies on the History of Society and Culture).

In Transylvania 'to die unmarried is to die perilously', and so it is the duty of the living to placate the soul of the young departed by performing a symbolic marriage during their funeral. Through her observation of such rituals, the author seeks to show how life-cycle occasions, such as marriage and death, come to realign social and economic relations within the community. In this scholarly study theory is skilfully and effortlessly blended with practical analysis in a series of contrasting doublets such as living/dead, men/women, nature/culture, nature/civilization, etc. The author's choice of the village of Ieud in Maramureş for her fieldwork is also significant since many of its inhabitants follow the Uniate (Greek Catholic) tradition in a country where it is the dominant Orthodox church which tacitly sanctions such popular ritual practices. The book is meticulously documented, exhaustively researched and exquisitely composed.

365   **The Tatars in Maramureş oral tradition.**
Joel Marrant.   *Mioriţa,* vol. 11 (1987), p. 37-50.

The author reveals how the peasants of Maramureş retain within their oral tradition a vivid memory of past invasions and, in particular, the Tatar incursions of the late Middle Ages, the Tatars still being remembered as 'the cruellest of all people'.

366   **National integration through socialist planning: an anthropological study of a Romanian new town.**
Steven L. Sampson.   Boulder, Colorado: East European Monographs, distributed by Columbia University Press, 1984. 352p. maps. bibliog. (East European Monographs, no. 148).

This study, which is based on eighteen months fieldwork undertaken in Braşov county and, more specifically, in the village of Feldioara, twenty-two kilometres north of Braşov, examines how the planning process of systematization worked in this area. The methodological approach is anthropological but the author also throws considerable light onto the ideology of Romanian socialism and the process of modernization in a rural area. An earlier version of this book appeared as *The planners and the peasants, an anthropological study of urban development in Romania* (Esbjerg, Denmark: Sydjyk Universitetsforlag, 1982. 96p. [Monographs in East-West Studies, no. 4]).

367   **Were-wolf and vampire in Romania.**
Harry A. Senn.   Boulder, Colorado: East European Monographs, distributed by Columbia University Press, 1982. 148p. maps. bibliog. (East European Monographs, no. 99).

A scholarly study based on extensive fieldwork conducted in a number of villages throughout Romania. The subject of the author's research are magical and nightmarish beings such as living *strigoi* (witches and wizards), dead *strigoi* (vampires) and *pricolici* and *tricolici* (werewolves). Senn examines the origins of such phenomena and the roles they are ascribed by popular belief. A number of appendices further detail the findings of his research listing the legends and beliefs surrounding were-beings, wolves, witches, vampires, fairies, dragons, their characteristics, behaviour patterns and reasons for their existence.

368 **Romanian peasant houses and households.**
Georgeta Stoica. Bucharest: Meridiane Publishing House, 1984.
149p. bibliog.
This beautifully illustrated book observes the effect modernization and changing life styles have had on the Romanian peasant house and household. In this study the author monitors these changes by examining the interior of peasant houses, the new patterns of organization of space and the adaptation of the traditional culture to the new needs and pace of life.

369 **The 'etatization' of time in Ceauşescus's Romania.**
Katherine Verdery. In: *The politics of time.* Edited by Henry J.
Rutz. Washington, DC: American Anthropological Association,
1992, p. 37-61. (American Ethnological Society Monograph Series,
no. 4).
The main aim of the author in this innovative study is to explore how the Ceauşescu régime came to expropriate the control of time from the people. In the case of Romania this was part of a wider struggle through which the state sought to subjugate the people, but, in the process, time came to stand still entrapped within the Party's walls of silence.

370 **Hommage to a Transylvanian peasant.**
Katherine Verdery. *East European Politics and Societies*, vol. 3,
no. 1 (Winter 1989), p. 51-82.
The peasant in question is 'Bade Petru' [Uncle Peter], Petru Bota, the dedicatee of Verdery's earlier book, *Transylvanian villagers: political, economic and ethnic change 1700-1980* (q.v.). Petru was born in 1894, farmed a small property all his life and died in 1987. Raised when Transylvania was still part of the Austro-Hungarian Empire, this 'humble and mischievous peasant' lived through the demise of this Empire and the incorporation of Transylvania into the new Romanian state, the troubled interwar years and the imposition of communist collectivization. This article contains an abridged version of Petru's life story as told to the author in a two-hour tape-recorded interview, a little over half of which is devoted to his experiences during the First World War.

371 **Funeral trees in Romanian traditional culture.**
Romulus Vulcanescu. *International Folklore Review*, vol. 1 (1981),
p. 77-79.
This article explores the significance of funeral trees in Romanian death customs. The tree, usually a fruit tree or a substitute bough which was once part of a living tree, underlines the responsibilities of the donor as well as the rights and commitments of its recipient (normally a member of the family of the deceased). The proffering of trees is an old custom which both symbolizes the passage from life to death and celebrates the memory of the deceased within the community.

Minorities

General

372 **The nationalities problem in Transylvania, 1867-1940, a social history of the Romanian minority under Hungarian rule, 1867-1918 and the Hungarian minority under Romanian rule, 1918-1940.**
Sándor Bíró, translated from the Hungarian by Mario D. Fenyo.
Boulder, Colorado: Social Science Monographs; Highland Lakes, New Jersey: Atlantic Research and Publications, distributed by Columbia University Press, 1990. 744p. maps. (East European Monographs, no. 333).
The question of minority rights in Transylvania is longstanding, vexed and contentious. In this study the author approaches the problem by offering a comparative study of how the Romanian population of this region fared under Austro-Hungarian rule and the Hungarians under Romanian rule after the formation of Greater Romania. Emphasis is placed on the legal position of religious institutions, the provisions made for education and minority language use, and the degree of legal and civil rights enjoyed by the minorities. In respect of the latter the Hungarian author seems to suggest that the Romanians in Austro-Hungary fared better than the Hungarians in Greater Romania.

373 **Some geographical remarks on education and prints in the language of ethnic groups in Romania.**
Mircea Buza, I. Ianos. *GeoJournal*, vol. 34, no. 4 (Dec. 1994), p. 457-65.
Comparing returns from the January 1992 census with figures from the 1980s, the authors offer a broad survey of current education provisions and publications in the languages of the ethnic minorities in Romania. Although the number of children

receiving education in most minority tongues has decreased, in keeping with a nation-wide decline in the number of pupils, the number of teachers seems to have grown – the authors aver that the number of Hungarian teachers rose by 816 per cent between 1989/90 and 1992/93. This information and other figures relating to education are presented in a number of useful tables and maps. There is also a valuable listing of publishing houses and state-sponsored minority language publications.

374 **Transylvania: the roots of ethnic conflict.**
Edited by John F. Cadzow, Andrew Ludanyi, Louis J. Elteto. Kent, Ohio: Kent State University Press, 1984. 368p. maps.

According to the authors the aim of this volume is to dispel some of the myths surrounding Transylvania and provide a scholarly up-to-date insight into life and developments in the region. They highlight the importance of this task by suggesting that the European order established by the Treaty of Versailles, the Second World War and the Helsinki Accords of 1975 is fundamentally 'challenged by the confrontation that has prevailed in Transylvania at least since 1918 between the Rumanian, Hungarian and German inhabitants'. The subsequent essays fall under four headings: 'the emergence of national consciousness'; 'the growth of modern nationalist orientations'; 'the impact of international relations'; and 'contemporary Romanian nationalities policy'. In the introduction the àuthors include a useful discussion about the politics behind the spellings Romania and Rumania. Noting that those who persist with the appellation Rumania tend not to accept the theory of Daco-Roman continuity, they themselves chose to use this spelling in this volume.

375 **The legislative and institutional framework for the national minorities in Romania.**
The Government of Romania. The Council for National Minorities. Bucharest: Romanian Institute for Human Rights, 1994. 174p.

Romania has a large number of ethnic minorities, the most important of which are the Hungarians who, according to census data (1992), number 1,620,199. The subject of minority rights has often aroused considerable controversy in the past and in this document the Government provides a useful and fairly comprehensive statement of the provisions it makes for its citizens who are not ethnic Romanians. After some background information on the articles of the constitution which relate to minority rights, there is a lengthy section on education that includes a list of schools which teach classes in minority tongues. Other sections cover topics such as religious institutions, cultural provisions, including museums, folk ensembles and theatre groups catering for the minorities, and the non-Romanian-language press, which contains a useful list of publications together with their annual subsidies in lei. The section on participation in political life contains a list of political parties representing minority interests and some interesting data on the ethnic background of local politicians. This reveals that after the 1992 local elections there were 184 Hungarian mayors in the country and 2,950 councillors. Finally, there are details on government institutions concerned with the minorities including the Council for National Minorities.

376 **National minorities in Romania: change in Transylvania.**
Elmér Illyés. Boulder, Colorado: East European Monographs,
distributed by Columbia University Press, 1982. 355p. maps. bibliog.
(Eastern European Monographs, no. 112).

After a brief introduction, in which the author states that the Hungarians were the first
to create a permanent state in the area, Illyés proceeds to investigate the minority
policies of the Romanian government with the chief emphasis being placed on the
period 1944-80. Amongst the issues discussed are territorial and population changes in
Transylvania since 1918, the situation of the national minorities between 1918 and
1956, Romanian policy towards the minorities since 1956, the provision of
educational facilities since the last war, the churches of the national minorities, and
publishing in Hungarian and German. The overall result is a detailed and forceful
catalogue of complaints about Romanian policy towards the minorities and,
especially, the Hungarian minority under communism, although the edge is somewhat
taken off the author's argument by his rather over romantic view of conditions in the
Austro-Hungarian monarchy. The selective bibliography is particularly valuable.

377 **The stolen revolution: minorities in Romania after Ceauşescu.**
Paul Leo. In: *The new political geography of Eastern Europe*.
Edited by John O'Loughlin, Herman van der Wustern. London;
New York: Belhaven, 1993, p. 143-65.

After a survey of the position of minorities in Romania after the Revolution, with
special emphasis on the Hungarian, German and Gypsy communities, the author offers
a history of minority relations in Transylvania since the 19th century.

378 **Socialist patriotism and national minorities: a comparison of the
Yugoslav and Romanian theory and practice.**
Andrew Ludanyi. In: *Society in change. Studies in honour of Béla K.
Király*. Edited by Steven Bela Vardy, Agnes Huszar Vardy.
Boulder, Colorado: East European Monographs, distributed by
Columbia University Press, 1983, p. 557-83. (East European
Monographs, no. 132).

Ludanyi examines and contrasts the position adopted by the two communist states on
the question of minorities. He concentrates particularly on the Hungarian minorities of
Transylvania and the Vojvodina, although this comparison is not entirely valid as the
size of the minority in Transylvania invests it with considerably more significance
than its Yugoslav equivalent. The author surveys the ideological position of both
states towards their minorities and their self-image before concluding that the
'Partisan myth' of the Yugoslavs is more inclusive than the equivalent 'August 23rd'
and 'Daco-Roman' myths of the Romanians, both of which are essentially exclusive in
nature.

379   **Minority rights and majority rule: ethnic tolerance in Romania and Bulgaria.**
       Mary E. McIntosh, Martha Abele Mac Iver, Daniel G. Abele, David B.
       Nolle.   *Social Forces*, vol. 73, no. 3 (March 1995), p. 939-68.

After a survey of the historic roots of the minorities problem in both countries, the
authors present the results of 1991 and 1992 surveys on tolerance amongst ethnic
Romanians and Bulgarians. They then advance their own model for assessing ethnic
intolerance based on a number of variables including political ideology, democratic
values, threat perception and social background.

The Hungarian minority

380   **Struggling for ethnic identity: ethnic Hungarians in post-Ceauşescu Romania.**
       Human Rights Watch.   New York: Human Rights Watch, 1993. 142p.
       (Helsinki Watch Report).

Although a certain amount of literature exists on the position of the Hungarian
minority under Ceauşescu, including an earlier report in this series, *Destroying ethnic
identity: the Hungarians of Romania* (New York: US Helsinki Watch Committee,
Human Rights Watch, 1989. 64p.), developments in post-1989 Romania have been
less well documented. An exception is this report by Human Rights Watch, written by
Holly Cartner and edited by Lois Whitman, Counsel and Department Director of
Helsinki Watch. This suggests that although the status of the Hungarian minority has
improved, especially in areas such as education, culture and freedom of speech, there
are still instances when human rights are not respected.

381   **The Hungarian minority's situation in Ceauşescu's Romania.**
       Rudolf Joó, revising editor Andrew Ludanyi, translated from the
       Hungarian by Chris Tennant.   Boulder, Colorado: Social Science
       Monographs, Atlantic Research and Publishing, 1994. 157p. (East
       European Monographs, no. 373).

A reworked version of a 'Report on the situation of the Hungarian minority in
Rumania' first published in Budapest in 1988 by the Hungarian Democratic Forum.
Notwithstanding the fact that it advances a Hungarian viewpoint on Transylvania, for
instance, the total Hungarian population of the region is cited as being 2,130,000, far
higher than the figure obtained from Romanian censuses, this is nonetheless an
important historical document. Firstly, in the context of Hungarian domestic politics,
it was the first serious attempt by an autonomous group outside the ranks of the ruling
Hungarian Socialist Workers' Party to challenge the policy of that party towards the
Hungarian minority of Transylvania, an issue which did much to undermine the
legitimacy of communist rule in Hungary. Secondly, in an area not blessed with well-
documented source material, it remains the best source for the Hungarian view of how
their co-ethnics were treated under Ceauşescu.

382 **The Magyars in Rumania: problems of a 'coinhabiting' nationality.**
Bennett Korvig. In: *Nationalitätenprobleme in Südosteuropa* (Problems of nationality in South-Eastern Europe). Edited by Ronald Schönfeld. Munich: Oldenbourg, 1987, p. 213-30. (Untersuchungen zur Gegenwartskunde Südosteuropas, no. 25).

Within a broad overview of the condition of the Hungarian minority in Romania, the author considers their history, number, which he argues has diminished, their legal, political and socio-economic status, educational and cultural provisions, dissent and repression, Romanian-Hungarian relations and the Western reaction to the plight of the minority. His findings lead him to conclude that 'resort to nationalism as the primary legitimising device in a polyethnic society is clearly a prescription for injustice, social tension and international opprobrium'. Another chapter concerned with Romania in this volume is Aurel Braun, 'Structural change and its consequences for the nationalities in Romania', p. 181-96. Focusing chiefly on the German and Jewish communities, Braun considers the impact of formal and informal structural changes on the minorities. Overall, his conclusions are as bleak as those of Korvig.

383 **Problems in the ethnic identity of the Moldavian Hungarians.**
Lászlo Lukács. In: *Encountering ethnicities: ethnological aspects on ethnicity, identity and migration.* Edited by Teppo Korhonen. Helsinki: Suomalaisen Kirjallisuuden Seura, 1995, p. 156-60. (Studia Fennica Ethnologica, no. 3).

Provides a Hungarian perspective on the question of the Csángó people who inhabit a number of valleys east of the Carpathian mountains in Moldavia. The Hungarians see the Csángó as Romanized Hungarians who settled on the other side of the Carpathians at about the same time as the arrival of the Székely in Transylvania. The number of Cś angó is difficult to determine. They are Catholics and as most Romanians are Orthodox this has led some Hungarians to suggest that virtually all the Roman Catholics in Moldavia, of which there are 180,000, are Csángó, giving an upper population figure of nearly 150,000. Most of this Catholic population speak Romanian but in this article, which is partly written in response to a series of articles and letters in the German newspaper *Frankfurter Allgemeine Zeitung*, the author suggests that there are still 40-50,000 Hungarian speakers in Moldavia. Some Romanians would assert that, in fact, there are only 6,000 Magyarized Romanians. A recent scholarly study into the origins of the Csángó is Robin Baker, 'On the origins of the Moldavian Csángós', *Slavonic and East European Review*, vol. 75, no. 4 (Oct. 1997), p. 658-80.

384 **Romania's ethnic Hungarians.**
George Schöpflin, Hugh Poulton. London: Minority Rights Group, 1990. 27p. maps.

This is a second edition of George Schöpflin's work, *The Hungarians of Romania* (London: Minority Rights Group, 1978. 20p. [MRG Report, no. 37]). Like the original it represents a commendable attempt to strike a balance between Hungarian and Romanian views on Transylvania and to offer an appraisal of the position of the Hungarians who live there, based on an assessment of the polemical and partial publications which have appeared in recent years.

385 **The grandchildren of Trianon: Hungary and the Hungarian minority in the communist states.**
Raphael Vago. Boulder, Colorado: East European Monographs, distributed by Columbia University Press, 1989. 297p. bibliog. (East European Monographs, no. 258).

Based on the author's PhD thesis on relations between Romania and Hungary since the Second World War, this study was expanded for publication to include two other communist countries which contained sizeable Hungarian minorities: Czechoslovakia and Yugoslavia. Within a wider study of interstate relations, the author places particular stress on cultural relations, which were invested with particular importance by the Hungarians as a potential shield preserving the Hungarian minority in Transylvania from assimilatory pressures.

386 **Witnesses to cultural genocide: first-hand reports on Rumania's minority policies today.**
New York: American Transylvanian Federation, Committee for Human Rights in Rumania, 1979. 209p. map.

An important collection of documents tracing the deterioration of ethnic relations in Romania during the 1970s and the rise of Magyar dissent. It includes 'Three letters to high-ranking Rumanian communist party officials' (p. 162-78) from Károly Király, a former alternate member of the Romanian Communist Party Political Executive Committee and vice-chairman of the Hungarian Nationalities Council, and extracts from the memorandum critical of Romanian nationalities' policy by Lajos Takács (p. 145-61), also a former vice-chairman of the Hungarian Nationalities Council, a candidate member of the RCP Central Committee and Rector of the university in Cluj.

The German minority

387 **Dual ethnic identity of the Transylvanian Saxons.**
Glynn Custred. *East European Quarterly,* vol. 25, no. 4 (Jan. 1992), p. 483-91.

A brief history of the community which focuses on their dual identity as both Saxons and Germans.

388 **Germanissimi Germanorum: Romania's vanishing German culture.**
William C. Dowling. *East European Politics and Societies*, vol. 5, no. 2 (Spring 1991), p. 341-55.

In this article Dowling discusses a book he believes to be a 'minor literary classic as well as a classic of social or ethnographic history', the autobiography of Andreas Nagelbach as told in an oral history published by his son Michael under the title *Heil! and farewell: a life in Romania, 1913-1946* (Chicago: Adams, 1986. 225p. maps. bibliog.). Nagelbach was born in Liebling in the Banat in 1913 but went to school at the gymnasium in Sibiu and later became a Pastor in the Transylvanian Saxon village of Wurmloch (Valea Viilor) near Mediaş. This gives him a fascinating view of both the Swabian and Saxon German communities of the country whose dialects were so disparate as to be mutually unintelligible. The honesty of Nagelbach's account means that he does not blanch from describing the enthusiasm of his compatriots for Hitler and this leads Dowling to astutely observe that the idea that the *Volksdeutsche* of Romania embody a lost German essence can not only be used to explain their seduction by Nazi Germany but also their more recent embrace by a postwar German society no less anxious about its identity.

389   **The Saxon Germans: political fate of an ethnic minority.**
       Marilyn McArthur.   *Dialectical Anthropology,* vol. 1, no. 2 (1976),
       p. 349-64.
This article traces the fortunes of the Saxon community of Transylvania under socialism, using the village of Marienberg (Feldioara) as a case-study. Even at the time of writing the author found the communal values of the Saxon minority already under severe strain, a finding which partially explains the subsequent post-1989 mass emigration to Germany.

390   **The Danube Swabians: German populations in Hungary, Rumania
       and Yugoslavia and Hitler's impact on their patterns.**
       G. C. Paikert.   The Hague: Martinus Nijhoff, 1967. 314p. bibliog.
       (Studies in Social Life, no. 10).
The second section of this book (p. 243-320) is concerned with the Swabian German minority in Romania. In contrast to their mostly Protestant Transylvanian brethren, the Swabian Germans are generally Catholics who settled in the Banat from the 18th century onwards. In this study the author discusses their relationship with the Romanian state from their incorporation into Greater Romania after the First World War until the end of the Second World War. Generally, relations seem to have been good, especially when they were fighting on the same side during the war, but after 1944 and the entry of Soviet troops into the country, almost half the Swabian community departed for Germany.

391   **The fate of the Germans in Romania: a selection and translation
       from Dokumentation der Vertreibung der Deutschen aus
       Ost-Mitteleuropa.**
       Theodore Schieder.   Bonn: Federal Ministry for Expellees, Refugees
       and War Victims, 1961. 355p.
An abridged English translation of the volume concerning Romania in a series which first began to appear in 1953. It contains the complete text of the introductory description and the annexes, together with a selection from the documents. The stress in the latter is on eye-witness reports of experiences. The material extends into the post-war period and includes a report on the forcible resettlement of Germans from the Banat into the Bărăgan steppe of south-east Romania in the summer of 1951.

392 **The unmaking of an ethnic collectivity: Transylvania's Germans.**
Katherine Verdery. *American Ethnologist*, vol. 12, no. 1 (Feb. 1985),
p. 62-83.
In this article the author investigates why the corporate ethnic identity of Romania's
German community has weakened so much compared to both its own past strength
and the continuing cohesion of the Hungarian minority. Verdery suggests that with the
German community the decline may be rooted in the weakening of the traditional
foundations of German ethic identity, such as privileged feudal rank, administrative
and religious autonomy, economic independence and linguistic separateness. She goes
on to compare the Germans with the Hungarians, suggesting there is nothing uniform
about the effects of socialism on various minorities and that unlike the Hungarians the
Germans have tended towards individualization.

The Jewish minority

393 **The 'Christian' regimes of Romania and the Jews, 1940-1942.**
Jean Ancel. *Holocaust and Genocide Studies*, vol. 7, no. 1
(Spring 1993), p. 14-29.
Examines the attitude of the Romanian Orthodox Church towards the persecution of
the Jews in Romania during the Iron Guard years (September 1940-January 1941) and
Antonescu's dictatorship (February 1941-August 1944). The author highlights the
anti-Semitism of the élite of the Romanian Orthodox Church who did not publicly
condemn the crimes against the Jews and took no firm action towards the
extermination policy of Antonescu. He concludes that, regretfully, only very few
intervened to aid the Jews.

394 **Plans for the deportation of the Rumanian Jews and their
discontinuation in light of documentary evidence (July-October
1942).**
Jean Ancel. *Yad Vashem Studies*, vol. 16 (1984), p. 381-420.
The author examines the reasons why the Antonescu Government failed to implement
plans to deport the 300,000 Jews of the Romanian wartime state to Belzec
concentration camp in Poland during the Second World War. By scrutinizing nine
official documents, in which both the German and Romanian authorities outline their
policies towards the Jews, Ancel puts forward several reasons for their inaction,
amongst which were: resentment of German meddling in Romanian internal affairs;
the continuing influence of a number of prominent local Jews; and pressure from the
United States.

395 **The Romanian way of solving the 'Jewish Problem' in Bessarabia and Bukovina, June-July 1941.**
Jean Ancel. *Yad Vashem Studies*, vol. 19 (1988), p. 187-232.

The author analyses the means by which during the Second World War, following their reoccupation of Bessarabia and Bucovina in the summer of 1941, the Romanians achieved a 'cleansing' of much of the pre-war Jewish population of these provinces. Ancel's account is supported by statistical tables detailing the number of Jews living in these areas during the December 1930, September 1941 and May 1942 censuses. These show that the Jewish population shrank from 314,933 in December 1930 to a mere 19,576 in May 1942.

396 **Genocide and retribution: the Holocaust in Hungarian-ruled Northern Transylvania.**
Randolph L. Braham. Boston, Massachusetts; The Hague; Dordrecht, the Netherlands; Lancaster, England: Kluwer Nijhoff Publishing, 1983. 260p. map. bibliog.

This book stands as a testament to the 'Judgement' pronounced by the People's Tribunal on 31 May 1946 by which those who had persecuted the Romanians and Jews of northern Transylvania during the Hungarian occupation of the area between September 1940 and the autumn of 1944 were sentenced to death or life imprisonment. The first part of the book contains a history of the Jews in Transylvania; the second comprises a word-for-word transcription of the judgement passed by the People's Tribunal.

397 **The tragedy of Romanian Jewry.**
Edited by Randolph L. Braham. Boulder, Colorado: Rosenthal Institute for Holocaust Studies Graduate Center, City University of New York, Social Science Monographs, distributed by Columbia University Press, 1994. 388p. (East European Monographs, no. 404).

This collection of essays deals, according to the editor, with 'one of the most neglected chapters in the history of the Holocaust', namely the fate of Romanian Jews during the Second World War. In this volume this difficult and controversial issue is lucidly and objectively analysed by: Stephen Fischer-Galaţi, 'The legacy of anti-Semitism', p. 1-28; Raphael Vago, 'Romanian Jewry during the inter-war period', p. 29-56; Radu Florian, 'The Antonescu regime: history and mystification', p. 77-115; Radu Ionaid, 'The Antonescu era', p. 117-71; Victor Eskenasy, 'The holocaust and Romanian historiography: communist and neo-communist revisionism', p. 173-236; Alexandru Florian, 'Treatment of the holocaust in Romanian textbooks', p. 237-85; Liviu Rotman, 'Romanian Jewry: the first decade after the holocaust', p. 287-331; and Michael Shafir, 'Anti-Semitism in the postcommuist era', p. 333-86.

398 **A TV documentary on rescue during the holocaust: a case of history cleansing in Romania.**
Randolph L. Braham. *East European Quarterly*, vol. 28, no. 2 (June 1994), p. 193-203.

Within a morass of claims and counterclaims, this article features a sustained and often bitter polemic against the revelation in a 1992 Romanian television documentary

that Rabbi Dr Mozes Carmilly-Weinberger and Professor Raoul Șorban assisted with
the rescue of Jewish people from areas of Transylvania occupied by the Hungarians
during the Second World War.

399 **The silent holocaust: Romania and its Jews.**
I. C. Butnaru, with a foreword by Elie Wiesel. New York; Westport,
Connecticut; London: Greenwood, 1992. 225p. maps. bibliog.
(Constributions to the Study of World History, no. 31).
In 1930 the Jewish population of Romania, which stood at 756,930, was the third
largest in Europe. By the census of 1942, following the yielding of territory to
Hungary, the USSR and Bulgaria, it had dwindled to a mere 292,149. After the war
and the re-annexation of northern Transylvania the figure was eventually to rise to
some 300,000. In this study the author, who is of Romanian Jewish extraction, as is
the Nobel laureate Elie Wiesel who supplies the foreword, traces the history of the
Jewish community in Romania with particular emphasis being placed on the Second
World War. He challenges the widely held perception that Romania protected her
Jewish population just because Antonescu refused to transfer the Jewish population of
the wartime Romanian state to Polish concentration camps. Instead, he argues that the
Romanians under Antonescu fully participated in the Holocaust, killing thousands of
Jews. Anti-Semitism in Romania for Butnaru was not a product of the people but of
the leaders and the so-called 'intellectual élite'.

400 **Waiting for Jerusalem: surviving the Holocaust in Romania.**
I. C. Butnaru. Westport, Connecticut; London: Greenwood, 1992.
264p. bibliog. (Contributions to the Study of World History, no. 37).
Whilst *The silent holocaust* (q.v.), the companion volume to this work, catalogues the
destruction of the Jewish community of Romania, in this book Butnaru celebrates the
people and organizations which managed to rescue 300,000 Romanian Jews. They
were a disparate group of Zionist organizations, Jewish resistance groups and
compassionate Romanians. In the process he reveals that just as Ceaușescu did
afterwards, Antonescu was even prepared to sell Jews, offering to permit 75,000-
80,000 to emigrate to Palestine for a payment of 200,000 lei each.

401 **The Jewish educational system in Romania during World War II
(1940-1944).**
Iaacov Geller. *Yad Vashem Studies*, vol. 20 (1990), p. 313-36.
When the Romanian army seized all the Jewish schools during the Second World War
and Jews were banned from all Romanian educational institutions, members of the
Jewish community managed to sustain a network of alternative schools by renting
private houses and converting synagogue halls and other communal buildings. A
number of high schools were also established by Jewish lecturers who had previously
taught at Romanian universities. In this article the author supports his research with
detailed statistical information, covering the number of schools, students and teachers,
as he effectively shows how a Jewish educational system managed to survive in a
hostile environment.

402 A **German evangelical minister's reminiscences of his youth in north Transylvania.**
Hans Holzträger. *Yad Vashem Studies*, vol. 14 (1981), p. 269-86.

These are the memoirs of a German priest from Zepling, a large village in the north of Transylvania in the Regen district. In these he ruefully describes the transformation of his village from a 'land of understanding' and a safe haven for Romania's many nationalities between the wars to an inhospitable place of anti-Semitism under the encouragement of Nazi propaganda. This is a poignant account based on the priest's own painful experiences as he was forced to endure seeing his Jewish friends being harassed and discriminated against, as they were forced to go out with the star of David sewn onto their clothing, if they had not already been deported. At this time even Jews who had converted to Christianity ran the risk of being cast out from society and interdicted.

403 **Jews in Romania 1866-1919: from exclusion to emancipation.**
Carol Iancu, translated by Carvel de Bussy. Boulder, Colorado: East European Monographs, distributed by Columbia University Press, 1996. 191p. bibliog. (East European Monographs, no. 449).

Drawing primarily on Romanian-language sources, this is an objective and well-balanced survey of the Romanian response to the vast influx of Jews from Russia and Poland into the north of Romania in the late 19th century. By 1878 the long-standing Jewish population of Iaşi had been swamped by the new arrivals as they topped 400,000, forty-seven per cent of the city's population. The new Jews functioned as a middle class, but they only gained the antipathy of both the Romanian peasants and intellectuals such as Romania's national poet, Eminescu. Article 44 of the treaty of Berlin held that citizenship be granted to all residents of Romania irrespective of their religious faith, but this was widely ignored by the Romanians. Under pressure from German Jews the issue was championed by Otto von Bismarck, but his primary aim was to force the Romanians to buy the loss-making German-built railway system. Once this was achieved, Bismarck lost interest in the matter and very few Jews received Romanian citizenship – only those who had fought in the 1877-78 war, those considered to be sufficiently assimilated and those wealthy enough to buy citizenship.

404 **Anti-Semitism and the treatment of the Holocaust in postcommunist Romania.**
Radu Ioanid. In: *Anti-semitism and the treatment of the Holocaust in postcommunist Eastern Europe.* Edited by Randolph L. Braham. Boulder, Colorado: The Rosenthal Institute for Holocaust Studies Graduate Center/The City University of New York, Social Science Monographs, distributed by Columbia University Press, 1994, p. 159-82.

After a brief discussion of the holocaust in Romania and Transnistria, the author reviews what he considers to be an alarming upsurge in anti-Semitism in post-communist Romania. He focuses in particular on the writings to be found in journals such as *România Mare* and *Europa* and the campaign to rehabilitate the wartime leader of Romania, Marshal Antonescu.

405 **How Romania reacted to the Holocaust, 1945-1992.**
Radu Ioanid. In: *The world reacts to the Holocaust, 1945-1992.*
Edited by David Wyman, Project director Charles H. Rosenzveig.
Baltimore, Maryland; London: Johns Hopkins University Press, 1994,
p. 225-55.

The emphasis in this chapter is not so much on the actual Holocaust but on the
Romanian reaction to the persecution of Jews in the period since the Second World
War. Ioanid argues that after the initial postwar trials of war criminals and the
publication of books such as Mathais Carp's *Cartea Neagra: suferințele evreilor din
România, 1940-1944* (The black book: the sufferings of the Jews in Romania, 1940-
44) (Bucharest: Socec, 1945-48. 3 vols.) documenting the persecution of Jews in
Romania and Romanian controlled areas, the subject disappeared from Romanian
historiography. In the words of Rabbi Rosen, paraphrasing Elie Weisel, 'Romanian
Jews were murdered twice, once in the holocaust and a second time through denial
and lies'. The author concludes by discussing the treatment of Romanian fascism and
anti-Semitism in Romanian historiography, including the forms it has taken since
1989.

406 **British diplomats and the Jews in Poland, Romania and Hungary
during the communist take-overs.**
Arieh J. Kochavi. *East European Quarterly*, vol. 29, no. 4
(Winter 1995), p. 449-64.

The largest Jewish population remaining in Eastern Europe at the end of the Second
World War, the estimated 430,000 Jews in Romania, attracted the attention of British
diplomats concerned about the possibility of an influx of refugees into Palestine.
According to a survey by British diplomats, the position of the 250,000 Jewish
residents who had survived the war in Romania was sufficient to secure for them a
reasonable future, particularly as many Jews were identified with the incoming
communists, but concerns were voiced about the prospects for the 60,000 returned
deportees and the 150,000 Jews who had fled from other countries. Immediately after
the war the authorities in all three Eastern European countries allowed Jews to leave
for Palestine, with about 250,000 fleeing, but with the onset of the Cold War
movement was restricted with the last shipload of 15,000 Romanian Jews sailing from
Bulgaria in December 1947. An earlier study by this author on the same subject is
Arieh J. Kochavi, 'Britain versus Roumania and the Soviet military authorities, 1945-
1947', *Balkan Studies*, vol. 29, no. 2 (1988), p. 283-97.

407 **The Jewish population in Romania during World War II/Populația
evreiască din România în timpul celui de-al doilea război mondial.**
Sabin Manuilă, Wilhelm Filderman, with an introduction by Larry
Watts, edited by Kurt W. Treptow. Iași, Romania: The Romanian
Cultural Foundation, 1994. 62p. maps. (Romanian Civilization Studies,
no. 1).

A reprint of a conference paper originally delivered in Stockholm in 1957 in which the
authors tried to establish the number of Jews who had perished in the Romanian lands
during the Second World War. The authors were well equipped to undertake such a
task. Wilhelm Filderman had been President of the Union of Jewish Communities of
Romania during the war and had himself spent some time in a concentration camp in

Transnistria. Sabin Manuilă was Romania's leading interwar demographer and statistician who had previously served as Director General of the Central Statistical Institute in Bucharest. Their findings were published in Rome and New York but in Romania they were largely ignored during the communist period – in his introduction Larry Watts suggests that this was because they did not overwhelmingly damn the Antonescu régime. After taking into account emigration, both official and unofficial, to Israel, the authors suggest that 209,214 of pre-war Romanian Jewry lost their lives during the war, that is approximately twenty-seven per cent of the total. Of these 15,000 died in the regions which remained part of the Romanian state throughout the war, 103,919 died in Bessarabia, Bucovina and the other lands which were first occupied by the Russians and then the Romanians with their German allies, and 90,295 in northern Transylvania which was occupied by the Hungarians, again in conjunction with their German allies. This suggests that of the twenty-seven per cent who died, two per cent were the responsibility of the Romanian authorities alone, thirteen per cent the Romanian-German administration in the East and twelve per cent the Hungarian-German authorities.

408 **Was the Transnistria rescue plan achievable?**
Ephraim Ophir. *Holocaust and Genocide Studies*, vol. 6, no. 1 (March 1991), p. 1-16.

The author traces the complex negotiations which lay behind the proposal to allow 70,000 Jews who were trapped and dying in Transnistria to emigrate from Romania. Ophir first examines the situation in Transnistria and then attempts to evaluate the several parallel negations which involved Romanian Jewish leaders, Romanian government officials, such as Radu Lecca, private entrepreneurs who were either German or Romanian intelligence agents and others. He concludes by stating that the initiative for such negotiations came from the Romanians in October 1942, but the Germans opposed it almost immediately and once it became public knowledge in February 1943, it had already been abandoned.

409 **Burning ice: the ghettos in Transnistria.**
Avigdor Shachan, translated by Shmuel Himelstein. Boulder, Colorado: East European Monographs, distributed by Columbia University Press, 1996. 510p. (East European Monographs, no. 447).

In this personal memoir, which is skilfully interwoven with historic narrative, the author addresses three major questions relating to the persecution of the Jews of Bessarabia and Transnistria in 1941-42. The first is whether this mass murder was previously planned by the Romanian authorities, the second is the number of Jews actually killed in Transnistria, and the third is why the local population turned against the Jewish community with which it had previously lived in peaceful co-existence for many years.

410 **Stefanesti: portrait of a Romanian shtetl.**
Ghitta Sternberg. Oxford; New York; Toronto; Sydney; Paris; Frankfurt: Pergamon Press, 1984. 289p. maps. bibliog.

A historical reconstruction, drawing on interviews and documentary evidence, of the author's home *shtetl* of Ştefăneşti, a small town in Botoşani county not far from Iaşi. The author presents a fascinating picture of a community clinging to its traditional values, customs, language and social stratification in a changing world. Forbidden from purchasing land outside the cities, most Jews channelled their energies instead into business ventures becoming merchants or shopkeepers. In consequence the Jews of Romania seem to have been generally better off than their compatriots living in the Pale of the Russian Empire (an area designated by Tsar Alexander I where Jewish people were allowed to settle) and to have enjoyed greater freedoms.

411 **The destruction of Romanian Jewry in Romanian historiography.**
Bela Vago. In: *Historiography of the Holocaust period: proceedings of the fifth Yad Vashem International Historical Conference, Jerusalem, March 1983.* Edited by Yisrael Gutman, Gideon Grief. Jerusalem: Yad Vashem, 1988, p. 405-32.
The author analyses the few references made to the Holocaust in Romanian historiography prior to the 1980s. He argues that the rarity of references may partly stem from a general reluctance to discuss the first half of the Second World War when Romania was allied to Germany. This paper is followed by a brief contribution by two Romanian historians, G. Zaharia and N. Copoiu, 'The situation of the Jews in Romania, 1938-1944, as reflected in Romanian historiography', (p. 423-32), in which, amongst other points, they stress the greater 'truthfulness' which has been evident in Romanian historiography since the 9th Party Congress of 1965 which elected Nicolae Ceauşescu as leader.

The Gypsy minority

412 **Racism and the formation of a Romani ethnic leader.**
Sam Beck. In: *Perilous states: conversations on culture, politics, and nation.* Edited by George E. Marcus. Chicago; London: University of Chicago Press, 1993, p. 165-91. (Late Editions: Cultural Studies for the End of the Century, no. 1).
A portrait of the Romanian gypsy activist, Nicolae Gheorghe, who the author has known since they began to conduct fieldwork together in 1979. Gheorghe was an activist under Ceauşescu when Romanies were a taboo subject even for Romanians and his activities brought both himself and the author to the attention of the *Securitate.* After a brief outline of the position of the Gypsies within Romanian society and Gheorghe's thoughts about creating a space in which they might express their identity as an ethnic group, the chapter concludes with the transcript of an interview between the author and Gheorghe in which the latter explores his own Gypsy identity.

413 **Destroying ethnic identity: the persecution of Gypsies in Romania.**
Holly Cartner. New York: Human Rights Watch, 1991. 125p.
(Helsinki Watch Report).
Deals with the position of the Gypsy minority in contemporary Romania. After an introduction tracing the history of the Gypsies in the country from their first migrations at the end of the 13th and beginning of the 14th century to the horrors of

the Second World War, some mention is made of the communist years before the bulk of the study considers the status of the minority in post-Ceauşescu Romania. The report offers evidence that Gypsies have been the victims of violent attacks by both ordinary Romanian citizens and the authorities, causing many to lose their property. They are also the victims of discrimination both as regards employment and the educational system. Although before the 1989 Revolution many Gypsies had a low level of ethnic conscience, this has been rising steadily in recent years, as can be seen from the growing number of Gypsy political parties, cultural organizations and newspapers which have at last started to raise the issue of ethnic discrimination and the long history of persecution as well as highlighting the shared cultural heritage of Gypsies and Romanians.

414 **The Gypsy historical experience in Romania.**
David Crowe. In: *The Gypsies of Eastern Europe.* Edited by David Crowe, John Kolsti, with an introduction by Ian Hancock. Armonk, New York; London: M. E. Sharpe, 1991, p. 61-79.

A chronological account which traces the presence of the Gypsies in Romania from the early 14th century and the first evidence of their arrival in the provinces of Wallachia and Moldavia until the present day. The author states that the Gypsy community in Romania numbers between 760,000 and one million and highlighting their previous isolation, he predicts that in the future they will continue to live on the margins of Romanian society. A similar analysis by the same author can be found in *A history of the Gypsies of Eastern Europe and Russia* (London; New York: I. B. Tauris, 1995. 317p.).

415 **Origins of the Roma's slavery in the Rumanian Principalities.**
Nicolae Gheorghe. *Roma,* vol. 7, no. 1 (Jan. 1983), p. 12-27.

Published in commemoration of the 125th anniversary of the emancipation from slavery of the Gypsies in Romania, which occurred by two acts of Parliament in December 1855 and February 1856. The author highlights the significance of this event not only for the Gypsies now living in Romania but also for those who have emigrated to Central Europe and the United States. Increasingly, the descendants of the nomadic slaves are joining the international Romani movement in the quest to affirm their own culture and ethnic identity as well as their human rights.

416 **Roma-Gypsy ethnicity in Eastern Europe.**
Nicolae Gheorghe. *Social Research,* vol. 58, no. 4 (Winter 1991), p. 829-44.

This article, written by a Romanian Gypsy activist, provides a useful historical review of the settlement of the Gypsies in Eastern Europe. The author traces the origins of the prejudices against the Gypsies, which remain strong until this day, especially in his native Romania, where Gypsies have frequently found themselves the scapegoats of a society in flux.

417 **The little maple tree: a Transylvanian Gypsy folk tale with songs.**
Katalin Kovalesik, Endre Tálos. *Journal of the Gypsy Lore Society,*
vol. 1, no. 2 (1991), p. 103-25.

An ethnological, ethnomusical and linguistic analysis of a Transylvanian Vlach Gypsy
folk-tale which belongs to the broader maple tree tradition. A king asks his three
daughters to gather strawberries, saying that the one who gathers most will be
rewarded. The youngest and most obedient daughter soon gathers a heavy basket but
she is killed by her jealous elder sisters who seize the fruit of her labours. A willow
tree grows on the young princess's grave and one day it tells a passing shepherd of the
girl's tragic fate. The shepherd journeys to the king to tell him the news but only after
the monarch himself has visited the tree does he believe the tale and punish his evil
daughters. The authors heard the song performed by a nineteen-year-old young man
who incorporated within it slow lyrical songs of the Vlach Gypsy tradition. However,
they contend that Hungarian patterns can also be discerned in the proportion and
positioning of loanwords and that the melody is related to Dorian and Phrygian pieces
on the periphery of the Hungarian lament style.

418 **Romani lexical items in colloquial Romanian.**
Corinna Leschber. In: *Romani in contact: the history, structure and
sociology of a language.* Edited by Yaron Matras. Amsterdam;
Philadelphia: John Benjamins Publishing Company, 1995, p. 51-76.
(Amsterdam Studies in the History of Linguistic Science. Series IV:
Current Issues in Linguistics, no. 126).

This article deals with the adoption of Romani loanwords into Romanian, looking at
the semantic and structural changes they undergo. After discussing the status of the
Romani language as well as the methodology employed, the author embarks upon a
detailed linguistic examination of a number of Romani words. She concludes that
most frequently they tend to be used in a colloquial (slang or jargon) rather than a
literary context.

Other minorities

419 **Islam in Romania.**
Gyorgy Lederer. *Central Asian Survey,* vol. 15, no. 3-4 (Dec. 1996),
p. 349-68.

Romania's Islamic population can be divided into native and immigrant groups. In this
study the author looks principally at the former, who mostly live in the Dobrogea and
by their own estimates number some 40,000 Tartars, 10,000 Turks and 15,000 Muslim
Gypsies. Like so many others they suffered under communism, when religion could
not be taught in schools and the number of mosques declined from approximately 150
in 1944 to 50 today. The situation has improved somewhat since 1989 with the
establishment of a political grouping to represent Islamic interests, the Muslim
Democratic Union of Romania, and the appearance of an eight-page newspaper
Karadeniz (Black Sea). The key issue, though, remains education and there are still no

Turkish educational institutions and the Turkish language is only taught for four to six hours a week in a few selected schools.

420 **Shattered eagles, Balkan fragments.**
Tom Winnifrith. London: Duckworth, 1995. 171p.
Amongst the essays in this book, which is concerned with Balkan Latinity and minorities in South-Eastern Europe, there is one on the Vlachs of Romania. Whether this group should even be considered as a minority is difficult to say because, as the author himself states, 'The relationship between Vlachs and Romanians is difficult to disentangle; more difficult to explain'. The Vlachs and Romanians speak a similar tongue and in the past the Romanians have generally failed to distinguish the Vlachs or, if they have, it has only been as Macedonian Romanians. Recently, however, a few activists have tried to reassert a distinct ethnic identity amongst this ethnic group. The Vlachs come to be in Romania because at the end of the 19th and the beginning of the 20th century the Romanians invested a great deal of money in educating the Vlach-speaking population of Macedonia. The area could never realistically have been a part of any Romanian state but it is possible they may have hoped to use a 'Romanian' minority in the area as a bargaining counter in any territorial exchanges. However, when this last portion of the Ottoman Empire in Europe was carved into nation states during the Balkan Wars, many of those Vlachs educated in Romanian schools chose to move to their 'mother country' with the majority settling in the Dobrogea. A full-length study of the Vlachs by the same author is *The Vlachs: the history of a Balkan people* (London: Duckworth, 1987. 180p.).

421 **Hungarian-Bulgarians? Ethnic identity and the process of acculturation among the Bulgarians of the Banat region.**
Vivien Zatykó. In: *Encountering ethnicities: ethnological aspects on ethnicity, identity and migration.* Edited by Teppo Korhonen.
Helsinki: Suomalaisen Kirjallisuuden Seura, 1995, p. 193-99.
(Studia Fennica Ethnologica, no. 3).
Aims to show how the Bulgarian minority of the Banat preserved their ethnic consciousness despite prolonged exposure to Hungarian and Romanian culture. The Bulgarians, who were all converts to the Catholic faith, settled in two villages in the area in 1737 and 1741. The biggest role in preserving their identity was played by their language, which is written in Latin rather than in the Cyrillic script, but their strong sense of historical awareness was also important. In the future, the author suggests, their identity will be shaped by their Romanian citizenship, cultivation of the Banat Bulgarian tradition and their growing awareness of belonging to the broader Bulgarian nation.

Romanians Abroad

422 **Peasants and strangers: Italians, Rumanians and Slovaks in an American city, 1890-1950.**
Josef J. Barton.   Cambridge, Massachusetts: Harvard University Press, 1975. 217p. (Harvard Studies in Urban History).
This work of social history traces the fortunes of the Romanian, Italian and Slovak immigrant communities in the industrial American city of Cleveland. The author illustrates the experiences of both the first generation immigrants, who left their rural homes in search of a new life, and of the second generation, who were torn between the traditional forces of their communities and the need to integrate into the rhythm and customs of American urban life. The Romanian settlement differed from the other two in that the more secular orientation of their ethnic culture tended to ease their passage to middle-class status.

423 **Significance and possibilities for existence of a national minority: the Romanian subculture in the USA. Theory and perspectives.**
Stephen Fischer-Galati.   In: *Society in change: Studies in honour of Béla K. Király.*   Edited by Steven Bela Vardy, Agnes Huszar Vardy. New York: Columbia University Press, 1983, p. 217-29. (East European Monographs, no. 132).
Examines the cultural, economic, social and political development of the Romanian community in the United States. Although, at least up until the Second World War, the Romano-American population largely consisted of unskilled and illiterate workers, they also held some influence and made an impact on events not only in America but also in Romania. The author concludes that gradually the two cultures are converging and that under the pressure of assimilation the values of the Romanians are changing to fit American norms.

424 **Ethnic civil religion: a case study of immigrants from Rumania in Israel.**
Rina Neeman, Nissan Rubin. *Sociology of Religion*, vol. 57, no. 2 (Summer 1996), p. 195-212.

Taking as a case-study a cultural association of 2,000 Israelis of Romania, most of whom have lived in Israel for over ten years, the authors show how these non-religious Jews manipulate traditional Jewish motifs within a secular context to redefine their identity and achieve ethnic integration and self-legitimization.

425 **The persistence of white ethnicity in Canada: the case of the Romanians.**
G. James Patterson. *East European Quarterly*, vol. 21, no. 4 (Jan. 1986), p. 493-500.

In this article the author traces the fortune of two groups of immigrant Romanians in Canada. He judges that one group, consisting of descendants of Bucovina peasants who settled in Saskatchewan and Alberta at the turn of the century, are fully assimilated. However, the other group, made up of more recent postwar emigrants who have tended to settle in larger cities in the East, have, in the face of a continuing influx of new emigrants, developed a 'third culture' which is neither Romanian nor Canadian. A lengthier study by the same author on this subject is *The Romanians of Saskatchewan: four generations of adaptation* (Ottawa: National Museum of Canada, 1977).

426 **Romanian-American literature.**
Alexandra Roceric. In: *Ethnic perspectives in American literature. Selected essays on the European contribution.* Edited by J. Robert Di Pietro, Edward Ifkovic. New York: The Modern Language Association of America, 1983, p. 197-209.

A short introduction to the Romanian contribution to American literature during the 20th century. At present there are an estimated 200,000 Romanians in the United States and in this essay the author highlights the apparent innate ability that writers within this community possess of preserving their traditional roots and cultural identity whilst at the same time integrating into American society. Amongst the poets and authors discussed are: Codrescu, Neagoe, Eliade, Novac, Daschievici, Floran and Damian-Tait.

Language

General

427 **Transformational grammar and the Rumanian language.**
Edited by Sorin Alexandrescu. Amsterdam: Peter De Ridder Press,
1977. 97p. bibliog.

This book consists of eight articles on various aspects of the Romanian language:
James E. Augerot, 'Modern linguistics and the Rumanian language' (p. 5-15); Robert
Bley-Vroman, 'Rumanian pronoun morphology from a generative point of view'
(p. 17-37); Helmuth Frisch, 'Phonetic alterations within the Rumanian inflection
system' (p. 39-44); Sanda Golopenția-Eretescu, 'Transformational grammar and
language parts' (p. 45-57); Jacques Goudet, 'An attempt at interpreting the
periphrastic verbal system: a fi+ gerund' (p. 59-73); Herwig Krenn, 'The genitive
article and modern syntax' (p. 75-82); Lorenzo Renzi, 'Remarks on the Rumanian
article' (p. 83-88); and E. Vasiliu, 'Connectives and modalities' (p. 89-97).

428 **Romanian phonology: a generative phonological sketch of the core
vocabulary of Standard Romanian.**
James E. Augerot. Bucharest: Editura Academiei Republicii
Socialiste Romănia; Moscow, Idaho: Idaho Research Foundation,
University of Idaho, 1974. 86p. (Language Series).

A highly specialized monograph on the pronunciation of the Romanian language.
Although some dialectical and historical information is occasionally cited in the text,
the main subject of the book is the synchronic phonological process of Standard
Romanian.

429 **Elements of national history reflected in Romanian proverbs.**
Al. Stănciulescu-Bîrda. *East European Quarterly*, vol. 24, no. 4
(Jan. 1991), p. 513-28.

The author draws upon a large number of Romanian proverbs in his efforts to
demonstrate that they reflect the nation's history. However, his highly subjective
interpretations and the lack of any real exploration of the origins and context in which
the proverbs were used means that this study is primarily interesting for the rich
number of examples cited.

430 **Romanian-language teaching: a century of pedagogical materials
published outside Romania.**
Charles M. Carlton. *Modern Language Journal*, vol. 68, no. 4
(Winter 1984), p. 354-69.

The article contains an exhaustive and meticulous listing of teaching aids for the study
of the Romanian language published outside Romania (although some editions
circulated through the Biblioteca Centrală Universitară of Bucharest are also
discussed). The author critically examines the full range of grammars, dictionaries,
textbooks and other materials available to the non-native speaker. He also discusses
the layout of a typical Romanian textbook in order to highlight the diversity available
and to guide the student. Each book is evaluated on its merit and the long bibliography
at the end of the article, although inevitably now rather dated, is still useful for those
looking for material.

431 **Prominence vs. rhythm: the predictability of stress in Romanian.**
Ioana Chitoran. In: *Grammatical theory and Romance languages.
Selected papers from the 25th Linguistic Symposium on Romance
Languages, Seattle, 2-4 March 1995.* Edited by Karen Zagona.
Amsterdam; Philadelphia: John Benjamins, 1995, p. 47-58. bibliog.
(Amsterdam Studies in the History of Linguistic Science. Series IV:
Current Issues in Linguistics, no. 133).

Aims to present a simplified but also sophisticated analysis of the Romanian stress
system, a subject which hitherto has been seen as being too complicated for such
endeavours. By pointing out the close dependence of primary stress (stress on any of
the last three syllables) on the morphology of the language and its independence of
secondary stress (the stress present on the initial syllable of words longer than three
syllables and trisyllabic verbs), the author suggests that 'primary stress marks
prominence while secondary stress denotes initial word boundary and rhythm in the
rest of the word'.

432 **Advances in Roumanian linguistics.**
Edited by Guglielmo Cinque, Giuliana Giusti. Amsterdam;
Philadelphia: John Benjamins Publishing Company, 1995. 173p.
(Linguistik Aktuel/Linguistics Today, no. 10).

A compilation of papers presented at a conference on Romanian Linguistics held by
the University of Venice on 6 June 1992. Amongst the articles included are:
Alexandra Cornilescu, 'Rumanian genitive constructions', p. 1-54; Carmen Dobrovie-
Sorin, 'Clitic clusters in Rumanian: deriving linear order from hierarchical structure',

p. 55-82; Donka Farkaş and Draga Zec, 'Agreement and pronominal reference', p. 83-102; Giuliana Giusti, 'Heads and modifiers amongst determiners: evidence from Rumanian', p. 103-26; Alexander Grosu, 'Free relatives with "missing prepositions" in Rumanian and universal grammar', p. 127-60; and Virginia Motapanyane, 'NP-movement from finite clauses in Rumanian', p. 161-70.

433 **The development of modern Rumanian: linguistic theory and practice in Muntenia 1821-1838.**
Elizabeth Close. London: Oxford University Press, 1974. 316p. bibliog.

This is the best study in English of the development of modern literary Romanian during the first half of the 19th century. The main emphasis is on the work of Ioan Heliade Rădulescu (1802-72) and his associates who helped shape the development of the language.

434 **Romanian in the Romance family: from isolation to integration.**
Elizabeth Close. *Journal of the Institute of Romance Studies,* vol. 2 (1992), p. 11-24.

This study surveys foreign (non-Romance, Romance and Latin) influences on the Romanian vocabulary and the reception they have had since the 17th century. Particular attention is paid to the influence of other languages, especially French, on Romanian syntax.

435 **Remarks of the determiner system of Romanian: the demonstratives al and cel.**
Alexandra Cornilescu. *Probs,* vol. 4, no. 3 (1992), p. 189-260.

A well-researched and well-documented study of the syntax of two Romanian particles, which are described by the author as expletive determiners. 'Al' (e.g. 'un student al Mariei' = 'a student of Mary's'), which is the 'genitive' article as it always precedes a noun or a pronoun in the genitive, and 'cel' (e.g. 'cerul cel albastru' = 'the blue sky'), which is the 'adjectival' article since it precedes an adjective which follows a noun.

436 **Clitic doubling, wh- movement and quantification in Romanian.**
Carmen Dobrovie-Sorin. *Linguistic Inquiry,* vol. 21, no. 3 (Summer 1990), p. 351-97.

A comparative study of the differences between Romanian wh- structures, which distinguish between movement and quantification, and similar structures in English which do not have such properties. The same subject is also addressed by: Ileana Comorovski, 'Multiple wh- movement in Romanian', *Linguistic Inquiry,* vol. 17, no. 1 (Winter 1986), p. 171-77; and William Kemp, 'Headless relatives and reduced relatives in Quebec French, Rumanian, and Spanish' in *Linguistic symposium on Romance languages: 9,* edited by William W. Cressey, Donna Jo Napoli (Washington, DC: Georgetown University Press, 1981, p. 248-64).

Language. General

437   The syntax of Romanian: comparative studies in Romance.
Carmen Dobrovie-Sorin.   Berlin; New York: Mouton de Gruyter,
1993. 296p. bibliog. (Studies in Generative Grammar, no. 40).
A highly scholarly attempt to provide the answer to the question of why certain
syntactic or grammatical structures are specific to Romanian and cannot be found in
other Romance languages. The aim of the author in investigating such comparative
data is to determine the specific parameters of Romanian. Issues considered include:
auxiliary constructions, cliticization, the infinitive and subjunctive structure, the
middle/passive voice, the wh- movement and others. Similar research can be found in
a book which was first published in Romania in 1969 by Emanuel Vasiliu and Sanda
Golopenţia-Eretescu, *The transformational syntax of Romanian* (Bucharest:
Academiei Republicii Socialiste România; The Hague; Paris: Mouton, 1972. 198p.
bibliog.).

438   A Latin source for the conditional auxiliary in Romanian.
Mark J. Elson.   *Zeitschrift für romanische philologie*, vol. 108,
no. 5-6 (1992), p. 560-75.
The author here argues that the perfect indicative of the verb 'habere' ('have') in
Latin is the origin of the conditional auxiliary in Romanian. Although this is a detailed
and exhaustive study, the fact that it involves so many hypothetical stages renders it
less than authoritative and convincing.

439   Subjunctive complements in Rumanian.
Donka F. Farkas.   In: *Papers from the XIIth Linguistic Symposium
on Romance Languages*.   Edited by Philip Baldi.   Amsterdam;
Philadelphia: John Benjamins, 1984, p. 355-72. (Amsterdam Studies in
the History of Linguistic Science. Series IV: Current Issues in
Linguistics, no. 26).
This study questions whether subjunctive complements in Romanian have anything in
common besides the mood of the verb. In Romanian, like the other Romance
languages, the subjunctive is used in complement clauses and takes over the function
of the infinitive. In a comprehensive study of the morpho-syntactic problems relating
to the subjunctive, the author argues that the 'Romance side' of the Romanian
subjunctive is connected to 'intentionality' whereas the Balkan side is connected to
'dependent time and subject reference', and that the distinction between the finite and
non-finite clauses in Romanian is a matter of degree and not a matter of morphology.

440   Rumanian.
Graham Mallinson.   London; Sydney; Dover, New Hampshire: Croom
Helm, 1986. 371p. (Croom Helm Descriptive Grammars).
An examination of a number of syntactic, morphological and phonological issues
relating to the Romanian language. The aim of the book is to explore the innovation as
well as the conservatism which is apparent in today's Romanian. To this end, attention
is paid to influences from other languages, especially French, since it has been
estimated that thirty-eight per cent of Romanian vocabulary is now French-based.
Mallinson's conclusion is that because of these many borrowings the specifically
Balkan features of the Romanian language are in decline.

441   **From staging strategies to syntax: clitic copying and prepositional direct objects in Romanian.**
Maria Manoliu-Manea.   In: *Historical Linguistics. Papers from the 9th International Conference on Historical Linguistics, Rutgers University, 14-18 August 1989.* Edited by Henk Aertsen, Robert J. Jeffers. Amsterdam; Philadelphia: John Benjamins, 1993, p. 297-312. bibliog.
The author of this paper amasses evidence to support the hypothesis that the fortune of clitics (words pronounced with so little emphasis that they form part of the preceding or antecedent word) in contemporary Romanian has been determined by socio-historical conditions which favoured the standardization of oral features. A further detailed linguistic study by the same author is 'Genetic congruence versus areal convergence: the misfortune of Latin AD in Romanian' in *Historical Linguistics 1993. Selected papers from the 11th International Conference on Historical Linguistics, Los Angeles, 16-20 August 1993*, edited by Henning Andersen (Amsterdam; Philadelphia: John Benjamins, 1995, p. 269-81. [Amsterdam Studies in the History of Linguistic Science. Series IV: Current Issues in Linguistics, no. 124]).

442   **An a-position for Romanian subjects.**
Virginia Motapanyane.   *Linguistic Inquiry*, vol. 25, no. 4 (Fall 1994), p. 729-34.
In this paper the author examines word-order in Romanian. Although Romanian can display both Subject, Verb, Object and Verb, Subject, Object word-orders, the author questions the theory that there is a single preverbal position in which dislocated phrases of all categories, such as Adverb, Preposition or Prepositional Phrases, are found in a-position. Another detailed and well-documented study on the subject of word-order is John Myhill, 'The two VS constructions in Rumanian', *Linguistics*, vol. 24, no. 2 (1986), p. 331-50.

443   **Outline history of the Romanian language.**
Alexandru Niculescu, translated by Andrei Bantaș.   Padua, Italy: Unipress, 1990. 239p. maps. bibliog.
This is an ambitious study which, drawing upon much of the secondary literature on the subject, examines the evolution of the Romanian language from its early Dacian and Roman origins to the present day. The book, which is a reprint of a 1981 edition published in Bucharest, also includes four major appendices comprising articles and papers previously delivered at conferences, all of which deal with the Latin element in Modern Romanian.

444   **Covert semantic and morphophonemic categories in the Romanian gender system.**
Jan-Louis Perkowski, Emil Vrabie.   *Slavic and East European Journal*, vol. 30, no. 1 (Spring 1986), p. 54-67.
Offers a simplified rule for distinguishing inanimate masculine nouns in Romanian. Arguing that the many so-called exceptions can be codified, the author divides them into ten broad categories grouped according to their semantic and morphophonemic function: those expressing bilaterality, anatomy, compacted spheroidal units, celestial entities, microparticles, implanted and hanging verticality, units of measure, names of letters, organized objects of the same kind and flour products.

445 **The historical development of Rumanian /i/.**
Peter R. Petrucci. In: *Contemporary research in Romance Linguistics: papers from 22nd Linguistic Symposium on Romance Languages. El Paso/ Cd. Juárez, February 1992.* Edited by Jon Amastae, Grant Goodall, Mario Montalbetti, Marianne Phinney. Amsterdam; Philadelphia: John Benjamins, 1995, p. 167-76. (Amsterdam Studies in the History of Linguistic Science. Series IV: Current Issues in Linguistics, no. 123).

In this paper a plethora of examples are employed in order to illustrate that the Romanian /i/ (e.g. *'cînd'* = 'when', *'rîu'* = 'river', etc.) is not a borrowing from the Slavic but instead can be taken as a segment which developed internally within the language itself. This question is not purely of academic interest because 'î' has been at the centre of all recent orthographic reforms in Romania. Usually it has been seen as of Slavic origin whilst the similar 'â' is said to have derived from Latin. During the Stalinist era 'î' was promoted with even the spelling of the country changed to 'Romînia' in an effort to highlight links with Slavic Russia. More recently, after the Revolution of 1989, the tide has swept in the other direction, and 'î' has now almost universally given way to 'â', with, for instance, the town of Tîrgu Jiu now being known as Târgu Jiu.

446 **Vowel nasalisation and its implementation in Romanian.**
Rodney Sampson. *Neuphilologische Mitteilungen*, vol. 90 (1989), p. 185-93.

Emphasizes that vowel evolution significantly modified by the action of nasality is not just a feature of Portuguese and French but also of Romanian, where vowels followed by a nasal consonant adopt a higher point of articulation. A later article on the same subject by this author is 'Romanian vowel nasalization and the palatal nasal /n/', *Slavonic and East European Review*, vol. 73, no. 4 (Oct. 1995), p. 601-12.

447 **Soft consonants: a comparison between Russian, Bulgarian and Rumanian.**
Roel Schuyt. In: *South Slavic and Balkan linguistics.* Edited by A. A. Barentsen, R. Sprenger, M. G. M. Tielemans. Amsterdam: Rodopi, 1982, p. 267-77. (Studies in Slavic and General Linguistics, no. 2).

The author closely examines the three languages in order to show that the suggested correlation between 'soft' and 'hard' consonants in fact only applies to Russian. In the case of Romanian this issue is discussed in reference to two main points: the consonant plus -ea construction (*leagän* = cradle) and the consonant plus 'short' final -i construction (*pomi* = trees).

448 **The concept of politeness and its formulas in the Roumanian language.**
Tatiana Slama-Cazacu. In: *The Fergusonian impact: in honor of Charles A. Ferguson on the occasion of his 65th birthday. Vol. I: from phonology to society; vol. II: Sociolinguistics and the sociology of language.* Edited by Joshua A. Fishman, André Tabouret-Keller, Michael Clyne, Bh. Krishnamurti, Mohamed Abdulaziz. Berlin: Mouton de Gruyter, 1986, p. 35-58.
This is a very interesting study of the many expressions denoting politeness to be found in Romanian. Originally verbal invocations to the deities to prevent evil befalling the interlocutor, these formulas now function as a means of creating and maintaining social relationships. Under a number of broad categories, such as 'thanking', 'greetings', 'wishes', etc., the author notes that some of the formulas can be found in other Balkan languages, primarily on account of the Turkish influence, whilst others are of Latin origins, although in modern Romanian they have adopted new meanings and forms.

449 **On the distribution of the neuter plural endings in Modern Standard Romanian (MSR).**
Emil Vrabie. *Slavic and East European Journal*, vol. 33, no. 3 (Fall 1989), p. 400-10.
This paper examines the distribution of the neuter plural endings -e and -uri in Romanian. The findings are supported by a long list of neuter nouns in the plural divided into two categories. Another article by the same author is 'New and revised Romanian etymologies', *General Linguistics*, vol. 31 (1991), p. 153-62, which deals with the etymology of Romanian words of Slavic origins.

Grammars and courses

450 **Modern Romanian.**
James E. Augerot, Florin D. Popescu. Seattle, Washington: University of Washington Press, 1971. 329p.
A practical graded manual of Romanian for English speakers. Rich in exercises and conversational drills, it is divided into two parts of sixteen lessons. There is also an appendix on pronunciation and inflexion, and an extensive Romanian-English vocabulary. It is perhaps more suitable for the class than for self tuition.

451 **Discover Romanian: an introduction to the language and culture.**
Rodica Boțoman. Columbus, Ohio: Ohio State University Press, 1995. 408p. maps.
This attractive and engaging textbook, which revolves around the adventures of two American students, Andrew and Aemilia, in Romania, is a practical and functional

means to learn Romanian in a relaxing and methodical manner. What makes this textbook particularly praiseworthy is not only the user-friendly absence of grammatical and syntactic clutter, which usually tends to impede rather than encourage the cognitive skills of the student, but also the heavy emphasis placed throughout on Romanian culture. This allows learning the language to be related to broader aspects of Romanian life. Each of the twenty units is divided into a dialogue, a cultural topic, an explanation of grammatical points together with exercises, conversation topics, and, finally, Aemilia's *'Jurnal'*, an account of her life in Romania, written in Romanian and applying the new grammar and vocabulary introduced in the unit. The textbook is accompanied by a 141-page student workbook.

452 **Colloquial Romanian.**
Dennis Deletant.   London; Boston, Massachusetts; Melbourne: Routledge & Kegan Paul, 1983. 335p.

This coursebook on the Romanian language is an effective and practical aid aimed primarily at the autodidact. The emphasis throughout is placed on everyday usage, with the author encouraging the student to experiment in speaking the language at the earliest possibility. The book is divided into twenty-five lessons, each of which contains conversations and texts in Romanian, a vocabulary, a section introducing grammatical and syntactic points and some exercises designed to reinforce the new elements introduced in each unit. The dialogues and texts are carefully selected to reflect daily life in Romania so that the student soon becomes familiar with some of the habits and customs of the country. An appendix carries a verb table, a list of the Romanian words used in the lessons, and an extensive Romanian-English vocabulary which contains words useful for both the student and the tourist. An audio cassette is also available to accompany this excellent textbook.

453 **Teach yourself Romanian: a complete course for beginners.**
Dennis Deletant, Yvonne Alexandrescu.   London; Sydney; Toronto: Hodder & Stoughton, 1992. 245p.

Another excellent guide for those who wish to learn or brush up their Romanian. Highly practical and user-friendly, it can also be used in conjunction with an accompanying audio cassette for more effective learning. The textbook is divided into twenty major units, each of which contains a contents' table, a list of key words, grammatical and syntactic information with tips on pronunciation and intonation, a dialogue and some exercises. At the back of the book the reader can find the answers to the exercises, a list of verbs and an English-Romanian and Romanian-English vocabulary.

454 **Hugo Romanian phrase book.**
Compiled by Lexus Ltd with Dennis Deletant and Yvonne Alexandrescu.   Woodbridge, England: Hugo's Language Books, Lexus, 1993. 128p.

Arranged under various headings, such as hotels, motoring, post offices and banks, this book contains a judicious selection of commonly used words and phrases. The menu guide lists nearly 400 dishes and methods of cooking or presentation, and the last section contains a 2,000 word mini-dictionary. The particular characteristics of Romanian pronunciation are illustrated in the introduction and to help the traveller throughout the book all Romanian words are 'imitated in English sound syllables'.

The word lists are also supplemented by some particularly sound and useful tips for the traveller, which range from not using street dealers to change money to avoiding 'astringent' local shampoos. This book is also available with an audio cassette in a Hugo travel pack.

455 **Le Roumain avec ou sans professeur/ Romanian with or without a teacher/ Româna cu sau fără profesor.**
Liana Pop. Cluj, Romania: Echinox, 1993. 2nd ed. 300p.
A comprehensible textbook divided into thirty-two lessons each of which include a dialogue, a short Romanian text, a word-list and a section dedicated to grammatical, syntactic and lexical explanations – which at times are expansive and rather jargonistic. At the end of the book there is an interesting selection of excerpts from Romanian newspapers, prose and poetry. The Romanian word-lists contain both English and French equivalents.

Dictionaries

456 **DEX: Dicţionarul explicativ al limbii române.** (DEX: an explicatory dictionary of the Romanian language.)
Academia Română. Institutul de Linguistică 'Iorgu Iordan'.
Bucharest: Editurii Univers Enciclopedic, 1996. 1,192p.
The second edition of this exhaustive and comprehensive one-volume monolingual lexicon is enriched with the neologisms, jargon and slang which have entered the Romanian language since the war. It is user-friendly and reliable, but unfortunately lacks a phonetic pronunciation guide.

457 **Dicţionar Englez-Român: 35,000 cuvinte.** (English-Romanian dictionary: 35,000 words.)
Andrei Bantaş. Bucharest: Editura Teora, 1996. 480p.
A comprehensive and easy-to-use dictionary with the entries clearly arranged in three columns on each page. In each case the various meanings of a word are arranged according to frequency of usage. The phonetic pronunciation of the Romanian words is provided throughout. A companion dictionary by the same author, *Dicţionar Român-Englez* (Romanian-English dictionary) (Bucharest: Editura Teora, 1993), has also been produced.

458 **NTC's Romanian and English dictionary.**
Andrei Bantaş. Lincolnwood, Illinois: NTC Publishing Group, 1995. 668p.
This bilingual dictionary which covers about 15,000 entries in each language is a reprint of an earlier 1968 edition. Apart from everyday language it also draws upon scientific, medical, literary and legal terminology. Unfortunately, although the phonetic pronunciation of the English words is given, this is not the case with the Romanian, where only meaning is indicated.

459 **Dicţionar maritim Român-Englez.** (Romanian-English maritime dictionary.)
Anton Beziris, Constantin Popa, Gheorghe Scurtu, Gheorghe Bamboi.
Bucharest: Editura Tehnică, 1985. 510p. bibliog.

A detailed and exhaustive word-list of terms, both common and technical, used in all forms of maritime activity. Only words in current usage are provided as the authors state they have made a conscious effort to avoid archaisms. The dictionary does, however, contain terms drawn from specialized fields such as cartography, hydrology and meteorology.

460 **Dicţionar Român-Aromân.** (Romanian-Aromanian dictionary.)
Apostol N. Caciuperi. Bucharest: Editura Atlas, 1996. 366p.

Although its compiler did not live long enough to see the fruit of his twenty-five-years labour, through the efforts of his widow this Romanian-Aromanian dictionary has been produced to complement its predecessor, published by Tache Papahaghi in 1963. The Aromanians, often known as Vlachs, are a people from northern Greece, southern Albania and the south of the Republic of Macedonia, who speak a Latin language similar to Romanian. Indeed, the Romanians have long considered them kin and in this dictionary the author's main interest is to show the mutual influences which have shaped the two languages. This dictionary contains 17,500 words and provides a large number of synonyms, based principally on the frequency of their usage.

461 **Dicţionar Englez-Român de verbe complexe.** (English-Romanian dictionary of complex verbs.)
Mihai Copăceanu. Iaşi, Romania: Editura Moldova, 1993. 432p. bibliog.

Intended primarily for Romanians, this dictionary nevertheless has some use for English speakers as well. Under each heading the various meanings of English verbal phrases, such as 'drop out' or 'carve up', are given in Romanian together with a passage from English literature demonstrating the usage of the construction.

462 **Dicţionar Englez-Român de expressi verbale.** (English-Romanian dictionary of verbal expressions.)
Ileana Galea, in co-operation with Irina Criveanu, Angela Ivaş, Maria Voia. Cluj, Romania: Echinox, 1991. 344p.

This informative, concise and explanatory dictionary concentrates on phrasal verbs and their meaning in English and Romaniah. Intended primarily for Romanian students learning English, the exercises provided at the back of the book would be of great help for those who wish to master the peculiarities of the English language in its application of prepositions.

463 **Dicţionar Englez-Român, 70,000 cuvinte.** (English-Romanian dictionary, 70,000 words.)
Leon Leviţchi, Andrei Bantaş. Bucharest: Editura Teora, 1992. 332p.

This large-format dictionary, which contains around 70,000 words arranged in four separate columns on each page, is the most comprehensive available for the student learning Romanian. It is easy to use, provides phonetic pronunciation for the English entries and, apart from offering the most common meaning(s) of the words, is also flexible enough to cover idiomatic expressions in both languages.

464   **Business Romanian dictionary. Romanian-English, English-Romanian.**
      Alex Macedonski.   Teddington, England: Peter Collin Publishing, 1996. 249p.

This practical and functional dictionary, covering such areas as banking, telecommunications, sales and trade, both export and import, provides a basic business vocabulary of 12,000 words. When appropriate, some legal terminology from these fields is also included. The publication of this volume was supported and partially funded by the British Government's Know How Fund.

465   **Romanian-English, English-Romanian dictionary.**
      Mihai Miroiu.   New York: Hippocrene Books, 1996. 567p.

A basic, easy to use dictionary which, alongside the meaning of each word, also provides a guide to pronunciation. However, the absence of synonyms and antonyms inevitably renders this work rather restrictive in its scope, as specialized nuances are often ignored. A simple guide to Romanian pronunciation can be found at the beginning of the book, whilst at the end there is a list of geographical names in both languages.

466   **Dicţionar Englez-Român.** (English-Romanian dictionary.)
      Irina Panovf.   Bucharest: Editura Holding Reporter, 1991. 423p.

This handy and practical dictionary provides the most common Romanian meanings for a large number of English words. Phonetic pronunciation is given throughout and at the beginning of the book there are some useful tips on English pronunciation and grammar. In the following year the publishers produced the companion volume, *Dicţionar Român-Englez* (Romanian-English dictionary) (Bucharest: Editura Holding Reporter, 1992. 462p.) by the same author.

143

Religion

467 Religion and politics: Bishop Valerian Trifa and his times.
Gerald J. Bobango.   Boulder, Colorado: East European Monographs,
distributed by Columbia University Press, 1981. 294p. (East European
Monographs, no. 92).

The author intends this to be an objective and balanced, yet critical, account of the
controversy surrounding Bishop Valerian Trifa, head of the Romanian Orthodox
Episcopate of North and South America. This chiefly revolved around accusations that
Trifa, amongst other things, had been a member of the Iron Guard and a war criminal.
Although the author seems to suggest that these charges mostly resulted from political
pressures brought by the communist régime then in power in Bucharest, the Bishop
was forced to retire and on 13 August 1984, after thirty years in the United States, he
was deported from the country.

468 The Latin-rite Roman Catholic Church of Romania.
Janice Broun.   *Religion in Communist Lands*, vol. 12, no. 2
(Summer 1984), p. 168-84.

The majority of Romania's Roman Catholics are non-Romanians, mainly Hungarians
but also, formerly, Germans. The question of the Roman Catholic Church in Romania
has thus usually been linked to the minorities issue. In this article, the author gives an
overview of the difficulties the Catholic Church faced in Romania under communism.
Somewhat surprising, despite harassment by the state, the number of Roman Catholics
actually increased over this period. According to the author this was not only due to a
general increase in the population but also because a significant number of Eastern-rite
Catholics (Uniates or Greek Catholics) preferred to join their Latin-rite counterparts
rather than be incorporated into the Romanian Orthodox Church. A reputation for
good organization coupled with an absence of corruption also, in the opinion of the
author, helped make the Catholic Church in Romania a highly respected and attractive
body.

469 Ethnicity and religion in Central and Eastern Europe.
Edited by Maria Crăciun, Ovidiu Ghitta. Cluj, Romania: University of Cluj Press, 1995. 399p.

An interesting collection of articles which were first presented at a conference in Cluj in June 1995. Amongst those written in English are: Christine Peters, 'Mural paintings, ethnicity and religious identity in Transylvania: the context for Reformation', p. 44-63; Maria Crăciun, 'Orthodox piety and the rejection of Protestant ideas in XVIth century Moldavia', p. 70-91; Graeme Murdock, 'International Calvinism, ethnic allegiance, and the Reformed Church of Transylvania in the early seventeenth century', p. 92-100; Pompiliu Teodor, 'The Romanians from Transylvania between the tradition of the eastern church, the counter Reformation and the Catholic Reformation', p. 175-86; Bogdan Murgescu, '"Phanariots" and "Pământeni". Religion and ethnicity in shaping identities in the Romanian Principalities and the Ottoman Empire', p. 196-204; Ladislau Gyémánt, 'Religious denomination and national Renaissance. The Transylvanian Romanians in the XVIIIth and XIXth centuries', p. 276-83; Mirela Luminiţa Murgescu, 'Educational goals and the priorities in the Romanian school during the XIXth century', p. 284-91; and Kevin Adamson, 'The political functions of ethnic conflict: Transylvania in Romanian politics', p. 381-98.

470 Persecution and life.
R. E. Davies. *Baptist Quarterly*, vol. 33, no. 6 (1990), p. 287-319.

Protestant sects such as the Baptists are proving increasingly popular in post-communist Romania. In this article the author surveys the often troubled history and the many travails of the Baptist Church in Romania since the foundation of its first church in the country in the 1880s.

471 Time to build bridges in Romania.
Tom Gallagher. *Studies: an Irish Quarterly Review,* vol. 81, no. 323 (Autumn 1992), p. 268-75.

A survey of the fortunes of the Uniate, also known as the Greek Catholic, Church in Romania with the emphasis falling on its recent quarrels with the Romanian Orthodox Church. Drawing upon parallel cases of friction between different Christian faiths in countries such as the Netherlands, Switzerland, Scotland and Ireland, the author suggests that if the Orthodox Church retreats with dignity from the position it was thrust into by the communists, then the sporadic clashes between the rival churches and their followers will soon be replaced by peaceful coexistence.

472 Religion and nationalism in Romania.
Trond Gilberg. In: *Religion and nationalism in Soviet and East European politics.* Edited by Pedro Ramet. Durham, North Carolina; London: Duke University Press, 1989, p. 328-51. (Duke Press Policy Studies).

After a brief historical introduction the author considers religious life in the Ceauşescu era. In particular, he highlights the dilemmas facing an ostensibly atheist régime as it embraced a nationalism imbued with Orthodox religious values.

473 **The Romanian Orthodox Church and the state.**
Keith Hitchins. In: *Religion and atheism in the USSR and Eastern Europe.* Edited by Bohdan R. Bociurkiw, John W. Strong, assisted by Jean K. Laux. Toronto: University of Toronto Press; London: Macmillan, 1975, p. 314-27.

When the Romanian Communist Party gained power in Romania, the position of the Orthodox Church *vis-à-vis* the state was totally transformed. Under the new régime the Church was made subservient to the state, and the Party preached that religion was an 'obsolete' product of the class system. The two sides eventually entered into a more balanced and harmonious relationship, largely as a result of the leadership given by Patriarch Justinian, but also because a renewed emphasis by the Party on nationalism made the Church, a traditional repository of such values, more relevant. During this period, the Romanian Orthodox Church enjoyed far greater tolerance from the Party than any other Orthodox Church in the socialist bloc. However, Hitchins cautions that this does not mean that the Church has any real independence of action. He concludes that 'this relative prosperity has largely been at the pleasure of the state' and that 'as never before in history, the Church is part of the State and is deeply dependent for its continued existence upon changes in the State's domestic priorities and the vicissitudes of its international relations'.

474 **The Romanian Greek-Catholic Church.**
Serge Keleher. *Religion, State and Society,* vol. 23, no. 1 (March 1995), p. 97-108.

This article serves as a passionate defence of the position of the Greek Catholic, also known as the Uniate, Church of Romania. The Church had been banned under communism, and, although the original 1948 prohibition was revoked soon after the 1989 Revolution, the position of the Church in Romania remains difficult. In particular, a number of contentious issues, such as the ownership of church buildings, sour relationships with the Orthodox Church which the author describes as 'abysmal'. In the hope of improving matters, he concludes by reproducing a fourteen-point proposal for reconciliation.

475 **The Lutheran Church in Romania in the aftermath of communism.**
Paul Philippi. *Religion, State and Society,* vol. 22, no. 3 (1994), p. 345-52.

The author traces the history of the Lutheran Church in Romania. Once one of the pillars of the Saxon community, it has been transformed by the mass exodus of its followers to Germany from 'a national church with a very distinctive tradition to a Diaspora church of love'. Now the approximately 30,000, mostly elderly, believers who remain, served by only fifty-five priests, face the daunting task of preserving the rich historical heritage of their church.

476   **Protestantism in Romania.**
Earl A. Pope.   In: *Protestantism and politics in Eastern Europe and
Russia. The communist and postcommunist eras.*   Edited by Sabrina
Petra Ramet.   Durham, North Carolina; London: Duke University
Press, 1992, p. 157-208. (Christianity Under Stress, no. 3).

Reviews the role of both the traditional branches of the Protestant faith in Romania,
the Lutheran, Reformed and Unitarian Churches, and the more recently arrived neo-
Protestant sects, such as the Adventists, Baptists, Christians according to the Gospel,
and the Pentecostal Church, and their relationship with the state. The chapter also
underlines the tensions that continue to exist between the Evangelical communities
and the Romanian Orthodox Church over the complex and vexed issue of proselytism.
In a country where two and a half million people are already Protestants (ten per cent
of the population) and where there is an omnipresent void after forty years of
corruption, paranoia and atomization, the Protestant faiths are increasingly presenting
a message that is seen as relevant by many Romanians.

477   **Petre Țuțea (1902-1991): the urban hermit of Romanian
spirituality.**
Alexandru Popescu.   *Religion, State and Society*, vol. 23, no. 4
(Dec. 1995), p. 319-41.

A scholarly study of the life and works of Petre Țuțea which focuses on his
intellectual and spiritual development and in particular his seminal work, *Omul: tratul
de antropologie creștină* (The human being: a treatise on Christian anthropology).
Persecuted throughout the communist era and prevented from publishing, Țuțea
nevertheless remained an influential figure in the intellectual underground, and in the
few short years between 1989 and his death, he was able to gain wider popular
recognition.

478   **The Romanian Orthodox Church.**
Alan Scarfe.   In: *Eastern Christianity and politics in the twentieth
century.*   Edited by Pedro Ramet.   Durham, North Carolina; London:
Duke University Press, 1988, p. 208-31. bibliog. (Christianity Under
Stress, no. 1).

In this chapter the author examines the relationship of the Romanian Orthodox Church
with the Catholic Church, the Iron Guard, communism and nationalism, not only from
a political but also from a philosophical point of view. The central thesis of his
argument is that the Romanian Orthodox Church should be truly representative of the
people and should break out of its tendency for submitting to Caesaropapism (the
acceptance of the supremacy of civil power in ecclesiastical affairs).

479 **The post-revolution conflict between the Orthodox and Eastern-rite Catholics in Romania.**
Fiona Tupper-Carey. In: *Towards a new community. Culture and politics in post-totalitarian Europe.* Edited by Peter J. S. Duncan, Martyn Rady. London: School of Slavonic and East European Studies, University of London; Hamburg; Münster, Germany: LIT Verlag, 1993, p. 93-100.

Suggests that as conflicts between people belonging to different political affiliations and ethnic groups escalated in Romania after the Revolution, so tensions arose between the Romanian Orthodox Church – which represents seventy-five per cent of the population – and a number of smaller religious denominations which it saw as a threat. Amongst the most significant of these other churches was the Eastern-rite Catholic Church, which is also known as the Greek Catholic or Uniate Church. In the first part of this article Tupper-Carey provides a useful history of the Church which was founded at the end of the 17th century. In its rite it follows the Orthodox faith but it also accepts the supremacy of the Pope and three points of Catholic dogma, the Latin doctrine of the Trinity, belief in Purgatory and the acceptance of unleavened bread during the communion. In the second part of the study the author deals with the frustrations and the insecurities of the Church in post-communist Romania. Long banned, it is now legal once more and is seeking to regain property and a congregation lost under communism but with few allies; since the Roman Catholics refuse to actively intervene in its support, it faces a bleak future. The author suggests that the problem can only be solved by the appointment of an impartial mediator to adjudicate between the two Churches, but this cannot be the Romanian government, which has a political stake in this dispute. This collection of papers from a conference held to celebrate the seventy-fifth anniversary of SSEES also contains an article by Dennis Deletant, 'Convergence versus divergence in Romania: the role of *Vatra Românească* (Romanian Hearth) movement in Transylvania', p. 101-20. In this he looks at the rise of *Vatra* in Romania and other manifestations of nationalism in post-communist Romania including the Greater Romania Party.

480 **World Christianity: Eastern Europe.**
Philip Walters, with a foreword by Michael Bourdeaux. Eastbourne, England: Missions Advanced Research & Communication Center (MARC), Monrovia, California, 1988. 317p. (World Christianity Series).

Drawing upon material housed at Keston College as well as other official and unofficial sources, this book offers a comprehensive and authoritative introduction to the history of Christianity in Eastern Europe. Chapter seven (p. 249-70) discusses issues relating to Romania, such as the country and its people, the status of Christianity under communism and the various churches and religious activities to be found in the country.

481 **Prophecy and propaganda in the Romanian Orthodox Patriarchate.**
Alexander F. C. Webster. *East European Quarterly,* vol. 25, no. 4 (Jan. 1992), p. 519-24.
A brief, but generally optimistic, survey of the state of the Romanian Orthodox Church after communism. The author reports on his meetings with the former régime propagandist Metropolitan Antonie Plămădeala of Ardeal, the well-known dissident priest Fr. Gheorghe Calciu-Dumitreasa and, what Webster terms, a progressive realist, the Metropolitan of Moldavia and Bucovina, Daniel Ciobotea.

Society and Social Change

General

482 What brought Romanians to revolt.
Sam Beck. *Critique of Anthropology*, vol. 11, no. 1 (1991), p. 7-31.
Investigates the factors that made the Romanian people shake off their apparent apathy and take to the streets in the December 1989 Revolution. Beck considers that the roots of the movement can be traced to the appalling living conditions engendered by Ceauşescu's policies and the prospect that unless action was taken these might continue indefinitely, with Romania left as an island of Stalinism amidst a newly liberated Eastern Europe. The importance of external influences is also evaluated, particularly news broadcasts by foreign radio stations such as Radio Free Europe and the BBC.

483 Prison conditions in Romania.
Holly Cartner. New York; Washington, DC: Human Rights Watch, 1992. 71p. (A Helsinki Watch Report).
This is a well-documented Helsinki Watch Report based on fieldwork undertaken in Romania during October and November 1991. It graphically catalogues the horrendous conditions to be found in Romanian prisons, the result of decades-long neglect amidst a collapsing economy. The author highlights not only the overcrowding and wretched conditions but also the cell-boss system by which certain prisoners, supposedly the more educated but often in reality the more assertive, are appointed to keep discipline amongst their fellow prisoners, a practice which clearly contravenes internationally accepted norms. Other practices that he encountered, which also breached international conventions, were the use of restraints such as handcuffs and leg-irons for very long periods solely as a form of punishment and the forcing of prisoners to stand for up to seventeen hours at a time in isolation for periods of ten/twenty days because they had infringed prison regulations.

484 **The Romanian communal village: an alternative to the zadruga.**
Daniel Chirot.   In: *Communal families in the Balkans: the zadruga.*
Essays by Philip E. Mosley and essays in his honor.   Edited by R. F.
Byrnes, introduction by Margaret Mead.   Notre Dame, Indiana:
University of Notre Dame Press, 1976, p. 139-59.
The Zadruga was an extended patrilineal household unit comprising a father and his
married sons and their offspring. Arising perhaps from defensive needs, it was
common in Bulgaria or Serbia, but cannot be traced in Romania. In this chapter the
author investigates the reasons for this, concluding that it seems to be linked to the
presence of communal villages, which were historically the predominant Romanian
settlement pattern.

485 **Social change in a peripheral society: the creation of a Balkan**
colony.
Daniel Chirot.   New York, San Francisco; London: Academic Press,
1976. 179p. maps. bibliog. (Studies in Social Discontinuity).
This thought-provoking study of social change in Wallachia between 1250-1917 is
based on a brilliant synthesis of Romanian- and foreign-language secondary sources.
Following Immanuel Wallerstein's core-periphery model, the author presents the
political and economic development of Wallachia as a gradual process of colonization
by the capitalist world.

486 **Economy, society and culture in contemporary Romania.**
Edited by John W. Cole.   Amherst, Massachusetts: University of
Massachusetts, 1984. 174p. (Research Report, no. 24).
This volume includes chapters by: David A. Kideckel and Sam Beck, 'Fieldwork in
Romania: political, practical and ethical aspects', p. 85-102; Regina Coussens, 'Folk
culture as a symbol in contemporary Romania', p. 129-38; and John W. Cole, 'In a
pig's eye: daily life and political economy in Southeastern Europe', p. 159-74. Earlier
John Cole and Sam Beck had edited another volume, *Ethnicity and nationalism in*
Southeastern Europe (Amsterdam: University of Amsterdam, Anthropology–
Sociology Centre, 1981. 144p. bibliog. [Papers on European and Mediterranean
Societies, no. 14]). Two papers in this volume relate directly to Romania: Katharine
Verdery, 'Ethnic relations and hierarchies of dependence in the late Habsburg Empire:
Austria, Hungary and Transylvania', p. 1-28; and Sam Beck, Marilyn McArthur,
'Romania: ethnicity, nationalism and development', p. 29-70.

487 **Incidence and duration of unemployment in Romania.**
John S. Earle, Catalin Pauna.   *European Economic Review*, vol. 40,
no. 3-5 (April 1996), p. 829-38.
Using a sample of 11,504 cases, the authors identify the socio-economic
characteristics of the registered unemployed in Romania during the current transition
period. Amongst the most vulnerable of groups are vocationally trained workers with
non-transferable skills, although the highest rate of unemployment is to be found
amongst those laid off from de-collectivized farms. The article is supported by a
number of informative statistical tables.

488 **The social structure of Eastern Europe: transition and process in Czechoslovakia, Hungary, Poland, Romania and Yugoslavia.**
Edited by Bernard L. Faber. New York; London: Praeger, 1976. 423p.

This volume contains two articles relating to Romania. In 'Cooperative farming and family change in Romania', p. 259-79, Mihail Cernea surveys the effect collectivization had on the traditional structure of peasant families during the years 1949-62. He finds that the effects varied, but that in general workers were individualized (that is, they acted more like individuals, capable of independent thought and action) once they stopped working within the bounds of the traditional social unit. In the new organizational structures the family head no longer determined work patterns, which were set by farm officials, and this inevitably brought changes in family relationships and values. In 'Ethnic minorities in Romania under socialism', p. 195-218, Trond Gilberg examines the socio-economic changes brought about by rapid industrialization and their effects on minority relations. In general, he concludes that the process did not result in cultural assimilation, although there were variations between minorities with the Jews and Gypsies, showing at least outwardly a greater tendency towards assimilation than the Hungarians and Germans. Gilberg's essay also appeared as an article in *East European Quarterly*, vol. 7, no. 4 (Winter 1973), p. 435-58.

489 **The changing Romanian village: the case of Semlac in Arad County, Romania.**
Ioan Ianos. *GeoJournal,* vol. 38, no. 2 (Feb. 1996), p. 175-79.

Romanian villages have suffered two traumatic shocks in the last half century; first, collectivization under communism; and then privatization and the reintroduction of a market economy during the recent political changes. Drawing on his findings from research in the village of Semlac, Arad, the author strikes an optimistic note as he argues that after the upheavals of the first years of the post-communist period there are signs of a growing prosperity in Romanian villages with higher incomes from agriculture benefiting the rural economy as a whole.

490 **Social change in Romania, 1860-1940: a debate on development in a European nation.**
Edited by Kenneth Jowitt. Berkeley, California: Institute of International Studies, University of California, 1978. 207p.

A collection of articles based on papers delivered at a conference on social change in Romania which highlight aspects of the relationship between economic growth and political independence. There are contributions by: Kenneth Jowitt, 'The socio-cultural bases of national dependency in peasant countries' (p. 1-30); Daniel Chirot, 'Neoliberal and social democratic theories of development: the Zeletin-Voinea debate concerning Romania's prospects in the 1920s and its contemporary importance' (p. 31-52); John Michael Montias, 'Notes on the Romanian debate on sheltered industrialization: 1860-1906' (p. 53-71); Andrew C. Janos, 'Modernization and decay in historical perspective: the case of Romania' (p. 72-116); Virgil Nemoianu, 'Variable socio-political functions of aesthetic doctrine: Lovinescu vs. Western aestheticism' (p. 174-207); Philippe C. Schmitter, 'Reflections on Mihail Manoilescu and the political consequences of delayed-dependent development on the periphery of Western Europe' (p. 117-39); and Keith Hitchins, '*Gîndirea:* nationalism in a spiritual guise' (p. 40-73).

491 **Drinking up: alcohol, class and social change in rural Romania.**
David A. Kideckel. *East European Quarterly*, vol. 18, no. 4
(Jan. 1985), p. 431-46.
Examines patterns of alcohol consumption in the Ţara Oltului region of Southern
Transylvania. The author aims to show that drinking alcohol has been transformed
into a social ritual through which drinkers seek to forge new relationships and find
meaning, identity and status. A further study in this issue on alcohol consumption,
which also touches upon Romania, is Sam Beck, 'Changing states of drinking: alcohol
use in the Balkans', *East European Quarterly*, vol. 18, no. 4 (Jan. 1985), p. 395-413.
In this Beck illustrates over-indulgence by relating the story of a funeral he attended
in Romania where the grave-digger was so drunk that he refused to come out of the
grave despite the threats and curses of the village priest.

492 **Prisons in Eastern Europe: some reflections on prison reform in
Romania.**
Roy D. King. *Howard Journal of Criminal Justice*, vol. 35, no. 3
(Aug. 1996), p. 215-31.
The author surveys changes in prison conditions in Eastern Europe since 1989 with
the emphasis on prison reform in Romania. In particular, he considers the contribution
made by two projects organized by the Netherlands Helsinki Committee and Penal
Reform International working in co-operation with the Romanian Penitentiary
Administration. The first of these was a training seminar organized for prison
governors and the second helped plan the régime for a new prison being constructed in
Bucharest.

493 **Prospects for Vrancea: a traditional mountain community in
Romania.**
Cristina E. Muica. *GeoJournal*, vol. 29, no. 1 (Jan. 1993), p. 69-82.
A study of the physical and cultural landscape of the 'republic' of Vrancea which lies
east of the subcarpathian hills in the south-west corner of Moldavia. The relative
backwardness and isolation of the region ensured that archaic community structures
were preserved even under communism. After 1989 these have been further reinforced
by a reassertion of traditional values and agricultural policies following the breaking
up of the collective farms. These changes also bring new challenges as it appears that
the best long-term chances for the region lie with tourism, small-scale service and
manufacturing industries.

494 **The family estate in an upland Carpathian village.**
Steven G. Randall. *Dialectical Anthropology*, vol. 1, no. 2 (1976),
p. 277-85.
On account of its geographical location in the Carpathian mountains and local
environmental conditions, the village of Paltin remained uncollectivized, even though
it was only a short distance from Braşov. However, this does not mean that the
introduction of socialism did not bring profound changes to the village. In this paper
the author traces some of these, showing that whilst older houses tended to be on the
hillside so as to be close to crops and away from the risk of flooding, newer ones are
situated in the valley bottom because of the need to commute to factory jobs which
have brought the relative security of wage labour.

Society and Social Change. General

495 **Muddling through in Rumania (or: why the mamaliga doesn't explode).**
Steven L. Sampson. *International Journal of Rumanian Studies*, vol. 3, no. 1-2 (1981-83), p. 165-85.

During the 1980s a question which puzzled many external observers of the Romanian scene was why the population remained so passive in the face of such hardship and suffering. A number of reasons for this phenomenon were advanced varying from the fearsome coercive apparatus deployed by the state to a political culture which stressed conformity. In this paper the author suggests that whilst both of these explanations may carry an element of truth, a further alternative is that, at least in the early 1980s, the Romanian people were somehow managing to 'muddle through'. By this the author means that they were 'confronting the unpleasant aspects of their system by going round it'. Sampson then proceeds to explain how this occured by looking at four factors: social mobility; the linkage between formal and informal systems; the diffusion of information through society; and the psychological adjustments embodied in the Romanian term *dedublarea* (duplicity). A later article which continues this innovative analysis of state and society in Romania is 'Regime and society in Rumania', *International Journal of Rumanian Studies*, vol. 4, no. 1 (1984-86), p. 41-51.

496 **Rumours in Socialist Romania.**
Steven L. Sampson. *Survey,* vol. 28, no. 4 (123) (Winter 1984), p. 142-64.

In communist Romania, and indeed until this day, the absence of credible formal news sources has meant that rumour has often been the chief form of social communication. In this excellent article, that will give food for thought to all who study modern Romania, the author argues that rumours gained such significance because they combined 'news' with expressions of 'societal anxiety and conflict'. They were a 'resurgent form of folk expression' but one used as much by intellectuals as by peasants. Examining the sociology of rumours, Sampson divides them into three catagories – pipe-dreams, bogies and wedge-drivers – illustrating these with some particularly choice examples, many of which described the antics of the Ceauşescu clan.

497 **Traditional Romanian village communities: the transition from the communal to the capitalist mode of production in the Danube region.**
Henri H. Stahl, translated by Daniel Chirot, Holley Coulter Chirot. Cambridge, England: Cambridge University Press; Paris: Editions de la Maison des Sciences de l'Homme, 1980. 227p. map.

Focusing on the village communities of Wallachia and Moldavia, this study monitors the evolution of Romanian peasant society from the 13th century to the present day. By comparing those communal villages whose population was subjected to serfdom with those which were free and had private property, the author gives a fresh interpretation of Romanian agrarian history.

Women

498 **Class, gender and fertility: contradictions of social life in contemporary Romania.**
John W. Cole, Judith A. Nydon. *East European Quarterly*, vol. 23, no. 4 (Jan. 1990), p. 469-76.
Investigates why a pronatalist policy was introduced during the Ceauşescu period and the reasons for its failure. The authors expand Janos Kornai's model of socialist economies of shortage to include labour and conclude that 'pronatalism develops as unemployment and underemployment are being eliminated, women are being brought into the work place, and state planners can predict the emergence of labor shortages and even population decline'. However, the absorption of women into the labour force is fundamentally anti-natal and this produces a conflict between productive and reproductive forces. In Romania few provisions were made for the pro-natal campaign with there being insufficient benefits for mothers, few extra health care facilities and no new schools for children. Instead, there was a continued stress on industrial growth and women, pressured by work, household and children, responded by limiting the number of the latter.

499 **Women's health and reproductive rights: the Romanian experience.**
H. P. David, A. Baban. *Patient Education and Counselling*, vol. 28, no. 3 (1996), p. 235-45.
The authors conducted in-depth interviews with fifty women aged between eighteen and fifty-five years old to discover the consequences of communist Romania's pronatalist policies which saw a ban on contraception, strict limits placed on the availability of abortions and a tax on childless couples. They found that despite the exhortations of the state most of the women had been able to retain control over their own fertility, although often at considerable personal cost and with serious risks to their health.

500 **Participation of women in the workforce: the case of Romania.**
Doina Pasca Harsanyi. In: *Family, women and employment in Central-Eastern Europe.* Edited by Barbara Łobodzińska.
Westport, Connecticut; London: Greenwood Press, 1995, p. 213-17.
(Contributions in Sociology, no. 112).
In this brief chapter the author argues that whilst the communists might have officially declared equality between women and men, in fact 'gender roles remained largely unchanged and unchallenged'. Indeed, the post-communist transition only seems to be confirming stereotypes because a pattern has emerged of greater redundancies amongst the female rather than the male workforce, with the effect that women are once more being pushed back into the home.

501   **The politics of reproduction in Ceauşescu's Romania: a case study in political culture.**
Gail Kligman. *East European Politics and Societies*, vol. 6, no. 3 (1992), p. 364-418.

This article highlights the consequences of the Ceauşescu régime's pronatalist policy based on the strict anti-abortion law of 1966. The author argues that the official ban did not deter women from having an abortion, instead it only made the phenomenon invisible. However, the consequences of state interference in the private life of families was tragic. It not only led to high maternal and infant mortality rates, an AIDS epidemic, and a large number of abandoned children but also to the social atomization and the dehumanization of Romania's population. However, despite all this, Kligman states that such consequences are neither fully specific to former communist states nor to what she calls Ceauşescuism. Two other articles by the same author on this subject are 'Abortion and international adoption in post-Ceauşescu Romania', *Feminist Studies*, vol. 18, no. 2 (Summer 1992), p. 405-19, and 'Women and reproductive legislation in Romania: implications for the transition' in *Dilemmas of transition in the Soviet Union and Eastern Europe*, edited by George W. Breslauer (Berkeley, California: University of California, 1991, p. 141-66).

502   **Women, states and party in Eastern Europe.**
Edited by Sharon L. Wolchik, Alfred G. Meyer. Durham, North Carolina: Duke University Press, 1985. 453p.

This collection of essays contains four chapters relating specifically to the position of women in communist Romania: Mary Ellen Fischer, 'Women in Romanian politics: Elena Ceauşescu, pronatalism, and the promotion of women', p. 121-37; Daniel N. Nelson, 'Women in local communist politics in Romania and Poland', p. 152-67; Robert J. McIntyre, 'Demographic policy and sexual equality: value conflicts and policy appraisal in Hungary and Romania', p. 270-85; and Gail Kligman, 'The rites of women: oral poetry, ideology, and the socialization of peasant women in contemporary Romania', p. 323-43.

Society and Social Services

503 **Psychiatry under tyranny: a report on the political abuse of Romanian psychiatry during the Ceaușescu years.**
N. Adler. *Current Psychology*, vol. 12, no. 1 (Spring 1993), p. 3-17.
This is an informative report about the victimization of both psychiatrists and their patients in Ceaușescu's Romania. Either willingly or unwillingly most of the 1,000 psychiatrists practising in Romania participated in the political abuse of their profession by signing papers ordering the detention in psychiatric hospitals of dissidents or political opponents of the régime. Now with the ending of the communist era, the prime need is for legislation to be amended in order to restore the rule of law to the practice of psychiatry in Romania. The author also states that moves are being made to compensate those who were victims of psychiatric abuse and to bring their abusers to account.

504 **Romanian health and social care system for children and families: future directions in health care reform.**
Children's Health Care Collaborative Study Group. *British Medical Journal*, vol. 304, no. 6826 (Feb.1992), p. 556-59.
Drawing upon data from the reports of international agencies on the status of children in Romania, official (unpublished) statistics from the Romanian Ministry of Health and a survey conducted in 1991 of randomly selected institutions which cared for children aged between 0-3, this study provides an analytical account of the Romanian health and social care system for children. The authors then look to the future, exploring the measures the system must take to avoid the crises of the past. Vital first steps would seem to be the restructuring and modernization of the care institutions together with the creation of a new management information system.

157

505 **Developing alternatives to residential care in Romania.**
Jonathan Dickens, Julia Watts. *Adoption and Fostering*, vol. 20, no. 3 (Autumn 1996), p. 8-13.

The authors, who have both worked for the Romanian Orphanage Trust in Timișoara and Iași, discuss the activities of the British-based Trust since its foundation in March 1990. They trace a tendency for the Trust to move from the direct provision and management of institutions to encouraging and supporting Romanian based initiatives. Despite the high number of children who remain in institutional care – some 42,000 in 1994 – and continuing poverty, the main reason for children being placed in care, they suggest that adoption and fostering should make headway in Romania in the future.

506 **Acquired immunodeficiency syndrome in Romania.**
Bradley S Hersh, Florin Popovici, Roxana C. Apetrei, Laurentiu Zolotusca, Nicolae Beldescu (et al.). *The Lancet,* vol. 338, no. 8768 (Sept. 1991), p. 645-49.

Prior to December 1989 only thirteen cases of AIDS had been reported in Romania but in just one year this figure was to grow to 1,168. Of these new cases 93.7 per cent were children under thirteen and, of these the vast majority were less than four years old. A little over half were children held in orphanages and other state institutions and it was the images of their suffering which were to provoke such an outpouring of sentiment in the West. Most of the children seem to have contracted the disease through unscreened blood transfusions or from the use of contaminated needles and syringes during therapeutic injections. Once the true extent of the problem became apparent a national AIDS surveillance unit was established to better define the epidemiology of AIDS in Romania and the purpose of this paper is to describe both the work of this organization and the nature of the AIDS cases reported.

507 **Developing a child care management training course in Romania.**
Malcom Hill, Anne Cairns-Smith. *Social Work in Europe*, vol. 2, no. 1 (1995), p. 20-27.

After a brief overview of child care provisions in Romania, the authors consider in detail a training scheme established in Scotland for the Romanian staff of *Pentru Copiii Nostri* (For Our Children), an organization funded by the Romanian Orphanage Trust.

508 **Reproductive health in Romania: reversing the Ceaușescu legacy.**
Charlotte Hord, Henry P. David, France Donnay, Merill Wolf. *Studies in Family Planning*, vol. 22, no. 4 (July-Aug. 1991), p. 231-40.

Under Ceaușescu, with abortion restricted and modern forms of contraception virtually unavailable, Romania had the highest rate of maternal mortality in Europe with 159 deaths per 100,000 live births in 1989 – 87 per cent of these because of abortions. After 1989 the figure dropped to 83 per 100,000, and in this article the authors review the changes that contributed to this improvement. However, whilst noting the improvement in contraceptive and abortion services, they also suggest that further advances in reproductive healthcare are still needed. The conclusion highlights a number of important lessons which can be learned from the Romanian experience.

509 **Foster care and adoption policy in Romania: suggestions for international intervention.**

Alice K. Johnson, Richard L. Edwards, Hildegard Puwak. *Child Welfare*, vol. 72, no. 5 (Sept.-Oct. 1993), p. 489-506.

Under communism institutionalization remained the norm for abandoned children and in this article the authors first look at the macroeconomic policies which led to the placing of such large numbers of Romanian children in care – a figure of 100,000 is cited in this article. After 1989 a new adoption law opened up the possibility of family foster care as an alternative, although to prevent a trade in babies from developing the law actually forbids private adoption, stipulating that it can only occur through an adoption agency recognized by the Romanian government. Following cases in the United States, where a number of children adopted after the Revolution have developed health problems, the authors challenge international adoption agencies involved in Romania to be more vigorous in the future in their examination of the health of those children who might be adopted, especially given the prevalence of HIV infection in the country.

510 **Contraception and abortion in Romania.**

Brooke R. Johnson, Mihai Horga, Laurentia Andronache. *The Lancet*, vol. 341, no. 8849 (April 1993), p. 875-78.

Seeking the views of Romanian women on the twin topics of contraception and abortion, the authors conducted in-depth interviews with 1,080 respondents in Bucharest, Moldavia and Transylvania between November 1991 and April 1992. Within these interviews the women revealed a clear preference for modern contraception methods over abortion. However, due to the pronatalist campaign of the Ceauşescus contraception had previously been virtually unavailable and many of the women had in the past been forced to resort to abortions – forty-seven per cent had previously had legal and twenty-five per cent illegal abortions. This high level of abortion has in turn bred a remarkably casual attitude towards the termination of pregnancies, leading one gynaecologist to state 'between going to the hairdressers and going to·the manicurist, they are having abortions'. Negative perceptions of contraception were also frequently encountered by the authors either because of the poor quality of previously available products or due to a hangover from the pronatalist rhetoric of campaigns of the past. Popular superstitions also hold that sterilization causes madness. The authors highlight the need for more information on contraceptive methods and for greater education and counselling. The same authors later produced another paper on this topic using this data: 'Women's perspectives on abortion in Romania', *Social Science and Medicine*, vol. 42, no. 4 (1996), p. 521-30.

511 **Health-care and nursing in Romania.**

C. K. Lakey, P. K. Nicholas, K. A. Wolf, J. D. Leuner. *Journal of Advanced Nursing*, vol. 23, no. 5 (1996), p. 1,045-49.

Like so much else in Romania, 1989 found healthcare in a state of crisis. In this article the authors investigate the main factors which led to that crisis and the steps being taken by the Ministry of Health to remedy matters.

512 **Romanian babies: robbery or rescue?**
Vivien Pullar. Wellington: Daphne Brasell Associates, 1991. 140p. bibliog.

In the aftermath of the Revolution few images from Romania made more impact than the pictures of suffering that emerged from institutions housing Romanian children. In the West many couples finding it increasingly difficult to locate babies to adopt in their own countries saw in these disturbing pictures not only a chance to help children in real need but also an answer to their own personal prayers. In the post-Revolution anarchy which gripped Romania, large numbers of babies were passing out of the country to new homes in the West. However, in Romania, where deep suspicions were rarely far from the surface after years of communist isolation, the actions of these putative foster parents were often seen in a less benevolent light and soon allegations of baby trafficking arose amidst a feeling that Romania was being plundered like some Third World country. If the issue was sometime emotive in Romania, it was often doubly so in the country of the adoptive parents as is revealed in this book which traces the fortunes of two New Zealanders, Andrew and Helen Gardyne, in their eventually successful attempts to adopt Dana, a six-year-old part-African girl from a Bucharest institution. Their struggles, often carried out in the spotlight of media attention, were not just with Romanian bureaucrats but also increasingly with their New Zealand counterparts who regarded adoption from abroad as the last possible option and who did their utmost to dissuade it.

513 **Children of the nightmare.**
Diana Reich. *Adoption and Fostering*, vol. 14, no. 3 (1990), p. 9-14.

The author, who is of Romanian extraction, estimates that in 1989 there were some 104,000 children aged 0-18 housed in institutions in Romania. At the time of the Revolution there were incorrectly termed by the Western press as orphanages. In fact, only about two to three per cent of the children were actual orphans with the rest having been sent to the homes by their parents, usually because of poverty or marital breakdown. Nevertheless, many Western couples tried to adopt children, although the process was fraught with difficulties, partly due to the number of records that had to be checked to identify parents, whose permission had to be gained. In surveying these developments, the author questions whether international adoption should be encouraged and argues that, if it does occur, then special attention should be paid to maintaining links with the child's country of origin.

514 **Who needs social protection in Eastern Europe?: a constrained empirical analysis of Romania.**
Richard Rose. Glasgow, Scotland: Centre for the Study of Public Policy, University of Strathclyde, 1992. 64p. bibliog. (Studies in Public Policy, no. 202).

In post-communist Eastern Europe, virtually the whole population faces some degree of economic hardship. In the transition some are more at risk than others and given the budgetary constraints faced by all the governments of the region, it is important that the resources available for social protection are targeted at the most vulnerable groups. However, the lack of reliable data and especially the size of the secondary or 'grey' economy makes it extremely difficult for such groups to be accurately identified. Instead, in this study the author suggests that the emphasis should be placed on macroeconomic strategies that boost national and, therefore, household income, noting that 'when definitions of need identify the majority of the population as requiring social protection, the less relevant becomes programmes targeted at individuals and families'. Throughout this study the author's findings are backed by a large amount of statistical data.

515   **The impact of recent policy changes on fertility, abortion and contraceptive use in Romania.**
Florina Serbanescu, Leo Morris, Paul Stupp, Alin Stanescu.   *Studies in Family Planning*, vol. 26, no. 2 (March-April 1995), p. 76-87.

The authors draw upon a 1993 survey of 4,861 Romanian women to study the impact of policy changes on fertility, abortion and contraceptive use before and after the Revolution. They find that abortion levels have doubled since 1989 and that contraceptive use has increased by twenty per cent. However, a lack of resources, limited sex education and mistrust of modern methods means that the rate of unintended pregnancies is still high, although the total fertility rate has dropped below the replacement level.

516   **Sophie's journey: the story of an aid worker in Romania.**
Sophie Thurnham.   London: Warner Books, 1994. 244p.

A heart-breaking tale which resonates with both the beauty and ugliness of human nature. The author first travelled to Romania to see the country as it slowly emerged from the trauma of the Ceaşescu régime. However, after three months her travels came to an abrupt end when, following a visit to Yonashen children's home, she felt compelled to stay and help care for the destitute children. She was to stay at Yonashen for over a year working with a group of volunteers to bring some comfort and order not only to the chaos of the children's home but also to the nearby adult institution called Podriga. Thurnham describes her life in Romania as a constant battle against a non-functioning system manned by unqualified and lazy workers who did little with the few inadequate resources they had.

Politics

Communist period

517 **How can one be a Romanian? Modern Romanian culture and the West.**
Matei Calinescu. *Southeastern Europe*, vol. 10, no. 1 (1983),
p. 25-36.

The question in the title comes from Cioran's provocative essay, 'A little theory of Destiny' in *The temptation to exist* (London; New York: Quartet, 1987. 222p.). The principal theme of the author is the ambiguity of cultural modernization in Romania. This article is also significant because it marked the first use in Western literature of the term 'protochronist' which came to be applied to the small group of intellectuals in late Ceaușescu Romania who advocated the pseudo-supremacy of Romanian (Dacian) thinking in all fields from political economy to philosophy and who argued that a strong indigenous culture could only grow in isolation from contaminating foreign values.

518 **The origins of Stalinism: from Leninist revolution to Stalinist society.**
Pavel Câmpeanu, translated by Michel Vale. Armonk, New York;
London: M. E. Sharpe, 1986. 184p.

Despite the so-called Romanian deviation from Soviet norms, which was mostly evident in foreign policy, Marxist intellectuals in Romania wrote few original works of analysis. An exception to this rule were three stimulating volumes produced by Pavel Câmpeanu, who had previously been a researcher at the Party's Academy in Bucharest. This is the first volume in the series. The others, all translated by Michel Vale, are *The genesis of the Stalinist social order* (Armonk, New York; London: M. E. Sharpe, 1988. 165p.) and *Exit: towards post-Stalinism* (Armonk, New York; London: M. E. Sharpe, 1990. 169p.). Earlier some of the principle theses behind Câmpeanu's analysis had been published under the pseudonym Felipe García Casals in a book translated from the French by Guy Daniels and with a foreword by Alfred G. Meyer, *The syncretic society* (Armonk, New York: M. E. Sharpe, 1980. 90p.).

519 **The political economy of Romanian socialism.**
William E. Crowther.   New York; Westport, Connecticut; London:
Praeger, 1988. 205p. bibliog.

An excellent study of the political development of Romania from the inception of communist rule until the early 1980s. The author's main thesis is that communism in the country can only be fully understood through reference to the historical development of Romanian society and politics, particularly as regards nationalism and authoritarianism – 'the synthesis of Leninist Party organization and Romania's endogenous political legacy transformed the regime's original Marxist ideology and shaped its political strategy'. Earlier the author presented some of his findings in 'Romanian politics and the international economy', *Orbis*, vol. 28, no. 3 (Fall 1984), p. 553-74.

520 **Socialism in one family.**
René de Flers.   *Survey,* vol. 28, no. 4 (123) (Winter 1984), p. 165-74.

A constant allegation during the 1980s was that power in Romania had become increasingly concentrated in the hands of the Ceauşescu dynasty which, according to rumour, had grown to embrace much of the top leadership through marriage. In this article the author presents biographies of the chief members of the family and in an objective fashion assesses the evidence that others within the leadership were related to the Ceauşescus. He concludes that many of those who were said to have family links, including Manea Manescu, Ilie Verdeţ, Cornel Burtica and Ion Ioniţa, in fact had no such ties with the ruling couple.

521 **Rewriting the past: trends in contemporary Romanian historiography.**
Dennis Deletant.   *Ethnic and Racial Studies*, vol. 14, no. 1 (Jan. 1991), p. 64-86.

The Daco-Roman continuity theory, which lies at the heart of theories of Romanian ethnogenesis, holds that the modern Romanians are descended from both the Roman conquerors and the indigenous local population of Dacia. In Romanian historiography the relative importance ascribed to the Romans and the Dacians as the progenitors of the nation has varied over the years and in this article the author examines their fortunes during the communist era. In particular he assess the changes during the last years of the Ceauşescu régime when there was a renewed emphasis on the Dacian past. He suggests that this change was associated with Nicolae Ceauşescu's brother, Ilie, and that it was primarily designed to give added legitimacy to the ruling régime.

522 **Why Romania could not avoid bloodshed.**
Jonathan Eyal, with a preface by Vaclav Havel.   In: *Spring in winter: the 1989 revolutions.*   Edited by Gwyn Prins.   Manchester, England; New York: Manchester University Press, 1990, p. 139-60.

Eyal first surveys the last years of the Ceauşescu régime and its disastrous effects on Romanian society. Turning to the Revolution he argues that it returned Romania to 1945 and reopened the country's historical wounds. He considers that the events were a revolution, as they achieved a redistribution of power, although by its autocratic nature the National Salvation Front régime that arose all too readily conformed with the past traditions of Romania. The author offers a similar analysis in the chapter entitled 'Romania: when communism gives way to communism' (p. 11-41) in his book, *Vicious circles: security in the Balkans* (London: Royal United Services Institute for Defence Studies, 1992. 108p. bibliog. [Whitehall Papers Series, no. 15]).

523 **Nicolae Ceauşescu: a study in political leadership.**
Mary Ellen Fischer. Boulder, Colorado; London: Lynne Rienner, 1989. 325p. bibliog.

Ironically this, the most thorough academic study of Nicolae Ceauşescu and his régime, was published in the very year of the Romanian dictator's demise, although this in no way detracts from its considerable value. In searching for an explanation for the deformities of the late Ceauşescu years, the author suggests they arose because Ceauşescu was so successful in manipulating the political system that he removed all opposition. As the centre of power narrowed to Ceauşescu, his wife and a few sycophants, he was effectively allowed to do as he pleased – hence the grotesque extremities of the cult and the thoughtless destruction of the centre of Bucharest. This is not a conventional biography in that it is not chronologically arranged. Concerned mostly with the years prior to the 1980s the focus is on the strategy of leadership and political control adopted by Ceauşescu together with his role as a political leader and public figure.

524 **Politics, history and nationalism: the origins of Romania's socialist personality cult.**
Vlad Georgescu. In: *The cult of power: dictators in the twentieth century*. Edited by Joseph Held. Boulder, Colorado: East European Monographs, distributed by Columbia University Press, 1983, p. 129-42. (East European Monographs, no. 140).

Explores the approach to leadership adopted by earlier Romanian rulers, including the boyars, in an effort to shed some light on the personality cult of Nicolae Ceauşescu. In his analysis the author not only emphasizes historical patterns but also trends within Romanian political culture which lead towards conformity. Taking Ceauşescu as his model, Georgescu then draws some conclusions about communist régimes in general, suggesting that they have a propensity to be breeding grounds for personality cults built around uncharismatic dictators.

525 **Romania: 40 years (1944-1984).**
Edited by Vlad Georgescu, with a foreword by Eugen Weber. New York; Philadelphia; Eastbourne, England; Toronto; Hong Kong; Tokyo; Sydney: Praeger, Center for Strategic and International Studies, Georgetown University, Washington, DC, 1985. 92p. (The Washington Papers, no. 115).

A collection of perceptive analyses of the conditions in Romania in the early 1980s written by experts from Radio Free Europe at a time when the full enormity of the Romanian tragedy was just becoming evident to the world. After an introduction by the editor the other chapters are: Serban Orescu, 'Multilaterally developed Romania: an overview', p. 12-32; Paul Grafton, 'Romania's socialist agriculture: the balance sheet', p. 33-39; George Ciorănescu, 'Romania and its allies', p. 40-59; Nestor Ratesh, 'The American connection', p. 61-78; and Simona Schwerthoeffer, 'The nationalities policy: theory and practice', p. 79-92.

526 **Nationalism and communism in Romania: the rise and fall of Ceausescu's personal dictatorship.**
Trond Gilberg. Boulder, Colorado; San Francisco; Oxford: Westview Press, 1990. 289p. bibliog.
This volume provides a comprehensive survey of Ceauşescu's Romania. The author argues that the path of Romanian development from 1965 to 1989 was determined by a curious mixture of traditional Romanian nationalism, orthodox Marxism and the personal values of Ceauşescu. These merged to produce a political system which, although it shared many of the attributes of other Eastern European states, also had its own peculiarities. In this volume Gilberg looks at the roots of this ideology, the means by which it was implemented (the Party), and its effects, both inside the country and in the world at large. He concludes by tracing the collapse of the Ceauşescu régime.

527 **Romania: democracy and the intellectuals.**
Doina Harsanyi, Nicolae Harsanyi. *East European Quarterly*, vol. 27, no. 2 (June 1993), p. 243-60.
A hostile and highly critical study of the role intellectuals have played in modern Romanian politics. The authors argue that they succumbed too readily to their own diagnosis of fatalism in the Romanian psyche and fell into a 'political torpor', especially during the late Ceauşescu years, when a more open oppositional stance would have reaped greater rewards. The questionable nature of this analysis, which overlooks the bravery of many Romanian intellectuals, some of whom the authors grudgingly admit did suffer 'slight harassment' at the time, is further underlined by the faulty comparison made with the confrontational stance adopted by the German authors who formed the *Aktionsgruppe Banat*. By publishing their work in West Germany the members of this group secured a degree of protection through international publicity which would have been impossible for most Romanian authors, and yet, by the mid-1980s, nearly all the more prominent members of the group had still been forced to emigrate. Although the authors' accusations that Romanian intellectuals were guilty of élitism and standing aloof from the realities of society are not without foundation, it can also be argued that by adopting such a stance the intellectuals were effectively propagating an alternative set of values to the prevailing peasant nihilism of the later Ceauşescu years.

528 **Revolutionary breakthrough and national development: the case of Romania, 1944-1965.**
Kenneth Jowitt. Berkeley, California: University of California Press, 1971. 371p. bibliog.
The author offers a challenging and innovative analysis of communist Romania in which he places emphasis on the concept of 'revolutionary breakthrough'. The aim of this process is the complete transformation of societal structures and values to remove alternative centres of power, 'breakthrough' being conditioned by the Party's achievement of absolute power, industrialization and collectivization. These ideas were further developed by Jowitt in a book which, although it is not specifically concerned with Romania, still draws largely on the Romanian experience: *The*

Leninist response to national dependency (Berkeley, California: Institute of International Studies, University of California, 1978. 85p. [Research Series, no. 37]).

529 **A history of the Romanian Communist Party.**
Robert R. King. Stanford, California: Stanford University Press, Hoover Institution Press, 1980. 190p. bibliog. (Histories of the Ruling Communist Parties).

As assistant director of research and senior analyst for Romania at Radio Free Europe, the author amassed a detailed knowledge of Romanian political affairs which he ably demonstrates in this well-written study. Relying extensively on Romanian sources, he charts the political and organizational development of the Party from its accession to power in 1944 to its increasing identification with Romanian nationalism during the late 1960s. The Party's exploration of the limits of Soviet indulgence, first under Gheorghiu-Dej, and later under Ceauşescu, enabled it to increase its popular support in Romania but, as the author notes, in the late 1970s the onset of economic problems was already beginning to tarnish its image.

530 **Democratic centralism in Romania: a study of local communist politics.**
Daniel N. Nelson. Boulder, Colorado: East European Monographs, distributed by Columbia University Press, 1980. 186p. bibliog. (East European Monographs, no. 9).

This book looks at the relationship between political and economic change in communist Romania. For his research the author studied local party élites and their relationship with the central authorities in four Romanian counties: Braşov, Cluj, Iaşi and Timiş. Generally, he found that despite a high level of centralization, the process of 'modernization' in Romania was not a uniform phenomenon. It tended to be most pronounced in those counties in which the local élites emphasized socio-cultural issues whereas in those counties where political and economic issues predominated, change was more muted.

531 **Romania in the 1980s.**
Edited by Daniel N. Nelson. Boulder, Colorado: Westview, 1981. 313p.

A collection of articles by a group of leading American specialists on Romania which has proved more long-lasting than the strict chronological bounds set by the title might suggest. The book is divided into three sections: 'The setting of Romanian communism', which includes amongst others papers by Stephen Fischer-Galati, 'Romania's development as a communist state' (p. 4-16), and by Paul A. Shapiro, 'Romania's past as challenge for the future: a developmental approach to interwar politics' (p. 17-67); 'Leaders and citizens in Romanian politics', which includes John W. Cole, 'Family, farm and factory: rural workers in contemporary Romania' (p. 71-116), Mary Ellen Fischer, 'Idol or leader? The origins and future of the Ceauşescu cult' (p. 117-41), Trond Gilberg, 'Political socialization in Romania: prospects and performance' (p. 142-73) and Daniel N. Nelson, 'Workers in a workers state' (p. 174-97); and finally a section entitled 'Foreign policy and economic policies', which includes Walter M. Bacon Jnr., 'Romanian military policy in the 1980s' (p. 202-18), Ronald H. Linden, 'Romanian foreign policy in the 1980s' (p. 219-53) and Marvin R. Jackson, 'Perspectives on Romania's economic development in the 1980s' (p. 254-305).

532 **Romanian politics in the Ceauşescu era.**
Daniel N. Nelson. New York: London, Paris, Tokyo; Montreux,
Switzerland; Melbourne: Gordon and Breach, 1988. 244p. bibliog.

An important collection of essays on the politics of communist Romania in which the author tackles questions relating to the nature of élite-mass relations, the structure of local politics and the focus of Romanian defence policy. Although all the chapters had been revised for publication in this volume, many had already appeared elsewhere. These previously published papers, together with their place of original publication, included: 'Worker-Party conflict in Romania', *Problems of Communism,* vol. 30 (Sept.-Oct. 1981), p. 40-49; 'Development and participation in communist systems: the case of Romania', in *Political participation in communist systems,* edited by Donald Schulz, Jan Adams (New York: Pergamon, 1981, p. 234-58); 'The politics of trade unions in Romania', in *Trade unions in the communist states,* edited by Alex Pravda, Blair Ruble (New York: Allen & Unwin, 1986, p. 107-23); 'An overview of survey research in Romania', in *Survey research and public attitudes in communist Europe,* edited by William Walsh (New York: Pergamon, 1981, p. 436-81); 'Issues in local communist politics: the Romanian case', *Western Political Quarterly,* vol. 3 (Sept. 1977), p. 384-96; 'Background characteristics of local communist elites: change vs. continuity in the Romanian case', *Polity,* vol. 3 (Spring 1978), p. 398-415; 'The national conference of the Romanian Communist Party', *The Journal of Communist Studies,* vol. 4, no. 3 (Sept. 1988), p. 331-35; and 'Women in local communist politics in Romania and Poland' in *Women, states and party in Eastern Europe* (q.v.), p. 152-67.

533 **Intellectual life under dictatorship.**
Andrei Pleşu. *Representations,* vol. 49 (Winter 1995), p. 61-71.

The author attempts to provide an answer to the question of a friend, Bruce Ackerman, Professor of Law at Yale University, as to how he survived intellectually during forty-five years of totalitarian rule. His line of argument rests on the preachings of his philosophy teacher, Constantin Noica, who said that 'for intellectual life bad conditions are good and good conditions are bad'. After a convincing exposition on his own techniques of intellectual survival, Pleşu warns the reader that in his opinion many Western scholars also run the risk of having their freedom curtailed by being scholarly without displaying what Cicero called *'curiositas nulla utilitate obiecta'* (a curiosity which is the source of disinterested knowledge).

534 **Romania: a case of 'dynastic communism'.**
New York: Freedom House, 1989. 119p. bibliog. (Perspectives on Freedom, no. 11).

This is the transcript of a wide-ranging round-table discussion about conditions in late Ceauşescu Romania organized by Freedom House. Participating were some of the most acute observers of the Romanian scene then living in the West: Mihai-Horia Botez, Andrei Brezianu, Matei Calinescu, Laszlo Hamos, Istvan Hosszu, Eugene Mihaesco, Nestor Ratesh, Gheorghe A. Sencovici, Vladimir Tismaneanu and Dorin Tudoran. The second part of the book (p. 95-113) comprises an article by Laszlo Hamos, 'Persecution of Romania's Hungarian minority'. The volume is illustrated throughout by some particularly striking and graphic images by Eugene Mihaesco depicting the plight of Romania at the time.

535 **Romania: human rights violations in the eighties.**
London: Amnesty International, 1987. 27p.
A damning report highlighting the abuse of human rights in communist Romania.
Among details provided are those concerning the confinement of prisoners of
conscience in psychiatric institutions, the number of prisoners, the location of prisons,
prison conditions and actions taken by Amnesty International in support of human
rights in Romania. An earlier report by Amnesty International is *Amnesty
International briefing: Romania* (London: Amnesty International, 1980. 19p.).

536 **The Romanian Revolution from a theoretical perspective.**
Steven D. Roper. *Communist and Post-Communist Studies,* vol. 27,
no. 4 (Dec. 1994), p. 401-10.
Investigates whether any of the major theories of revolution are applicable to the
Romanian Revolution of 1989. In conclusion, Roper argues that the events should be
judged as a revolution and that rather than searching for new theories of revolution to
explain the events of 1989 in Eastern Europe, those that exist should be further
refined.

537 **Romania: house of cards.**
Steven L. Sampson. *Telos,* vol. 79 (Spring 1989), p. 217-24.
The author paints a graphic picture of conditions in Romania in the late 1980s, as he
suggests that under Ceauşescu Romania was being 'Africanized' with life being
reduced to the bare subsistence level. With great prescience Sampson also describes
the ruling régime as a 'house of cards' which only needs one concerted push for it to
collapse. Turning to the absence of perestroika in Romania, the author argues this is
not just due to Ceauşescu's dogmatic Stalinism but also because no alternative
programme has been articulated by a society which lacked an effective internal or
even external voice.

538 **The men of the Archangel revisited: anti-Semitic formations
among communist Romania's intellectuals.**
Michael Shafir. *Studies in Comparative Communism,* vol. 16, no. 3
(Autumn 1983), p. 220-39.
The author investigates the reasons behind the publication by the Bucharest cultural
weekly *Săptămîna* of a fiercely anti-Semitic editorial 'Ideals'. He finds that it is linked
to proposals to publish the ninth volume of the collected works of Eminescu which
covers his often anti-Semitic journalistic activities between 1870-77. Another article
by the same author discussing the rise of anti-Semitism in Romania at this time is
'From Eminescu to Goga via Corneliu Vadim Tudor: a new round of anti-Semitism in
Romanian cultural life', *Soviet Jewish Affairs,* vol. 14, no. 3 (1984), p. 3-14.

539 **Romania.**
Michael Shafir. In: *Leadership and succession in the Soviet Union,
Eastern Europe and China.* Edited by Martin McCauley, Stephen
Carter. Armonk, New York: M. E. Sharpe, 1986, p. 114-35.
The author offers an informed analysis of Nicolae Ceauşescu's rise to the leadership
of Romania. Highlighting the manipulations by which he gained power, Shafir also
considers the strategies he employed to consolidate his power once he was in office.

540 **Romania: politics, economics and society.**
Michael Shafir. London: Frances Pinter; Boulder, Colorado: Lynne
Rienner, 1985. 232p. map. bibliog.
An innovative and informative political analysis of communist Romania which
contains some ideas on political culture which are still relevant to today's post-
communist society. Shafir characterizes the Ceauşescu régime as one of 'political
stagnation' where political pressures were either absent or neutralized. Political
stagnation produced political quiescence for many years but in the absence of any
'real' change, system maintenance was based on the régime's ability to defend its
position rather than on its ability to govern. As such it was primarily concerned not
with regulating the political process but directing it to ensure its own survival. This
merely served to mask the gradual disintegration of the Romanian state which was
eventually to reach such an acute state of breakdown that it was toppled in 1989 by a
relatively weak and unorganized, but numerous, oppositional grouping. Earlier Shafir
had outlined some of his ideas about Romanian political culture in 'Political culture,
intellectual dissent, and intellectual consent: the case of Romania', *Orbis*, vol. 27,
no. 2 (Summer 1983), p. 393-420.

541 **Romanian Revolution or coup d'état: a theoretical view of the
events of December 1989.**
Peter Siani-Davies. *Communist and Post-Communist Studies*, vol. 29,
no. 4 (Dec. 1996), p. 453-65.
The exact nature of the events of December 1989 in Romania has long been the
subject of intense speculation and in this article the author seeks to contribute to this
ongoing debate by considering the previously rather neglected question of whether it
can be justifiably termed a revolution from a theoretical point of view. Utilizing the
current literature on theories of revolution, Siani-Davies examines whether the events
constituted a revolution or some other form of irregular political challenge such as a
coup d'état or popular uprising. His overall conclusion is that although a revolutionary
situation arose in the country in 1989, a revolutionary outcome is not yet assured.

542 **Byzantine rites, Stalinist follies: the twilight of dynastic socialism
in Romania.**
Vladimir Tismaneanu. *Orbis*, vol. 30, no. 1 (Spring 1986), p. 65-90.
The author chronicles the tragic plight of Romania in the 1980s when he suggest the
nation was in the grip of a 'psychology of national despair'. Highlighting the
legitimacy crisis of the régime and the absurdities of the Ceauşescus' personality cult,
which had blossomed at the expense of the Party, he locates the roots of the elevation
of Nicolae, Elena and Nicu to semi-divine status in the quasi-mystic traditions of
Romania's Byzantine past. An earlier study by Tismaneanu of the nature of Romanian
communism can be found in 'The ambiguity of Romanian national communism',
Telos, no. 60 (Summer 1984), p. 65-80.

Politics. Communist period

543 **From arrogance to irrelevance: avatars of Marxism in Romania.**
Vladimir Tismaneanu. In: *The road to disillusion: from critical
Marxism to postcommunism in Eastern Europe.* Edited by Raymond
Taras. Armonk, New York; London: M. E. Sharpe, 1992, p. 135-50.
The author surveys Marxist thought in Romania from its origins in the studies of
Constantin Dobrogeanu-Gherea to the more recent work of Silviu Brucan and Pavel
Câmpeanu. Despite the ostensibly independent stance of Romanian communism, it
noticeably failed to produce a strand of critical Marxism comparable to the Budapest
School, the Praxis group of Yugoslavia or figures of the stature of Leszek Kołakowski
and Jacek Kuroń in Poland. Instead, any challenges to Marxist orthodoxy in Romania
remained restricted to the academic level. By the late 1980s, as elsewhere in Eastern
Europe, Marxism in Romania had lost all appeal. The author writes that 'In Romania
at this moment the name of Karl Marx is a subject of irreverent derision or bitter
memory' and in this article he traces the causes of this disenchantment.

544 **Miron Constantinescu or the impossible heresy.**
Vladimir Tismaneanu. *Survey,* vol. 28, no. 4 (123) (Winter 1984),
p. 175-87.
A survey of the varied career of the leading Romanian Marxist intellectual, Miron
Constantinescu (1917-74). Expelled from the Romanian Communist Party Central
Committee in 1958 for his reformist views, he was rehabilitated by Ceauşescu in 1965
and became a staunch supporter of his régime.

545 **Personal power and political crisis in Romania.**
Vladimir Tismaneanu. *Government and Opposition,* vol. 24, no. 2
(Spring 1989), p. 177-98.
Emphasizing the continuity between the régimes of Gheorghiu-Dej and Ceauşescu, the
author characterizes the latter as 'neo-Stalinist radicalism cloaked in nationalist
language'. He also makes the remarkably prescient observation that 'One of the most
likely candidates for Ceauşescu's successor is Ion Iliescu, once the President's protégé
and presumably the favourite of the Party apparatus'.

546 **From parent-state to family patriarchs: gender and nation in
contemporary Eastern Europe.**
Katherine Verdery. *East European Politics and Societies,* vol. 8,
no. 2 (Spring 1994), p. 225-55.
In this study of the interaction between gender and nationalism, the author contends
that socialism neither liberated women nor ended the nationalist discourse but that it
did reshape the relationship between the two. Although all of Eastern Europe is
covered within the paper, as might be expected from a Romanian specialist, a great
deal of the material relates to Romania and the gendered nationalist discourse within
that country. Drawing upon an extract from one of Ceauşescu's speeches, the author
demonstrates how history in Romania has long been presented as a succession of male
heroes. This conclusion is then reinforced by a passage from Ion Lăncrănjan's
nationalist polemic, *Cuvînt despre Transilvania* (A word about Transylvania)
(Bucharest: Editura Sport-Turism, 1982) in which 'male heroes burn with ardour for a
"feminized Romania"'.

547 **National ideology under socialism: identity and cultural politics in Ceauşescu's Romania.**
Katherine Verdery. Berkeley, California; Los Angeles; Oxford: University of California Press, 1991. 406p. bibliog. (Societies and Culture in East-Central Europe).
One of the most discussed features of late Ceauşescu Romania was his blending of socialism with rampant nationalism. It has been widely argued that this was little more than a cynical ploy designed to bolster the fading legitimacy of the Romanian Communist Party régime. However, in this masterly study of the intellectual life of the period, Verdery, whilst not entirely dismissing this line of thought, advances the novel idea that the strength of the nation as a 'master symbol' has been so great in Romania that it has traditionally subsumed all other discourses, including, in this case, the official Marxist-Leninist ideology. Thus, the Party did not just turn to a national ideology as a source of legitimization but '. . . to a considerable extent it was forced onto the terrain of national values (not unwillingly) under pressure from others, especially intellectuals whom it could fully engage in no other way'. Drawing on the work of Pierre Bourdieu, Verdery describes the cultural politics of the period as a struggle for different definitions of cultural value, competence and authority. Although not all intellectuals were involved in this conflict two broad groupings did emerge. On the one side there were a small group known as the protochronists, who gained the support of the régime, and on the other a wider grouping with a broader European orientation. In order to clarify her often complex ideas, Verdery goes on to discuss a number of case-studies, including the divergent visions of Horea's uprising in Romanian historiography and the interpretations given to the philosophy of Constantin Noica.

Post-communist period

548 **Romania since the Revolution.**
Mark Almond. *Government and Opposition,* vol. 25, no. 4 (1990), p. 484-96.
As much a piece of reportage as a work of contemporary history, this article offers a sketch of the first nine months of post-communist Romania. Amongst other issues the author discusses the question of whether the events of 1989 were really a popular anti-communist uprising or a carefully planned *coup d'état* by a shady group of neo-communists.

549 **Towards a civil society: the struggle over University Square in Bucharest, Romania, June 1990.**
Sam Beck. *Socialism and Democracy,* vol. 13 (May 1991), p. 135-54.
The author, on the basis of his own eye-witness observations, offers an anthropological assessment of the prolonged occupation of University Square in the centre of Bucharest by students and other opponents of the National Salvation Front. It was this demonstration that was forcibly and bloodily broken up by the miners in June

Politics. Post-communist period

1990. The author surveys the causes of the conflict between the students and the authorities and the role it played in the growth of a democratic discourse amongst the population as a whole. Assessing the occupation in terms of public space, he argues that it not only challenged the régime but also perceptions of normality amongst the wider populace.

550 **National fervor in Eastern Europe: the case of Romania.**
Pavel Câmpeanu. *Social Research*, vol. 58, no. 4 (Winter 1991), p. 804-28.
Written with a long introduction, which includes the contentious argument that the events of 1989 are 'a new conclusion to the Second World War' with 'Germany and the USSR reversing their principal historical roles', this is nevertheless an interesting work. It offers a challenging interpretation of post-1989 nationalism in Romania, arguing that the new National Salvation Front régime sought legitimacy in nationalist ideologies more consistently than its predecessors. Câmpeanu has also contributed several other studies to this journal which largely relate to Romania: 'The comfort of despair', *Social Research*, vol. 57, no. 3 (Fall 1990), p. 719-32; and with Ștefana Steriade, 'The revolution: the beginning of the transition', *Social Research*, vol. 60, no. 4 (Winter 1993), p. 615-32.

551 **Irregularities or rigging: Romania's 1992 parliamentary elections.**
Henry F. Carey. *East European Quarterly*, vol. 29, no. 1 (Spring 1995), p. 43-66.
At the onset the author states that the 'purpose of this essay is [to] present evidence of irregularities in the procedures and results of the 1992 Romanian parliamentary elections'. In support of his hypothesis he firstly draws upon the disparities between the IRSOP-INFAS exit poll and the official results. Secondly, he assesses a number of irregularities in the actual voting procedures. Amongst these he points to the inordinately high number of cancelled ballots (thirteen per cent) – an interesting table shows that this process tended to be highest in the poorest and most pro-Iliescu areas – the ability of those who were either not on the registrar or away from their homes to vote on a special list (ten per cent or 1.5 million) as well as various other 'obstacles to accountability'. The large amount of circumstantial evidence amassed leads the author to imply fraud, although he is careful to caution that 'I leave it to the reader to conclude whether the irregularities were intentional and therefore rigged'.

552 **Assessing democracy assistance: the case of Romania.**
Thomas Carothers. Washington, DC: Carnegie Endowment, 1996. 144p.
A clearly written and informative book in which the author surveys the various American-funded democratic assistance programmes which have been active in Romania since the Revolution. Until the date of publication these had spent a total of $13.5 million on projects covering fields such as: political parties, elections, the rule of law, parliament, civil society, trade unions and the media. In each case an outline of the range of assistance offered and the institutions involved is followed by an attempt to gauge the success of the various projects. Sadly, Carothers is forced to conclude that little has been achieved. Often this has been as a result of poor targeting by the Americans but elsewhere, as in the rule of law programme, bureaucratic obstruction has been chiefly to blame. The limitations of such democratic assistance programmes

are clearly visible. They cannot in themselves instigate change, but can only help sustain the pace of reform, if this is the wish of the government in power.

553 **Since the revolution: human rights in Romania.**
Holly Cartner. New York: Helsinki Watch, 1991. 68p.

Following the overthrow of the Ceaușescu régime, it was widely expected both by the Romanians themselves and the international community that, free from the shackles of communism, the country would be able to fully guarantee human rights. Sadly, in the years immediately after 1989, although the situation did improve, this was not to be the case. In this careful study the author catalogues continuing human rights violations and reveals that nearly two years after the Revolution many ordinary Romanians still lived in fear that they might again lose their recently gained and still fragile freedom.

554 **The curtain rises: rethinking culture, ideology, and the state in Eastern Europe.**
Edited by Hermine G. Desoto, David G. Anderson. Atlantic Highlands, New Jersey: Humanities Press, 1993. 341p.

Contains two chapters which are specifically concerned with Romania. In 'Once again the land: decollectivization and social conflict in rural Romania', p. 62-75, David A. Kideckel examines the impact of post-1989 changes on rural life. He suggests that the rejection of collectivization cannot solely be seen in terms of a desire for individual ownership. Instead, it is better to view it as an instant response to past wrongs and that in the long-term the peasants may not be so willing to renounce all the securities and rights that came from being a member of a collective. Sam Beck, in 'The struggle for space and the development of civil society in Romania, June 1990', p. 232-65, builds on his earlier analysis, *Towards a civil society, the struggle over University Square in Bucharest, Romania, June 1990* (q.v.) and offers a first-hand ethnographic account of the 1990 demonstrations in University Square, Bucharest. He argues that it was the lack of institutional means to structure the dissent that led to it being crushed so easily. This chapter concludes with an appendix (p. 247-62) entitled 'Oral History', in which Beck gives his own eye-witness impressions of the events and presents a compendium of interviews gathered on 5 June 1990 from demonstrators in the Square.

555 **Romania: the anguish of postcommunist politics.**
Mary Ellen Fischer. In: *Establishing democracies.* Edited by Mary Ellen Fischer. Boulder, Colorado; Oxford: Westview Press, 1996, p. 178-212.

The author examines events in Romania since 1989, with the emphasis on the period from the Revolution until the end of 1992, in an effort to assess the prospects for democratic consolidation in the country. Whilst most theorists in 1990 were generally pessimistic about Romania's chances, by 1995 they were markedly more hopeful, and the author concludes: 'Romania in 1995 was not yet a consolidated democracy, but the country had accomplished far more since 1989 than most observers could have expected'.

556 **Romania after Ceauşescu: the politics of intolerance.**
Tom Gallagher. Edinburgh: Edinburgh University Press, 1995. 267p.
map. bibliog.

Although the author deals with the whole of Romania, the real strength of this study
lies in the insight it offers into the politics of Transylvania, the region in which he
conducted most of his fieldwork. The emphasis throughout is on the abiding place of
nationalism in the Romanian political discourse. In support of his thesis Gallagher first
looks back to the interwar 'experiment' with democracy and the communist era, when
the Romanian Communist Party under Ceauşescu looked for legitimacy through
nationalism more than Marxism. Assessing the National Salvation Front's
consolidation of power after 1989, he notes their embracing of nationalism, especially
after the March 1990 inter-ethnic riots in Târgu Mureş. He argues that the authorities
played a leading role in fomenting these disturbances that ruptured the previous good
relations with neighbouring Hungary and drove the Hungarians of Transylvania into
the arms of the opposition. The remaining chapters examine the records of the ruling
National Salvation Front and the derivatives by which it was succeeded, the
opposition and the ultra-nationalist parties. Gallagher's rather bleak assessment is that
in Romania 'an agenda of limited change has been pursued by reluctant democrats
who have bowed to prevailing circumstances rather than voluntarily renouncing
authoritarian behaviour and embracing pluralism'. Earlier Gallagher had presented his
observations on the May 1990 elections in 'The disputed election of 1990',
Parliamentary Affairs, vol. 44, no. 1 (Jan. 1991), p. 79-93.

557 **Vatra Românească and resurgent nationalism in Romania.**
Tom Gallagher. *Ethnic and Racial Studies*, vol. 15, no. 4 (Oct. 1992),
p. 570-98.

Offers a good overview of the rise of the Romanian nationalist organization, *Vatra
Românească*, and its political arm, the Party of Romanian National Unity. After the
Revolution of 1989, *Vatra* sought to be the voice of Transylvanian Romanians. It
achieved some success in this task because by adopting the rhetoric of nationalism
previously used by the Ceauşescu régime, it provided a familiar set of values at a time
of great uncertainty. Indeed, as the author shows in this article, so potent was its
message that its discourse was eventually embraced by the Iliescu régime.

558 **Cultural and political trends in Romania before and after 1989.**
Andrei Marga. *East European Politics and Societies*, vol. 7, no. 1
(Winter 1993), p. 14-32.

A survey of the main intellectual groupings to be found in Romania prior to 1989. The
author identifies six categories: Particularist Marxism, which supported the cultivation
of national peculiarities within a Marxist framework; Orthodox Marxism; Revisionist
Marxism, which drew upon the works of Lukács, Marcuse and Gramsci;
Protochronism, a modified nationalism; Noicism, as taught by the followers of the
philosopher Constantin Noica; and Critical Rationalism. The author argues that 1989
brought no great changes and that many of these ideological trends continued to
feature prominently in Romania, particularly communism and nationalism. Looking to
the future he concludes with a series of propositions under the heading 'What is to be
done'.

559 **Mental stereotypes in the first years of post-totalitarian Romania.**
Ioan Mihăilescu. *Government and Opposition*, vol. 28, no. 3
(Summer 1993), p. 315-24.

Analyses of the transition in former communist countries usually focus on the process
of political and economic change but in this article the author turns his attention to
mental attitudes, as he suggests that they are the key to the slow pace of change in
post-1989 Romania. Mihăilescu argues that communism left deep mental scars and
that most Romanians are still not immune to the old stereotypes. Until these are
broken, change will remain a slow and painful process.

560 **The emergence of political pluralism in Romania.**
L. Mihut. *Communist and Post-Communist Studies*, vol. 27, no. 4
(Dec. 1994), p. 411-22.

Comparing the process of democratization in Romania to Eastern Europe as a whole
the author argues that although it may lag somewhat behind some of the other
countries, it is essentially taking the same form. In reviewing the growth of pluralism,
Mihut places particular emphasis on the elections and the adoption of a new
constitution.

561 **Correspondence from Bucharest: intellectuals as political actors in
Eastern Europe: the Romanian case.**
Alina Mungiu. *East European Politics and Societies*, vol. 10, no. 2
(Spring 1996), p. 333-64.

A searching inquiry into the role of intellectuals in contemporary Romania, both
before and after 1989. The author focuses chiefly on those intellectuals she considers
to have been anti-communists, identifying a number of groups, including
conservatives, liberals, leftists and nationalists as well as the apolitical. The basis of
these divisions lies in the postures the various groups adopted to such questions as
religion, nationalism and collaboration with the communists.

562 **Letter from Bucharest.**
Alina Mungiu, Andrei Pippidi. *Government and Opposition*, vol. 29,
no. 3 (Summer 1994), p. 348-61.

This 'letter' from Romania assesses developments in the country since the Revolution
of 1989. The authors state that just as the speed of the original overthrow of
Ceauşescu delighted the watching world, so the slowness of the changes in the four
years since the Revolution has been a disappointment. They place the blame for this
on a complex historical legacy and a post-1989 political system which too often
closely resembled the former communist régime, not only in terms of personnel.

563 **Romania.**
Daniel N. Nelson. *Electoral Studies*, vol. 9, no. 4 (Dec. 1990),
p. 355-66.

Within the context of a report on the May 1990 elections, the author offers a survey of
political developments in Romania during the first six months after the Revolution. In
a balanced and objective appraisal of the elections Nelson endorses the view that
'whilst the *campaign* was imperfect, including many incidents that endangered the

opposition's capacity to mount a nationwide effort [...] election monitors acknowledged that the 20 May vote was generally clean'. Another useful study of the election, based on the eye-witness account of an observer, is Dennis Deletant's article, 'The Romanian elections of May 1990', *Representation,* vol. 29, no. 108 (1990), p. 23-26.

564   **Romania after tyranny.**
      Edited by Daniel N. Nelson.   Boulder, Colorado: Westview Press, 1992. 311p.

This volume contains an important collection of essays on post-communist Romania by leading American and Romanian commentators. The contributions include: Mary Ellen Fischer, 'The new leaders and the opposition', p. 45-65; David A. Kideckel, 'Peasants and authority in the new Romania', p. 67-81; Trond Gilberg, 'Romanians and democratic values: socialization after communism', p. 83-94; Larry L. Watts, 'The Romanian Army in the December Revolution and beyond', p. 95-126; Petre Datculescu, 'Social change and changing public opinion in Romania after the 1990 election', p. 127-48; Mugur Isarescu, 'The prognoses for economic recovery', p. 149-65; Daniel N. Nelson, 'Post-communist insecurity and the Romanian case', p. 169-85; Walter M. Bacon, 'Security as seen from Bucharest', p. 187-202; Ronald H. Linden, 'After the revolution: a foreign policy of bounded change', p. 203-38; William Crowther, 'Romania and Moldovian political dynamics', p. 239-59; Sorin Mircea Botez, 'An alternative Romanian foreign policy', p. 261-70; Ioan Mircea Pascu, 'Romania's response to a restructured world', p. 271-84; and Daniel N. Nelson, 'Conclusion: a chance for Romania', p. 285-91.

565   **Rebuilding democracy: the OMRI annual survey of Eastern Europe and the former Soviet Union, 1995.**
      Open Media Research Institute, with an introduction by J. F. Brown.
      Armonk, New York: M. E. Sharpe, 1996. 325p.

During its brief existence, the successor to the Radio Free Europe/Radio Liberty Research Unit, OMRI, produced the highest quality research on Eastern Europe, principally in its fortnightly journal *Transition.* The section on Romania in the current volume is drawn from that publication and contains an overview of the political developments of 1995 by OMRI researchers Michael Shafir and Dan Ionescu, a profile of the leader of the Greater Romania Party, Corneliu Vadim Tudor, entitled 'A menace to genuine democracy', and a partial translation of an editorial by Andrei Pleşu from the journal *Dilema* in which he discusses the state of relations between the Greater Romania Party and the then ruling Party of Social Democracy in Romania.

566   **The challenges of transition.**
      Vladimir Pasti.   Boulder, Colorado: East European Monographs, distributed by Columbia University Press, 1997. 344p. (East European Monographs, no. 473).

The author, as Director of the Directorate for Social Reform, was an influential voice in the administration of the Party of Social Democracy in Romania which in various guises ruled Romania from the Revolution until 1996. The inside knowledge that Pasti brings from his close ties to government, together with his training as an academic sociologist, makes this a thoughtful and illuminating picture of Romania in transition. After presenting an analysis of Romanian society under communism, Pasti argues that contrary to popular perceptions the transition has in fact been a remarkably stable process in Romania as the main actors have remained the same throughout. In his analysis of events since 1989, he highlights the gap that has frequently existed between politics and reality and the general weakness of government which has failed to effectively control the reform process. Indeed, he argues that the reforms *per se* have achieved little and that the process of change has been largely carried forward by a totally unmanaged spontaneous transition. This usefulness of this important work is weakened by the poor index.

567 **The bloody flag: post-communist nationalism in Eastern Europe. Spotlight on Romania.**
Juliana Geran Pilon, with a foreword by Robert Conquest and an afterword by Vasile Popovici. New Brunswick, New Jersey; London: Social Philosophy and Policy Center, Transaction Publishers, 1992. 126p. map. bibliog.
Written in a slightly polemical vein, this study of Romanian nationalism begins with a theoretical look at the subject, which is mainly philosophical in nature, but has some historical allusions. This is followed by a survey of the wider East European context and a more detailed examination of nationalism in Romania. The book concludes with a chapter entitled 'Some notes on harmony' in which the author, drawing on the work of Ludwig von Mises, suggests some classical liberal 'solutions' to the 'problem'.

568 **Post-totalitarian pathology: notes on Romania, six years after December 1989.**
Andrei Pleşu. *Social Research,* vol. 63, no. 2 (Summer 1996), p. 559-71.
In this article, which is arranged under headings such as 'From neurasthenia to hysteria', 'Culture in transition: the garlic effect' and 'The problem of happiness', the author once again displays the political wisdom, analytical patience and empathy of one who experienced the 'illness' of communism and is still trying to come to terms with the alien 'pathological symptoms' of transition. In a sophisticated, but also down-to-earth argument, Pleşu underlines how adapted the Romanians had become to a life under dictatorship and how unprepared they were to receive democracy. However, he is also a cautious optimist who believes that the formulation of new mentalities, the recovery of democratic instincts, and the fostering of pluralistic institutions is only a matter of time and that a transitional period of confusion and 'contortion' is just a step on the road to a real democracy.

569 **The Romanian party system and the catch-all party phenomenon.**
Steven D. Roper. *East European Quarterly,* vol. 28, no. 4 (Jan. 1995), p. 519-32.
An analysis of party formation in Romania since 1989 which focuses primarily on the question of whether the Democratic Convention of Romania is able to transform itself into a 'catch-all' party which is attractive to the maximum number of voters.

570 **The inheritors: the Romanian radical right since 1989.**
Michael Shafir. *East European Jewish Affairs,* vol. 24, no. 1
(Summer 1994), p. 71-89.

The author has divided the post-communist right in Romania into those who seek
'radical continuity' – a continuation of the Ceauşescu line in foreign and internal
policy, but with a stronger emphasis on xenophobia – and those who favour 'radical
return' – a rejection of the Ceauşescu model in preference to a real return to the
prescriptions of the far right of the interwar years. Focusing on the latter group, Shafir
surveys the growth of interest in the Iron Guard in Romania since 1989 and the
fortunes of the political groupings that seek to be its heirs: the Movement for
Romania, founded in 1991 by the former student leader, Marian Munteanu; and the
Party of the National Right, led by the journalist Radu Sorescu. A further study of the
right in Romania since the Revolution by Shafir is 'The revival of the political right in
post-communist Romania' in *Democracy and right-wing politics in Eastern Europe in
the 1990s,* edited by Joseph Held (Boulder, Colorado: East European Monographs,
distributed by Columbia University Press, 1993, p. 153-74. [East European Monographs, no. 376]).

571 **Romania in transition.**
Edited by Lavinia Stan. Aldershot, England: Dartmouth, 1997. 218p.

This volume of essays is divided into two sections, one covering political aspects of
the Romanian transition from an authoritarian to a pluralist society and the other
dealing with economic aspects of the transition from a command to a free market
economy. The chapters cover a broad range of topics and the hope of the editor is that
they are 'not quickly outdated by the evolution of reform policies'. The contents
include: Robert Weiner, 'Democratization in Romania', p. 3-24; Tom Gallagher,
'Nationalism and post-communist politics: the Party of Romanian National Unity,
1990-1996', p. 25-48; Francisco Veiga, 'On the social origins of ultranationalism and
radicalism in Romania, 1989-1993', p. 49-66; Georgeta Pourchot, 'Mass media and
democracy in Romania: lessons from the past, prospects for the future', p. 67-90;
Daniel Daianu, 'Macro-economic stablization in post-communist Romania', p. 93-
126; Lavinia Stan, 'Romanian privatization program: catching up with the East',
p. 127-62; Russell Pittman, 'Competition law and policy in Romania', p. 163-82;
Dana-Nicoleta Lascu, Zafar U. Ahmed, Mircea Vatasescu, 'Application of the
marketing concept philosophy in Romania', p. 183-90; and Russell W. Belk,
'Romanian consumer desires and feelings of deservingness', p. 191-208.

572 **The quasi-revolution and its discontents: emerging political
pluralism in post-Ceauşescu Romania.**
Vladimir Tismaneanu. *East European Politics and Societies,* vol. 7,
no. 2 (Spring 1993), p. 309-48.

The author reviews contemporary Romanian politics from the late Ceauşescu years
through the Revolution to the re-emergence of pluralism. He argues that the main
source of instability in post-revolution Romania 'has been the NSF's [National
Salvation Front] hegemonic ambitions and its refusal to dismantle the Securitate
radically'.

573 **Romanian exceptionalism? Democracy, ethnocracy and uncertain pluralism in post-Ceauşescu Romania.**
Vladimir Tismaneanu. In: *Politics, power, and the struggle for democracy in South-East Europe*. Edited by Karen Dawisha, Bruce Parrott. Cambridge, England: Cambridge University Press, 1997, p. 403-51. (Democratization and Authoritarianism in Postcommunist Societies, no. 2).

Discusses the main causes of the collapse of the Ceauşescu régime and the progress of the political transition in Romania until the elections of 1996. In general, the assessment offered of recent Romanian history is largely negative. Indeed, charting what he considers were Iliescu's attempts to establish a semi-authoritarian régime, Tismaneanu raises the possibility that Romania might have proved an exception to the general rule of the countries of the region, making a successful transition to free market democracies on the Western model. Such an analysis, as the author admits, has recently been challenged by the 1996 election result, in which opposition groupings under Emil Constantinescu secured a famous victory – 'After seven years of missed opportunities, institutionalized squalor, and disgraceful plundering of national resources by those who were supposed to administer them, Romanians voted for renewal'. However, maintaining his pessimism to the end, Tismaneanu then casts doubts on the possibilities of such a renewal really occurring because of the weakness of the alliance between the two main constituents of the new ruling coalition, the Democratic Convention of Romanian and the Social Democratic Union.

574 **Faith, hope, and *Caritas* in the land of pyramids – Romania, 1990 to 1994.**
Katherine Verdery. *Comparative Studies in Society and History*, vol. 37, no. 4 (1995), p. 625-69.

In a thought-provoking article the author explores the infamous *Caritas* pyramid scheme. Based in Cluj this was established in April 1992 and lasted just over two years, until it finally collapsed in May 1994. Originally depositors were promised an eight-fold return on their investment in only three months and this proved so attractive that the author estimates that twenty per cent of Romanian households placed money in the scheme. Such an enterprise obviously had important ramifications not least because on paper it was attracting a large proportion of the Romanian gross domestic product. In this article the author discusses not only the history of the pyramid scheme, which is still shrouded in mystery, as were the origins of its founder Ion Stoica, but uses it as a vehicle to explore wider issues pertaining to the transition in Romania. A further study of *Caritas* by the same author is '"Caritas" and the reconceptionalization of money in Romania', *Anthropology Today*, vol. 11, no. 1 (Feb. 1995), p. 3-7.

575 **Nationalism and national sentiment in post-socialist Romania.**
Katherine Verdery. *Slavic Review*, vol. 52, no. 2 (Summer 1993), p. 179-203.

The author challenges the widely held thesis that post-communist nationalism is merely a revival of ancient ethnic hatreds which had long been smothered under the blanket of communism. Instead she suggests that nationalism was not so much suppressed under socialism as altered and enhanced and that this process has continued during the transition to democratic politics and a market economy. Turning to Romania, Verdery suggests that the reasons for the salience of national sentiment in the country 'lie equally in the historical and structural situation of groups in the polity, in calculations of advantage and the rhetoric that promotes them, in social construction of "self" and "person" and in people's representation of their life circumstances in which images of other social groups serve as primary symbols'.

576 **Romania after Ceauşescu: post-communist communism?**
     Katherine Verdery, Gail Kligman.   In: *Eastern Europe in revolution.*
     Edited by Ivo Banac.   Ithaca, New York; London: Cornell University
     Press, 1992, p. 117-47.

Despite the early assertion that their essay raises more questions than it answers, the authors, two of the foremost writers on the subject, provide an incisive look at post-communist Romania. They briefly consider the 'Revolution' of 1989 and the plethora of plots and conspiracy theories that surround it, the relationship of the National Salvation Front with the defunct Communist Party and the continued maintenance of structures from the former régime. A fuller analysis is then offered of the events of 13-15 June 1990 which saw the Jiu Valley miners' invasion of Bucharest. According to the authors the weakness of the government in early post-communist Romania can be largely ascribed to an ongoing power struggle within the leadership of the National Salvation Front and the temporary ungovernability of the Romanian people freed from the constraints of communism. After considering some of the many problems facing Romania during the post-communist transition, they conclude by highlighting the importance of state-society relations before tentatively suggesting some steps for the future.

577 **What was socialism, and what comes next?**
     Katherine Verdery.   Princeton, New Jersey: Princeton University
     Press, 1996. 298p.

A useful collection of recent papers and articles on post-communist society and politics in Romania augmented by a short introduction and afterword by this thoughtful and innovative commentator on the Romanian scene. All the papers have been published elsewhere except for chapter five, 'Civil society or nation? "Europe" in the symbolism of postsocialist politics' (p. 104-29), which dates from 1993 and builds on the analysis presented in *National ideology under socialism* (q.v.) and chapter eight, 'A transition from socialism to feudalism? thoughts on the postsocialist state' (p. 204-28), parts of which appeared in 'Notes towards an ethnography of a transforming state, Romania 1991' in *Articulating hidden histories, exploring the influence of Eric R. Wolf,* edited by Jane Schneider and Rayna Rapp (Berkeley, California; London: University of California Press, 1995. 400p.).

Constitution and
Legal System

578 **Parliamentary rules and judicial review in Romania.**
Stanley Bach, Susan Benda. *East European Constitutional Review*,
vol. 4, no. 3 (Summer 1995), p. 49-53.
The new post-communist institutions of Romania are still struggling to establish the
parameters of their authority, and in this article the authors examine this process with
a case-study involving the Constitutional Court and the parliament. Focusing on a
May 1994 ruling by the Constitutional Court that a large number of parliamentary
rules were unconstitutional, the authors discuss the remit of the Court and the
parliamentary response to the decision. They conclude that the parliament's
acceptance of the ruling showed a commitment to constitutional order and that the
resolve by both sides to follow the letter of the constitution bodes well for the
establishment of the rule of law in Romania.

579 **Constitution of Romania 1991.**
Bucharest: Monitorul Oficial, 1995. 2nd ed. 79p.
An English translation of the current Romanian constitution. Adopted by a Constituent
Assembly on 21 November 1991, it was passed by a popular referendum on 8
December 1991 with 77.3 per cent voting in favour on a 69.1 per cent turnout. The
legislation under which elections are contested has also been published in a number of
bilingual English-Romanian editions, such as, for instance, *Romanian legislation.*
Volume 4: political elections (Bucharest: The Parliament of Romania, 1992. 142p.).

580 **Reform of property rights and corporate governance restructuring
in Romania.**
Alberto Gabriele. *Moct-Most*, vol. 5, no. 3 (1995), p. 1-23.
This lucid and informative paper argues that despite a slow start and persisting
political, social and economic instability, the Romanian government has nevertheless
developed a fairly consistent programme of privatization. However, the author
cautions that unless a macroeconomic stability is achieved and a true free market is
established, it will be difficult to complete this programme.

181

581 **An overview of developments in Romania.**
Steven M. Glick. In: *Privatisation in Central and Eastern Europe: a collection of the papers delivered at the International Bar Association regional conference Prague, Czechoslovakia 23-26 June 1991.* Edited by Stephen A. Rayner. London: International Bar Associates, Butterworths, 1992, p. 22-35.

A brief overview of Romanian legislation on economic reform in 1990, when over sixty laws were promulgated, is followed by a translation of the draft privatization law.

582 **Romania's evolving legal framework for private sector development.**
Cheryl Williamson Gray, Rebecca J. Hanson, Peter G. Ianachkov. Washington, DC: World Bank, 1992. 27p. (Policy Research Working Papers).

The process of privatization in Romania has faced many obstacles and in this World Bank pamphlet, the authors highlight the problems posed by the lack of a legal framework in which the private sector can develop. Although the outline of such a framework has now been established, they argue that it cannot begin to function properly until the Romanians themselves accept that the laws are binding and obligatory.

583 **Exercises in cynicism and propaganda: law, legality, and foreign correspondence in Romania.**
Peter Gross. *Political Communication and Persuasion*, vol. 6, no. 3 (July 1989), p. 179-90.

The first press law for communist Romania did not appear until 1974, twenty-seven years after the Romanian Communist Party assumed power. The new law was heavily modelled on other socialist press laws, and in this angry protest at the state of journalism in communist Romania, the author calls for either its abrogation or its substantial revision. Gross warned that if the situation was allowed to continue, Romanian journalism would never begin the long and painful road towards resurrecting its standards and there would never be an opportunity for either Romanian or foreign journalists to cover stories openly.

584 **The Romanian procuratura.**
H. B. Jacobini. *East European Quarterly*, vol. 14, no. 4 (Winter 1980), p. 439-59.

The role of the *procuratura* in Romania can be compared to that of the Attorney General in England or the State's attorney in the USA. In this study the author investigates in meticulous detail the procuracy's role in criminal proceedings, its supervision of court decisions, and the actions it takes in reference to complaints against state officials.

585 **Romanian public law: some leading internal aspects.**
H. B. Jacobini. Boulder, Colorado: East European Monographs,
distributed by Columbia University Press, 1987. 187p. bibliog.
(East European Monographs, no. 223).

The definition of public law in Romania, which was still a communist country at the
time this study was written, is different from what is understood by the term in the
West, since it comprises both civil and criminal codes. This book, which surveys
aspects of Romanian public law, is divided into four major sections. A historical
introduction to the Romanian legal system is followed by expositions on the
development of Romanian legal institutions, the Romanian procuracy and Romanian
administrative law.

586 **Interview with Ion Muraru, President of the Romanian
Constitutional Court.**
Alina Mungiu Pippidi. *East European Constitutional Review*, vol. 6,
no. 1 (Winter 1997), p. 78-82.

This special edition of this journal devoted to the Constitutional Courts of Eastern
Europe contains an informative interview with Ion Muraru, Professor of Constitutional
Law at the University of Bucharest, member of the Constitutional Court since its
foundation in 1992 and, at the time of writing, its President. Within a wide-ranging
discussion the topics covered include the external model for the court (it seems that
the inspiration came from the French system), the means by which the court operates
and its remit – it can rule on the constitutionality of decrees but not on government
decisions. The interview also contains the revelation that a Constitutional Court judge
in Romania receives a salary of only $200 per month.

587 **Organs of the state in Romania.**
Daniel N. Nelson. *International and Comparative Law Quarterly*,
vol. 25, no. 3 (July 1976), p. 651-64.

Although in communist states neither constitutional nor administrative law could
really curtail the powers of the authorities, contrary to popular perception, they did
influence life outside the bounds of the Party. This article also deals with the function-
ing of the bureaucracy in a communist society.

588 **Protection of intellectual property in Central and Eastern
European countries: the legal situation in Bulgaria, CSFR,
Hungary, Poland and Romania.**
Organisation for Economic Co-operation and Development. Paris:
Organisation for Economic Co-operation and Development, 1995.
137p. (OECD Documents).

A useful overview of the laws enacted to protect intellectual property in the five ex-
communist states mentioned in the title. Section E (p. 62-72) is concerned with
Romania. It includes general remarks on the situation under Ceauşescu as well as
more detailed comments on trademark and copyright law, patent law and laws
protecting industrial designs. Two annexes offer an up-to-date (at the time of writing)
survey of post-communist changes in the law of all the countries.

589 **The role of the constitutional court in the consolidation of the rule of law: proceedings of the UniDem Seminar organized in Bucharest on 8-10 June 1994 in co-operation with the Romanian Constitutional Court with the support of the Ministry of Foreign Affairs of Romania.**
Strasbourg: Council of Europe, 1994. 149p. (Science and Technique of Democracy, no. 10).

After a number of introductory statements, including one by the then President, Ion Iliescu, this book is a record of the proceedings and decisions of a conference on constitutional reform organized by the University of Democracy (UniDem). The main topic under consideration was the activities of constitutional courts and, in particular, their role, competencies, operational guidelines, decision-making powers and relations with other courts. The final conclusions of the participants in the seminar are phrased within an understanding that a common body of European law will form a necessary precondition for an integrated Europe.

590 **Romania: organizing legislative impotence.**
Elena Stefoi-Sava. *East European Constitutional Review*, vol. 4, no. 2 (Spring 1995), p. 78-83.

In an issue of this journal devoted to the organizational dilemmas of post-communist assemblies, this article reviews the performance of Romanian's new parliament. Generally, the author finds that it has been ineffective and that this has led to growing public alienation and an erosion of the constitutional balance of power as the executive has gained at the expense of a weak legislature. The problem seems to lie with both the constitutional provisions appertaining to the parliament and the rules it adopted governing procedures. A combination of these has meant that until now there has been little co-ordination between the two chambers and that the committee system has yet to function effectively.

591 **Legal sources and bibliography of Romania.**
Virgiliu Stoicoiu. New York: Praeger, 1964. 237p.

An invaluable catalogue of selected publications, mostly in Romanian, on the corpus of laws enacted in the Danubian principalities from the 17th century to 1918, and in Romania from 1918 to 1963. Section 9 incorporates lists of the principal laws, decrees and resolutions in force in the People's Republic of Romania from 1 January 1963. Some items in English, French, German, Italian and Russian are also included.

592 **Constitutional pillars for new democracies: the cases of Bulgaria and Romania.**
Tony Verheijen. Leiden, Netherlands: DSWP Press, 1995. 238p. (Studies in Government, no. 10).

Despite the promise of the sub-title, in fact only three chapters of this study touch upon Romania. Chapter two offers a comparative survey of the post-communist transition in Romania and Bulgaria, chapter six analyses the 1991 Romanian constitution and the last chapter, the conclusion, also makes some further comments. In reviewing Romania's constitutional development, the author offers some historical parallels between the 19th century and post-1989 attempts to adopt a democratic constitution. He also argues that despite its shortcomings, the December 1991 constitution offers a clear framework for Romania's political and administrative structures without which wider democratization is impossible.

Administration and
Local Government

593 Local government and the centre in Romania and Moldova.
Adrian Campbell.   In: *Transformation from below: local power and
the political economy of post-communist transitions.*   Edited by John
Gibson, Philip Hanson.   Cheltenham, England; Brookfield, Vermont:
Edward Elgar, 1996, p. 73-112. (Studies of Communism in Transition).
The first half of this article is concerned with Romania. After reviewing the structure
of local government and the state of relations with the central authorities, the author
looks specifically at a conflict between the two which arose in the last months of 1994
and the first part of 1995. At issue was the continuing failure of the central authorities
to pass laws on local finance and municipal property, the latter being a particularly
divisive issue at a time of privatization when state holdings were being converted to
liquid assets. The author concludes that the régime was serious in its professed aim of
decentralization but only if it could 'minimize the potential of local authorities to pose
a political threat, and ... keep intact central government's machinery of co-
ordination, monitoring and control'.

594 Local government in Romania.
Adrian Campbell.   In: *Local government in Eastern Europe:
establishing democracy at the grassroots.*   Edited by Andrew
Coulson.   Aldershot, England: Edward Elgar, 1995, p. 76-101.
(Studies of Communism in Transition).
Drawing on a number of interviews with mayors and other local officials, the author
presents an overview of the development of local government structures in Romania
since 1989. He argues that although a framework for local political institutions was
soon put in place, it has yet to function properly. Chief amongst the reasons for this is
an absence of resources due to budgetary constraints, but Campbell also points to a
lack of competence at a local level due to inexperience. The situation was also
complicated at the time of writing by the fact that many of the largest cities and towns
were in the hands of the then opposition Democratic Convention of Romania which
made the ruling Democratic National Salvation Front government even more reluctant

to devolve powers. The result was that the newly elected local governments in 1992 could rarely fulfil the promises they made during the electoral campaign and this, in part, may explain the apparent popular alienation from local politics which led to a relatively low turnout at the next local elections in 1996. Further problems also arose from the fact that spheres of competence between local and national authorities remained ill-defined as did the exact status of the quasi-autonomous organizations which were the major suppliers of public services.

595 **The volatile administrative map of Rumania.**
Ronald A. Helin. *Annals of the Association of American Geographers*, vol. 57, no. 3 (Sept. 1967), p. 481-502.

The author believes that public administration lends itself to geographical as well as to political analysis and in this article he sets out to fulfil three objectives: to show, cartographically, the seven major changes that have occurred in the administrative map of Romania since the First World War; to describe the specific circumstances that triggered these territorial reforms; and to note how and to what extent the reforms have reflected the political needs of the governments responsible for their implementation as well as broader geographical and socio-economic criteria. Throughout parallels are drawn with the United Sates and the experience of local government in that country.

Defence and
Armed Forces

596 The Romanian Army.

Alex Alexiev.   In: *Communist armies in politics.*   Edited by Jonathan
R. Adelman.   Boulder, Colorado: Westview, 1982, p. 149-66.

Reviews the evolution of the Romanian army from the communist take-over to the
early 1980s. The author suggests that Romania's well-known foreign policy deviation
was matched by a military deviation from Warsaw Pact norms. In particular, the
Romanian Army seems to have been able to maintain a degree of professional
autonomy and its position as the guardian of the nation's interests. Another chapter
on this subject written by this author is 'Party-military relations in Eastern Europe: the
case of Romania' in *Soldiers, peasants and bureaucrats: civil-military relations in
communist and modernizing societies*, edited by Roman Kolkowicz and Andrzej
Korbonski (London: George Allen & Unwin, published under the auspices of the
Center for International and Strategic Affairs, University of California, Los Angeles,
1982, p. 199-227).

597 Romanian secret police.

Walter M. Bacon.   In: *Terror and communist politics: the role of the
secret police in communist states.*   Edited by Jonathan R. Adelman.
Boulder, Colorado: Westview, 1984, p. 135-54.

The author offers a brief history of the secret police in Romania from the *Siguranţa* of
the interwar period to the *Securitate* of the Ceauşescu era. He concludes that Romania
in the 1980s is a 'state in which terror has disappeared but where the institutions of
terror remain'.

598   **The military and the Party in Romania.**
Walter M. Bacon Jnr.   In: *Civil-military relations in communist systems.*   Edited by Dale R. Herspring, Ivan Volgyes.   Boulder, Colorado: Westview, 1978, p. 165-80.

Although this study is concerned with the relationship that existed between the Romanian Communist Party and the Romanian Army, the author chooses to concentrate primarily on the Army which he described as 'an articulating interest group with access to the policymaking process'. As well as areas of common interest between the two institutions, the author also discusses areas of potential conflict, arguing that it was within Romania's relationship with the USSR that the chief points of tension would arise. This chapter also appeared under the title 'Civil-military relations in Romania' in *Studies in Comparative Communism*, vol. 11, no. 3 (Autumn 1978), p. 237-49.

599   **The defence policy of Romania.**
David P. Burke.   In: *The defence policies of nations: a comparative study.*   Edited by Douglas J. Murray, Paul R. Viotti.   Baltimore, Maryland; London: Johns Hopkins University Press, 1982, p. 323-41.

The author argues that Romania's political situation within Eastern Europe in the late 1970s and early 1980s was more complex and 'deviant' than was often realized. In particular, Romanian defence policy was clearly shaped to deter invasion by what it saw as its most likely adversaries – its own nominal allies in the Warsaw Pact. The Warsaw Pact was thus not as monolithic as normally perceived at the time and Burke argues that if this fact is taken into account, it should lead to a readjustment of Western military strategy which had usually been based on the assumption that NATO would face the combined might of all Pact forces in any confrontation. In support of his contention, Burke then provides an overview of Romania's foreign and defence policy. This chapter on Romania did not appear in a subsequent volume of this book and it was originally adapted from a previous article by Burke, entitled 'Defence and mass mobilization in Romania' in *Armed Forces and Society*, vol. 7, no. 1 (Fall 1980), p. 31-49.

600   **Romanian military doctrine: past and present.**
Ilie Ceaușescu.   Boulder, Colorado: East European Monographs, distributed by Columbia University Press, 1988. 246p. (East European Monographs, no. 238).

One of the features of the Ceaușescu cult was a desire to appear in print. Nicolae Ceaușescu's speeches and other writings, quotation of which was mandatory in most Romanian publications, were translated into numerous languages and Elena Ceaușescu was presented to the world as a scientist of international repute with a stream of publications to her name. Not wishing to be outdone, Ceaușescu's brother, Ilie, who had been elevated to the rank of Major-General without having manifested any great military inclinations, put his name to a number of books and articles on history and military matters. Inevitably, these were usually translated into English and other Western languages and even, in this case, published in the West. Such works have some interest as examples of the development of ideology in late-Ceaușescu Romania, particularly as Ilie took an even more extreme Daco-centric position than his brother. Typical of the style is the following passage: 'To defend the ancient land, its independence, sovereignty, and territorial integrity has always been a fundamental and priceless virtue of the Romanians. Since the time of the first centralized and independent Dacian state and, then for more than two millennia, the Romanian people had waged fierce fights against numerous foreign invaders. The idea of independence and sovereignty has always been the most salient feature of the Romanian past and present, which are intertwined in an indestructible continuity'. Similar sentiments are voiced in another book in this series, edited by Ilie Ceauşescu, *War, Revolution, and society in Romania: the road to independence* (Boulder, Colorado: Social Science Monographs, distributed by Columbia University Press, 1983. 298p. [East European Monographs, no. 135]).

601   **The 'popular war' doctrine in Romanian defense policy.**
Ari Chaplin.   *East European Quarterly*, vol. 17, no. 3 (Sept. 1983), p. 267-82.
An examination, largely from a legal standpoint, of the 'Popular War' doctrine adopted by Romania in response to the Warsaw Pact invasion of Czechoslovakia in 1968. Essentially a defensive strategy designed to deter invasion, it was based on the idea of mustering a large proportion of the country's population in the nation's defence. This study looks at both theoretical and practical aspects of the strategy and concludes that Romania has made 'a great contribution to the concept of "popular war"'.

602   **'Ceauşescuism' and civil-military relations in Romania.**
William Crowther.   *Armed Forces and Society*, vol. 15, no. 2 (Winter 1989), p. 207-25.
This is now a rather outdated but nevertheless prophetic account of the uneasy relations that existed between Ceauşescu and the Romanian army. The author suggests that the forces of the Ministry of the Interior represented the main pillar on which the régime's survival rested rather than the Army, which was increasingly losing its autonomy, prestige and privileges.

603   **Romania: between appearances and realities.**
Jonathan Eyal.   In: *The Warsaw Pact and the Balkans: Moscow's southern flank*.   Edited by Jonathan Eyal.   Basingstoke, England: Macmillan, Royal United Services Institute for Defence Studies, 1989, p. 67-108. (RUSI Defence Studies).
Written on the eve of the Romanian Revolution and the breaching of the Berlin Wall, this book inevitably was almost instantly rendered out-of-date. However, this chapter still retains value as an excellent analysis of Romania's strategic importance during the Cold War. Too insignificant and geographically remote to be an influential player in its own right, Romania, nevertheless, managed for much of the Ceauşescu epoch to successfully straddle the divide between the Superpowers. Yet, the much vaunted semi-independent foreign policy was ultimately dependent on the support of the West and when, following the Soviet-American *rapprochement* of the 1980s, this disappeared, Romania quickly lost strategic significance.

604 **The Romanian Navy during the War of Independence, 1877-1878.**
Mihai Georgescu. *Warship International*, vol. 23, no. 4 (1986),
p. 359-68.

A survey of the role played by four ships on the Danube during the Russo-Turkish War of 1877-78 after which Romania secured its full independence. The ships were crewed and officered by Russians, but after the war they were to form the nucleus of the navy of the new Romanian state. Two other articles by the same author on related matters in this journal are: 'Elisabeta', *Warship International*, vol. 21, no. 2 (1984), p. 158-67; and 'The Romanian torpedo boat "Rindunica"', *Warship International*, vol. 24, no. 4 (1987), p. 350-55.

605 **Eastern European military assistance to the Third World.**
Trond Gilberg. In: *Communist nations' military assistance.* Edited by John F. Copper, Daniel S. Papp. Boulder, Colorado: Westview, 1983, p. 86-87.

Discusses the military aid given by Romania during the communist period to a number of African and Asian states. In particular, in Africa the Romanians supported guerrilla movements in Zimbabwe, Angola, Mozambique and Namibia. Economic and political support was also extended to a number of Latin American countries and a significant number of Third World students attended Romania's military academies.

606 **Security implications of nationalism in Eastern Europe.**
Edited by Trond Gilberg, Jeffrey Simon. Boulder, Colorado; London: Westview Press, 1986. 327p. bibliog.

This book contains two chapters which refer to Romanian topics. In 'Nationalism in the Romanian military: Ceauşescu's double-edged sword', p. 277-94, George W. Price discusses the use of nationalism by the Ceauşescu régime and its effect on the military. The dilemma faced by the authorities was that although an emphasis on nationalism and a corresponding downplaying of Marxism-Leninism helped to legitimize the régime, it also tended to encourage the military to identify with the nation rather than the Party. This reinforced perceptions within some segments of the military that it could be an autonomous actor in Romanian political life, a tendency that could pose a challenge to the continuing hegemony of the Party, as it might conceivably lead to a military coup. Another chapter in this book by Stephen Fischer-Galaţi, 'Marxist thought and the rise of nationalism', p. 69-79, also contains material relevant to Romania.

607 **Romania.**
Christopher D. Jones. In: *Warsaw Pact: the question of cohesion.*
Phase II – Volume 2: Poland, German Democratic Republic, and
Romania. Edited by Teresa Rakowska-Harmstone, Christopher D.
Jones, Ivan Sylvain. Ottawa: Department of Defense, 1984,
p. 348-411. (ORAE Extra-Mural Paper, no. 33).

The author is primarily concerned with Romania's military relation with its Warsaw Pact allies. He contends that by the early 1980s Romania had placed four main barriers in the path of its military relations with the USSR. These were: a series of treaty obligations which freed Romania from its Warsaw Pact commitments; a number of initiatives aimed at securing arms control agreements which would lessen the prospect of East-West conflict in the Balkans; the creation of a national military doctrine which made no provision for coalition warfare; and, finally, signs of disengagement from Warsaw Pact programmes designed to prepare for coalition warfare. Each of these are investigated in turn in this chapter, which offers a comprehensive survey of Romanian defence policy and the country's weapon production programme.

608   **Ceauşescu and the Romanian Army.**
       Daniel Nelson.   *International Defense Review*, vol. 22, no. 6
       (Aug. 1989), p. 737-41.
The author reviews the defence policy of the Ceauşescu régime, paying particular attention to the links between the Romanian Communist Party and the military and the political role of the Romanian Army. Nelson considers the condition of the Army and the Patriotic Guard and the rising levels of popular discontent before pondering the particularly pertinent question of the likelihood of a military coup. He considers such an occurrence to be unlikely and instead stresses the Army's role as modernizers; indeed, it can be argued that this was the position that they did come to adopt in the Revolution, as they swung behind the technocratically orientated Iliescu régime.

609   **Nationalism and the military in the 1990's: the unique case of Rumania.**
       Donald C. Snedeker.   *History of European Ideas,* vol. 18, no. 2
       (1994), p. 241-54.
Based on interviews, press reports and secondary sources, this article examines the role played by the Romanian Army both during and after the Revolution of 1989. The author argues that more than in any other country in the Soviet bloc, the Army in Romania played a key role in the collapse of the communist régime. In the post-revolutionary period the Army has reasserted its position in domestic politics as a respected autonomous institution, embodying the patriotic values of the nation.

610   **New Romanian Navy: a weapon without a target.**
       Robert Van Tol, Jonathan Eyal.   *RUSI Journal*, vol. 132, no. 1
       (March 1987), p. 37-46.
Examines Romania's apparently baffling decision in the 1970s to construct a new fleet of warships, including the 4,500-ton destroyer, *Muntenia*. The authors question the rationale behind the decision and, after considering a number of possible reasons, they conclude that the answer must lie in Ceauşescu's increasingly martial personality cult and his infatuation with major industrial projects. From a military point of view they agree that the money, which seems to have mostly come from foreign subsidies, would have been better spent on bolstering the country's air defences and territorial forces.

Foreign Relations

611 **Romanian and East German policies in the Third World: comparing the strategies of Ceauşescu and Honecker.**
Thomas P. M. Barnett. Westport, Connecticut; London: Praeger, 1992. 173p. bibliog.

The author sets out to investigate why Romania and East Germany pursued such ambitious Third World policies in the 1970s and 1980s when they committed a major proportion of their foreign policy resources to the nations of the South. Identifying a number of internal and external policy objectives, he argues that it was primarily done in the hope of increasing domestic legitimacy and thus ultimately improving their position *vis-à-vis* the Soviet Union. In the words of the author, it was an attempt at 'leverage deficit reduction'. However, in both cases the policy achieved little as it was limited by the dynamics of the détente process and the constraints imposed by the international economy.

612 **Romanian foreign policy since 1965: the political and military limits of autonomy.**
Aurel Braun. New York: Praeger, 1978. 218p. bibliog.

A detailed and comprehensive analysis of Romanian foreign policy during the first decade of Ceauşescu's rule. The Romanian 'deviation' from the Soviet foreign policy line is considered against the background of Soviet policy towards Eastern Europe as a whole and an attempt is made to define the political and military limits of Romania's autonomy.

613 **Romania, CSCE and the Most-Favoured-Nation process, 1982-1984.**
Lynne A. Davidson. In: *The diplomacy of human rights.* Edited by David D. Newsom. Lanham, Maryland: University Press of America, 1986, p. 187-200.

The granting of 'Most-Favoured-Nation' trading status by the United States has often been used to secure concessions on human rights issues from non-market, often communist, trading partners. In this article the author assesses how this tool was employed in the case of Romania in the period 1982-84. Davidson concludes that although it was an effective policy, the 'Most-Favoured-Nation' mechanism is no magic wand, and that human rights violations have continued to occur in Romania. However, since it did have some influence, it should continue to be seen in a constructive light.

614 **Pinstrips and reds: an American Ambassador caught between the State Department and the Romanian Communists, 1981-1985.**
David B. Funderburk, with a foreword by Philip M. Crane.
Washington, DC: Selous Foundation Press, 1987. 226p. bibliog.

Before being appointed as ambassador, Funderburk had been a Fulbright fellow in Romania studying the history of the country. This meant that he entered his new job with a considerable background knowledge and this is visible in this book which is not just anecdotal account of his experiences but a serious critique of the State Department's working practices and its policies towards Romania in the 1980s. The author, who is a self-confessed conservative anti-communist, pulls no punches in his description of Romania in the 1980s – one chapter is entitled 'Mad-man Ceauşescu'. Whilst in office his actions were constantly thwarted by an élite group within the foreign policy establishment intent on pushing through their own agenda on Romania but whom Funderburk considered were having the wool pulled over their eyes in their eagerness to believe that Romania could be decoupled from the USSR.

615 **Romania.**
Anneli Ute Gabanyi. In: *Central and Eastern Europe and the European Union.* Gütersloh, Germany: Bertelsmann Foundation, 1995, p. 109-33. (Strategies for Europe).

Within a general survey of political and economic developments in post-communist Romania, the author assesses the attitude of Romanians towards the EU. According to Gabanyi, Europe is a highly value-orientated concept for the Romanians, particularly because of their own self-perception of Romania as a bridge between Western and Eastern Europe and the Byzantine and Latin cultural spaces. Somewhat surprisingly, she also reveals that the positive image of the EU held by eighty-eight per cent of the population according to opinion polls – amongst the highest figures in Eastern Europe – is based not on vague assumptions but on a remarkably high level of information.

616 **Romania: background to autonomy.**
Graeme J. Gill. *Survey*, vol. 21, no. 3 (Summer 1975), p. 94-113.

This excellent analysis of Romania's foreign policy during the communist era argues that the country was able to take a partially independent stance largely because of the prevailing international circumstances. In particular, Romania effectively exploited the opportunities presented by the Sino-Soviet rift by adopting an essentially neutral position. At the same time Khruschev did not develop significant control mechanisms to replace those of Stalin and peaceful coexistence and détente allowed for greater autonomy in relations with the West. Destalinization then allowed Dej to launch his Romanization campaign which sought to align the Romanian Communist Party with more traditional national aspirations. This led to the rejection of the Soviet model and the quest for a national road to socialism. However, by the mid-1970s, circumstances were forcing a change of policy. The success of China's post-Cultural Revolution diplomacy, which saw its admittance to the UN, moved the Sino-Soviet split into the world arena, thereby downgrading the importance of countries such as Romania. Furthermore, evident Russian hostility towards his flirtation with China persuaded Ceauşescu that geopolitical considerations prevented any effective playing of the 'China Card'. The deterioration in Romania's economic situation gave less leeway for an independent economic policy and the era of détente saw Russia forging its own relations with the West with the result that it effectively appropriated Romania's policies.

617   **American-Romanian relations, 1984-1994.**
      Joseph F. Harrington, Edward Karns, Scott D. Karns.   *East European Quarterly*, vol. 29, no. 2 (Summer 1995), p. 207-35.

This article brings up to date Harrington's extensive coverage of modern Romanian-American relations. The chief issue between the two countries has been the question of Most-Favoured-Nation status with Romania seeking to regain what it had renounced in 1988. Despite a number of minor setbacks, the return of big business to support the Romanian cause led to MFN status finally being reinstated on 8 November 1993. Indeed, following the roller-coaster relations of 1990-91, the author reveals that the decisive moment in post-1989 Romanian-American relations was the August 1991 Moscow coup which was vigorously condemned by the Romanian leadership. Fears that such a coup might be repeated in Romania, with Iliescu cast in the guise of Gorbachev but with no Yeltsin waiting in the wings to come to the rescue, led the Americans to adopt a more pro-Iliescu policy and this line was later cemented in the Gulf War when the Romanians gave strong backing to the West. Similar ground is covered in another article by the same authors, 'Romania, America, and MFN, 1989-1994' in *Romanian Civilization,* vol. 4. no. 1 (Spring 1995), p. 3-20.

618   **MFN and human rights: Romanian-American relations, 1975-1988.**
      Joseph F. Harrington, Scott D. Karns.   *Southeastern Europe*, vol. 15, no. 1-2 (1988), p. 71-97.

The granting of Most-Favoured-Nation trading status has long been used as a political weapon by the US authorities. Traditionally, it was used as a prize to a non-market economy for a foreign policy independent of Moscow, with Romania being one of the nations so rewarded for its 'deviation' in foreign policy. However, the collapse of the Romanian economy in the 1980s meant that few American businessmen were willing to lobby for the Ceauşescu régime to continue to enjoy such favours and, with the arrival of a conservative American Ambassador in Bucharest in 1988, the Romanian régime unilaterally withdrew from the agreement to forestall Congress from scrutinizing its human rights record. The abrogation of the agreement did not halt all trade, but it damaged two-way trade and removed a lever by which the US had been able to curtail some of the worst human rights abuses by the Romanian authorities.

619   **Tweaking the nose of the Russians: fifty years of American-Romanian relations, 1940-1990.**
      Joseph F. Harrington, Bruce J. Courtney.   Boulder, Colorado: East European Monographs, distributed by Columbia University Press, 1991. 657p. (East European Monographs, no. 296).

A very detailed and comprehensive study of Romanian-American relations in the second half of the 20th century. The subject is considered within the wider context of

East-West trade, American security policy (chiefly as regards the USSR) and US policy towards Eastern Europe in general, as well as Bucharest-Moscow relations. The title comes from a comment by Corneliu Bogdan, a former Romanian Ambassador to the United States (1967-76), who suggested that President Richard Nixon made his famous visit to Romania in 1969 to 'tweak the nose of the Russians'. Two previous articles published by the same authors on this subject are: Joseph F Harrington, 'Romanian-American relations during the Kennedy administration', *East European Quarterly*, vol. 18, no. 2 (June 1984), p. 215-36; and Joseph Harrington, Bruce Courtney, 'Romanian-American relations during the Johnson administration', *East European Quarterly*, vol. 22, no. 2 (June 1988), p. 213-32.

620 **United States-Romanian trade relations: development and use of Most-Favoured-Nation trading status.**
Stephen P. Heuston. *George Washington Journal of International Law and Economics,* vol. 22, no. 2 (1988), p. 379-415.

In 1988 Romania unilaterally renounced its 'Most-Favoured-Nation' trading status with the United States to forestall Congress investigating human rights abuses. In this article the author analyses the consequences of this decision and argues that both the economies of the United States and Romania will ultimately suffer. However, he wholeheartedly supports the position that grants of such status should continue to be linked to human rights concerns.

621 **Romanian perspectives on security risks.**
Roxana Iorga. *International Spectator,* vol. 29, no. 4 (Oct.-Dec. 1994), p. 81-105.

The author assesses both internal and external influences on Romanian security policy, placing particular emphasis on the issues most likely to destabilize the country. These include outstanding border disputes, the minorities question and the processes of democratization and economic reform. The focus is on 'Romanian perceptions of these problems and on the likely response to Romanian policy not only from the neighbouring countries, but also from international organizations'.

622 **The future of Romanian-Soviet relations in the post-Ceauşescu era.**
Robert R. King. In: *East-Central Europe and the USSR.* Edited by Richard F. Staar. New York: St Martins Press, 1991, p. 229-47.

Romania's autonomy from the USSR provided an important source of legitimacy for the Ceauşescu régime and because the country was a disruptive factor within the Warsaw Pact, it grew in importance for the West. This position resulted, at least initially, in some economic benefits and led to Romania being regarded as a regional power. The collapse of the Warsaw Pact and the disintegration of the Soviet Union brought about a radical change to this situation and in this study King outlines the new geopolitical reality facing the country, which is now just one of several medium-sized states in the region, with a limited influence in the Balkans. In the future, Bucharest's relations with Moscow will continue to be much more important for Romania than Russia, not least because of differences over Moldavia.

623 **Romania versus the United States: the diplomacy of the absurd, 1985-1989.**
Roger E. Kirk, Mircea Raceanu. New York: St Martin's Press, 1994. 320p.

An informative eye-witness account of the breakdown of American-Romanian relations during the 1980s by two of the chief protagonists; Kirk was American Ambassador in Bucharest and Răceanu the Romanian Foreign Ministry expert on American affairs. The causes of the breakdown are traced to the personality of Nicolae Ceaușescu and the lack of a meeting of minds – Ceaușescu saw negotiations as little more than photo-opportunities, whilst the Americans viewed them as a chance to berate the Romanians over human rights abuses. A number of appendices contain the text of official communications from the US government to Ceaușescu and statistical information on the number of Romanians emigrating to the US, Israel and West Germany in the period 1975-88. In January 1989, Răceanu, whose father Grigore Răceanu was one of the signatories of the Letter of the Six condemning Ceaușescu's policies, was arrested and charged with spying for the Americans. Sentenced to death, he was granted an amnesty after the Revolution and left for the United States. The authors present a summary of some of their thoughts in 'Dealing with dictatorships: lessons from Ceaușescu's Romania', *Mediterranean Quarterly,* vol. 5, no. 2 (Spring 1994), p. 25-36.

624 **The challenge to Soviet interests in Eastern Europe: Romania, Hungary, East Germany.**
F. Stephen Larrabee.   Santa Monica, California: Rand Corporation, 1985. 118p.

Pages 23-55 of this book contain a concise analysis of the potential military, political and economic challenge that Ceaușescu's Romania posed to the USSR. Although Romania appeared by virtue of her semi-autonomous foreign policy to be the most troublesome of allies for the Soviet Union, it was in fact in the weakest position of the three countries under investigation. It was not strategically important to the USSR, and with a rapidly weakening economy and diminishing Western support, the author concludes that in the future it was most likely to return to a closer alignment with its powerful Eastern neighbour.

625 **National independence and reciprocal advantages: the political economy of Romanian-South relations.**
C. W. Lawson.   *Soviet Studies,* vol. 35, no. 3 (1983), p. 362-75.

This article investigates the circumstances surrounding Romania's membership of the less developed negotiating group at the United Nations Conference on Trade and Development (UNCTAD) North-South discussions. The author argues that Romania's prime rationale for joining the group was economic, as the country needed to diversify its trade and hoped to benefit directly from any West-South trade concessions on offer. However, the consequences seem to have been largely political, as in joining the group Romania deviated from CMEA policy and thereby increased intra-bloc stresses. There also remained an inherent paradox between the continuing need to demonstrate substantial economic growth for the Romanian domestic audience whilst still maintaining levels of economic development concomitant with its position as a developing country. The policy seems to have brought a few advantages to Romania through the creation of extra political links, the diversification of trade and the further projection of the much vaunted independent foreign policy, but at the cost of raised tensions within CMEA and a series of commitments to less developed countries which were to place a heavy burden on the Romanian economy.

626 Communist states and international change: Romania and Yugoslavia in comparative perspective.
Ronald H. Linden.   Boston, Massachusetts; London; Sydney; Wellington: Allen & Unwin, 1987. 201p.

This study of the impact of international change on Romania and Yugoslavia 'does not narrate the history of these two countries' involvement in international relations but addresses itself to how they adapted when the many international environments within which they operated changed'. In particular, the promises of détente proved ephemeral as communist régimes, such as Romania and Yugoslavia, made the disastrous policy choices of staking their future prospects on continuing low interest rates and cheap oil.

627 Romania and the Yugoslav conflict.
Ioan Mircea Pascu.   In: *The search for peace in Europe. Perspectives from NATO and Eastern Europe based on a conference co-sponsored by the Institute for National Strategic Studies and the George C. Marshall European Center for Strategic Studies.*   Fort Lesley, Washington, DC: National Defense University Press; Pittsburgh: McNair, 1993, p. 233-45.

This volume arose from a conference held in 1993 that was convened with the twin aims of healing the divisions of the Cold War, that had split Europe between East and West, and controlling the nationalism that was threatening the new post-1989 political order. The short paper by Pascu surveys the implications of the Yugoslav conflict for Europe as a whole before considering its impact on Romania.

628 Britain's 'political romance' with Romania in the 1970s.
Mark Percival.   *Contemporary European History*, vol. 4, no. 1 (March 1994), p. 67-87.

British-Romanian relations reached their apogee, or their nadir, depending on the point of view, with the state visit of Nicolae and Elena Ceaușescu in 1978 during which they lodged with Queen Elizabeth II in Buckingham Palace. In this study the author looks at the details of this visit, including a rather ham-fisted effort to prevent any protests, and tries to divine why Britain chose to take such a positive view of Romania during the 1970s. Although his research is hampered by the thirty-year-rule preventing the release of British government papers on the subject, he suggests that the main reason was a desire to promote trade.

629 The United States and Romania: American-Romanian relations in the twentieth century.
Edited by Paul D. Quinlan.   Woodland Hills, California: American-Romanian Academy of Arts and Sciences, 1988. 180p. (American-Romanian Academy of Arts and Sciences, no. 6).

Amongst the papers included in this volume are: Joseph F. Harrington, Bruce J. Courtney, 'Romania's changing image: Bucharest and the American press: 1952-1975',

p. 105-23; Robert Weiner, 'The U.S. policy of differentiation towards Romania', p. 129-46; David B. Funderburk, 'Relations between the United States and Romania during the first half of the 1980's', p. 147-60; and Nestor Ratesh, 'The rise and fall of a special relationship', p. 161-75.

630 **Romania: boundary disintegration between East and South.**
Robin Alison Remington. In: *The Soviet Bloc and the Third World: the political economy of East-South relations.* Edited by Brigitte H. Schulz, William W. Hansen. Boulder, Colorado: Westview, 1989, p. 197-211.
Deals with Romania's relations with the Third World. Within it the author argues that unless Romania's ambitions in the 'South' are modified they will only exacerbate the economic disaster facing the country.

631 **Romanian foreign policy under Dej and Ceauşescu.**
Michael Shafir. In: *The Soviet Union and Eastern Europe.* Edited by George Schöpflin. New York; Oxford: Facts on File, 1986, p. 364-77. (Handbooks to the Modern World).
An elegant essay on the course of Romanian foreign policy from the advent of communism until the mid-1980s. The author argues that contrary to some assertions the first signs of a Romanian 'deviation' from the Soviet line cannot be traced until the late 1950s, when there was a distinct lessening in the volume of trade between the two countries. After 1968 and Ceauşescu's denunciation of the Warsaw Pact invasion of Czechoslovakia, relations with the Soviet Union were based on an explicit rejection of the 'Brezhnev Doctrine', a policy which was coupled with an elaborate courting of the West.

632 **The EU and Romania and Bulgaria: stuck between Visegrad and Minsk.**
Tony Verheijen. In: *Prospective Europeans: new members for the European Union.* Edited by John Redmond. New York; London; Toronto; Sydney; Tokyo, Singapore: Harvester Wheatsheaf, 1994, p. 151-74. (The European Initiative).
In treating Romania and Bulgaria as a unit, the author is aware that the two are really only paired because of their geographical separation from the northern tier of Eastern Europe states, which are seen as the first candidates for EU entry, and their shared Ottoman heritage and Orthodox faith. In this chapter Verheijen examines the history of the EU's relations with the two countries and the possible effect of these on future developments, the various trade and co-operation agreements signed by Romania and Bulgaria with the EU and the importance of current EU assistance programmes, including PHARE. An overview of the complex negotiations surrounding the signing of association agreements is then followed by an assessment of the likelihood of either of the countries being offered EU membership in the near future on the basis of their post-1989 economic and political reforms. At this point Verheijen makes a strong argument for the two countries being decoupled when it comes to assessing the possibility of EU entry, because Bulgaria is far ahead of Romania in the reform process – a graphic example of how treacherous the sands of forecasting are in Eastern Europe, as Romania, having narrowly missed being amongst the first entrants to

NATO, was seen in 1997 as being far more likely to be invited to join the EU than its southern neighbour.

633 Romanian foreign policy and the United Nations.

Robert Weiner. New York: Praeger, 1984. 206p. bibliog.

Fascinated with the question of how internal neo-Stalinist orthodoxy can still produce a foreign policy not tied to the dictates of the Warsaw Pact, Weiner is primarily concerned in this scholarly study with identifying linkages between domestic variables and Romanian foreign policy at the United Nations. He also examines the extent to which Romanian policy differs from that of the USSR at the UN and the place the latter institution occupied within the overall framework of Ceauşescu's foreign policy.

Economy

Economic history

634 **British economic interests in the Lower Danube and the Balkan shore of the Black Sea between 1803 and 1829.**
Paul Cernovodeanu. *Journal of European Economic History*, vol. 5, no. 1 (Spring 1976), p. 105-19.

The author surveys the many oscillations in British policy towards the region from 1803, when the right of free passage to the Black Sea was first obtained, until 1829 and the Treaty of Adrianople which formalized trading structures, opening the region to international commerce.

635 **Vickers' Balkan conscience: aspects of Anglo-Romanian armaments, 1918-1939.**
R. P. T. Davenport-Hines. *Business History*, vol. 25, no. 3 (Nov. 1983), p. 287-319.

According to the author this article has three aims: firstly, to describe the 'business conditions, baffling politics and social complexity that confronted British manufacturers trying to win contracts and sell products in Romania between the two World Wars'; secondly, to cast light onto attempts immediately after 1918 to develop Eastern Europe as a market for British heavy industry; and thirdly, to show how Vickers' relations with the Romanian *Uzinele Metalurgice din Copșa Mică și Cugir Societate Anonimă* were of considerable significance during the interwar years.

636   **Germany's informal empire in East-Central Europe: German
       economic policy towards Yugoslavia and Rumania 1933-1939.**
       William S. Grenzebach.   Stuttgart, Germany: Steiner Verlag, 1988.
       269p.

This scholarly study is based upon the author's PhD thesis. Although it is weighted
slightly more towards Yugoslavia than Romania, it still contains a great deal of
information about the extent of Germany's economic penetration of the latter country
in the 1930s. The author concludes that Germany's trade drive to the East was initially
an aggressive response to the Depression. However, economic policy naturally had
important political consequences and it eventually led to German dominance in a
region which had been abandoned by France and Great Britain to face the
consequences of the economic downturn without help.

637   **Industrial output in Romania and its historical regions, 1880-1930.**
       Marvin R. Jackson.   *Journal of European Economic History*, vol. 15,
       no. 1 (Spring 1986), p. 59-111; vol. 15, no. 2 (Fall, 1986), p. 231-57.

The aim of this paper is to trace Romania's industrial growth record. Part one deals
with Wallachia and Moldavia between 1880 and 1915 whilst part two considers the
country after the creation of Greater Romania. Although the limits of the data make
growth rates difficult to surmise, the author suggests that prior to the First World War
they averaged at between six and eight per cent per annum but that, after the War, they
slumped to only two per cent, before picking up again in the late 1920s. The article is
supported by copious statistics recording the number of factories and levels of
employment in industry as well as industrial output. A useful annex summarizes the
most important information from the Romanian Survey of Industry of 1901-02.

638   **Xenophobia or nationalism? The demands of the Romanian
       engineering profession for preference in government contracts
       1898-1905.**
       John H. Jensen, Gerhard Rosegger.   *East European Quarterly*,
       vol. 19, no. 1 (March 1985), p. 1-14.

The authors examine how economic development in Romania during the late 19th
century resulted in the rise of an educated Romanian élite headed by local
industrialists such as I. B. Cantacuzino, the owner of the country's largest cement
factory. In times of economic difficulty this élite, through recourse to nationalism,
proved itself sufficiently powerful to gain government contracts in the face of foreign
competition. Eventually, this was to lead to the nationalization of the Romanian
modernization process with the first Romanian-built railroad being constructed in
1880s. However, extensive sub-contracting gave room for considerable corruption.

639   **Balkan economic history 1550-1950: from imperial borderlands to
       developing nations.**
       John R. Lampe, Marvin R. Jackson.   Bloomington, Indiana: Indiana
       University Press, 1982. 728p. maps. bibliog.

This pioneering study of remarkable range and depth fills a significant vacuum in
scholarship on Southeast Europe. The authors have assembled an impressive amount
of data from primary and secondary sources, many of which are in the languages of
the region, to produce a book that is not only unique in any language but also

intelligible to those who are not economists. The historical survey, supported by some 130 statistical tables, emphasizes the factors of modernization in the area and finds many parallels in regional development patterns, despite past ideological divisions.

640 **Crafting the third world: theorizing underdevelopment in Rumania and Brazil.**
Joseph L. Love. Stanford, California: Stanford University Press, 1996. 348p. (Comparative Studies in History, Institutions and Public Policy).

This learned study in economic history shows how the major concerns of developmental economists in Romania in the interwar years were translated to Latin America and especially Brazil. In particular, the author looks at the work of Mihail Manoilescu, whose seminal work was *Théorie du protectionnisme et de l'échange international* (Theory of protectionism and international exchange) (Paris, 1929), and its influence on Raúl Prebisch and the Latin American structuralist school of economists. Although the author is a Latin American specialist, his study of Manoilescu's ideas and the Romanian background in which they were shaped is particularly thorough and informative. The link between Romania and Brazil is not always easy to establish, but Love does successfully show how economists, faced with similar problems in different countries, often came to the same conclusions.

641 **Oil and the Romanian state.**
Maurice Pearton. London: Oxford University Press, 1971. 361p. bibliog.

The most comprehensive and detailed study of the Romanian oil industry from its birth in the final decade of the last century to its nationalization under the communist government in 1948. Drawing on a wide range of sources, including unpublished material, the author displays an authoritative knowledge of the subject, combining erudition, as an economic historian, with first-hand experience of the oil industry. A later article by the same author on this subject is 'Liberal nationalisation and British interests in the Romanian oil industry', *Revue Roumaine d'Histoire*, vol. 28, no. 1-2 (Jan.-June 1989), p. 113-21.

642 **The Reșita industrial complex: perspectives in historical geography.**
David Turnock. *GeoJournal*, vol. 29, no. 1 (Jan. 1993), p. 83-102.

This piece of historical geography studies the development of the town of Reșița, one of Romania's oldest industrial complexes and the administrative centre of the county of Caraș-Severin. Starting from the mid-18th century decision by Habsburg monarchs to construct an iron works to exploit local natural resources, the article monitors the creation of today's large-scale metallurgical and engineering complex. Covering all aspects of the geography of Reșița, the article also surveys the urban development of the town (population 96,800, at the time of writing) and the local infrastructure as well as tourism in the surrounding mountains.

643 **The Romanian economy in the twentieth century.**
David Turnock.   New York: St. Martin's Press, 1986. 296p. maps.
bibliog.
The author, drawing upon his many years of research on Romanian geography, offers
an illuminating survey of economic development in the country during this century.
Most sectors of the economy are covered and considerable attention is also given to
patterns of transport and settlement. Throughout Turnock's findings are backed by a
considerable amount of statistical data.

Communist period

644 **The second economy in Romania.**
Horst Brezinski, Paul Petersen.   In: *The second economy in Marxist
states.*   Edited by Maria Łos.   London; Basingstoke, England:
Macmillan, 1990, p. 69-84.
The second economy, hidden and unaccountable, was of enormous importance in
communist Romania. In this article the authors analyse the activities of this economic
sector and looks at the reasons for its emergence, including popular distrust of official
institutions and the disastrous performance of the first, official, economy under
socialism. Brezinski and Petersen also touch upon the legal implications of the
existence of such an economy.

645 **The orthodox model of the Socialist enterprise in the light of
Romanian experience.**
David Granick.   *Soviet Studies,* vol. 26, no. 2 (April 1974), p. 205-23.
This specialist article looks at the performance of managers in Romanian industry
during the early Ceaușescu period. The author argues that with regard to the rewarding
of managers, Romanian practices deviated from the norm of the Soviet bloc in that
their potential variable income was far less than in other countries. This meant that
Romanian managers, unlike those elsewhere, were not seeking to maximize their
bonuses, because no money was available. Generally, it seems that managers in
Romania had limited functions with power being more centralized than was the case
in most of the other East European states. Unusually for the times, these findings were
made on the basis of a large number of interviews with Romanian managers.

646 **New horizons in East-West economic and business relations.**
Edited by Marvin R. Jackson, James D. Woodson Jnr.   Boulder,
Colorado: East European Monographs, distributed by Columbia
University Press, 1984. 277p. (East European Monographs, no. 156).
Contains papers presented at the third Romanian American conference on trade and
economic co-operation, Bucharest 1978. The contributions include the following:
J. C. Brada, M. R. Jackson, A. E. King, 'The Romanian balance of payment crisis:
and econometric study of its causes and cures'; E. Neuberger, A. Ben-Ner, 'Romania's

reactions to international commodity inflation'; P. Marer, 'U.S. market disruption procedures involving Romanian and other CPC products with policy recommendations'; G. P. Lauter, 'East-West trade: organizational structures and problems of United States multinational corporations'; S. G. Walters, 'Management issues in U.S.-Romanian trade and co-operation'; R. C. Amacher, 'International markets versus the new international order: challenges to independence of nation states'; and H. S. Tapia, 'The experience of Latin America in marketing exports to the U.S.: some lessons for Romania'.

647 **Economic development in communist Romania.**
John Michael Montias. Cambridge, Massachusetts: MIT Press, 1967. 327p. bibliog.

An objective evaluation of Romanian economic development from the inception of communist rule to the mid-1960s with the emphasis on the expansion of Romanian industry which resulted in the doubling of industrial output between 1953 and 1963. The effects of collectivization on Romanian agriculture are also surveyed.

648 **Pressures for reform in the East European economies: study papers submitted to the Joint Economic Committee, Congress of the United States.**
Washington, DC: US Government Printing Office, 1989. 2 vols. 284p. 633p.

In keeping with the objectives of Stalinism, both the régimes of Gheorghe Gheorghiu-Dej and Nicolae Ceauşescu sought rapid industrial development combined with growth in other sections of the economy, such as agriculture and population resources. Ideological considerations meant that the Romanian Communist Party continued to follow the same objectives until its demise but whereas in the past growth targets had often been met, in the 1980s the economy was in apparently terminal decline. The second volume of this work contains two articles dealing with the Romanian economy at this time. In the first, 'Romania: the search for economic sovereignty', p. 291-306, Ronald Linden provides a general historical introduction to economic policy before Ceauşescu, an analysis of the economic performance during the first fifteen years of his rule, an outline of the adjustments made to cope with growing external and domestic difficulties, and a projection of the reforms necessary in order to secure a better economic future. In 'Statistics and political economy in Romania: what comes next – relief or more exploitation?', p. 307-27, Marvin R. Jackson suggests that it is difficult, if not impossible, to offer an accurate prognosis for the Romanian economy because of the absence of reliable statistics. To rectify this problem he then advances a model aimed at 'deflating Romania's official statistics and developing appropriate categories of distribution suited for analysis of the country's political economy'.

649 **Economic reform in Rumanian industry.**
Iancu Spigler. Oxford; New York: Oxford University Press, 1973. 176p. bibliog. (Institute of Soviet and East European Studies, University of Glasgow, Economic Reforms in East European Industry Series).

This work complements and expands Montias' earlier work on the economy (see item no. 647) by analysing developments from the mid-1960s until the early 1970s. It presents detailed information on Romanian macro-, micro- and branch-planning, outlines industrial management practices, discusses the criteria for investment allocation, and surveys budgetary procedures and banking.

650 **Romania: the industrialization of an agrarian economy under socialist planning.**
Andreas C. Tsantis, Roy Pepper. Washington, DC: The World Bank, 1979. 707p. bibliog.
The most comprehensive study in English of the Romanian economy under communism. Presented in a historical framework, the book describes the growth and changes within the economy from the communist take-over until the late 1970s. In addition, it contains a comprehensive database of the economy and describes the planning and management systems. Also covered are foreign trade, human resources, the construction industry, housing, tourism, transport and energy. Separate appendices describe local government and financing, national accounting, planning, investment, the social welfare system, and overall development prospects. This assessment of the Romanian economy was made before Romania's large external debt began to impose burdens on the economy, burdens that have made it more difficult to maintain the high growth rates of the past. Indeed, by 1982 rationing of bread, milk, cooking-oil, flour, sugar and petrol had been introduced in many areas of the country and by 1989 the whole economy was teetering on the brink of disaster.

Post-communist period

651 **The introduction of markets in a hypercentralized economy: the case of Romania.**
Avner Ben-Ner, John M. Montias. *Journal of Economic Perspectives*, vol. 5, no. 4 (Fall 1991), p. 163-70.
After a brief overview of the Romanian economy under communism, the authors offer their assessment of the first year of the transition to a market economy during which, in common with much of Eastern Europe, the country witnessed a fall in industrial output of over twenty per cent. The authors suggest that amongst the factors behind this fall were the shortening of the working week, a weakening of discipline in the workplace, a shortage of inputs, dislocation caused by the restructuring of large companies, the shortcomings of new managers thrust into office by the Revolution and the general difficulties experienced by all managers in adjusting to the new economic environment.

652 **The Romanian economic reform program.**
Dimitri G. Demekas, Moshin S. Khan. Washington, DC: International Monetary Fund, 1991. 36p. (IMF Occasional Paper, no. 89).
This study is based on information gathered by IMF researchers during a number of visits to Romania in 1990 and 1991. The result is a broad outline of the major

Economy. Post-communist period

characteristics of the Romanian economy prior to the restructuring process and an evaluation of the reform process as it evolved against a background of economic, institutional and social chaos. Although the programme has sometimes appeared erratic, the authors argue that it is generally coherent, and they finish with an optimistic conclusion given the many problems faced by Romania. A more recent report by the IMF on the Romanian economy is *Romania: recent economic developments and selected background studies* (Washington, DC: International Monetary Fund, 1996. 112p. [IMF Staff Country Reports, no. 96/9]).

653 **Macromodels of the Romanian transition economy.**
Emilian Dobrescu.   Bucharest: Romanian Academy Institute of Economic Research, 1996. 159p.
The bulk of this volume is concerned with a highly complex macroeconomic model of the Romanian economy. However, in the introduction the author presents an interesting view of the Romanian economy in transition which, he argues, suffers from an extremely weak structure. In particular, he points to poorly defined ownership rights, a market mechanism of limited effectiveness, persisting unofficial structures, continuing political influence on resource allocation, a deep fracture between real and nominal sectors, and continuing activity outside official institutions.

654 **Company management and capital-markets development in the transition in Romania.**
Irina Dumitriu.   *Russian and East European Finance and Trade*, vol. 29, no. 2 (Summer 1993), p. 49-58.
The author outlines some of the problems facing the Romanian economy in its transition from a command to a market economy. Amongst other factors she points to the enormous gap between, on one hand, the government's intentions in its legislation and macroeconomic measures and, on the other, the microeconomic reality on the ground in enterprises. Another factor is the persistence of traits from the communist past, including strategies employed by the bureaucracy so as not to lose control over economic assets.

655 **Privatization in a hypercentralised economy: the case of Romania.**
John S. Earle, Dana Săpătoru.   In: *Privatization in the transition to a market economy: studies of preconditions and policies in Eastern Europe.*   Edited by John S. Earle, Roman Frydman, Andrzej Rapaczynski.   London: Pinter in association with Central European University, 1993, p. 147-70.
The authors address the hypothesis that those countries which remained most ideologically orthodox and centralized under communism were in a position to undertake a quicker transition to a market economy than those which experienced a certain degree of liberalization and decentralization, because in the former property rights were more explicit and the central government still possessed the powers to rapidly enact a radical reform package. Whilst this hypothesis might have some bearing on the Czech case, the authors find it less readily fits hypercentralized Romania where a lack of clarity of purpose and political will threatens to fritter away the 'advantages of backwardness'.

656 **The privatization process in Central Europe.**
Roman Frydman, Andrzej Rapaczynski, John S. Earle (et al.).
Budapest, London; New York: Central European University Press,
1993. 262p. (CEU Privatization Reports, no. 1).

The first fruits of the Central European University privatization project, this volume is
concerned with the early years of post-communist economic reform. The view given of
Romania (p. 208-62) is very much the official government line, as the team of authors
includes the then Prime Minister, Teodor Stolojan. As well as a general overview of
economic performance, backed by a considerable amount of data, there is also a useful
official view of the workings of the privatization process and the intended relationship
between the State and Private Ownership Funds (SOF and POFs).

657 **Forecasting economies in transition: the case of Romania.**
Stephen G. Hall, John O'Sullivan. *Economics of Planning,* vol. 27,
no. 3 (1994), p. 175-84.

Using the case of Romania, the authors of this complex and highly specialized article
suggest that the accepted econometric model is valid because of its ability to adjust its
parameters in the face of economic change. Their argument is supported by a large
amount of quantitative data and it is followed by a comment by Constantin Ciupagea
(p. 185-88) in which he suggests that the models capture the main trends but do not
always succeed in predicting values accurately.

658 **Private economy in an etatist environment: the case of Romania.**
Gábor Hunya.   In: *The economic impact of new firms in post-socialist
countries. Bottom-up transformation in Eastern Europe.*   Edited by
Horst Brezinski.   Cheltenham, England: Edward Elgar, 1996,
p. 107-15.

Examines the slow pace of economic reform in Romania and the small size of the
market economy. Hunya argues that social behaviour in Romania lacks many of the
attributes necessary for market exchange, such as sincerity and trust. The presence of
widespread corruption also means that the private economy and continuing state
control have evolved in a kind of symbiosis. Amongst the issues which he considers to
be the main obstacles to the development of the private sector are the incompleteness
of macroeconomic liberalization and stabilization policies, the delay in privatization,
the bankruptcy of state-owned enterprises and the continuing persistence of
widespread state interference in the economy.

659 **Problems of economic and political transformation in the Balkans.**
Edited by Ian Jeffries.   London; New York: Pinter, 1996. 199p. maps.

Contains three informative papers relating to Romania. Per Ronnås, 'Romania:
transition to underdevelopment?' (p. 13-32), argues that post-1989 governments in
Romania have failed to build on a widespread desire for improved economic
conditions and have neither carried out significant restructuring nor depoliticized the
economy. Andrei Musetescu, 'Romania: the emergence of a pluralist party system:
challenges and crises, 1989-1994' (p. 33-44), discusses the evolution of political
parties after the Revolution. Whilst pointing towards a tendency towards atomization,
he also correctly notes that a significant bipolar cleavage has already appeared which
does not fully fit the traditional left-right divide. Finally, Alan Smith, 'Problems of the

transition to a market economy in Romania, Bulgaria and Albania: why has the transition proved so difficult?' (p. 111-30), compares the process of economic reform in South-Eastern Europe with the Central-East European economies of Poland, the Czech Republic, Slovakia and Hungary, and asks why it has been so difficult to implement 'shock therapy' in Romania, Bulgaria and Albania.

660   **Socialist economies and the transition to the market: a guide.**
Ian Jeffries.   London; New York: Routledge, 1993. 562p. bibliog.

Two chapters in this volume focus on the transition to a market economy in Romania. The first (p. 307-16) provides an analysis of the basic features of the communist command economy in the country. In the second (p. 450-59), Jeffries focuses on the post-communist transition to a market economy, assessing the process under such headings as: political background, austerity programme, marketization, labour relations, privatization, foreign trade and agriculture. The same author has also recently produced a companion to this volume which includes a chapter on Romania (p. 505-20): *A guide to the economies in transition* (London; New York: Routledge, 1996. 816p.). However, with sources mostly derived from newspapers and government publications, this is more a review of the current state of the transition process than a sustained piece of analysis.

661   **Romania: an economic assessment.**
Organisation for Economic Co-operation and Development.   Paris: Organisation for Economic Co-operation and Development Centre for Co-operation with European Economies in Transition, 1993. 122p.

This first comprehensive OECD report on the Romanian economy in transition provides a balanced and informative account of the early post-Revolution reform process and its effects. The legacy of the Ceauşescu régime meant that Romania had greater problems to face than most of the former communist countries. Indeed, the suffering had been so great during the 1980s that the Romanian government suggested that the inability of the population to bear any more hardship explained why it could not adopt a 'shock therapy' economic reform programme. Instead, they adopted a policy of 'gradualism', but over time this has become associated with even higher costs as Romania lagged behind the reform process elsewhere in Eastern Europe. Two recent studies of the Romanian economy in transition are: Dan Grindea, *Shock therapy and privatization: an analysis of Romania's economic reform* (Boulder, Colorado: East European Monographs, distributed by Columbia University Press, 1997. 133p. [East European Monographs, no. 459]); and Raphael Shen, with a foreword by Ivanciu Nicolae-Valeanu, *The restructuring of Romania's economy: a paradigm of flexibility and adaptability* (Westport, Connecticut: Praeger, 1997. 230p.).

662   **Macroeconomic policy in a transitional environment: Romania, 1989-1994.**
Clifford Poirot.   *Journal of Economic Issues*, vol. 30, no. 4 (Dec. 1996), p. 1,057-76.

'Through an examination of the political and economic situation in the former socialist country of Romania, this paper explores the inherent difficulty in carrying out a coherent and consistent stabilization policy in an environment characterised by radical uncertainty in all sections of the economy'. Poirot argues that defining and creating an institutional framework in which macroeconomic policies can function is more important than implementing IMF stabilization policies. Indeed, 'without the presence of institutions that can effectively link policy to the behaviour of the economy as a whole, macroeconomic stabilization has limited and potentially desultory results as regards creating the conditions for economic recovery'.

663 **An essay on the conceptual framework and the principles of restructuring the Romanian economy.**
Romanian Ministry of Economy and Finance. *Russian and East European Finance and Trade,* vol. 28, no. 2 (Summer 1992), p. 19-79.
A translation of part of an article which originally appeared in an official publication of the Romanian Ministry of Economy and Finance in September/October 1991. In it the authors describe the then government's economic policies and lay down the theoretical premise behind restructuring at both the national and regional levels.

664 **Towards a market economy: the Romanian effort.**
Maria-Cristina Sîrbu. *East European Quarterly,* vol. 28, no. 4 (Jan. 1995), p. 471-518.
A lengthy and detailed overview of the problems faced by Romania during its transition towards a market economy. The author surveys the legacy of communism, the process of transition and the macroeconomic stabilization measures adopted before closing with a conclusion which is perhaps a little over-optimistic in its prognosis.

665 **Economic change in the Balkan states.**
Edited by Orjan Sjöberg, Michael Wyzan. London: Pinter, 1991. 256p.
The results of a conference held in June 1990, this volume contains two papers relating to Romania. In the first by Per Ronnås, 'The economic legacy of Ceauşescu', p. 47-68, the author argues that whilst politically Ceauşescu may have changed tack, at least in the eyes of the West for whom he changed from maverick to tyrant, in his economic policies he was in fact remarkably consistent in the dogmatic inflexibility he displayed in the face of changing conditions. In short, the legacy of Ceauşescu can only be described as 'an unmitigated disaster on all fronts'. In the second paper by Alin Teodorescu, 'The future of a failure: the Romanian economy', p. 69-82, extra poignancy is added to the author's discussion of the Romanian economy by some revelations about his own pitiful family budget in January 1985, when during a bitterly cold winter the temperature in their flat remained a constant eight degrees centigrade and they slept in overcoats.

666 **Market economy and economic reform in Romania: macroeconomic and microeconomic perspectives.**
Yves G. Van Frausum, Ulrich Gehmann, Jürgen Gross. *Europe-Asia Studies,* vol. 46, no. 5 (1994), p. 735-56.
The first half of this study looks at the Romanian economy from a macroeconomic perspective, summarizing the main economic trends and analysing the strengths and weaknesses of the reform programme. The second part takes a microeconomic view appraising the performance of enterprises. The authors conclude that, in general, shortcomings at the national level merely reinforce shortcomings at the local level and

that it is the quality of management which will ultimately determine the progress of economic reform and restructuring.

667 **Privatization in NACC countries: defence industry experiences and policies and experiences in related fields, colloquium 29-30 June, 1 July 1994.**
Edited by Reiner Weichhardt. Brussels: NATO, 1994. 311p.

Every year NATO holds a colloquium which discusses an issue relevant to the economies of Eastern Europe. In 1994 the topic was the restructuring of the defence sector in the region. The key-note speaker at the colloquium was Mircea Cosea, the then Romanian Deputy Prime Minister and President of the Council for Coordination Strategy and Economic Reforms. His speech, 'The policy for privatization and restructuring the arms industry in Romania', can be found on p. 17-21 of this volume which also contains a paper by Daniel Daianu, 'Post-communist defence industry restructuring: the role of foreign direct investment', on p. 251-55. The papers from the 1993 colloquium, *Economic developments in cooperation partner countries from a sectoral perspective, colloquium 30 June, 1 and 2 July 1993* (Brussels: NATO, 1993), contains a paper by Dragos Negrescu, 'Creating the framework for effective industrial restructuring: the case of Romania', p. 125-31 and the 1990 volume, *The Central and Eastern European economies in the 1990s: prospects and constraints, colloquium 4-6 April 1990* (Brussels: NATO, 1990), features a paper by Alan H. Smith, 'The Romanian economy: policy and prospects for the 1990s', p. 117-28.

668 **Romania, human resources and the transition to a market economy.**
World Bank. Washington, DC: World Bank, 1992. 242p. maps.
(A World Bank Country Study).

This World Bank report was prepared by Louise Fox, who participated in an economic mission to Romania in October and November 1990. The study provides the first comprehensive post-1989 review of Romania's social sector, analysing amongst other issues labour markets, social insurance, education, health, scientific research and family planning. Throughout the findings are supported by statistical data.

Trade and Industry

Foreign trade

669 **An elasticity approach to the analysis of Romanian foreign trade policy during the years of transition.**
Constantin Ciupagea. *Economics of Planning*, vol. 27, no. 3 (1994), p. 227-50.
A highly specialized paper which looks at fluctuations in Romania's exchange rate in the period 1990-93 and the effect it had on international trade. In the first part of the paper the author advances a new theoretical model, whilst in the second section he offers an econometric attempt to establish the relationship between imports and output and price competitiveness in the energy sector, which accounts for thirty-three per cent of Romania's commodity imports.

670 **Romanian economic relations with the EEC.**
Alan H. Smith. In: *Jahrbuch der Wirtschaft Osteuropas* (vol. 8). Munich; Vienna: Günter Olzog, 1979, p. 323-61.
This detailed examination of Romania's trade relations with the EEC during the 1960s and 1970s shows how in 1967 Romania embarked on a programme of acquiring Western technology by importing substantial amounts of machinery and entering into a series of joint ventures with Western companies. This policy led to an initial growth in Romanian-EEC trade, but as Romania experienced difficulties in marketing its predominately agricultural exports, this declined.

671 **Trade policy review: Romania 1992.**
Geneva: General Agreement on Tariffs and Trade, 1993. 2 vols. 170p. 157p.
At the Uruguay Round of trade talks, in April 1989, it was agreed to establish a new Trade Policy Review Mechanism which would monitor the adherence of the

211

contracting parties to GATT rules and disciplines. Under this mechanism the performance of the four largest trading entities (the EU being considered as one unit) were to be reviewed every two years whilst smaller countries, such as Romania, were to be evaluated every six years. These two volumes are the fruits of the first review of Romania under this mechanism. The first contains the report of the GATT Secretariat, the second the report of the Government of Romania and the proceedings of the GATT council meeting of 17-18 December 1992 in which delegates were broadly supportive of the policies pursued by the Romanian Government whilst raising a number of concerns. The reports show that during the 1980s and 1990s Romania's trading patterns were in a state of flux. First, during the 1980s, as Ceauşescu squeezed the economy to pay foreign debts, the country's share of world trade slipped from 0.6 per cent to only 0.2 per cent. Then, after the fall of communism, there was a realignment of trade away from the former Soviet bloc towards the EU, although it was noticeable that in 1991 the former Soviet Union still remained the single most important market for both imports and exports.

Industry

672 **Energy policies of Romania: 1993 survey.**
International Energy Agency. Paris: OECD/IEA, 1993. 196p.
This valuable study, which is accompanied by full supporting statistics, is the result of a survey undertaken by the International Energy Agency at the behest of the Romanian Government. The authors investigated the post-1989 structure of the Romanian energy industry, examining current supply and demand as well as future prospects. Their main conclusion was that the development of a successful energy policy in Romania could not be divorced from the reform process in the economy as a whole.

673 **Rebuilding Romania: energy, efficiency and the economic transition.**
Walter C. Patterson. London: Royal Institute of International Affairs, Earthscan Publications, 1994. 212p.
Motivated by the belief that 'Romania is a country worth knowing better', this volume skilfully combines historical background with the argument that the use or misuse of energy is crucial to the country's successful transition to a market economy. The book, which is also published in Romanian, is well supported by statistical tables and charts.

674 **The Romanian enterprise.**
Alan H. Smith. In: *Industrial reform in socialist countries. From restructuring to revolution.* Edited by Ian Jeffries. Aldershot, England: Edward Elgar, 1992, p. 201-18.
In this chapter the author first outlines the strategy of industrialization and the system of industrial administration followed by the communist régime, and then surveys the

progress of post-communist industrial reforms in the 1990s. A previous chapter by Smith on this subject is 'The Romanian industrial enterprise' in *The industrial enterprise in Eastern Europe,* edited by Ian Jeffries (Eastbourne, England; New York: Praeger, 1981, p. 63-83).

675   **Industrial restructuring in Romania: diagnosis and strategies.**
      Yves G. Van Frausum.   *Europe-Asia Studies*, vol. 47, no. 1 (1995),
      p. 47-66.

Between 1992 and 1993 several foreign consultancy companies drew up a number of restructuring reports for the Romanian Ministries of Industry and Agriculture. The sectors investigated included food processing, agricultural machinery, textiles, petrochemicals, motor vehicles, steel, coal mining, commercial banking and petroleum refining. This specialized article draws upon the findings of these reports to suggest a possible restructuring strategy for Romania.

Agriculture and Food

676 **Spatial variations in the progress of land reform in Romania.**
Floarea Bordanc. *GeoJournal,* vol. 38, no. 2 (Feb. 1996), p. 161-65.
A survey of post-communist land privatization and the problems that confront the
newly restructured Romanian agriculture. The author suggests that the tendency has
been for individual smallholdings to predominate in hill and mountainous zones,
whereas in the main cropping areas small units of land have often been grouped into
larger units for more efficient management by associations. Thus, although the general
desire amongst the population is for owner-occupation, at the moment forty per cent
of the land allocated to individual peasants is being worked by some 20,000
associations. The author supports her findings with specific case-studies drawn from a
number of counties, including Giurgiu and Prahova.

677 **Romanian agricultural policy in the quest of 'the multilateral
developed society'.**
Trond Gilberg. In: *Agricultural policies in the USSR and Eastern
Europe.* Edited by Roland A. Francisco, Betty A. Laird, Roy D.
Laird, with a conclusion by Karl-Eugen Wädekin. Boulder,
Colorado: Westview, 1980, p. 137-64.
Although now very much of historical interest only, this chapter provides a useful
summary of agricultural policy under communism and the position the sector was
designated within Ceaușescu's vision of a 'multilaterally developed society'. The text
is supported by a considerable amount of statistical information. A previous study by
the same author on the issue of collectivization is 'The costly experiment:
collectivisation of Romanian agriculture' in *The political economy of collectivised
agriculture: comparative study of communist and non-communist systems,* edited by
Ronald A. Francisco, Betty A. Laird and Roy D. Laird (New York: Pergamon, 1979,
p. 23-62. [Pergamon Policy Studies, no. 14]). Gilberg also contributed an essay on the
same subject entitled 'Rural transformation in Romania' in *The peasantry of Eastern
Europe, volume II: 20th century developments,* edited by Ivan Volgyes (New York:
Pergamon, 1979, p. 77-122. [Comparative Rural Transformation]).

678   New developments in Romanian agriculture.
Gábor Hunya.   *East European Politics and Societies*, vol. 1, no. 2
(Spring 1987), p. 255-76.
Assesses the catastrophic decline in Romanian agriculture during the late 1980s,
although the actual scale of the collapse was difficult to determine because of the
absence of credible statistics. After the Revolution of 1989, the harvest of that year,
which Ceauşescu had trumpeted as being a record 60 million tonnes, was downgraded
to a meagre 17 million tonnes.

679   East European communities: the struggle for balance in turbulent
times.
Edited by David A. Kideckel.   Boulder, Colorado; San Francisco,
Oxford: Westview, 1995. 248p.
This collection of essays about the post-communist transition in the countryside of
Eastern Europe includes two chapters specifically relating to Romania: David A.
Kideckel, 'Two incidents on the plains in southern Transylvania: pitfalls of privatisa-
tion in a Romanian community', p. 47-64; and Steven Sampson, 'All is possible,
nothing is certain: the horizons of transition in a Romanian village', p. 159-76.

680   The social organization of production on a Romanian cooperative
farm.
David A. Kideckel.   *Dialectical Anthropology,* vol. 1, no. 2 (1976),
p. 267-76.
During his fieldwork conducted in Hîrseni, one of four villages organized into an
agricultural co-operative within a five-village commune in the Făgăraş area, the author
examined the organization of the co-operative in relation to both national policy and
the needs of the local community. Despite their previous autonomy, maintained
through a network of family, kindred and ritual kin relationships, Hîrseni and the other
three villages were finally collectivized with, at first sight, moderate success. However, difficulties soon arose in the relationship between the managerial class of the
Cooperativa agricola de productie (CAP) and the workers, and it is this factor which,
in the author's view, remained the major obstacle to achieving the desired production
targets and building socialism in the Romanian countryside.

681   The ecological consequences of privatisation in Romanian
agriculture.
Cristina Muica, Ion Zavoianu.   *GeoJournal,* vol. 38, no. 2 (Feb. 1996),
p. 207-12.
A survey of the ecological consequences of privatization on Romanian agriculture.
Noting that the economic hardships of the transition have limited ecological concerns,
the authors stress the importance of continuing research so as to monitor the impact of
the changes and provide a basis for recommending appropriate conservation measures.
They conclude with a case-study drawn from Buzău county.

682 **Corn and the development of agricultural science in Romania, 1864-1939.**
Ecaterina Petrina. *Agricultural History,* vol. 69, no. 1 (Winter 1995), p. 54-78.

Within this detailed and meticulous study the author challenges the line adopted by Romanian scholars under communism that agricultural science remained underdeveloped in the country prior to 1945. A combination of a favourable climate, fertile soil, improved methods of cultivation and a ready labour force all helped make Romanian agriculture highly productive. In 1900 Romania stood third behind the USA and Russia in grain production. By 1914 corn (maize) – the basis of the Romanian national dish *mămăliga* – was planted on more than fifty per cent of the total arable land and Romania had become one of the world's most important corn exporting nations. From the mid-1920s until 1939 it was ranked only second behind Argentina. Research for the improvement of corn yields began in 1919 and became steadily more systematic until the establishment of the Romanian Institute of Agricultural Research in 1927 which facilitated the transfer of scientific knowledge from countries such as Germany, the USA and France.

683 **The changing Romanian countryside: the Ceauşescu epoch and prospects for change following the Revolution.**
David Turnock. *Government and Policy,* vol. 9, no. 3 (Aug. 1991), p. 319-40.

The author reviews rural economic planning under Ceauşescu and the resulting radical shift of population away from the countryside to the towns as agricultural employment declined. He concludes by outlining the prospects for development after the Revolution of 1989 which should be more beneficial to the countryside.

684 **Forest exploitation and its impact on transport and settlement in the Romanian Carpathians.**
David Turnock. *Journal of Transport History,* vol. 12, no. 1 (March 1991), p. 37-60.

Argues that an increasing energy deficit and a persistent shortage of raw materials are forcing Eastern European countries to maximize the use of natural resources, as is the case of timber in Romania. In this article Turnock examines the growth of the wood-processing industry in the Carpathians and assess the significance of forest exploitation for the opening up of the region as a whole. The article is divided into four major sections: 'Market opportunities for Romanian timber'; 'Development of processing and transport technology before 1945'; 'Development of processing and transport technology since 1945'; and 'Humanising the Carpathians', in which he focuses on the role the industry has played in promoting increased settlement in the region.

685 **The introduction of maize into the food of the Rumanian people and its impact.**
Ofelia Văduva. In: *Food in perspective: proceeding of the Third International Conference on Ethnological Food Research, Cardiff, Wales, 1977.* Edited by Alexander Fenton, Trefor M. Owen. Edinburgh: John Donald, 1981, p. 333-41.

The author argues that it was because the Turks preferred wheat for their own personal consumption that the Romanian lands under Ottoman occupation developed the cultivation of maize as their main food staple. More recently the national consumption of maize has declined sharply in favour of wheat, which has been cultivated in Romania since the 4th century BC, but the country still ranks as the eighth largest producer of maize in the world.

686 **Popular Romanian food in the late eighteenth and early nineteenth centuries: traditional and incoming elements.**
Ofelia Văduva. In: *Food in change: eating habits from the Middle Ages to the present day.* Edited by Alexander Fenton, Eszter Kisbán. Edinburgh: John Donald in association with the National Museums of Scotland, 1986, p. 99-103.

A brief study of changes in the Romanian diet which was traditionally based on indigenous cereals, vegetables and dairy products. However, as early as the 17th century, a North American bean variety was introduced and potatoes followed in the next hundred years as, along with other Western customs, different foods were also introduced. From the late 18th century an embryonic food processing industry appeared in the cities, bringing specialist bakers and other shops. However, local traditions also persisted, especially in rural areas, where Ottoman mutton was more common than Western beef. The author also distinguishes between ordinary and celebratory foods, revealing that at this time even amongst the nobility it was not uncommon to find feasts held in the oriental fashion with twelve to eighteen courses beginning and ending with borsch.

687 **The elasticity of land: problems of property restitution in Transylvania.**
Katherine Verdery. *Slavic Review*, vol. 53, no. 4 (Winter 1994), p. 1,071-109.

Based on fieldwork carried out in the Transylvanian village of Vlaicu, this is a well researched foray into the complexities of land restitution in post-communist Romania. The lack of documentation or the presence of conflicting records and the obliteration of many markers between plots has made actual restitution – the return of the same land to those who owned it prior to collectivization – a process fraught with many difficulties. Over the years the land itself has also changed shape, stretching or contracting. This process can take either a physical form, as with the erosion of fields by the local River Maroș and the reclamation of agricultural land from a marsh, or a metaphorical guise, as in the case of so-called 'hidden land' – areas which remained undeclared to the central authorities so as to enable collective farms to meet over-ambitious production targets. The article deals with those who have gained and lost in the process of restitution together with the strategies and justifications they employ. The image of decollectivization conjured up by the author comes from the villager's own biblical image of the apocalypse and she resignedly notes 'Transylvanians will probably never see the full restitution of their earlier rights to land'.

Transport

688 **Transferring technology to a peripheral economy: the case of Lower Danube transport development, 1856-1928.**
John H. Jensen, Gerhard Rosegger. *Technology and Culture*, vol. 19, no. 4 (Oct. 1978), p. 675-702.

Examines some of the technical, economic and socio-political forces which shaped the development of a modern transport system in the Lower Danube basin. Within this development the authors look at the 'competition' between the river, as the traditional means of transport, and the railways, as the technological intruder, and their interrelation in terms of commercial and political viability. The authors divide the process of development into three chronological stages: first, the period of foreign engineers and their enterprises between 1856 and 1865; secondly, that of Romanian engineering and capital inputs between 1882 and 1913; and finally, the difficult time of recovery and renewal after the First World War.

689 **Transylvanian railways and access to the Lower Danube.**
Gerhard Rosegger, John H. Jensen. *East European Quarterly*, vol. 29, no. 4 (Winter 1995), p. 427-48.

Continuing their detailed study of technological and economic change in the Danubian basin (see also preceding entry) the authors of this article focus on the late Habsburg Empire. Amongst the factors that shaped railway development at the time, they highlight the constant need to compromise between economic rationality and political reality, the questionable abilities of many of the entrepreneurs and their lack of integrity, the failures of engineers, who did not live up to reputations they had carried from the West, and the frequent overriding of local regional interests in favour of broader central government policy.

690 **Sustainable transport in Central and Eastern European cities: proceedings of the workshop on transport and environment in Central and Eastern European cities, 28th-30th June 1995 Bucharest, Romania.**
Paris: Organisation for Economic Co-operation and Development, 1996. 429p.

A collection of papers from a conference organized to examine urban transport trends and related environmental, economic and social issues as well as suggest possible future transport policies for the cities of the region. The last section of the book is devoted to a case-study of Bucharest and contains two papers: Octavian Udriste, 'The metro: an essential part of the Bucharest public transport system and its future', p. 389-408; and Constantin Popescu, 'Integrated public transport in the municipality of Bucharest and agro-industrial suburbs', p. 409-29.

691 **The Romanian railway debate: a theme in political geography.**
David Turnock. *Journal of Transport History*, n.s., vol. 5, no. 2 (Sept. 1979), p. 105-21.

This paper, supported by a number of maps, examines the historical evolution of the Romanian railway system against a background of fluctuating political boundaries. The latter has been a particularly significant factor in the development of the railways, because most of the network was constructed prior to the First World War, when large swathes of the country still lay under Austro-Hungarian and, in the case of Bessarabia, Russian rule. Problems associated with the amalgamation of these different systems after 1918 slowed the development of the railways during the interwar years, as did a shortage of funds and the priority given to industrial and military schemes. Nevertheless, the deterioration in international security was eventually to lead to some renewed state investment in the railways prior to the Second World War in an effort to improve the country's defences. Since 1945, construction has generally been limited to a few branch lines and filling in the gaps left in the old system, with the only major project being a new direct line between Craiova, Bucharest and Tecuci.

Trade Unions

692 **Collective labor disputes in post-Ceauşescu Romania.**
Larry S. Bush. *Cornell International Law Journal*, vol. 26, no. 2
(Spring 1993), p. 373-420.
After the Revolution it seemed that the workers in nearly every industrial enterprise
created their own trade union. Only slowly have these consolidated into a number of
union blocs in a process which has been sadly neglected by scholars. Thus, although
in this article Bush is mostly concerned with Law 15/1991 and its effects on collective
labour disputes, he still manages to give the best overview of the process of union
formation after the Revolution. As regards the law, his argument is that it was aimed
at neutralizing strikes as a weapon so as to prevent the unions from challenging
government policies.

693 **Romania.**
Stephen Fischer-Galati. In: *European labor unions*. Edited by Joan
Campbell, General Consultant John P. Windmuller. Westport,
Connecticut: Greenwood Press, 1992, p. 371-80.
Before industrialization under communism, trade unions tended to play a marginal
role in Romanian history. In this brief overview the author provides an account of the
development of the union movement, focusing particularly on the years prior to 1944.
The chapter closes with a list of labour organizations including some of the current
bodies, which like the political parties of Romania, seem to be constantly forming and
reforming into new blocs.

694 **Workers' rights East and West: a comparative study of trade union and workers' rights in Western democracies and Eastern Europe.**
Adrian Karatnycky, Alexander J. Motyl, Adolph Sturmthal. New Bruswick, New Jersey: Transaction Books; London: League for Industrial Democracy, 1980. 150p.

The aim of this study, which examines the status of workers' and trade union's rights in both Western and Soviet bloc countries, was to move the issue of workers' rights to a more prominent position and link it more closely with the human rights debate. The book is divided into two sections. In the first, between pages 78-86, the authors consider the laws safeguarding workers' rights in Romania and how they are frequently ignored as 'workers' rights are being systematically denied'. In the second section, made up of documents, the charter of the Free Trade Union (SLOMR), which a number of workers and intellectuals tried to establish in 1979, is reproduced alongside a communiqué issued by the union and the transcript of a telephone call from Romania describing its brutal suppression.

Statistics

695 **Methodological and conceptual approaches of the Romanian labour force survey.**
Filofteia Panduru, Dan Ghergut. *Statistics in Transition*, vol. 1, no. 4 (June 1994), p. 491-508.

In an issue of this journal devoted to labour force survey methodology, this paper describes the statistical sampling patterns and questionnaires used in Romania for both the trial survey of October 1993 and the full survey of March 1994. The introduction of this revised labour force survey should not only provide more accurate estimates of employment and unemployment but also other important statistical information. This article is followed by comments by Giulio Ghellini (p. 503-06) and Richard Platek (p. 507-08).

696 **Romanian statistical yearbook.**
Bucharest: National Commission for Statistics, 1997. 965p.

This bilingual English-Romanian annual publication contains a useful summary of statistical information arranged in various categories: geography and environment, population, labour force, income and consumption, social services, health, education, trade, industry and agriculture.

697 **Report on Romania's national accounts by institutional sectors.**
Florina Tănase, Constantina Bugoi. *Statistics in Transition*, vol. 2, no. 3 (Aug. 1995), p. 383-92.

This special issue of the Polish Journal, *Statistics in Transition*, is largely devoted to the proceedings of a workshop on the change-over in Eastern Europe from the former communist accounting Material Production System [MPS] to the System of National Accounts [SNA] and European System of Integrated Accounts [ESA] so as to bring the transition economies into line with practices in Western Europe. In Romania the switch occurred in 1991 and within this issue, in a number of highly technical papers, Romanian experts relate their experiences. Alongside the article by Florina Tănase and Constantina Bugoi this issue also contains: Adriana Ciuchea, 'The final consumption of households in the general framework of the Rumanian national accounts', p. 401-408; Vasile Gh. Dumitrescu, 'Underground economy in the general framework of the Rumanian national accounts', p. 429-34; and Florina Tănase, 'The institutional sector "General Government" in Romania', p. 465-70. A further related article in the same issue is Florina Tănase, Clementina Ungureanu, Adriana Ciuchea, 'An analysis of the economic system of Romania within a SAM framework', p. 495-505.

Environment

698 **The distribution of solar global radiation over Romania.**
V. Bădescu. *Energy Sources*, vol. 12, no. 1 (1990), p. 83-95.

This study, which is based on meterological data amassed from twenty-nine localities, measures the monthly distributions of solar global radiation over Romania with the intention of correcting the world map of solar global radiation prepared by H. E Landsberg, H. Lippmann, K. H. Paffen and C. Troll, *World maps of climatology* (Berlin: Springer Verlag, 1965). Bădescu argues that Romania has a solar potential higher than that attributed to it by the world map, with the Carpathians together with the Black and the Mediterranean Seas having a major, although variable in their intensity, effect on the country's global radiation levels.

699 **Studies concerning the empirical relationship of cloud shade to point cloudiness (Romania).**
V. Bădescu. *Theoretical and Applied Climatology*, vol. 44 (1991), p. 187-200.

From records establishing the relationship between sunshine duration and cloud cover at a few selected locations, scientists are able to compute global solar radiation over a far wider geographical area. This article analyses the relationship between cloud shade and point cloudiness as recorded at twenty-nine weather stations in Romania and then extrapolates these results to cover other regions of the country.

700 **Focus and effectiveness of environmental activism in Eastern Europe: a comparative study of environmental movements in Bulgaria, Hungary, Slovakia and Romania.**
Liliana Botcheva. *Journal of Environment and Development*, vol. 5, no. 3 (Sept. 1996), p. 292-308.

A well-balanced and lucidly-argued essay about the activities of environmental groups in Bulgaria, Hungary, Slovakia and Romania after 1989. In particular, the author examines the apparent decline in support for such groups after their initial post-communist

224

popularity. She suggests that environmental issues attract wider popular support only when they are linked with political problems, and this thesis is substantiated in a series of convincing case-studies which include the Romanian town of Copşa Mică, where serious pollution problems have led to it being labelled 'the blackest town in the world' and where life expectancy is nine years lower than the Romanian average.

701   **The Danube Delta: geographic characteristics and ecological recovery.**
Petre Gastescu. *GeoJournal,* vol. 29, no. 1 (Jan. 1993), p. 57-67.
The Danube Delta covers 4,152 square kilometres and is the second largest delta in Europe. The vast majority of the wetland lies in Romania and in this article the author considers its development from its earliest geographical origins as an off-shore bar. Under communism the Delta was ruthlessly exploited as a source of natural resources. Reeds were harvested for cellulose, with the harvesting initially being performed by prisoners from labour camps, and fishing and agriculture were both intensified. Not only were all of these schemes economically unsuccessful but they also had a detrimental effect on the region's environment, in particular, because they disturbed the circulation of water, essential for a healthy ecosystem. The author concludes by stating that since 1989 there has been a welcome new emphasis on conservation in government policy, with much of the Delta now being protected as a biosphere reserve.

702   **Quality of the environment in Romania.**
Teodor Ognean, Angheluţă Vădineanu.   In: *Coping with crisis in Eastern Europe's environment.*   Edited by Joseph Alcamo.   New York; Carnforth, England: International Institute for Applied Systems Analysis & Parthenon, 1992, p. 245-58.
Written by two experts from the Romanian Ministry of the Environment, this is a highly informative paper on the catastrophic effect that unchecked industrialization has had on the Romanian environment. Surveying the effects of pollution on water, air and soil quality, they find that the deterioration in water quality has left fifty-one per cent of the hydrological network degraded in some areas, such as Ialomiţa. Furthermore, each year an estimated 1.8 million tonnes of pollutants are spewed into the air and there is also widespread soil erosion. The same volume also contains a second paper by Angheluţă Vădineanu, 'Priorities for environmental protection in Romania', p. 259-63, in which she sketches the measures proposed to improve the environment, although the author is careful to note that 'These actions also require substantial support from the European Community and other international organizations . . . involved in environmental protection at the regional and global levels'.

703   **Background to catastrophe: Romanian modernization policies and the environment.**
William O. Oldson.   *East European Quarterly,* vol. 30, no. 4 (Winter 1996), p. 517-27.
The environmental disasters of the Ceauşescu régime are well known. From the 2,400 tons of poisonous polychlorinated biphenyls dumped at the mouth of the Danube in Sulina to the blackened landscape around the chemical plant at Copşa Mică, they form a grim legacy which 'manifests a tone of ruthless industrial expansion, even of criminal exploitation'. However, according to the author, the experiences of the

Environment

Ceauşescu years were not unique; instead, they form part of a wider pattern which has seen Romanian governments consistently willing to sacrifice environmental considerations in the quest for a rapid industrialization in order to augment national security and ensure economic growth. The fact that this imperative is as strong today as it was before 1989 leads Oldson to conclude that the events of that year were nothing more than a bureaucratic *coup d'état*.

704 **Romania.**
David Turnock. In: *Environmental problems in Eastern Europe.*
Edited by Francis W. Carter, David Turnock. London; New York:
Routledge, 1996, p. 135-63.

The author catalogues the levels of air, water, soil and noise pollution present in Romania as well as the effects that deforestation, a poorly regulated chemical industry and the mismanagement of hydroelectric, land drainage and irrigation projects have had on the environment. Although industrialization has always brought some environmental costs, these rose to unacceptable levels under communism. Assessing the extent of the problem is made difficult by the lack of statistical information, but since the 1989 Revolution, the local press has heightened public awareness of environmental issues. However, the author prophesizes that the process of environmental improvement will be slow given the financial constraints faced by Romania.

Education

General

705 **Education in the Rumanian people's republic.**
Randolph L. Braham.   Washington, DC: US Government Printing
Office, 1963. 229p.
A detailed presentation of the educational system of communist Romania that also
includes information on pre-war structures. It highlights the steps taken to wipe out
illiteracy under communism and the progress that was achieved. It also contains an
interesting list of textbooks used in primary and secondary education during the
1950s.

706 **Ideological training in communist education: a case study of
Romania.**
Martin J. Croghan, Penelope P. Croghan.   Washington, DC:
University Press of America, 1980. 201p. bibliog.
Drawing on Martin Croghan's extensive fieldwork in Romania, this book offers a
valuable insight into all levels of the communist education system, from the
kindergarten to the university, as it developed under Ceauşescu. The principle aim of
the system was to mould a generation of ideologically and nationally minded young
citizens. Amongst other details, the authors reveal that even in kindergartens local
Party secretaries were instructed to read to the children highlights from the week's
news which inevitably focused on the activities of the Ceauşescus.

Higher education

707 **Higher education reform in Romania.**
T. O. Eisemon, I. Mihailescu, L. Vlasceanu, C. Zamfir, J. Sheehan,
C. H. Davis. *Higher Education*, vol. 30, no. 2 (Sept. 1995),
p. 135-52.
A detailed assessment of the situation of near crisis which has confronted Romanian higher education since 1989, with many institutions facing a challenging environment with only limited resources. Amongst the features the authors discuss here are the growth of student numbers, the rise in enrolments in the social sciences and the creation of private higher education institutions. The responses of the authorities to these changing circumstances have included reforms of the procedures for university funding, academic employment and university accreditation. The authors conclude by advancing a number of proposals for further reforms.

708 **The present state of Romanian studies in the United States and
Canada.**
Michael H. Impey. *Modern Language Journal*, vol. 59, no. 5-6
(Sept.-Oct. 1975), p. 262-72.
This is a survey of the growth of Romanian studies in the universities of the United States and Canada during the 1970s. The author records the ever increasing number of students who wish to study not only Romanian history but also literature and culture, and monitors the academic contributions of a number of scholars both in America and in Canada.

709 **The social sciences in a changing Romania.**
I. Mihailescu. *International Social Science Journal*, vol. 44, no. 131
(Feb. 1992), p. 153-58.
In this short article concerned with post-revolutionary developments in the social sciences, the author argues that a general review of both theory and methodology is a pressing necessity. However, such a process is hampered by a tendency amongst Romanian social scientists to disagree as regards research priorities.

710 **Legacy and change: higher education and restoration of academic
work in Romania.**
Jan Sadlak. *Technology in Society*, vol. 15, no. 1 (1993), p. 75-100.
Examines both the past constraints placed on higher education in Romania, especially under Ceauşescu, and the current difficulties. Backing his argument with statistical data on students, academic staff and research, the author discusses both the strengths and the weaknesses of the current reform programme. The changes will alter the character, institutional structure and mission of higher education in Romania, but substantial challenges still lie ahead.

711 **The use and abuse of the university: higher education in Romania, 1860-1990.**
Jan Sadlak. *Minerva*, vol. 29, no. 2 (Summer 1991), p. 195-225.
The author offers a broad survey of the fortunes of higher education in Romania since the foundation of the first university in Iași in 1860. Soon afterwards, in 1864, a university was founded in Bucharest and in 1867 this was followed by a polytechnic for the training of engineers and other vocational subjects. In the Austro-Hungarian lands, which were later destined to become Romanian, a university was founded at Cluj in 1872 and Cernăuți in 1875. Amongst other topics Sadlak considers the internal structures of the universities, the role of academics in politics, the system of control introduced by the communists and the decline of higher education under Ceaușescu, before finishing with some remarks about future prospects.

Science and Technology

712 **Information technology and business strategy in Romania.**
C. R. Franz, R. Klepper. *International Journal of Information Management*, vol. 15, no. 6 (1995), p. 451-61.

Romania, like the rest of Eastern Europe, entered the 1990s far behind the West in terms of the provision of information technology. Moreover, the systems that were available were more suited to the needs of the command economy than the market. In a series of case-studies the authors assess the progress six Romanian companies have made in adapting their information systems to the new post-communist environment and find that they have had only limited success in this task.

713 **Telecommunications in Central and Eastern Europe. Similarities, peculiarities and trends of change in the countries of transition.**
Gyula Sallai, Ivan Schmideg, George Lajtha. *Telecommunications Policy*, vol. 20, no. 5 (June 1996), p. 325-40.

In the mid-1990s the countries of Central and Eastern Europe, including Romania, were still relatively backward when it came to telecommunications. Indeed, in numbers of telephones per head of population Romania, proportionally, even lags behind neighbours like Bulgaria, although Poland also registers a similarly low figure. In this article the authors review the telecommunication development strategies announced by Romania and the other countries of the region with the aim of helping further the harmonization of services.

230

Literature and Philosophy

General

714   **The poetic return: variations on a theme by three Romanian poets abroad.**
Rodica Boțoman.   *Miorița*, vol. 8, no. 1-2 (1983), p. 1-13.
A study of the experience of poetic return in the works of three Romanian poets, Aron Cotruș, Vintilă Horia and Vasile Posteucă.

715   **Romanian contributions to the European avant-garde.**
Vera Călin.   *Cross Currents*, vol. 4, no. 5 (1985), p. 337-50.
A survey of the Romanian avant-garde from Urmuz, an unassuming substitute judge who fought in the First World War and committed suicide in 1923, to the better known Tristan Tzara and Eugene Ionescu. Although in his few short works Urmuz produced 'an anti-style which overthrew conventional and traditional concepts of literature', he died unknown. Tzara, who is credited as the creator of Dadaism, found fame in France as did Benjamin Fondane (Barbu Fundoianu), a representative of Romanian symbolism. Indeed, the author argues that the origins of the Romanian avant-garde can be seen as coming from 'a typical Balkan mixture of permissiveness with French sophistication'. During the 1930s the movement was particularly productive in Romania, encompassing artists such as Victor Brauner and Marcel Iancu, poets such as Ilarie Voronca and playwrights of the calibre of Eugene Ionescu.

716   **History of Romanian literature.**
G. Călinescu.   Paris: UNESCO, Nagard, 1987. 893p. bibliog.
This monumental and authoritative study, first published in Romania in 1941, covers the development of Romanian literature from the religious works of the 16th and 17th centuries through the Dadaists, surrealists, memorialists and other movements of the early 20th century to the 'literature of experience' of the 1930s. Within a lucid and highly informative exposition, each of the authors is assessed on their own merit and

then placed in the context of the literary trend which they represent. Accompanied by photographs of the writers, documents and manuscripts, this masterly work is indispensable for the student of Romanian literature.

717 **Romanian literature: dealing with the totalitarian legacy.**
Matei Calinescu. *World Literature Today*, vol. 65, no. 2
(Spring 1991), p. 244-48.
In this essay the author attempts to evaluate the so-called 'cultural crisis' that some have claimed has beset post-Ceaușescu Romania. Surveying the history of Romanian literature since the communist take-over, the author traces the fortunes of various literary groups, those who collaborated, those who were accused of bourgeois leanings and those who were active dissidents. In the process, he concludes that the purported 'cultural crisis' is, in fact, a superficial manifestation and expresses full confidence in the new generation of writers who were less affected by the Ceaușescu legacy.

718 **Romania's 1930's revisited.**
Matei Calinescu. *Salmagundi,* vol. 97 (Winter 1993), p. 133-51.
Mihail Sebastian's novel, *De două mii de ani* (For two thousand years), published in 1934, serves as the starting point for a wide-ranging review of Romanian literature from the 1930s onwards. After pointing out the limited options that men of letters had under communism, including, amongst other things, acceptance of the official line, emigration and traditionalism, the author, borrowing a metaphor from Ionesco's play 'Rhinoceros', laments the infectious 'rhinoceritis' which has beset succeeding generations of Romanian writers, journalists, philosophers and artists. This disease led them first to conform to the ideological regimentation of fascism and then communism.

719 **The Romanian ballad 'Cicoarea'.**
Ana Radu Chelariu. *Romanian Civilization*, vol. 4, no. 2
(Summer 1995), p. 71-74.
An analysis of the ballad 'Cicoarea' (Chicory) in which the sun is rejected by his lover, a fairy. Recorded in Transylvania by G. Dem. Teodorescu, it was first published in Bucharest in 1885. Although similar ballads are encountered elsewhere in South-Eastern Europe, the author suggests that this form is specific to the Romanian lands.

720 **Aspects of erotic and Bacchic poetry in Roumanian and Modern Greek literature at the end of 18th century.**
Maria Pia Chișu. *Balkan Studies*, vol. 27, no. 1 (1986), p. 61-75.
A comparative study of the poetry of Romanian pre-modernists poets such as Ienăchiţa (1740-98), Alecu Văcărescu (1762-1800), Costache Conachi (1778-1849), Nicolae Dimache (1776-1836) and Ioan Cantacuzino (1757-1828), and their Greek counterparts Athanasios Christopoulos (1772-1847), Ioannis Vilaras (1771-1823) and Athanasios Psalidas (1764-1829). The author suggests that the markers of eroticism, such as flirting, hugging, kissing and so on, which feature in the work of all these poets, acquired a new 'meaning' at the end of the 18th century on account of the peculiar spiritual and historical circumstances of the Balkan area, and became signifiers of political passion, fear, anxiety, frustration and even desperation.

721 **The personality of Romanian literature: a synthesis.**
Constantin Ciopraga, translated from the Romanian by Ştefan
Avădanei. Iaşi, Romania: Junimea Publishing House, 1981. 357p.
The first part of this book contains a series of scholarly meditations on the 'personality'
of Romania literature. Amongst the themes considered are the degree of Balkan-Oriental
influence, which the author considers has been important 'only figuratively', and the use
of the fantastic and myth. The second section, 'Reverberations', is a series of case-studies
of the 'giants' of pre-communist Romanian literature from Cantemir and Eminescu
through Caragiale and Rebreanu to Blaga and Barbu.

722 **A tragic love for German: Holocaust poetry from the Bukovina.**
Amy Colin. *Cross Currents*, vol. 10 (1991), p. 73-84.
The best known poet from Bucovina is Paul Celan, but in this article the author
surveys the work of some of his German-Jewish contemporaries: Alfred Margul-
Sperber, Moses Rosenkranz, David Goldfield, Isaac Schreyer, Alfred Kittner, Rose
Ausländer, Immanuel Weissglas and Alfred Gong. The traditions of Bucovina were of
a rich interplay of cultures – German, Romanian, Ukrainian and Yiddish – in which
'everybody, the liberals as well as the fanatics, peacefully coexisted in the mutual
consent of cynicism'. This world was shattered by the Second World War with the
experiences of the Jewish population of the region producing some haunting elegiac
poetry, as in Gong's *Israel's last psalm* in which the victim's prayers to God turn into
doubts: 'Soon we will be yours alone . . . /Death hums in the pipes./Out of the flue the
greasy smoke will rise . . . /O Yahwe, can you hear our voices'.

723 **Narration across the totalistic gap: on recent Romanian fiction.**
Marcel Cornis-Pop. *Symposium*, vol. 43, no. 1 (Spring 1989), p. 3-19.
The author uses a brief critical analysis of the literary works of authors such as
Eugene Ionescu, D. R. Popescu, Mircea Eliade, Ov. S. Crohmalniceanu and Augustin
Buzura to illustrate some aspects of the 'periphrastic' style within their writings. He
starts from the premise that the 'discourse' between Romanian literature and politics
has never been direct but instead hides behind metaphoric explorations and symbolic
disguises. This article, alongside other previously published work, much of which is
concerned with the critical analysis of modern Romanian literature, has recently been
published in Marcel Cornis-Pope *The unfinished battles: Romanian postmodernism
before and after 1989* (Iaşi, Romania: Polirom, 1996. 190p.).

724 **Literature and society in Romania since 1948.**
Dennis Deletant. In: *Perspectives on literature and society in Eastern
and Western Europe.* Edited by Geoffrey A. Hosking, George F.
Cushing. Basingstoke, England: Macmillan in association with the
School of Slavonic and East European Studies, University of London,
1989, p. 121-61.
A knowledgeable survey of the travails of Romanian literature under communism and,
in particular, the attempts of a number of writers under Ceauşescu to expand the bounds
of permitted literature. Their efforts achieved some success in the late 1960s and until
the 1980s the Writers' Union was able to stave off Party attempts to dictate who should
be elected as president. Within his general survey of politics in literature, Deletant pays
special attention to a few individual works such as Augustin Buzura's *Absenţii* (The

absent ones) and *Feţele tăcerii* (The faces of silence) and Marin Preda's *Delirul* (The delirium) and *Cel mai iubit dintre pămînteni* (The most beloved of earth dwellers).

725   **A concise history of Romanian literature.**
      Ion Dodu Bălan.   Bucharest: Editura Ştiinţifică şi Enciclopedică, 1981. 119p.

This informative study, which is arranged chronologically, provides details on the life and works of many of the most influential figures of Romanian literature. Although it lacks a bibliography, the entries are expansive and often include extracts in translation from the works of the authors.

726   **The fate of Romanian culture.**
      Mircea Eliade, translated from the Romanian by Bogdan Ştefănescu.
      Bucharest: Editura Athena, 1995. 47p.

The basic thesis of Eliade's text, originally written in the 1950s, is that it is only the vicissitudes of history which have prevented the Romanian people from developing their genius and making a full contribution to Western culture. Instead, foreign domination has left cultural development in the Romanian lands rooted at the peasant level with the real treasures being folk ballads such as 'Mioriţa' and 'The legend of Master Manole'. Moreover, this painful past has also had the further effect of raising the Romanian people to a special historic and spiritual significance because '. . . by taking shelter into their own self, focusing on their traditions, defending themselves against the world outside . . . the Romanians preserved, deepened and put to good use a Christian vision of Nature, such as it had been expressed during the first centuries of Christianity. Therefore, the conservativsism and archaism of Romanian folklore saved a patrimony of the general Christianity, annihilated by historical processes'.

727   **Partei und literatur in Rumänien seit 1945.** (Party and literature in Romania since 1945.)
      Anneli Ute Gabanyi.   Munich: R. Oldenbourg Verlag, 1945. 209p.
      (Untersuchungen zur Gegenwartskunde Südosteuropas. Herausgegeben vom Südost-Institut München, no. 9).

A comprehensive and systematic analysis of the development of Romanian literature under the communist régime between 1945 and the 1970s and its influence on various literary genres, especially that of literary criticism. This is an indispensable guide for all those interested in the literature and politics of this period.

728   **Semiotics in Romania.**
      Sanda Golopenţia-Eretescu.   In: *The Semiotic sphere.*   Edited by Thomas A. Sebeok, Jean Umiker-Sebeok.   New York; London: Plenum Press, 1986, p. 417-72.

Semiotics is the study of symbols and signs and the twentieth chapter of this book, outlining the progress of semiotics research in a number of countries, is dedicated to Romania. The author starts with a historical introduction examining the philosophical style of Lucian Blaga, the scientific aesthetics of Pius Servien, Constantin Brăiloiu's structural ethno-musicology and Mircea Eliade's work on the history of religions, before giving an account of current research including Solomon Marcus' work on mathematical poetics and formal semiotics.

729 Milan Kundera's wisdom of uncertainty and other categorical imperatives: the experience of the contemporary Romanian novel.
Michael H. Impey. In: *Literature and politics in Eastern Europe.*
Selected papers from the fourth world congress for Soviet and East European Studies, Harrogate, 1990. Edited by Celia Hawkesworth.
New York: St. Martin's Press, 1992, p. 59-73.
This is an appraisal of the contemporary Romanian novel according to the principles of aesthetics expounded by Milan Kundera, the renowned Czech novelist and literary critic. The author, examining the fiction of writers such as Popescu, Ionescu, Buzura, Preda and Breban, reaches the conclusion that on the basis of their supra-natural context and their spirit of continuity, these novels are not bound by time or place but are in fact capable of passing beyond the limitations of any bourgeois or socialist experience.

730 Recent Romanian-German poetry: Bossert, Hodjak, Modoi, Britz.
H. Konig-Fritz. In: *The Germanic mosaic: cultural and linguistic diversity in society.* Edited by Carol Aisha Blackshire-Belay.
Westport, Connecticut: Greenwood, 1994, p. 33-44.
Analyses the poetry of a number of German-Romanian poets including Rolf Bossert, Frank Hodjak, Juliana Modoi and Helmut Britz. Emphasizing their talent in employing irony, innuendoes and long, eloquent pauses or, as the author terms them, 'articulate omissions', Konig-Fritz argues that these proved potent weapons in the battle against the censor, allowing the poets to safeguard their artistic expression. Another chapter in this book which deals with a topic relating to Romania is Adrian Poruciuc, 'Linguistic aspects of the Romanian-Saxon contact in Transylvania' (p. 95-104).

731 Romanian literature and the publishing industry since 1989: assymetries between history and rhetoric.
Ion Lefter Bogdan. *Canadian Review of Comparative Literature,* vol. 22, no. 3-4 (Sept.-Dec. 1995), p. 867-79.
This learned and erudite article starts from the premise that, when political and social oppression is successfully challenged and freedom of speech is once again regained, a new literary reality must necessarily follow. However, in the case of post-1989 Romania, the author argues that this does not seem to have occurred and instead an 'asymmetry' has arisen. In examining why this might be, he suggests that prior to the Revolution, Romanian writers, both at home and abroad, had already embraced what was essentially a post-communist discourse, so that after 1989, although there were great changes in the country as a whole, literature has not felt the need to make enormous readjustments.

732 Allegories of subversion: hermeneutics and the politics of critical reading. A Romanian case.
Christian Moraru. *Symposium,* vol. 49, no. 1 (Spring 1995), p. 35-50.
Discussing recent critical analyses of the literary output of Ion Luca Caragiale, the leading Romanian playwright of the 19th century, the author argues that the interpretative methods and epistemiological strategies employed by Romanian literary

critics and theorists since the 1960s have been borrowed from the West and, more specifically, from French structuralism and poststructuralism. He then suggests that these influences have in turn acted as a catalyst for the political radicalization of Romanian intellectuals.

733 **Patterns of minority life: recent Hungarian literary reports in Romania.**
Károly Nagy. In: *Society in change: studies in honour of Béla K. Király.* Edited by Steven Bela Vardy, Agnes Huszar Vardy. Boulder, Colorado: East European Monographs, distributed by Columbia University Press, 1983, p. 585-95. (East European Monographs, no. 132).

The author offers a brief introduction to the broad topic of 'sociographic' prose in Romania and, in particular, the literary output of writers within the Hungarian community, including Árpád Farkas, Gyula Szabó, László Király, András Sütő and Zoltán Tófalvi. Excerpts from their work are used to illustrate the vicissitudes of the Hungarian community during the Ceauşescu years.

734 **The persistence of archaic traits among gypsy story-telling communities in Romania.**
Olga Nagy. *Journal of the Gypsy Lore Society,* Fourth Series, vol. 1, no. 4 (1978), p. 221-39.

In this article the author tests the hypothesis that what at first sight appears fixed and unchanging in a folk-tale, is in fact, when viewed over a longer time-scale, in a state of continuous flux. To this end, 156 fairy-tales collected from five Transylvanian gypsy communities, Mera, Suceagu, Sîncraiul de Mureş, Band and Brîncoveneşti, are examined in order to gauge the persistence of archaic traits.

735 **Mihai Şora and the traditions of Romanian philosophy.**
Virgil Nemoianu. *Review of Metaphysics,* vol. 43, no. 3 (March 1990), p. 591-605.

Starting from the premise that Romanian philosophy is a natural bridge between Eastern and Western thought, the author offers a historical examination of Romanian philosophers and their work from the 17th until the 19th century. He then provides a survey of the main features of the modern school of Romanian philosophy, as it crystallized from the 1930s onwards, and, in particular, explores the writings of Mihai Şora, a representative member of this school, whose writings not only shaped the themes of modern Romanian philosophy but also gave a kind of retrospective coherence to the whole philosophical tradition.

736 **Symposium/colloque. Studies on Romanian modernism.**
Edited by Virgil Nemoianu. *Southeastern Europe,* vol. 11, no. 2 (1984), p. 127-68.

This edition of this journal contains a number of articles drawn from a symposium on Romanian Modernism, including: Marcel Cornis-Pop, 'Long rehearsed "Revolution of Sensibility": postmodernism and the Romanian historical Avant-Garde', p. 127-48; Dan Cristea, 'The heretical poetry of Gellu Naum', p. 149-58; and Dan Petrescu, 'Le paradoxe de la première répétition' (The paradox of the first repetition), p. 159-68. There is also a short note by Zoe Apostolache-Stoicescu and Nicolae Dunăre on 'A Romanian sociologist – Dimitrie Gusti: his contacts with American scholars and institutes', p. 225-36.

737　**Coming home into exile: the end of Romanian-German culture.**
Erika Nielsen.　In: *Cultural transformations in the new Germany: American and German perspectives.*　Edited by Friederike Eigler, Peter C. Pfeiffer.　Columbia, South Carolina: Camden House, 1993, p. 81-90.

This chapter forms a memorial to a literary genre that is already dying and very soon, according to the author, will be dead – Romanian-German literature. Ironically, it was in the very last decades of its existence that this community experienced a remarkable flowering of its culture, as individual writers blended their own personal experiences in narratives which chronicled the suffering of their German community as a whole. However, after years of remorseless pressure under the Ceauşescu régime both writers and audience have now departed to their historic homeland.

738　**Nikolaus Berwanger and the contemporary German literary scene in West Romania.**
Peter Pabisch.　*World Literature Today*, vol. 59, no. 1 (Winter 1985), p. 30-34.

Focuses on the activities of the German literary circle in Timişoara during the communist period. In particular, the author appraises the role and contribution of the German, Nikolaus Berwanger, a prominent cultural figure and editor-in-chief of the newspaper *Neue Banater Zeitung*. A political and spiritual leader as well as a poet, writer of short stories and dramatic texts, Berwanger became a symbol for all those who contributed to the new Romanian-German literature, such as Otto Aczel, Magdalene Ballmann, Jakob Dietrich, Marianne Ebner and Erika Scharf.

739　**The Romanian novel.**
Sorin Pârvu, with an introduction by Kurt W. Treptow.　Boulder, Colorado: East European Monographs in co-operation with the Romanian Cultural Foundation Publishing House, distributed by Columbia University Press, 1992. 161p. (East European Monographs, no. 329).

The aim of this volume is to make available in English translation extracts from the works of some of Romanian leading authors so as to bring them to the attention of non-Romanian speakers. The extracts, which all date from before the Second World War, are arranged chronologically and in each case are accompanied by a critical analysis considering the literary strategies and structural devices employed. Amongst the novels selected are Ionel Teodoreanu's *La Medeleni* (At Medeleni), Mihail Sadoveanu's *Hanu-Ancuţei* (Ancuţa's Inn), and *Fraţii Jderi* (The Jderi Brothers) and Mateiu Caragiale's *Craii de Curtea Veche* (Kings of the old court).

740 **Hard lines: Romanian poetry, truth, and heroic irony under the Ceauşescu dictatorship.**
Adam J. Sorkin. *The Literary Review*, vol. 35, no. 1 (Fall 1991), p. 26-38.

In the face of the censorship of the Ceauşescu régime writers developed certain 'protective mechanisms' or to use the author's expression 'ventriloquism of irony' to safeguard themselves and their muse. In this article Sorkin traces these techniques of oblique discourse and polysemous meaning within a number of poems including Angel Dumbraveanu's *The imperial winter*, Mircea Dinescu's *Death reads the newspaper*, Ioana Ieromin's *Monday mornings*, Marin Sorescus's *Icarus* and Virgil Mihaiu's *Lighthouse*. More recently Sorkin, together with Irina Grigorescu Panaea, edited a collection of poems by Angel Dumbraveanu entitled *Selected poems of Anghel Dumbraveanu in Romanian and English: love and winter* (Lewiston, New York: Edwin Mellen Press, 1992. 205p.).

741 **The oldest illuminated Moldavian manuscript.**
Émil Turdeanu. *Slavonic and East European Review*, vol. 29, no. 73 (June 1951), p. 456-70.

A detailed and critical examination of one of the earliest known books from the Romanian lands, a Greco-Slavic gospel copied in Neamţ in 1429 which is currently held by the Bodleian Library, Oxford. Amongst the other issues discussed by this distinguished literary historian are the history of the manuscript, the identity of the copyist and the date of its production. This article is also reproduced in a collection of sixteen essays by the same author, although all the others are in French, under the title *Études de littérature roumaine et d'écrits slaves et grecs des principautés roumaines* (Studies of Romanian literature and Slavic and Greek texts from the Romanian Principalities) (Leiden, Netherlands: E. J. Brill, 1985. 509p.). Early Moldavian literary endeavours are placed in a wider context in another article by this author, 'Centres of literary activity in Moldavia, 1504-1552', *Slavonic and East European Review*, vol. 34, no. 82 (Dec. 1955), p. 99-123.

Anthologies

742 **Like diamonds in coal asleep: selections from 20th century Romanian poetry.**
Compiled and introduced by Andrei Bantaş, translated from the Romanian by Andrei Bantaş, Dan Duţescu and Leon Leviţchi.
Bucharest: Minerva Publishing House, 1985. 375p.

This wide-ranging anthology contains poems by nearly seventy of the most influentia Romanian poets of the 20th century, including the four men whom the compile considers to be the 'pillars' of this poetry: Tudor Arghezi, George Bacovia, Ion Barbı and Lucian Blaga. The title is borrowed from Mihai Codreanu's eponymous poen which opens the volume.

743   **An anthology of contemporary Romanian poetry.**
Translated from the Romanian by Andrea Deletant, Brenda Walker.
London; Boston, Massachusetts: Forest Books, 1984. 99p.

The aim of the translators in this work was to familiarize a wider public with the
literary output of Romanian poets of the calibre of Ana Blandiana, Ioan Alexandru,
Constanța Buzea, Nina Cassian, Ștefan Augustin Doinaș, Marin Sorescu, Nichita
Stănescu and Ion Stoica. Many of these poets first made their mark in the late 1960s,
when conditions in Romania eased somewhat and censorship was imposed slightly
less vigorously. However, the formative years of all these poets were spent under the
harshest years of communism and despite their differing techniques, styles and
influences, the common thread that binds them together is an 'anguish of being', as
they use verse to explore themes such as solitude, destruction and death.

744   **Silent voices: an anthology of contemporary Romanian women
poets.**
Translated by Andrea Deletant and Brenda Walker with an introduction
by Fleur Adcock.   London; Boston, Massachusetts: Forest Books,
1986. 161p.

This anthology features the poetry of fourteen of the finest postwar Romanian female
poets, including Nina Cassian, Ana Blandiana and Daniela Crăsnaru. Addressing a
variety of social, moral and philosophical issues, these women were able through their
poems to blunt the controls imposed by the state publishing houses so that even in the
darkest days of the Ceaușescu era, their work possessed a remarkable freedom of
spirit. Full of linguistic vigour, irony and humour, the poems reflect the joys and
sorrows of motherhood, childhood, love, family life and marriage. Within many of the
poems the theatre serves as a metaphor to explore public life and wider human
experiences.

745   **The pied poets: contemporary verse of the Transylvanian and
Danube Germans of Romania.**
Selected and translated by Robert Elsie.   London; Boston,
Massachusetts: Forest Books, 1990. 192p.

It is not an exaggeration to say that the sixteen poets presented in this book represent
both the zenith of German-language poetry in Romania and also its epitaph, as since
1989 the communities they speak for have seeped away to their German homelands.
Indeed prior to 1989 many of these German poets, under pressure from the Ceaușescu
régime, had already found exile in the West, especially the members of the literary
circle *Aktionsgruppe Banat* including Richard Wagner, William Totok, Nikolaus
Berwanger and Johann Lippet. Given the experience of their nation the themes of
exile and leaving inevitably loom large in many of the works. In his poem
'Departure', Totok writes 'Your womb, your breasts – my homeland/Slips away in the
melting snow' and in the poem 'Perhaps I'd take my coffee mug', Frieder Schuller
longs for the day a German passport will arrive. However, elsewhere the lesser
preoccupations of daily life shine through.

746 **When the tunnels meet: contemporary Romanian poetry.**
Edited by John Fairleigh. Newcastle upon Tyne, England: Bloodaxe
Books, 1996. 112p.

In this volume ten leading Irish poets – including the Nobel laureate Seamus Heaney –
have produced English versions of poems by ten Romanian poets. Amongst the
Romanian poets are well known figures such as Ana Blandiana and Marin Sorescu,
but also included are less translated poets such as Cezar Baltoz and Ileana Malancioiu.
Although this is at first sight a rather unusual collaboration, involving lands from the
opposite extremities of Europe, in fact, in both countries poets are expected to play a
remarkably similar role, articulating private thoughts whilst also acting as a public
conscience. Both Romania and Ireland, in spite of an often tragic history, also share
the trait of being places of escape for the romantic imagination.

747 **The phantom church and other stories from Romania.**
Edited and translated by Georgiana Farnoaga, Sharon King, selection,
introduction, chronology and biographical notes by Florin Manolescu.
Pittsburgh, Pennsylvania: University of Pittsburgh Press, 1996. 240p.
bibliog. (Pitt Series in Russian and Eastern European Studies).

This volume seeks to make available to a Western audience a representative sample of
some of the best of Romanian short-story writing during the last half century. Stories
are included from writers such as Fănuş Neagu, Petru Dumitriu, Dumitru Radu
Popescu, Ana Blandiana, Dumitru Ţepeneag and Gabriela Adameşteanu, many of
whom have rarely, if ever, appeared in English translation before. Although various
themes and styles appear, satire, allegory, parable and metaphor predominate as the
writers responded to the political dogmatism preached by the communist régime.

748 **Balade populare româneşti: Romanian popular ballads.**
Translated by Leon D. Leviţchi, Andrei Bantaş, Dan Duţescu, Alfred
Margul-Sperber, W. D. Snodgrass. Bucharest: Minerva, 1980. 471p.

A bilingual anthology (Romanian and English) of Romanian folk ballads which date
from as early as the 16th century. The entries are grouped thematically under broad
categories such as pastoral, religious, notorious outlaws, fantastical tales, etc.

749 **Anthology of contemporary Romanian poetry.**
Edited, translated and with an introduction by Roy MacGregor-Hastie.
London: Peter Owen, 1969. 166p.

The first anthology of 20th-century Romanian verse to be published in the United
Kingdom, this volume contains a judicious selection of poems drawn primarily from
poets who were active in the years after the Second World War.

750 **An anthology of Romanian women poets.**
Edited by Adam J. Sorkin, Kurt W. Treptow. Boulder, Colorado:
East European Monographs in co-operation with the Romanian
Cultural Foundation Publishing House, distributed by Columbia
University Press, 1994. 157p. (East European Monographs, no. 397;
Classics of Romanian Literature, no. 7).

In keeping with the aim of this series, which is to present some of the most important
works of Romanian literature to an international audience, this volume offers a taste of
the achievements of Romanian female poets over the last two centuries. Starting from
the work of Veronica Micle and Matilda Cugler-Poni in the 19th century, it proceeds
through interwar poets such as Magda Isanos to contemporary figures of the stature of
Ana Blandiana and Daniela Crăsnaru. Finally, it looks to the next generation of
Romanian women poets by including younger writers such as Carmen Firan and
Carmen Veronica Steiciuc.

751 **Transylvanian voices: an anthropology of contemporary poets
from Cluj-Napoca.**
Edited and translated by Adam J. Sorkin, Liviu Bleoca. Iaşi,
Romania: Romanian Cultural Foundation, 1994. 112p. (Romanian
Civilization Studies, no. 4).

This anthology, reflecting the varied ethnic composition of the city, contains the work
of sixteen Cluj-based poets, ten Romanians, five Hungarians and one German. In his
introduction Sorkin notes that whilst communism had the deleterious effect of
breaking cultural ties with the West, it also provided a 'bracing tonic, a goad to poetic
inventiveness and the natural ingenuity, indirectness, and the metaphorical and
ironical obliqueness of the art, forcing poets . . . to find ways around the regime's
prohibitions and follies'. He sees the communist period as a time when poetry was a
'witness to the spiritual terror and material deprivation of the police state and an
essential participant in the resistance of the human psyche to the denial of its integrity
and its freedom'.

752 **Young poets of a new Romania.**
Selected and edited by Ion Stoica, translated from the Romanian by
Brenda Walker with Michaela Celea-Leach, introduced by Alan
Brownjohn. London: Forest Books, 1991. 131p.

This is a collection of verse by a group of poets who at the time of writing were in
their late thirties. Although they form no single literary group and have disparate and
diverse ideas as to the way poetry should be written, they are nevertheless bound
together by their shared experiences of oppression during the late Ceauşescu years.
Indeed, even in these days of darkness, their abilities were such that with the aid of
some sympathetic members of the Writers' Union, their talents were still able to shine.

Individual authors

753 **Demon in brackets.**
Maria Banuş, translated from the Romanian by Dan Duţescu with a
preface by Nicolae Manolescu. London: Forest Books, Romanian
Cultural Foundation, 1994. 228p.

This parallel Romanian and English text contains only Banuş' earliest works with her
later poems written under communism being excluded. Banuş, a talented poet, essayist
and translator, made her debut in 1937 with 'Girls' land', a collection of intelligent
verses about female sensation and sensibility. With a simplicity of method and a pure
lyricism, her poetry explores the eternal themes of life and death, love and disillusion-
ment, joy and fear.

754 **At the court of yearning.**
Lucian Blaga, translated from the Romanian with an introduction by
Andrei Codrescu and an afterword by Marcel Cornis-Pop. Columbus,
Ohio: Ohio State University Press, 1989. 211p. (Romanian Literature
and Thought in Translation. A Sandstone Book).

One of the giants of the cultural life of interwar Romania, Lucian Blaga wrote
philosophy like a poet and poetry like a philosopher. This collection contains the bulk
of his poetry written prior to 1949, when he was stripped of his university chair at Cluj
by the communist authorities. The poems are taken from seven collections: 'Poems of
light' (1919), 'The footprints of the prophet' (1921), 'In the great passing' (1924), 'In
praise of sheep' (1929), 'One the water divides' (1933), 'At the court of yearning'
(1938), and 'The unsuspected chair' (1943). The translator, a fellow poet, draws
parallels between Blaga's inability to speak until the age of four and the silence that
befell his poems under communism.

755 **The hour of sand: selected poems 1969-1988.**
Ana Blandiana, translated by Peter Jay and Anca Cristoforici.
London: Anvil Press, 1990. 103p.

Most of the poems in this volume originated in the collection, 'Ora de nisip', first
published in 1983. They were therefore written during the Ceauşescu years and
Blandiana's neo-romantic poetry is primarily a response to the suffering of that time.
The translators call it a 'poetry of epiphanies . . . minor personal epiphanies of
everyday life . . .'. Almost 'Eminescean' in its rhyme and construction, it blends
religious imagery with other symbols as Blandiana seeks to communicate to her
audience the possibility of achieving inner salvation amidst omnipotent destructive
forces which threaten the harmonious rhythms of existence.

756 **Peter Neagoe's relations with the American expatriate movement
in France.**
Rodica Boţoman. *Mioriţa*, vol. 5, no. 2 (July 1978), p. 163-71.

A survey of the life and work of the Transylvanian author Peter Neagoe who was born
in 1881 in Odrihei. After finishing school in Sibiu, Neagoe attended the Bucharest
Academy of Arts, where he was a contemporary of Brâncuşi, before emigrating to the
United States. Here he worked at a number of jobs whilst he mastered the English

language. From 1926 to 1935 he lived in France where he took up writing full-time and came to know many of the leading intellectuals of the day. As a result of these contacts he was asked in 1932 to edit a volume of short stories and poems by leading American expatriate writers, including Ernest Hemingway, Henry Miller and Ezra Pound. This appeared under the title *Americans abroad: an anthology* (The Hague: The Servire Press, 1932. 475p.). Shortly afterwards Neagoe published a volume of his own short stories, a number of which are set in his native Transylvania: *Storm* (Paris: Obelisk Press, c. 1934. 304p.). This volume was banned from the USA on account of its alleged obscenity and the author became something of a *cause célèbre* for a while. Afterwards Neagoe continued to publish a number of novels which drew on his Transylvanian roots, for example, *Easter sun* (q.v.).

757 **Refugees.**
Augustin Buzura, translated from the Romanian by Ancuţa Vultur and Fred Nadaban. Boulder, Colorado: East European Monographs, distributed by Columbia University Press, 1994. 461p. (Eastern European Monographs, no. 349).

Born in Berinţa, Maramureş in 1938, Augustin Buzura studied medicine at the University of Cluj before embarking on a literary career which was to make him one of Romania's leading novelists. Starting from the novel, *Absenţii* (The absent ones), published in 1970, his writings offered a critique of the Ceauşescu régime and the moral decline of Romanian society. *Refugees*, which was first published in Romania in 1984, marks a further step in this process as Buzura lambasts the passivity and social conformity of the Romanian people in the face of tyranny. Instead of a virtue he considers such character traits to be a mere shield for cowardice.

758 **Ionesco and Rhinoceros: personal and political backgrounds.**
Matei Calinescu. *East European Politics and Societies*, vol. 9, no. 3 (Fall 1995), p. 393-432.

'Rhinoceros', Ionesco's famous play of 1958, which was derived from an earlier short story of 1957, is examined in this essay not as a literary product but as a model for understanding how a glittering generation of Romanian intellectuals in the 1930s succumbed to the 'puerile, nebulous, primitive mysticism of the Iron Guard'. The author suggests that the play, which is concerned with the metamorphosis of people into animals, reflects the playwright's personal distress at the growing fanaticism of his close friends, since almost alone of his generation, Ionesco, born in Slatina in 1909, remained immune to the blandishments of the extreme right. This stance may be explained by his background; he had a French mother and a Romanian father and a youth spent in both countries made him both a 'reluctant Romanian and a nostalgic Frenchman'.

759 **The error of being: poems.**
Ion Caraion, translated from the Romanian by Marguerite Dorian and Elliott B. Urdang. London: Forest Books, Romanian Cultural Foundation, 1994. 142p.

Much of the poetry of Ion Caraion was composed during the eleven years he spent in prison and detention camps. Held in his memory until he was free to set it down, it inevitably often passes judgement on the conditions in which it was shaped. Caraion's was a powerful voice whose main source of energy came from his painful collision with what he saw as a distorted and depraved world. This collection reproduces his

Literature and Philosophy. Individual authors

poems in parallel Romanian and English texts. An earlier anthology of Caraion's poems, also translated by Dorian and Urdang, is *Ion Caraion, poems* (Athens, Ohio; London: Ohio University Press, 1981. 109p.).

760 **The trapped strawberry.**
Petru Cârdu, with an introduction by Daniel Weissbort, translated from the Romanian and Serbo-Croatian by Brenda Walker with Dušica Marinkov. London; Boston, Massachusetts: Forest Books, 1990. 84p.

Born in Yugoslavia of Romanian parents, Cârdu draws in his poetry upon the French surrealist tradition, a genre which has continued to flourish in Eastern Europe, and especially in Yugoslavia and Romania, long after its most productive moments passed in the West. Written in an almost prophetic fashion prior to the disintegration of Yugoslavia, Cârdu's short and pithy poems are laced with allusions and metaphors drawn from a wide range of mythical, biblical, historical and contemporary contexts. Through his poetry Cârdu speaks of the fears, predicaments and illusions of life but he stubbornly refuses to provide ready answers.

761 **An interview with poet Mircea Ivănescu.**
Thomas C. Carlson. *Cross Currents*, vol. 4, no. 5 (1985), p. 351-62.

The transcript of an interview with the poet, critic, editor and translator who was awarded the National Poetry Award in 1973 by the Writer's Union of Bucharest. During the interview Ivănescu reveals that he started to write verse only at the age of twenty-eight after a female colleague at a Bucharest weekly challenged him to write some poems about her, recording as an afterthought about this early outpouring of sentiment: 'Incidentally, they were terrible'.

762 **Waiting for the dawn: Mircea Eliade in perspective.**
Edited by David Carrasco, Jane Marie Law, foreword by Joseph Mitsuo Kitagawa. Niwot, Colorado: University Press of Colorado, 1991. rev. ed. 170p.

This book was born out of a year-long seminar about Mircea Eliade held at the University of Colorado in 1982 which was attended by the scholar himself shortly before his death. The volume contains a number of lectures by Eliade, some articles about his work and a selection of his literary works, including his last piece of fiction, the previously unpublished 'In the shadow of the Lily' which was translated from the Romanian by Mac Linscott Ricketts.

763 **Call yourself alive?**
Nina Cassian, translated from the Romanian by Andrea Deletant and Brenda Walker, introduced by Fleur Adcock. London; Boston, Massachusetts: Forest Books, 1988. 80p.

Born in Galați in 1924, Nina Cassian suffered through poverty during her early life. After her marriage to a communist activist, she herself became infused with political idealism and wrote several volumes of poetry in the socialist realist style, which she now rejects on aesthetic grounds. With an easing of censorship during the 1960s, she produced a string of verse collections, full of vigour and sensuality, but at times also startling and even shocking in their sheer physicality, with the body, as the source of the erotic, being emphasized as a complex but also flexible rhythm of expression. This collection of love poems, written at various times in Cassian's life, is thematically arranged into four main categories: 'Call yourself alive?', 'God, how well I remember the pain', 'And when summer comes to an end', and 'I left those walls . . .'.

764 **Cheerleader for a funeral.**
Nina Cassian, translated by Brenda Walker with the author.   London; Boston, Massachusetts: Forest Books, 1992. 67p.

In 1985, during a visit to the USA, Cassian learnt that a close friend in Romania, Gheorghe Ursu, had been arrested in Bucharest and his papers seized. Amongst these there was a diary which contained poems by Cassian mocking the Ceauşescus. Under brutal interrogation Ursu was to die and, fearing for her life, Cassian chose to remain in exile in the USA. This latest collection of poems includes 'Ars poetica – a polemic', 'Language' and 'Three dialogues' which were originally written in English. The poems are divided under three different headings: 'At dawn', 'At noon' and 'At night' and they are intended to be both an allegorical satire on the clumsiness of youth and a celebration of the 'youthfulness' of old age.

765 **Life sentence: selected poems.**
Nina Cassian, edited and with an introduction by William Jay Smith.
London: Anvil Press, 1990. 129p.

This further selection from this talented Romanian female poet is arranged under five different headings: 'The troubled bay', 'Burning amber', 'Tables wiped clean', 'The wheel not in my hands' and 'Life sentence'. In a lyrical, passionate language she speaks of love and loss, of death and life, using the memory of smells and past terrors to build up an immediacy which is designed to overwhelm her audience.

766 **On the heights of despair.**
E. M. Cioran, translated and with an introduction by Ilinca Zarifopol-Johnston.   Chicago; London: The University of Chicago Press, 1992. 128p.

During his long post-Second World War exile in France, Emil Cioran was to establish himself as one of the greatest philosophers of his generation. In this early book, written in Romania in 1934 when he was only twenty-two years old, he already shows an interest in themes which were to dominate his mature works: despair and decay, absurdity and alienation, futility and the irrationality of existence. Although Cioran's language is rarely straightforward, it is lucid and lyrical as humour and irony are adroitly intertwined to offer an insight into the anguish of the philosophical mind.

767 **From the familiar to the unfamiliar: a Rumanian contribution to European fantasy: 'Sarmanul Dionis' by Mihai Eminescu.**
Elizabeth Close.   *AUMLA: Journal of the Australasian Universities Language and Literature Association,* vol. 63 (May 1985), p. 43-52.

In this brief essay the author seeks to bring to public attention the fantastic tale by Mihai Eminescu, 'Sărmanul Dionis' (Poor Dionis). Although it is little known outside Romania, Close considers this story to be on a par with such celebrated 19th-century examples of that genre as 'Der goldene Topf' by Hoffmann, 'Vera' by Villiers de l'Isle Adam and 'Le Horla' by Maupassant, because of the skilful way in which Eminescu gradually leads the reader from the familiar to an unfamiliar universe.

768 **Alien candor: selected poems 1970-1995.**

Andrei Codrescu. Santa Rosa, Santa Barbara, California; Ann Arbor, Michigan: Black Sparrow Press, 1996. 303p.

This collection of poems is divided chronologically into five sections, each representing a time and place in the life of the poet. The first, entitled 'Personae: Sibiu to New York' (1970-72), is followed by 'San Francisco' (1973-74), 'Monte Rio' (1974-78), 'Baltimore' (1980-81) and 'Baton Rouge & New Orleans' (1986-95). In the first section, which reflects the author's experiences in his native Romania, Codrescu adopts the striking device of assuming a number of different personae and writing as four imaginary poets: Julio Hernandez, Peter Boone, Alice Henderson-Codrescu and Calvin Boone. When the author invites himself to pass judgement on 'their' work, he describes them as Romanian poems with an American mask. Amongst the most poetically and conceptually compelling of the poems in this section are 'License to carry a gun' and 'The history of the growth of Heaven'.

769 **The blood countess.**

Andrei Codrescu. London: Quartet Books, 1996. 347p.

The first novel of this well-known Romanian-born poet, essayist, National Public Radio commentator, script-writer, translator and all-round man of letters is set in his native Transylvania. In it he tells the tale of Elizabeth Báthory, a 16th-century Hungarian countess, whose quest for eternal beauty is said to have led her to imprison, torture and murder more than 600 young maidens in the belief that by bathing in their blood she could retain her youth. The book was first published in the USA by Simon & Schuster in 1995.

770 **The muse is always half-dressed in New Orleans and other essays.**

Andrei Codrescu. New York: St. Martin's Press, 1993. 199p.

This collection of essays is arranged under five headings: 'Live acts', 'Television and war', 'The suicide of communism', 'Culture and sport', and 'Where I hang my hat'. Much of the writing is intended to pass a moral message on contemporary America, where Codrescu now resides, but some of it also touches on his native Transylvania. Although Codrescu's humour and sarcasm are unremittingly black, the very elegance of his style makes his words soothing, even when he castigates. A further series of essays by the same author is *Zombification, stories from National Public Radio* (New York: St. Martin's Press, 1994. 307p.), and recent collections of poems include *Comrade Past and Mister Present* (Minneapolis, Minnesota: Coffee House Press, 1986. 110p.) and *Belligerence* (Minneapolis, Minnesota: Coffee House Press, 1991. 79p.).

771 **Paul Celan: holograms of darkness.**

Amy D. Colin. Bloomington, Indianapolis; Indiana, Indianapolis: Indiana University Press, 1991. 211p.

Paul Celan's whole poetic oeuvre was shaped by his own experiences during the Second World War and the persecution of the Jews by the Nazis. In this scholarly work the author pays particular attention to Celan's early, seldom studied German and Romanian texts (1938-47), as she examines his struggle to create a 'language' with which to encapsulate the enormity of the Holocaust. For an analysis, by the same author, of Celan's Romanian poems see 'Paul Celan's poetics of destruction' in *Argumentum e Silentio: International Paul Celan Symposium. Internationales Paul*

Celan-Symposium, edited by Amy D. Colin (Berlin; New York: Walter de Gruyter, 1987, p. 157-82).

772 **Marin Preda and the new poetics of contemporary political fiction.**
Marcel Cornis-Pop. *Critique*, vol. 27, no. 2 (Winter 1986), p. 117-28.
Marin Preda was one of the most outstanding Romanian novelists of his generation. Born in 1922 as Marin Călăraşu, he was the son of a peasant and his pen was to give eloquent voice to the social conflicts which scarred the Romanian countryside both before and during the communist era. Much of Preda's fiction can be read as a protest against the tyranny of the evil 'officials' who, as he saw it, had been sent into the provinces in order to destroy the moral fibre of the Romanian village. This perversion of values lies at the heart of Preda's novel, *Cel mai iubit dintre pâmînteni* (The most beloved man on earth), published in 1980. In his critical appreciation of this work, Cornis-Pop highlights how the narrator, who is Preda himself, adopts a number of discourses and personae in order to break free from established literary models and create a new tradition in his art. This in turn allows the hero of the novel, Victor Petrini, to polemically challenge such communist shibboleths as collectivization and the right of the *Securitate* to operate above the law. Preda was to die in somewhat mysterious circumstances in 1980.

773 **Letters from darkness.**
Daniela Crăsnaru, translated from the Romanian by Fleur Adcock, with a foreword by Fleur Adcock. Oxford; New York: Oxford University Press, 1991. 47p.
This slim volume of poems is divided into two parts. The first, 'public', section contains a selection drawn from two of Crăsnaru's most recent collections, 'Niagra de Plumb' (Leaden torrents) 1984 and 'Emisferde de Magdeburg' (1987). Because of the censorship then in operation, she perfected the art of shrouding her work in metaphors and imagery, but the bleak introspection of these poems eloquently testifies to the sense of hopelessness felt throughout Romania during the 1980s. The crude realities of everyday life are fully exposed in a series of explicit and stark vignettes in the 'private' poems of the second half of the book. Hidden in a box of onions in her aunt's cellar, these were to remain unpublished until after the overthrow of Ceauşescu.

774 **Exile on a peppercorn.**
Mircea Dinescu, translated from the Romanian by Andrea Deletant and Brenda Walker, introduction by Dennis Deletant with illustrations by Dixie. London; Boston, Massachusetts: Forest Books, 1985. 82p.
Dinescu's is an angry poetry delivered with violence and rage against the society that surrounds him. The poet cannot suppress his fury at the monstrosity and inhumanity of the modern world and sets out to parody the devices by which society manipulates human existence in the name of progress. With his strident and uncompromising voice, Dinescu won acclaim at the tender age of seventeen with his first poem, 'Family destiny', which caused a stir in the literary circles of Bucharest. In his verse, surrealism is artfully interwoven with realism in an explosive fusion where uncommon word-combinations, biting sarcasm, strange metaphors and similes, together with allusions to all forms of anger, abound. Although the poet makes no attempt at resolving the human predicament through his art, his is a poetry of protest at the plight of humanity, and this sense of indignation was later to make him one of the most outspoken critics of the Ceauşescu régime.

Literature and Philosophy. Individual authors

775 A visit with Ion Caraion.
Maguerite Dorian. *Cross Currents*, vol. 6, no. 6 (1987), p. 301-13.
The author records her impressions on meeting the poet and translator, Ion Caraion, in Switzerland after he and his family had been granted political asylum in 1981. Previously, after the communist take-over of power in Romania, Caraion had spent eleven years in prisons and labour camps and it is the hardship of his life which leads Dorian to conclude that 'Exile was a permanent state for him, his imprisonment in Romania being merely its confirmation. He could "Come home" only in his poetry'. Caraion died in Lausanne in 1986.

776 The freedom to pull the trigger.
Geo Dumitrescu, translated from the Romanian by Dan Duţescu, preface by Lucian Raicu. Bucharest: Cartea Românească, 1995. 175p.
A collection of Dumitrescu's poems with parallel texts in English and Romanian. His poetry is distinctive as it displays a humour which extends beyond the bounds of lyricism. At the end of the book there is a further selection of Dumitrescu's poems rendered into English by other translators.

777 The family jewels.
Petru Dumitriu, translated from the French by Edward Hyams in consultation with Princess Anne-Marie Callimachi. London: Collins, 1961. 448p.
The first part of Dumitriu's trilogy, *The boyars*, this historical novel, set in Romania between the years 1862 and 1907, tells the story of the rich land-owning Coziano family. A harsh critique of the social order of the time, it charts the decline and approaching ruin of a whole class through avarice and immorality whilst offering as a poignant counterpoint the misery and suffering of the disenfranchised peasantry. The second volume of the trilogy, translated by Norman Denny, appeared in the next year as *The prodigals* (London: Collins, 1962. 446p.). This followed the fortunes of the next generation of the family through the upheavals of interwar Romania when they 'betrayed themselves, one another, and ultimately their country with the same insouciance with which their ancestors plundered the peasants'. A further novel by Dumitriu, translated by Peter Wiles, is concerned with the lives of Romanian exiles outside Romania: *Westward lies heaven* (London: Collins, 1966. 380p.).

778 Incognito.
Petru Dumitriu, translated from the French by Norman Denny. London: Collins, 1964. 476p.
Dumitriu's masterpiece, this is a grimly realistic picture of life in Romania during the Second World War and the communist take-over. It marks the final evolution of the author from his earlier works such as *Dustless highway*, published in 1954. Written in the style of what he was to later term the 'repellent non-books of socialist realism', this had been a uncritical paean to the camaraderie of the work camps of the Danube-Black Sea Canal and their ability to transform simple peasants into class-conscious workers. In 1960 Dumitriu, perhaps the best known Romanian writer of his day, asked for political asylum whilst visiting West Germany. Amongst the reasons he gave for his defection was a desire to reveal the truth about the communism that blighted his native land and *Incognito* can partly be seen as the fulfilment of this wish.

779   **To the unknown God.**
Petru Dumitriu, translated from the French by James Kirkup.
London: Collins, 1982. 247p.

After a long period of silence and meditation, in which he wrote no works, Dumitriu narrates his own quest for God in this theological thriller, which also serves as personal meditation. Although he cannot claim to have found the answers to questions such as 'Can God's existence be rationalised without resorting to the preachings of the Bible?', within the pages of this novel the author, as protagonist, transforms himself from a non-believer into a Christian.

780   **Bengal nights.**
Mircea Eliade, translated by Catherine Spencer.   Manchester,
England: Carcanet Press; Chicago: University of Chicago Press, 1993.
176p.

Although written as a novel, this is an almost autobiographical account of Eliade's experiences in India in the 1930s. Fascinated and intrigued by the mysteries of the East, the young Romanian fell in love with a beautiful Indian poetess, only to come to the sad realization that the world of his dreams did not correspond with reality.

781   **Fantastic tales.**
Mircea Eliade, Mihai Niculescu, translated from the Romanian by Eric
Tappe. London: Forest Books, 1990. 99p.

This slender volume contains two short stories by Eliade, 'Twelve thousand head of cattle' and 'A great man', and one by Niculescu, 'The cobbler of Hydra'. The common strand between the three is that they all touch upon the fantastic. The presentation of a parallel Romanian text with the English translation makes this book a useful learning aid for anyone with a knowledge of Romanian grammar.

782   **Mystic stories: the sacred and the profane.**
Mircea Eliade, translated from the Romanian by Ana Cartianu, edited
by Kurt W. Treptow.   Boulder, Colorado: East European Monographs
in co-operation with Editura Minerva, Bucharest, distributed by
Columbia University Press, 1992. 302p. (Classics of Romanian
Literature, no. 2).

Although Mircea Eliade gained wide recognition as a distinguished scholar, he was less well-known as a novelist. This may be in part because he preferred to write his literature in Romanian, as he once noted, 'In exile, the native land is the language, is a dream'. This volume contains four of his novellas: 'Miss Christiana', 'Doctor Honigberger's secret', 'The gypsies' and 'Rejuvenation in lightening'. All are set in Romania and deal with different aspects of the fantastic.

783 **The old man and the bureaucrats.**
Mircea Eliade, translated by Mary Park Stevenson.   Notre Dame,
Indiana: University of Notre Dame Press, 1979; Chicago; London:
University of Chicago Press, 1988. 128p.

Eliade's accomplished novella is set in the Bucharest of the early 1950s. The central
character is a retired schoolmaster who, upon noticing that a major in the security
police has the same name as one of his former pupils, tries to contact him. However,
this apparent innocent quest soon leads to the schoolteacher's arrest and interrogation.
Under questioning he starts to talk about the past, but his apparently innocent
reminiscences only arouse the authorities' suspicions about personnel working for the
security police and even some high ranking party officials, several of whom are
subsequently removed from office. However, the schoolmaster is just a skilful story-
teller whose tales are all merely fabrications, but such is the paranoia of the system in
which he lives that his words are interpreted as significant.

784 **Youth without youth and other novellas.**
Mircea Eliade, translated from the Romanian by Mac Linscott Ricketts,
edited and with an introduction by Matei Calinescu.   London: Forest
Books, 1989. 304p.

This book contains three of Eliade's later novellas, 'The cape', 'Youth without youth'
and 'Nineteen roses', with some notes on the circumstances in which they were
written. Common to all three stories is Eliade's use of the fantastic and supernatural as
reality clashes with unreality, themes which are fully addressed in the lengthy introduction (p. XIII-XXXIX) by Matei Calinescu, entitled 'The fantastic and its
interpretation in Mircea Eliade's later novellas'. This work also appeared in an earlier
edition (Columbus, Ohio: Ohio State University Press, 1988. 288p.).

785 **The complete prose writings of Mihai Eminescu.**
Mihai Eminescu, translated from the Romanian by Ioan Giurgea.   Iaşi,
Romania: The Center for Romanian Studies, the Romanian Cultural
Foundation, Iaşi, 1995. 199p. (Romanian Civilization Studies,
Supplement II).

As well as being a poet, Eminescu was also an accomplished prose writer as is
revealed in this collection of thirteen works which include 'Prince Handsome – the
tear-begotten', 'Poor Dionis' and 'A burnt-out genius'. The stated aim of the translator
is not only to disseminate Eminescu's work to the wider English-speaking world but
also to open his work to scrutiny by Western analytical techniques.

786 **In celebration of Mihai Eminescu.**
Mihai Eminescu, translated from the Romanian by Brenda Walker and
Horia Florian Popescu, with a preface by Zoe Dumitrescu-Buşulenga.
London: Forest Books, 1989. 128p.

This collection of twenty-eight of Eminescu's poems was published to commemorate the
centenary of his death in 1889. Poems such as 'Calin', 'The evening star', 'Satires' and
'Ode' are selected on the basis that they are typical of Eminescu's output and best reflect his
relationship with God and society. Controversial issues such as Eminescu's nationalism,
xenophobia and attitude to women are all touched upon in the translators' introduction.

This well produced volume, attractively illustrated with black-and-white drawings by Sabin Balasa, provides a good introduction to the work of Romania's national poet.

787 **Poems.**
Mihai Eminescu, English versions by Corneliu M. Popescu. Paris: Editura Cartea Românească, UNESCO, 1989. 215p.
Another collection of poems produced to mark the centenary of Eminescu's death in 1889. Drawn from the works that originally appeared in the literary review *Convorbiri Literare*, this anthology includes poems such as 'Lucifer', 'Doina', 'Ode', 'Solitude' and 'How far I am from you'. The translations are all published posthumously, as the translator tragically died aged eighteen in the Bucharest earthquake of 1977. An earlier collection of Eminescu's poems from the same publisher can be found in *Poems*, translated from the Rumanian by P. Grimm (Cluj, Romania: Cartea Românească, 1938. 54p.).

788 **Paul Celan: poet, survivor, Jew.**
John Felstiner. New Haven, Conneticut; London: Yale University Press, 1995. 344p. bibliog.
Paul Celan was born Paul Antschel – in Romanian Ancel, of which Celan is an anagram – of Jewish parents in Cernăuți, Bucovina in 1920. After leaving school, he spent a brief interlude studying medicine in France before returning to study Romance languages and literature at his hometown university. In 1941, during the German occupation of Bucovina, Celan's parents were sent to an extermination camp and he only survived by fleeing to Bucharest, where he was held in a work camp. After the war he moved to the Romanian capital and began to work as a translator and publisher's reader. Here he also published his first poems, including the celebrated 'Death Fugue' which appeared in the periodical *Agora*. In December 1947 he moved to Vienna, and, one year later, Paris, where he remained for the rest of his life until his suicide in 1970. Celan's whole poetic oeuvre was shaped by the Holocaust. This book is not only a biography of this notoriously 'difficult' poet but also a critique of the more than 800 poems he wrote between 1938 and 1970. The same author's analysis of 'Death Fugue' can be found in John Felstiner, 'Paul Celan's Todesfuge', *Holocaust and Genocide Studies*, vol. 1, no. 2 (Fall 1986), p. 249-64.

789 **Contestatory visions: five plays by Georges Astalos.**
Georges Astalos, translated by Ronald Bogue. Lewisburg, Pennsylvania: Bucknell University Press; London; Toronto: Associated University Press, 1991. 207p.
The five plays contained in this volume are: 'What'll we do now Willi's gone', 'The apotheosis of the void', 'Mademoiselle Helsinka', 'Our daily tea' and 'The soldiers are coming'. The first and the last of these, which are the best known of the plays, were both written in Romania and are powerful attacks on the blatant abuse of political power. The others, written outside Romania, are no less strong critiques of Western subjects such as racism, mass media, self-improvement cults and advertising. Bearing the influence of both Eugene Ionescu and Samuel Beckett, these absurdist dramas provide a forceful analysis of dysfunctional societies.

790   **Exile in Hell: the early poetry of Paul Celan and Alfred Gong.**
Jerry Glenn.   In: *Psalm und Hawdalah zum werk Paul Celans: akten
des Internationalen Paul Celan-Kolloquiums, New York, 1985* (Psalm
and Hawdalah in the work of Paul Celan: proceedings of the
international colloquium on Paul Celan, New York, 1985).   Edited by
Joseph P. Strelka.   Bern; Frankfurt am Main; New York; Paris: Peter
Lang, 1987, p. 99-111. (Jahrbuch für Internationale Germanistik:
Kongressberichte, no. 20).

A comparative analysis of the work of two poets, Paul Celan and Alfred Gong, both
born in Bucovina in 1920, whose poetry was shaped by the Holocaust. Despite their
different experiences, with Celan composing his first verses in a work camp, whilst
Gong penned his in Bucharest where he lived under forged Aryan papers, Glenn
argues that in both cases their poetry can be termed 'exile literature'. He then attempts
to address two questions related to this classification: first, the nature of the
relationship between such 'exile literature' and the literature written by Jews in
concentration camps and ghettos or in the underground; and secondly, whether it is
necessary to apply sociological methods in order to arrive at an understanding and
appreciation of this literature.

791   **My childhood at the gate of unrest.**
Paul Goma, translated from the Romanian by Angela Clark.
Columbia, Louisiana; London: Readers International, 1990. 266p.

This, the first of Paul Goma's novels-cum-memoirs to be translated into English, is an
evocative account of life in his native Bessarabia during the Second World War.
Under communism, Goma, who had been in intermittent conflict with the authorities
since 1951, was the most significant Romanian dissident. His first novel, *Ostinato*,
was banned allegedly because it featured a character similar to Elena Ceauşescu.
Eventually it was published in Germany and all of his subsequent works were to first
appear outside Romania. In 1977 he wrote an open letter to the CSCE Belgrade
Conference protesting at human rights abuses in Romania. His appeal attracted nearly
200 signatories, but after a remorseless campaign of intimidation by the authorities he
was forced to abandon Romania and leave, with his wife and family, for France. This
novel first appeared in France in 1987 with the 'gate' in question being the doorstep of
Goma's family house, the centre of his childhood universe.

792   **God was born in exile: Ovid's memoirs at Tomis.**
Vintila Horia, translated from the French by A. Lytton Sells, with a
preface by Daniel-Rops.   London: George Allen & Unwin, 1961.
228p.

Although he was born in Romania, Vintila Horia was to gain literary fame in France,
where this book was a winner of the prestigious Prix Goncourt. In 1940 Horia was
sent as a press attaché to the Romanian Embassy in Rome. Recalled by the Iron Guard
administration, he was appointed in 1942 to the Embassy in Vienna only to be
interned by the Germans. From this point onward Horia was to remain in exile from
his native land, first in Italy then in Argentina and finally in Spain. It is therefore not
surprising that the theme of exile lies at the heart of this, his most famous novel. It
takes the form of an apocryphal journal kept by the Roman poet Ovid after he was
banished by the Emperor Augustus to Tomis, today's Constanţa. Faced with exile and

the prospect of a lonely death in a foreign land, Ovid undergoes a spiritual transformation as he embarks on a search for meaning in his own life and the nature of truth. Of course, Ovid's exile is merely a metaphor for the author's own experiences and much of the fascination of this book lies in the glimpses it gives of Horia's own personal evolution.

793 **When angels sing/când îngerii cântă: poems and prose/poezii și proză.**
Magda Isanos, edited and translated by Laura Treptow, Kurt W.
Treptow, illustrations by Ioana Lupușoru, postscript by Elisabeta
Isanos Goian.   Iași, Romania: Romanian Cultural Foundation, 1994.
143p. (Romanian Civilization Studies, no. 3).

Born in Iași in 1916, Isanos made her poetic debut at the age of fifteen whilst she was still a school pupil in Chișinău, where she had moved with her family. A first volume of poetry followed in 1943 but her life was tragically cut short when she died in Bucharest aged only twenty-eight. Subsequently, two further volumes of poetry were published posthumously. In this work, which contains parallel Romanian and English texts, the editors provide an enthusiastic introduction, a selection of Isanos' poems and three excerpts from a piece of prose, 'The town of miracles'.

794 **Benjamin Fondane: a poet in exile.**
William Kluback.   New York; Washington, DC; Baltimore,
Maryland; Bern; Frankfurt am Main; Berlin; Vienna, Paris: Peter Lang,
1996. 140p. (The Literature and Poetry of Exile, no. 1).

In the opinion of Kluback, Benjamin Fondane was the greatest poet of the Holocaust. Originally born Benjamin Wexler in Iași in 1898, he took the name Benjamin Fondane after emigrating to France in 1923. He was gassed in Birkeanau concentration camp on 3 October 1944. In a series of elegant essays Kluback meditates on the life and work of Fondane and especially his experience of exile, noting that 'Fondane found that nowhere could his exile be taken from him. He was always the stranger even in the land he loved'. A literary critic as well as a poet, Fondane wrote about Rimbaud and Baudelaire and under the influence of the philosophers Shestov and Bachelard, he played an essential part in the struggle to understand existentialism as a philosophical attitude. A brief but highly graphic pen-portrait of Fondane by a fellow Romanian exile is presented in 'Benjamin Fondane. 6 Rue Rollin' (p. 218-22) in Emil M. Cioran's *Anathemas and admirations,* translated from the French by Richard Howard (New York: Arcade Publishing & Little, Brown and Company, 1991. 256p.).

795 **Excerpts from a troubled book: an episode in Romanian literature.**
Irina Livezeanu.   *Cross Currents,* vol. 3, no. 4 (1984), p. 297-319.

This article relates the history of Mihai Sebastian's troubled 'Jewish Book', *De două mii de ani* (For two thousand years), first published in 1934. A novel about being Jewish in Romania in the 1930s, it is written in the form of a pseudo-journal. It became something of a *cause célèbre* in interwar Romania because of a preface furnished by Nae Ionescu. Sebastian had fallen under the influence of Ionescu as a student and aware of his knowledge of religions, including Judaism, about which he spoke respectfully in 1931, he asked him to write the preface. However, the finished work in 1934 fully reflected Ionescu's embracement of anti-Semitic views and the 500 pages of critical response which arose from the affair was to spawn a further volume

Literature and Philosophy. Individual authors

by Sebastian, *Cum ma devenit huligan* (How I became a hooligan) (Bucharest: Editura Hasefer, 1995. 360p.).

796 The black envelope.
Norman Manea, translated from the Romanian by Patrick Camiller.
London; New York: Faber & Faber, 1996. 329p.

Manea's full-length novel relates the attempts of Tolea Voinov to resolve the mystery surrounding the death of his father, a philosopher, who had fled Romania forty years earlier. Tolea, an intellectual who had been sacked from his teaching job and temporarily employed as a hotel receptionist, has to struggle with endless bureaucratic obscurantism and a tangled web of conspiracy as he seeks an elusive photographer who may have the answer to his quest.

797 Compulsory happiness.
Norman Manea, translated from the French by Linda Coverdale.
Evanston, Illinois: Northwestern University Press, 1994. 259p.
(Writings From An Unbound Europe).

This book in fact comprises four shorter novellas: 'The interrogation', about an imprisoned young woman forced to inform on her friends and whose main interlocutor is revealed to be as anxious and neurotic as his victim; 'Composite biography', about the careers of communist comrades working in the National Bank in Bucharest; 'A window on the working class', about a court case heard by the Supreme Court in Bucharest; and 'The trenchcoat', which captures the paranoia caused by the abandonment of a raincoat at a dinner party. All were written in the later Ceaușescu years and the theme throughout is the absurdity of the police state.

798 On clowns: the dictator and the artist.
Norman Manea. New York: Grove Weidenfeld, 1992; London;
Boston, Massachusetts: Faber & Faber, 1994. 186p.

In six disparate essays the author combines a judicious mixture of tragedy and comedy to produce a convincing picture of life under totalitarianism. The process of formation through deformation and the inherent conflict between individual aspirations and societal norms constitute the main leitmotifs of the book, as, preoccupied with the trauma of the Holocaust, the author contemplates his own vulnerability as both an artist and a human being. Manea finds all political labels manipulatory and so he himself is difficult to categorize but, although there is a moderate optimism in his writings, the pervading atmosphere is one of scepticism, even after the 1989 overthrow of the Ceaușescu régime.

799 Mihai Sadoveanu: 100 years since his birth.
Pompiliu Marcea. Bucharest: Cartea Românească, 1980. 55p. bibliog.

This is a fulsome and laudatory tribute to one of the best known Romanian novelists of the 20th century. Born in 1880 in Moldavia, Sadoveanu had his first work published in 1897 and during the next forty years there followed a string of highly acclaimed novels including *Baltagul* (The hatchet) (q.v.). As well as being a writer, Sadoveanu also pursued a political career. He entered parliament in 1926 and rose to become President of the Senate in 1930-31. After the Second World War he aligned himself with the Communist Party and henceforth his works were to conform with the dictates

254

of socialist realism. *Mitrea Cocor* (1949) tells the story of an orphan who finally fulfils his ambition of working on a collective farm. Sadoveanu died in 1961 and the second part of this volume contains a useful, detailed chronological listing of all this prolific author's many works.

800   **Through the needle's eye.**
Jon Miloş, translated from the Romanian and the Swedish by Brenda Walker.   London; Boston, Massachusetts: Forest Books, 1990. 93p.

Born of Romanian parents in former Yugoslavia but now resident in Sweden, Miloş publishes his poetry in Romanian, Serbo-Croatian and Swedish. Indeed his enormous versatility with language, which enables him not only to switch, apparently effortlessly, from one language to another but also to move from colloquialisms to learned Latin allusions, has led some literary critics, such as the Swede, Tommy Olofsson, to dubb him a 'chameleon'. Perhaps as a further reflection of his varied upbringing, Miloş's poetry explores a great variety of themes: women, love, death, life, but above all the degradation of man and nature. His poetry has been called 'full-bloodied' on the basis of its vigour and the surreal language employed, and this representative collection is divided under six major headings: 'On red carpet roads', 'A water party', 'Love with the auxiliary heat', 'The wolf doesn't frighten children anymore', 'Don't stay outside' and 'Stay in your own skin'.

801   **The land of green plums: a novel.**
Herta Müller, translated by Michael Hofman.   New York: Metropolitan Books, 1996. 242p.

Set in the bleak world of Ceauşescu's Romania, this is a powerful story of the difficulties faced by a group of young Germans who leave their provincial backwater to confront a hostile urban world. Here, faced with arrogant and bullying officials, they endure systematic discrimination, a metaphor for this being the 'plums' of the title, which the police gorge themselves on, even though they are green and unripe, just to demonstrate their ability to do as they please. The only escape from this grim society is through suicide or emigration, with the heroine, like the author, eventually finding salvation through the latter as she leaves for Germany.

802   **The passport: a surreal tale of life in Romania today.**
Herta Müller, translated by Martin Chalmers.   London: Serpent's Tail, 1991. 93p.

Based on everyday life in her native Banat during the demented days of the Ceauşescu régime, the author depicts life in a Swabian German village caught between the hopelessness of communist Romania and the glittering promise of life in the West. In a sparse and direct style, which resembles a prose poem as much as a novel, Müller writes of the problems faced by Windisch, the village miller, once he applies to emigrate to the West. When bribes of sacks of flour fail to budge the authorities, the miller even resorts to sending his young daughter to search for the requisite passport and birth certificate in beds of the local militiaman and priest.

803 **Zenobia.**
Gellu Naum, translated from the Romanian by James Brook and Sasha
Vlad. Evanston, Illinois: Northwestern University Press, 1995. 192p.
(Writings from an Unbound Europe).
Naum was a leading figure of the Romanian surrealist movement prior to the Second
World War. After the imposition of communism, he was unable to publish anything
other than children's books for over twenty years, and this novel did not appear in
Romania until 1985. In an evocative love story, in which carnal intimacies are
rendered in highly descriptive language, Naum presents a narrative of self-discovery
and revelation. A discussion of his work, together with some poems translated by
Liviu Bleoca, can be found in Ion Pop, 'A surrealist – Gellu Naum', *Transylvanian
Review*, vol. 5, no. 3 (Autumn 1996), p. 111-21.

804 **Easter sun.**
Peter Neagoe. London: Hutchinson, 1934. 288p. (First Novel
Library, no. 22).
Set in a village in the author's native Transylvania, this is a novel of all-consuming
passions and primitive suspicions. It tells the story of Ileana, the beautiful daughter of
one-eyed John. Ileana is said by the villagers to be carrying the evil eye, leading John
to become increasingly consumed by the thought that his daughter is possessed by the
devil. Meanwhile, Ileana is caught between the duplicitous Serafim Corbu, who
seduces her, despite the fact that he is pledged to marry Saveta who carries a rich
dowry, and the hunchback teacher Jancu Tedescu. Tedescu finally plucks up the
courage to tell Ileana that he loves her, only to see John in a fit of madness try to
murder his own daughter. Just in time John is overpowered, but the villagers become
convinced that his actions were driven by the devil within his daughter and so they
force Ileana and Tedescu to leave the village and became outcasts from their society.
Neagoe wrote a number of other novels set in Transylvania, including *There is my
heart* (London: J. M. Dent, 1936. 383p.).

805 **The royal hunt.**
Dumitru Radu Popescu, translated from the Romanian and with an
introduction by J. E. Cottrell and M. Bogdan. London; New York:
Quartet, 1987. 174p.
Popescu's allegorical composition explores the psychology of mass terror as it affects
both the individual and the community. Although the narrator is an adult, the story
unravels through the eyes of a child who recounts the events which caused the world
to be invaded by terror, in the guise of a plague of rabies, and how in the process a
new man is allowed to emerge. The title refers to the legend of the village, which
prohibits hunting on a certain day on pain of death, and the story begins with the
villagers, who had gone to hunt on this forbidden day, trying to 'fool' death by
sacrificing an inanimate puppet, Big Prince. Popescu, a former editor of *Tribuna* and
President of the Writers' Union, was a member of the Central Committee of the
Romanian Communist Party during the later Ceauşescu years.

806 **A juicier way. Romanian poems.**
    Mihai Radoi.   London; Boston, Massachusetts: Forest Books, 1996.
    59p.
This collection of poems is partly in Romanian and partly in English with the
Romanian poems not being translated on the instructions of the author. Prior to the
appearance of this book, Radoi was previously unpublished and many of the poems
date back as far as the 1960s. This is reflected in the book with the poems being
divided into various non-sequential periods. In his poetry Radoi mixes the crudeness
of the street and an often explicit sexual imagery with a more lyrical and sensitive
appreciation of love.

807 **Adam and Eve.**
    Liviu Rebreanu, translated from the Romanian by Mihai Bogdan, with
    a foreword by Mircea Zaciu.   Bucharest: Minerva Publishing House,
    1986. 263p.
This inventive novel is arranged as seven separate short, semi-autonomous
biographies in which the same hero appears in seven different guises, as an Indian
cowherd, a Babylonian scribe, an Egyptian high official, a Roman patrician, a
medieval monk, a French revolutionary physician and a Romanian philosopher.
Although there are signs of artificiality in the author's descriptions of the external
setting, his psychological analysis of the inner world is impressive.

808 **Ion.**
    Liviu Rebreanu, translated by A. Hillard.   London: Peter Owen, 1965.
    411p.
In this novel of village life, Rebreanu dwells on the greed and opportunism of a
peasant who abandons all values in his desperate search to escape poverty. Peasant
agitation against landlord abuses in 1907, the year of the last great peasant revolt, is
also the theme of another novel by Rebreanu, *The uprising,* translated by P.
Grandjean, S. Hartauer (London: Peter Owen, 1964. 385p.). A further novel, *The
forest of the hanged,* translated from the Romanian by A. V. Wise (London: Peter
Owen, 1967. 350p.), deals with the poignant issue of opposing loyalties, when a
young Romanian officer from Transylvania finds himself fighting against his fellow
Romanians during the First World War.

809 **The hatchet. Stephen the Great.**
    Mihai Sadoveanu, translated from the Romanian by Eugenia Farca.
    Boulder, Colorado: East European Monographs, distributed by
    Columbia University Press, 1991. 267p. (East European Monographs,
    no. 340; Classics of Romanian Literature, no. 3).
Contains two short stories written by this prolific Romanian novelist prior to the
Second World War. In both he demonstrates his characteristic ability to integrate
elements of history and folklore into a popular narrative. *The hatchet* is a 'detective
story' set amongst a community of shepherds in northern Romania. The subject is
Victoria Lipan's search for her missing husband who has been murdered by two of his
fellow shepherds who coveted his flock. As such it follows in the tradition of the folk
ballad *Miorița* which is concerned with resignation in the face of death. The second
work, *Stephen the Great,* is a historical novella set in the reign of this Moldavian king.

Literature and Philosophy. Individual authors

The hatchet has already appeared in two other editions in English, in 1965 (London: Allen & Unwin. 163p.), and in 1983 (Bucharest: Minerva Publishing House. 143p.).

810 **Tales of war.**
      Mihail Sadoveanu. New York: Twayne, 1962. 140p.
First published in 1905, this collection of thirteen stories are amongst the earliest of Sadoveanu's work. Nostalgic, but also tinged with bitterness, they tell of a soldier's life in the Russo-Turkish war of 1877 that led to Romania gaining full independence. The tales are arranged chronologically from the early preparation of entrenchments near Grivița through the bitter fighting of summer to the exhausted return home from Bulgaria during a cold winter.

811 **Introduction to Benjamin Fondane.**
      Leonard Schwartz. *Pequod. A Journal of Contemporary Literature and Literary Criticism*, vol. 34 (1992), p. 73-75.
Like his fellow Romanian émigrés in France, Eugene Ionesco and Emil Cioran, Benjamin Fondane was an explorer of despair *par excellence*. An influential poet who mixed existentialism and surrealism in his art, Fondane was also a philosopher. In this article and the selection of texts and poems which follows (p. 76-104), Schwartz highlights the scope and the internal coherence of Fondane's literary output, including his early poetry written in Romanian.

812 **Ioan Slavici's 'Zîna Zorilor': boundaries and blindness and the ambiguities of moral determination.**
      Norman Simms. *Miorița*, vol. 8, no. 1-2 (1983), p. 51-76.
Analysing Slavici's story 'Zîna Zorilor' (The dawn fairy), the author shows how folkloric imagery 'seeps through' the literary work of the author who was a master of powerful and dark prose. In 'The dawn fairy', Slavici sought to write not a children's fairy tale but a short story suitable for a wider audience, and in this article Simms explores the demarcation lines between these genres.

813 **The mill of luck and plenty and other stories.**
      Ioan Slavici, edited by Kurt W. Treptow.   Boulder, Colorado: East European Monographs in cooperation with the Romanian Cultural Foundation Publishing House, distributed by Columbia University Press, 1994. 301p. (East European Monographs, no. 351; Classics of Romanian Literature, no. 5).
From the publication of his first book, entitled *Nuvela din popor*, Ion Slavici was widely recognized as one of the leading prose writers of 19th-century Romania. Two of the stories from this first collection are to be found in this present volume: 'Mora cu noroc' (The mill of luck) and 'Badulea Taichii' (Papa's boy Budulea). The third story is 'Pădureanca' (The forest girl). Heavily influenced by Romanian folklore, in his work Slavici draws heavily upon the mores and customs of his native Transylvania.

814   **Hands behind my back. Selected poems.**
Marin Sorescu, translated by Gabriela Dragnea, Stuart Friebert and
Adriana Varga, introduced by Seamus Heaney.   Oberlin, Ohio:
Oberlin College Press, 1991. 168p. (Field Translation Series, no. 18).
The poems in this collection, which are drawn from a number of Sorescu's works, are
arranged in five main categories: 'After the creation', 'Subjectism', 'Where we
forget', 'History and therapy' and 'Miracle'. In the introduction to the volume, the
Nobel laureate Seamus Heaney says of Sorescu's poems that they '. . . begin in
delight, take an excursion through wisdom and end at the original starting point,
altogether invigorated'.

815   **Let's talk about the weather.**
Marin Sorescu, translated from the Romanian by Andrea Deletant and
Brenda Walker, introduction ('Poet to Poet') by Jon Silkin.   London;
Boston, Massachusetts: Forest Books, 1985. 84p.
This anthology contains poems drawn from a number of collections, including 'The
death of the clock', 'Poems', 'Don Quixote's youth', 'Cough!', 'Clouds' and
'Fountain in the sun'. Sorescu's work is clinical and direct, at times almost
emotionless, but it has an immediacy and imaginative allegorical wit which gives it
enormous strength and vision.

816   **Selected poems.**
Marin Sorescu, translated by Michael Hamburger.   Newcastle upon
Tyne, England: Bloodaxe, 1983. 83p.
This anthology contains works from a number of Sorescu's earlier collections:
'Poems' (1965), 'The death of the clock' (1966), 'Don Quixote's youth' (1968),
'Cough!' (1970), 'Soul, you are good for anything' (1972) and 'So' (1973). Born into
a peasant family in Bulzeşti, southern Romania in 1936, Sorescu published his first
poems in 1954 after studying modern languages at the University of Iaşi. Also a
talented playwright and essayist, Sorescu had an unconventional approach which leads
this translator to note that: 'Every kind of poetry takes its own risks, and Sorescu has
taken the very great risks involved in trying to wrench poetry out of its specialisation'.
Between 1993 and 1995 Sorescu served, often somewhat uncomfortably, as Minister
of Culture in the government of Nicolae Văcăroiou. He died in 1996. A later
anthology of Sorescu's poems by the same publisher is *The biggest egg in the world,*
English versions by Seamus Heaney, Ted Hughes, David Constantine, D. J. Enright,
Michael Hamburger, Michael Longley, Paul Muldoon, Williams Scammell with Joana
Russell-Gebbett (Newcastle upon Tyne, England: Bloodaxe, 1987. 79p.).

817   **Symmetries: selected poems.**
Marin Sorescu, translated from the Romanian by John Robert Colombo
and Petronela Negoşanu.   Toronto: Hounslow Press, 1982. 63p.
A compilation of fifty-four of Sorescu's poems. Their texture varies, but irony ('We
wonder at nothing/ We make constant progress'), anxiety ('They open two skies:/ One
to the right,/ The other to the left') and fatalism ('And although I endure/ With
sufficient stoicism/ My granite fate.') are amongst the strongest features of his poetic
expression.

818   **The thirst of the salt mountain: a trilogy of plays by Marin Sorescu.**
Marin Sorescu, translated from the Romanian by Andrea Deletant and Brenda Walker.   London; Boston, Massachusetts: Forest Books, 1985. 112p.

The three plays of this trilogy are: 'Jonah', 'The Verger' and 'The Matrix'. In the best-known, Jonah, a philosophical allegory, the biblical character escapes from the clutches of the whale only to find that it has been swallowed by a bigger fish. His predicament repeated, as this fish is in turn swallowed by an even bigger fish, Jonah eventually only finds release by taking his own life. For Sorescu the universe is a succession of finite realms in which the human is trapped, although Jonah can also be seen as a prisoner of the conventions that trapped Ceauşescu's Romania. After a six-week initial run, the play was only performed one more time during Ceauşescu's lifetime. Another play by Sorescu, available in a bilingual Romanian/English text, is *A cold/Răceala*, translated by Stavros Deligiorgis (Iaşi, Romania: Junimea, 1978. 149p.). Set in 1462, this uses the collapse of the Byzantine Empire and the first Ottoman incursions into the Romanian lands to explore the perennial issues of treachery, betrayal and sycophancy, all of which had resonance in Ceauşescu's Romania.

819   **Vlad Dracula the Impaler.**
Marin Sorescu, translated by Dennis Deletant.   Boston, Massachusetts: Forest Books, 1987. 111p. map.

Sorescu's drama about Vlad Dracul, the prince of 15th-century Wallachia, has nothing to do with the ghoulish character of Bram Stoker's popular novel. Despite the title Vlad is not a cruel man; instead he is a prisoner of his own misfortunes, who is condemned by the betrayal of his own people to sacrifice himself on the third stake (the original Romanian title of the play). In Sorescu's work Vlad is a machiavellian figure who foolishly set out to exterminate single-handedly deceit, greed and banditry, inherent conditions in Wallachia at the time. The world he inhabits is a dark land of treachery, suspicion and mistrust and, indeed, the play is primarily an allegory for the tragedy of people who fall foul of their times, an apt description of the Romanian experience under the Ceausescu régime. As the translator says in his introduction, 'Marin Sorescu's drama is a masterly encapsulation of the Romanian historical predicament. That artists of his stature have emerged in contemporary Romanian society is a testimony to that predicament'.

820   **The youth of Don Quixote.**
Marin Sorescu, English versions by John F. Deane.   Dublin: Dedalus, 1987. 67p.

Although this volume bears the title of only one collection of Sorescu's poetry, first published in Romanian in 1968, it does in fact contain poems from several of his earlier works including 'Poems' (1965), 'The death of the clock' (1966), 'Cough!' (1970), 'Soul, you are good for anything' (1972) and 'So' (1973). In his poetry Sorescu skilfully interweaves fantasy and irony to imbue the commonplace with double meanings. In its freedom of invention it is often enigmatic, almost surreal, but it is also humorous and sometimes unnerving.

821 **Panaït Istrati – portrait of a rebel.**
Boris Souvarine. *Dissent,* vol. 29, no. 3 (Summer 1982), p. 342-51.
In a fascinating memoir the author recalls his friendships with both the Romanian novelist Panaït Istrati and Christian Rakovsky, the early Romanian communist leader and one time Soviet Ambassador to France. In particular, he recalls the story behind Istrati's three-volume history of Soviet communism which was first published in France in 1929. Harbouring strong communist sympathies, Istrati travelled extensively in the 1920s in the Soviet Union, accompanied for much of the time by the Greek novelist Nikos Kazantzakis. Gradually, his idealism soured into doubts, especially after close friends in Moscow were persecuted because an official had her eyes on their flat. When he returned to France to pen his planned history, Istrati was only to write the first volume. The second was largely a collection of news clippings to which he put his name and the third, as is revealed in this article, was actually produced from the same sources by Souvarine. However, it was only the volume written by Istrati, in which he related the story of the persecution of his friends, that drew any attention. It was bitterly attacked by the French Stalinists, who accused Istrati of betraying the cause, and their hollow tirade continued to dog the novelist until his premature death in 1935.

822 **Ask the circle to forgive you: selected poems 1964-1979.**
Nichita Stănescu, translated from the Romanian by Mark Irwin and Mariana Carpinisan. Cleveland, New York; London: The Globe Press, 1983. 74p.
An anthology of poems drawn from four earlier collections of Stănescu's works: 'The state of poetry', 'The eleven elegies', 'Epica Magna' and 'Imperfect works'. Born in Ploieşti in 1933, Stănescu published sixteen volumes of verse between 1960 and his death in 1983, establishing himself as the most innovative of the postwar generation of Romanian poets. His work perhaps reached its apogee in the 'Eleven elegies' of 1966 in which he questions the very essence of language in his attempt to construct a new reality. A further collection of Stănescu's poems is *Bas-relief with heroes*, translated by Thomas C. Carlson and Vasile Poenaru (London: Forest Books; Memphis, Tennessee: Memphis State University Press, 1989. 156p.).

823 **As I came to London one midsummer's day.**
Ion Stoica, translated from the Romanian by Brenda Walker with the poet. London: Forest Books, 1990. 32p.
Inspired by a visit to the United Kingdom, this collection of poetry contains original and imaginative responses to places as far afield as Trafalgar Square, Stonehenge and Hadrian's Wall.

824 **Gates of the moment.**
Ion Stoica, translated from the Romanian by Brenda Walker and Andrea Deletant. London: Forest Books, 1993. 2nd ed. 128p.
A journalist by training, Stoica demonstrates in his poetry both the acquired skills of his profession and his innate talents as a poet. In this collection, presented with parallel Romanian and English texts, his fluidity of language comes to the fore as, in a series of lyrical works spiced with humorous overtones, he examines the relationship individuals enjoy with their spatial environment.

825 **Orient express.**
Grete Tartler, translated from the Romanian by Fleur Adcock.
Oxford; New York; Auckland: Oxford University Press, 1989. 45p.
This selection of forty-five relatively short poems is drawn from Tartler's two latest collections 'Substituiri' (1983) and 'Achene Zburătoare' (1986). According to the translator, Tartler's poetry 'lends itself most naturally to translation into English' as she expresses herself in a direct and unobscure language.

826 **One Moldavian summer.**
Ionel Teodorescu, translated by Eugenia Farca, edited by Kurt W.
Treptow. Boulder, Colorado: East European Monographs in co-operation with the Romanian Cultural Foundation Publishing House, distributed by Columbia University Press, 1992. 267p. (East European Monographs, no. 341; Classics of Romanian Literature, no. 4).
Ion Slavici considered Teodorescu to be a master at describing childhood and although this book, set during the traumatic years of the First World War, is not entirely autobiographical, it faithfully reproduces the upper middle class circumstances of the author, and the main protagonists, Dănuţ, Olguţa and Monica, can be seen as expressions of the soul of their creator.

827 **The miracle of Saint Sisoe.**
George Topîrceanu. *Romanian Civilization*, vol. 3, no. 2 (Fall-Winter 1994), p. 116-53.
Originally intended as a novel, this story was left unfinished when the author died in 1937. It tells the story of the saintly Sisoe who descends from heaven to earth only to be faced with a totally uncomprehending society. A collection of Topîrceanu's poems, translated by Dan Duţescu, appeared in *Romanian Civilization*, vol. 4, no. 1 (Spring 1995), p. 127-36, and the text of a lecture, 'How I became a Moldavian', originally given by Topîrceanu at the University of Iaşi in June 1935, translated by Mihail Bogdan, appeared in *Romanian Civilization*, vol. 2, no. 2 (Fall-Winter 1993), p. 59-70.

828 **Primele poeme/ First poems.**
Tristan Tzara, translated by Michael Impey and Brian Swann.
Berkeley, California: New Rivers Press, 1976. 82p. bibliog.
Tristan Tzara was born in Moineşti, Romania, in 1896 and probably first bore the name Sami Rosenstock, only taking his pseudonym in 1915. He made his literary debut with four symbolist poems in 1912. This is a collection of Tzara's very first poems which he wrote in Romanian before he left for Zurich and Western Europe in 1915. The themes include the futility of provincial life, his affections for his sister and the horrors of war, a subject which may have been inspired by the events of the two Balkan Wars of 1912 and 1913. Another recent selection of Tzara's poems, which mostly concentrates on his later works but also includes one of his earlier Romanian poems, is *Chanson Dada: Tristan Tzara. Selected poems,* translated by Lee Harwood (Toronto: Coach House Press, 1987. 141p.).

829 **Weird pages.**
Urmuz, translated from the Romanian by Stavros Deligiorgis.
Bucharest: Cartea Românească, 1985. 99p.
Urmuz was the pseudonym of Demetru Demetrescu-Buzău. Born into a middle-class
family in Curtea de Argeş on 17 March 1883, he graduated from the faculty of law at
the University of Bucharest and served as a judge in various provincial towns before
becoming clerk to Romania's Supreme Court. Tudor Arghezi, who suggested that
Demetrescu-Buzău took the pseudonym Urmuz, published his first poems in a 1922
issue of *Cugetul Românesc* but only one year later, in 1923, the young poet committed
suicide. This bilingual Romanian and English edition of his work, which covers the
full range of his surreal and often disturbing prose and verse, includes 'The funnel and
Stamate', 'Ismail and Turnavitu' 'After the Storm', and 'Algazy and Grummer'.

830 **The sky behind the forest: selected poems.**
Liliana Ursu, translated by Liliana Ursu with Adam J. Sorkin and Tess
Gallagher. Newcastle upon Tyne, England: Bloodaxe, 1997. 96p.
These poems, including some from Ursu's latest collection 'Port Angeles', are
presented under four major headings: 'In the forest', 'With one eye we cry, with the
other one we laugh', 'Bait', and 'Letter from the constellation of the swan'. The
language is spontaneous, if not audacious, but at the same time intricate as the poet
uses it as a tool to underline the starkness of everyday life in 1990s' Romania. Sorkin
and Ursu have also recently collaborated in the production of a volume of poetry by
poets from the Transylvanian city of Sibiu: *Focuri pe apă: 7 poeţi din Sibiu/Fires on
water: 7 poets from Sibiu*, translations by Adam Sorkin and Liliana Ursu, preface by
Liliana Ursu (Bucharest: Cartea Românească; Sibiu, Romania: Centrul European de
Poezie şi Dialog Cultural Est-Vest 'Constantin Noica' din Sibiu; distributed by the
European Association for the Promotion of Poetry, European Poetry House, 1992.
148p.).

831 **Tales of fantasy and magic.**
Vasile Voiculescu, translated from the Romanian by Ana Cartianu,
foreword by Mihai Zamfir. Bucharest: Minerva Publishing House,
1986. 303p.
In these unconventional fantastic tales, this well-known poet from the interwar years
displays his talents as a prose writer. Set in a mysterious 19th century, they speak of
hamlets which no longer register the passage of time and where extraordinary events
occur, as the patterns of everyday life are skilfully interwoven with myths and
legends. Voiculescu was arrested in the late summer of 1958 after being denounced
for reading poems of religious inspiration to a circle of friends. Released a few months
before his death, he never saw any of his major postwar works published.

832 **Memoirs of an anti-Semite.**
Gregor von Rezzori. London: Picador, Pan Books, 1983. 282p.
A highly acclaimed and rather controversial novel by von Rezzori who was born in
Bucovina, Romania, studied at the University of Vienna and for a time lived in
Bucharest before he moved to West Germany after the Second World War. The book
contains five short stories: 'Skushno', 'Youth', 'Pravda' (all translated from the
German by Joachim Neugroschel), 'Löwinger's rooming house' and 'Troth'.

The Arts

Visual and decorative arts

833 **Romanian icons 16th-18th century.**
Myrtali Acheimastou-Potamianou. Athens: Byzantine Museum of
Athens, 1993. 151p. bibliog.
This informative and visually striking catalogue was produced to accompany an
exhibition of post-Byzantine Romanian icons from Wallachia, Moldavia and
Transylvania held in Athens between 29 March and 29 April 1993. All the icons were
drawn from the collection of the National Museum of Art in Bucharest. A picture of
each icon is accompanied by a date and the name of the artist, if known, together with
details of the provenance of the work, the materials used, previous exhibitions and a
bibliography. There is also a detailed commentary in parallel English and Greek texts.

834 **Brancusi and Rumanian folk traditions.**
Edith Balas, with a foreword by Isamu Noguchi. Boulder, Colorado:
East European Monographs, distributed by Columbia University Press,
1987. 88p. bibliog. (East European Monographs, no. 224).
In an effort to correct what the author perceives to have been a 'Francophile' bias in
interpreting the work of Constantin Brâncuși (1876-1957), this scholarly study
emphasizes the role and significance of Romanian folk art elements in his sculpture
and underlines the artist's spiritual links with his homeland. Certainly, Brâncuși's art
can not be detached from his Romanian origins, but the whole debate over which of
his dual personalities is more predominant, the Romanian peasant or the Parisian
artist, is to a large extent fallacious, since it is this duality that characterizes every
aspect of his work. The book is divided into four major chapters: 'Brancusi and
Rumania', 'Brancusi as artisan', 'Brancusi and forms of Rumanian art' and 'Brancusi
and Rumanian folklore'. Four appendices complete the work: 'The Rumanian folktales
of Maiastra Bird', 'Where did the swan come from?', 'The swan maiden, the bird of
Heaven and the crown of paradise' and 'The little purse with two pennies'.

835 **Rumanian icons on glass.**
Juliana Dancu, Dumitru Dancu, translated from the Romanian by
Andreea Gheorghiţoiu. Detroit, Michigan: Wayne State University
Press, produced by the Meridiane Publishing House, Bucharest, 1982.
178p. bibliog.
A fascinating study of the long neglected Romanian folk art form of icon painting on
glass. More than mere decorative objects the icons represent for the authors a living
testament to the traditional culture of Romanian village communities. Aesthetically
and emotionally they serve as an 'artistic documentation of the spiritual world of the
Transylvanian peasant'. However, as artistic appreciation of the glass icons has
grown, so they have begun to lose this dimension, becoming instead of objects of
worship objects of study and research in museums of ethnography. This informative
book covers a host of topics relating to the icons from the techniques used in their
production to the various influences present in the art and the themes specific to the
different regions of Romania.

836 **Prehistoric art in Romania.**
Vladimir Dumitrescu. Bucharest: Meridiane Publishing House, 1985.
176p. bibliog.
The author surveys the various artefacts found in Romania dating from the period
between the Palaeolithic period and the Iron age which may be considered objects of
art. Made of clay, bone, shells, marble, copper and other materials, these objects are
usually non-functional in design and bear some magical, religious or ritualistic
significance. Copiously illustrated, this book readily conveys the beauty and also the
sense of timelessness that surrounds many of these precious artefacts. The volume is
completed by a short chapter on prehistoric architecture.

837 **Gheorghe Petraşcu.**
Vasile Florea, translated by Andrei Bantaş. Bucharest: Meridiane
Publishing House, 1990. 110p. bibliog.
Born in Tecuci in southern Moldavia, Gheorghe Petraşcu (1872-1949) went on to
establish himself as one of Romania's premier artists with colourful and vibrant
paintings which depict local subjects in a style reminiscent of the late French
impressionists. Indeed, Petraşcu sent four years in Paris at the turn of the century
when he met many of the leading artists of the day. After an extended biographical
essay and an appreciation of his work, this volume reproduces in 149 colour and
black-and-white plates a representative sample of Petraşcu's work

838 **Romanian painting.**
Vasile Florea, translated into English by Sergiu Celac. Bucharest:
Meridiane Publishing House, 1982. 154p. bibliog.
An ambitious survey of Romanian art from medieval times to the contemporary era,
covering a wide trajectory which ranges from religious paintings and the famous
exterior murals of the churches and monasteries of Bucovina to impressionism,
expressionism and other more modern artistic movements. An informative volume,
this book would be a useful companion for those who wish to know something of
Romania's artistic heritage.

839 **Horia Bernea.**
Bucharest: Muzeul Naţional de Artă al României, Departmentul Artă
Contemporană, 1997. 110p. bibliog.

In order to safeguard himself in Ceauşescu's Romania, Bernea, like so many other
artists, detached himself from his surroundings and shielded his art by resorting to
visual metaphors. True art for such an artist could be found in normal everyday life.
Most importantly art was also a device to help him survive spiritually – 'to look
beyond the visible and to help us believe in the unseen . . .'. The plates in this
beautifully produced book are accompanied by a number of essays by artists and
cultural figures in which they try to shed some illumination on Bernea's polysemic
and enigmatic world.

840 **Brancusi.**
Pontus Hulten, Natalia Dumitresco, Alexandre Istrati.   New York:
Harry N. Abrams, 1987. 336p. bibliog.

Profusely illustrated with a large number of photographs of Brâncuşi's sculptures, this
beautifully produced book covers the sculptor's life, work and artistic techniques.

841 **Constantin Brancusi. A survey of his work.**
Sanda Miller.   Oxford: Clarendon Press, 1995. 256p. bibliog.

This scholarly and lucid analysis of the artist's work is arranged in five different
chapters entitled 'The beginning: Romania', 'The crucial years: Paris', 'Maturity: the
motifs', 'A Romanian wood-carver', and 'Magnum opus: the Tîrgu-Jiu complex'. The
book closes with a particularly useful and exhaustive bibliography.

842 **Nicolae Grigorescu: argument, anthology of texts, selection of
illustrations and chronology.**
George Sorin Movileanu, translated from the Romanian by Andrei
Bantaş.   Bucharest: Meridiane Publishing House, 1986. 59p.

Nicolae Grigorescu (1838-1907) is often considered to be the first truly national
Romanian painter. After studying painting in France, he returned home to interpret the
landscapes and people of his own country. His is a bucolic art replete with shepherds
sporting fluffy sheepskin caps, carters driving yoked oxen along dusty country roads
and peasant women stirring pans of *mămăliga* before waiting, hungry children. Such
paintings led to Grigorescu gaining a reputation as being not only a faithful recorder
of the landscape and its traditions but also an interpreter of the very soul of Romanian
peasant life. He was a prolific artist and his total oeuvre is estimated to exceed 4,000
paintings and drawings.

843 **Nicolae Tonitza (1886-1940).**
Bucharest: Alcor Edimpex, 1996. 55p. bibliog.

A painter, graphic artist, professor and art critic, Nicolae Tonitza reached artistic
maturity during the interwar years. A contemporary of Gheorghe Petraşcu, Theodor
Pallady, Nicolae Dărăscu and J. Al Steriadi amongst others, Tonitza believed that
form is never perfect in itself, but only achieves perfection through what it succeeds in
expressing. This book, which is beautifully produced, reproduces a representative
selection of his oil paintings, drawings and sketches.

844 **Romanian folk costume.**
Paul Petrescu, Elena Secoşan.   Bucharest: Meridiane Publishing
House, 1985. 186p. bibliog.

Provides a socio-ethnographic overview of the development of Romanian traditional costume. The text, which is accompanied by a number of handsome coloured photographs, covers the historical and technical development of folk dress before offering an analysis of the differing designs to be found in both male and female costumes. The book closes with a short chapter on 'Fashion and functionality' in the Romania of today.

845 **Constantin Brancusi.**
Eric Shanes.   New York: Abbeville Press, 1989. 128p. bibliog.
(Modern Masters Series).

The author gives a balanced analysis of Brâncuşi's work, exploring not only the arresting forms of his sculptures but also the ideas that lay behind them. This book, which is written with a clarity of prose that serves well the clarity of the sculptures, is divided into seven major chapters covering: the artist's early life; his maturity; the natural world; the human world; the beginning of the world; the avenue of heroes; and the final years.

846 **Romanian metalwork.**
Victor Simion.   Bucharest: Meridiane Publishing House, 1990. 150p.
bibliog.

In this book the author attempts the ambitious task of surveying the artistic metalwork produced on Romanian soil from the prehistoric period (5500-2500 BC) to the present day. Beginning with the Iron Age and with items such as bracelets, rings, discs, pendants, buttons and funerary diadems, the author observes the development of technical skills and craftsmanship as well as the diversity of styles, the latter being the subject of a long section, chapter five (p. 63-148). The rest of the book is arranged under headings such as 'Artisans and customers' (p. 18-37) and 'Categories of objects' (p. 38-62).

847 **Constantin Brancusi 1876-1957.**
Friedrich Teja Bach, Margit Rowell, Ann Temkin, translations by
David Britt.   Philadelphia, Pennsylvania: Philadelphia Museum of
Art, c.1995; Cambridge, Massachusetts; London: The MIT Press, 1996.
406p. bibliog.

This book was published to mark a major retrospective exhibition of Brâncuşi's works shown first in Paris and then in Philadelphia during 1995. It contains three major essays on the artist's life and work by: Friedrich Teja Bach, 'Brancusi: the reality of sculpture'; Margit Rowell, 'Brancusi: timelessness in a modern mode'; and Ann Temkin, 'Brancusi and his American collectors'. The volume is completed by a catalogue of the photographs and illustrations and two brief articles on the artist's drawings and photography.

848 **Brancusi.**
Radu Varia. New York: Rizzoli International Publications, 1986. 320p.
Born in Hobița, a hamlet near Petroșani on the edge of the Jiu Valley in Wallachia, Constantin Brâncuși had no formal education, but as a child working as an errand boy in Târgu Jiu he learnt something of the skills of local woodcarvers. A local industrialist observed his exceptional craftsmanship and helped him attend the School of Arts in Craiova and then the National School of Fine Arts in Bucharest. A government scholarship led him to France, where he studied under Rodin, and he was to remain in this country for the next fifty years. In Paris he worked on many of his most important themes – the kiss, sleeping muse, torso, Mlle Pogany, the new-born, endless column and bird in space – producing a sculpture which was marked by its striking simplicity of form; as he himself was to declare, his work was not only 'a healing process' but also 'lovely to touch and friendly to live with'. In 1926 Brâncuși was to gain some notoriety and become a household name in the United States, when during a visit to that country a customs officer labelled one of his bird series 'a piece of metal' and levied a $10 import duty. Justifiably, Brâncuși has been hailed as a pioneer of modern sculpture, and this handsomely produced book contains illustrations of many of his best-known works.

Music and dance

849 **Rumanian folk music.**
Bela Bartók. The Hague: Martinus Nijhoff, 1967. 3 vols. 704p. 756p. 661p.
The well-known Hungarian composer Béla Bartók began collecting the tunes and lyrics of Romanian folk music in his native Transylvania whilst it was still under Austro-Hungarian rule in 1908. He only completed the task a bare six months before his death in September 1945 by which time he was in exile in the United States. This monumental three-volume work contains 2,400 melodies and 1,752 texts. All the volumes are edited by Benjamin Swchoff. Volume one, with a foreword by Victor Bator, covers instrumental melodies, volume two is concerned with vocal melodies and volume three covers the texts which are translated by E. C. Teodorescu.

850 **Text and music in Romanian oral epic.**
Margaret Hiebert Beissinger. *Oral Tradition*, vol. 3, no. 3 (Oct. 1988), p. 294-314.
In an effort to understand the process of composition in Romanian oral epic verse, the author of this scholarly article offers an analysis of the complex relationship that exists between text and music. Beissinger addresses such questions as: 'Does the music aid the singer in the composition of the text?' and 'What types of patterns are evident as singers combine text and music?' By comparing the different styles of peasant amateurs and professional singers (*lăutari*), she highlights the mechanisms and techniques employed to join text to music as an epic is performed. A previous article on the same subject by Beissinger is 'The Romanian epic song and ballad', *Miorița,* vol. 7, no. 2 (1981), p. 121-28.

851   **The Popeluc guide to Transylvania.**
Pete Castle, Lucy Castle, with the assistance of Ioan Pop.   Derby,
England: Steel Carpet Music, 1995. 40p. map. bibliog.

Driven by their love of the traditional music of Maramureş, the authors of this
entertaining work, together with Ioan Pop, have founded a group known as 'Popeluc'
– an acronym formed from their combined names. Performing at festivals in both
Romania and Great Britain, the group is led by Popica – the Romanian nickname of
Pop – who sings and plays the *zongora* (a guitar-like instrument used in Maramureş),
the *braci* (a viola with three strings used in Transylvania) and the *cetera* (a type of
fiddle). Lucy, a classically trained violinist, plays the fiddle, whilst her father, Pete,
accompanies them on the guitar, the *doba* (bass drum) and also sings. This informative
booklet contains examples of musical scores as well as a history of Transylvania
written, as the authors profess, to enhance their knowledge of the region and dispel
myths, such as those surrounding Dracula.

852   **George Enescu.**
Viorel Cosma, John Waterhouse.   In: *The new grove dictionary of
music and musicians.*   Edited by Sadie Stanley.   London: Macmillan,
1980, p. 163-66.

George Enescu (1881-1955), known outside Romania under the form of his name that
he adopted while resident in France, Georges Enesco, is considered to be Romania's
most accomplished musician and composer. This biographical entry provides details
of his career as a violinist and teacher in Paris, and of the character of his
compositions. It is supplemented by a list of his works and a bibliography of studies
about him.

853   **A cult instrument in Romania – the wooden plate.**
Constanţa Cristescu.   *Jahrbuch für Volksliedforschung*, vol. 39
(1994), p. 117-24.

The wooden plate, which can actually be either wooden or metallic, is an old
instrument known to people as varied as the Greeks, Armenians, Bulgarians and
Chinese amongst others. Beaten rhythmically by one or two mallets, it plays an
important role in Orthodox Church ritual, especially in monasteries, where it is used
either as a solo instrument or as an accompaniment to special songs called *toconelele*.
It is the repertoire of these songs that constitutes the main focus of this article.

854   **The national festival 'Song to Romania': manipulation of symbols
in the political discourse.**
Anca Giurchescu.   In: *Symbols of power: the aesthetics of political
legitimation in the Soviet Union and Eastern Europe.*   Edited by Claes
Arvidsson, Lars Erik Blomqvist.   Stockholm: Almqvist & Wiksell,
1987, p. 163-71.

'Song to Romania' was a national festival inaugurated in 1975 by the Department of
Propaganda of the Central Committee of the Romanian Communist Party. Its name
was derived from an anthem of the 1848 revolution, and the author in this article
suggests that the Ceauşescu régime used the festival to convey two messages: the first
was one of nationalism in terms of independence, unity and liberty; and the second,
patriotism in terms of devotion to the socialist state, party and leader, Ceauşescu. The

festival also served to symbolize the revolutionary links which supposedly bound the patriots of 1848 with the Ceauşescu régime. 'Song to Romania' presented Ceauşescu's Romania as an idyllic society replacing real events with a fictive history and, more importantly, a fictive present.

855 **Dance among the urban Gypsies of Romania.**
     Robert Grafias. *Yearbook for Traditional Music*, vol. 16 (1984),
     p. 84-96.

Urban Gypsy music and dance in Romania is compared not only with ethnic Romanian music and dance forms but also with those of their rural Gypsy counterparts. Another study in this volume concerned with the insularity of Gypsy musicians within their communities of residence, which also makes reference to Romania, is Bernard Lortat-Jacob, 'Music and complex societies: control and management of musical production', p. 19-33.

856 **Disemic features in the Romanian folk musical 'Jianii'.**
     Eugenia Judetz-Popescu. *Dance Studies*, vol. 17 (1993), p. 77-129.

Using the concept of 'disemia', which was first advanced by the anthropologist Michael Herzfeld and was itself derived from the linguistic term 'diglossia', used to indicate two levels of language, the author examines the disemic framework of the Romanian folk musical 'Jianii'. Originally performed in Moldavian villages on New Year's Eve and New Year's Day, it is now more commonly encountered on the theatre stage. The two opposite registers in this case are the 'urban', as represented by the Captain and his posse, and the 'folk', as represented by Jianu and his outlaws.

857 **Căluş. Symbolic transformation in Romanian ritual.**
     Gail Kligman. Chicago; London: University of Chicago Press, 1981.
     210p.

This is the most detailed study in English of the significance of the ritual dance *căluş*. Based on information gathered from thirty villages in Wallachia, where the dance is still performed, the writer's fieldwork enables her to compare the characteristics of the ritual village by village.

858 **A Romanian singer of tales: Vasile Tetin.**
     Eliza Miruna Ghil. *Oral Tradition*, vol. 1, no. 3 (Oct. 1986),
     p. 607-35.

A portrait of a peasant singer, Vasile Tetin, who hails from Teleorman county in southern Romania. His singing is particularly notable because he incorporates within his renditions of *cîntec bătrînesc* ('songs of old deeds') elements of the local epic poetic tradition. Indeed, the rhythmic structures seem to be the most stable element of his songs, because in the verbal component he displays such a high degree of flexibility that a song is never identical from one performance to another.

Film and theatre

859 An abridged history of Romanian theatre.
Edited by Simion Alterescu.   Bucharest: Editura Academiei
Republicii Socialiste România, 1983. 191p.
Romania has long had a lively theatre tradition and in this volume various contributors
trace the history of Romanian theatre from the rites and ceremonies of the Dacian
people to the contemporary communist theatre. Both popular and formal theatre are
featured in the essays in this book.

860 The Rumanian film today.
Colman Robert Andrews.   *East Europe*, vol. 18, no. 8-9 (Aug.-Sept.
1969), p. 21-24.
A survey of the Romanian film industry as it was in the early Ceauşescu years.
Although controls were slightly relaxed following the Stalinist period, which had
featured works of socialist realism such as 'Lupeni 29' starring Gheorghe Gheorghiu-
Dej's daughter, too often story lines still remained bound by ideology. Releases for
1966 included a love story of a worker and a widow on a railway project and the story
of the heroic deeds of a twelve-year-old girl during the Second World War. An
increasing number of co-productions with France gave the prospect of some hope for
the future but bureaucratic interference remained the main obstacle to be surmounted.

**861 Quick takes on Yuri Mamin's 'Fountain' from the perspective of a
Romanian.**
Andrei Codrescu.   In: *'Inside Soviet film satire'. Laughter with a lash.*
Edited by Andrew Horton.   Cambridge, England: Cambridge
University Press, 1993, p. 149-53.
At one level this is a review of Yuri Mamin's dark and surrealistic film, 'Fountain', a
satire about the 'terror' of being 'free' in the Soviet Union under *glasnost* and the
ruthlessness of the 'delights' on offer in this new state of being. However, the subtext
of this review is the author's own painful experiences in Romania under the oppressive Ceauşescu régime. The 'fountain' serves as a metaphor for 'existence' and once
the flow of water weakens, then the world fills with false illusions.

862 A concise history of theatre in Romania.
Medeea Ionescu.   Bucharest: Editura Ştiinţifică şi Enciclopedică,
1981. 69p.
This slim volume, which is arranged chronologically, contains four major chapters:
'Archaic and folk drama in Romania', 'The professional theatre and the Romanian
Principalities', 'The theatre in the inter-war period' and 'Post-war drama'.

**863 The Romanian popular theater: origins, structure and
characteristics.**
Horia Barbu Oprişan.   *Mioriţa,* vol. 6, no. 2 (July 1976), p. 21-31.
Until recently the study of Romanian popular theatre had been relatively neglected.
Previously, folklorists, with the notable exception of Tudor Pamfile in Moldavia, had

tended to concentrate their research on oral ballads. It was only in the 1940s that attention came to be focused on Romania's rich tradition of popular theatre and in this article the author outlines some of the main themes to be found in the repertoire. The Romanian popular theatre included both secular and religious plays with the best known being the 'Herod play' introduced with other Western works into Transylvania by Catholic priests after the union with Rome in the late 17th century. Bulgarian and Leventine influences were also prominent and can be seen in the use of masks, although during the 19th century in certain areas anybody caught wearing one could be subjected to forty days penance as this was associated with the devil.

864 **Balkan cinema, evolution after the revolution.**
Michael J. Stoil. Ann Arbour, Michigan: UMI Research Press, 1982. 160p. (Studies in Cinema, no. 11).

A scholarly study of the film industry in South-Eastern Europe which, the author suggests, has a cinematic tradition as old and as extensive as many Western European countries. Ever since the first motion pictures made in the area by the optician and photographer, Paul Menu, of a military parade in Bucharest in 1897, and the first classic of South-Eastern Europe cinema, 'Independent Romania', of 1912, Romania was at the forefront of the region's cinema and its achievements are heavily featured in this study. After covering the early days of the cinema and the political uses of the medium under Marxism-Leninism, the author devotes a number of chapters to various film genres: historical, anti-fascist, detective, spy, and films depicting rural life.

865 **History on the cutting-room floor.**
Bryant Jessie Wilder. *Literature Film Quarterly*, vol. 23, no. 4 (Oct. 1995), p. 243-46.

'The truth is not pretty, but it always surfaces like oil on water. Like blood . . .'. These were the prophetic words uttered by Dominic Paraschiv hours before his death as, tied to a bed naked and covered with a net, he was paraded before the world's press as the 'Butcher of Timişoara', an arch-counterrevolutionary, who was personally responsible for the massacre of eighty of his colleagues. Three months after Paraschiv's death, his childhood friend, the film director Robert Dornhelm, returned to his homeland determined to find the truth behind the incident. The result was an acclaimed docudrama, 'Requiem for Dominic' and in this article the director narrates the results of his research. It seems that Paraschiv, a deeply religious and essentially peaceable man, had joined a search party at the height of the Revolution looking for terrorists at the Solventul factory. On 24 December 1989, exhausted after two consecutive nights on guard duty without any sleep, Paraschiv seems to have suffered a temporary nervous breakdown and forced his colleagues to kneel in prayer and repent their sins, saying they had all collaborated in the forty-year lie of communism. Eventually, he was overpowered by soldiers, but in the process he was shot and taken to a local hospital where the situation somehow got completely out of control, and he was branded a *Securitate* killer. Believing these wild rumours, the staff of the hospital seem to have withdrawn treatment from Paraschiv and he was apparently allowed to bleed to death.

Architecture

866 **Casă Frumoasă: an introduction to the House Beautiful in rural Romania.**
Jan Harold Brunvand. In: *The old traditional way of life: essays in honor of Warren E. Roberts.* Edited by Robert E. Walls, George H. Schoemaker. Bloomington, Indiana: Trickster Press, Indiana University Folklore Institute, 1989, p. 191-207.

A study of the highly ornate, decorated houses that are still frequently encountered in Romanian villages even today. Although the author admits that the 'beauty' and aesthetics of these edifices remains a controversial subject, he examines the buildings both as examples of traditional Romanian peasant art and in relation to the current needs and preferences of the people who build and live in them.

867 **Romanian house decoration in stucco.**
Jan Harold Brunvand. *Miorița*, vol. 3, no. 1 (Jan. 1976), p. 2-11.

In this article the author discusses the exterior decorations to be found on Romanian houses that are faced with mud, plaster or cement. All these fall under the category of 'stucco' and Brunvand argues that the importance of this material lies in the fact that it lends itself even to modern building materials, allowing for the use of old decorative designs, such as the tree of life, horse and rider and solar spirals, on recent constructions. This author has also written a number of further studies of house decoration in Romania, including 'Gingerbread in Romania', *Natural History*, vol. 84, no. 6 (June 1975), p. 66-71.

868 **Traditional house decoration in Romania: survey and bibliography.**
Jan Harold Brunvand. *East European Quarterly*, vol. 14, no. 3 (Autumn 1980), p. 255-301. bibliog.

Whereas most traditional arts in Romania still reflect old skills and designs, house decoration is strongly influenced by contemporary life and individual tastes. This article compares the traditional and modern aspects of Romanian peasant houses, including details of their construction and decoration. It is supplemented by a bibliography of over 175 titles on folk architecture in Romania, arranged alphabetically by author.

869 **The wooden churches of Eastern Europe: an introductory survey.**
David Buxton. Cambridge, England; London; New York; Melbourne; Sydney: Cambridge University Press, 1981. 405p. maps. bibliog.

Wooden churches exist throughout much of Eastern Europe from the Baltic to the Danube but there is a particularly rich concentration in Romania. These churches are the chief subject of study in chapter five of this lavishly illustrated book, 'Rumania, Hungary and Yugoslavia' (p. 189-268). Buxton divides the churches of Romania into different groups. The first of these and the foundation from which the others evolved is the 'basic Balkan style' which can be mostly found in Wallachia. In neighbouring

Moldavia this style was influenced by a mixture of Byzantine and local traditions to produce more elaborate cupolared churches, perhaps, as the author suggests, because of Ukrainian influences. In Transylvania, which was under Habsburg rule, the basic wooden design was again influenced by local masonry equivalents. However, rather than Byzantine the influence this time was the Gothic style and from the 17th century onwards this produced a large number of wooden churches with magnificent soaring spires.

870 **Medieval architecture in Transylvania.**
John H. Harvey. *Transactions of the Ancient Monuments Society*, vol. 31 (1987), p. 175-210.

A methodical and attractively presented study of the medieval architecture of Transylvania illustrated with many photographs. The distinctive feature of the architecture of the region at this time, the fortified church, was primarily developed as a defence against the Tatars and Turks. In this study the author discusses in alphabetical order the churches and other buildings visited and includes in an appendix a listing of all the medieval monuments in Transylvania.

871 **Romania's rural rescue scheme.**
Ann Hills. *History Today*, vol. 44, no. 2 (Feb. 1994), p. 2-3.

This article underlines the acute conservation problems facing many former Saxon villages in Transylvania which have been abandoned by their inhabitants who have sought a new life in Germany. The author discusses in particular the case of the village of Homorod, where the old religious paintings and frescoes of the main church are almost irreparably damaged. The main problem is a lack of funds and the author concludes with a discussion of the activities of ECOVAST, the European Council for the Village and the Small Town, which is seeking to raise funds for projects in Romania.

872 **Folk wood carving in Romania.**
Cornel Irimie, Marcela Necula. Bucharest: Meridiane Publishing House, 1985. 105p. bibliog.

Examines one of the most popular genres of folk art in Romania, that of wood carving, an old artistic tradition which can be traced as far back as prehistoric times. The authors highlight the use of wood carving in architecture (house building), interior decoration (furniture and household utensils), technical equipment (tools and implements) and musical instruments as well as wood carving for purely ornamental reasons. The text of this study is accompanied by a number of handsome illustrations.

873 **Views on the dancing-houses in Transylvania.**
A. Kostyák, J. Gagyi, A. Horváth. *Folklorismus Bulletin*, vol. 2 (Oct. 1980), p. 18-21.

A brief account of the changing role of 'dancing-houses' in Transylvania. In the past they have been used as places of entertainment, music schools, centres for the exchange of ideas and socialist houses of culture.

874 **Historic buildings in Romania and their conservation.**
Gwyn I. Meirion-Jones. *Transactions of the Ancient Monuments Society*, vol. 26 (1982), p. 32-52.

After a brief introductory note on the history and geography of Romania, the author offers a detailed survey of the policies adopted by the Romanian government to conserve the country's wealth of historic buildings and other edifices in the face of the challenges posed by a fast modernizing society. He discusses the role of government bodies such as the then Council for Culture and Socialist Education, and the part played by the excellent open-air ethnographic museums which have also helped to preserve the country's rich architectural heritage.

875 **Wooden churches and their paintings in the Maramureş region of Romania: a preliminary study.**
Fran Weatherhead. *Antiquity*, vol. 67, no. 254 (March 1993), p. 368-77.

Built in the early 18th century, the magnificent wooden church of the Holy Archangels in Şurdeşti, Maramureş, is famous for its forty-five metre tower, which is the highest wooden structure in Europe. The church is also renowned for its interior wall murals and in this study, which is illuminated by some beautiful drawings and photographs, the author examines the state of the paintings and determines the degree of restoration needed to ensure their preservation. In outlining the various causes of the deterioration of the paintings, which include dampness and condensation, Weatherhead also points to neglect and suggests that in future the congregation must show a greater awareness of the artistic treasures which surround them.

Sports

876 Nadia: the autobiography of Nadia Comăneci.
Nadia Comăneci.   London; New York: Proteus Books, 1981. 141p.
When this autobiography was produced, gymnast Nadia Comăneci was not yet twenty years old, but she had already reached the pinnacle of her career, and in the process had become perhaps the best known Romanian in the world after Ceauşescu. In this book she describes the trials and tribulations of her early life and her subsequent Olympic triumphs. She also exposes her tempestuous relationship with the foreign press, which on the one hand lauded her but on the other carried a stream of rumours and gossip. This book, which is lucidly written and beautifully illustrated with photographs, is a testament to the talents of the greatest of Romanian gymnasts. Comăneci's life took another turn in the late 1980s, when she made a high-profile escape to the West. She now lives in the United States.

Libraries, Archives, Galleries and Museums

877 **The National Gallery: Romanian painting in the collection of the Art Museum of the Socialist Republic of Romania.**
Alexandru Cebuc, translated from the Romanian by Ştefan Stoenescu and Thomas C. Carlson. Bucharest: The National Gallery, 1984. 394p. bibliog.

This book, which describes the contents of the National Gallery of Romania in Bucharest, is very much the product of its time as, from the beginning, the author states that 'the present work has emerged from the ideas and recommendations put forth by Nicolae Ceaşescu, Secretary-General of the Romanian Communist Party, President of the Socialist Republic of Romania'. This rather inauspicious beginning soon leads to a rather cursory exposition on the development of Romanian art in the 18th, 19th and 20th centuries but this is then followed by a fine selection of plates reproducing works by painters such as Gheorghe Tattarescu, Ştefan Luchian, Gheorghe Petraşcu, Theodor Pallady, Nicolae Tonitza and Nicolae Grigorescu. The photographs are mostly in colour, but some black-and-white ones are also included. A catalogue devoted solely to the 19th-century paintings in the National Gallery, accompanied by 179 plates, is *The Art Museum of the Socialist Republic of Romania. Catalogue of the National Gallery. Painting, XIXth century*, edited by Paula Constantinescu and Ştefan Diţescu (Bucharest: The National Gallery, 1975. 95p.).

878 **Russia, the Soviet Union and Eastern Europe: a survey of the holdings at the Hoover Institution of War, Revolution and Peace.**
Edited by Joseph D. Dwyer. Stanford, California: Hoover Institution Press, 1980. 233p.

The section of this volume dealing with Romania (p. 120-34) includes details of the Hoover Institution's holdings on the country's history, foreign relations and political organizations. The editor reveals that the Hoover Institution has a particularly good coverage of material on the interwar political parties and that the archives include papers from the collections of: the former Prime Minister, Ion G. Duca; Jeanne Marie Lambrino, the first wife of Carol II; and the most influential interwar Foreign

Minister, Nicolae Titulescu. The contents of the archive of the Hoover Institution are also described in Charles G. Palm, Dale Reed, *Guide to the Hoover Institution archives* (Stanford, California: Hoover Institution Press, Stanford University Press, 1980. 418p. [Hoover Bibliographic Series, no. 59]).

879 **Some critical notes on Moses Gaster's correspondence with Jewish and Romanian intellectuals.**
Victor Eskenasy. *East European Quarterly*, vol. 21, no. 4 (Jan. 1988), p. 447-50.
A brief comment on the extensive document holdings concerning Romania which were bequeathed to London University by Rabbi Moses Gaster (1856-1939).

880 **Guide to libraries in Central and Eastern Europe.**
Compiled by Maria Hughes with the assistance of Paul Wilson.
London: The British Library, Science Reference and Information Service, 1992. 82p.
In compiling this list of libraries, the authors state that they were guided by a desire to include 'those libraries of use to Western governments, businesses and other bodies contributing to the economic restructuring of Central and Eastern Europe'. The pages concerned with Romania (p. 51-54) list sixteen libraries, most of which are attached to universities in Braşov, Bucharest, Cluj, Craiova, Iaşi, Timişoara and Târgu Mureş, although strangely, the largest holding of books and periodicals in Romania, the library of the Romanian Academy, is not included. At the end of this volume (p. 71-73) there is a short listing of libraries in the United Kingdom with large holdings of books on Eastern Europe.

881 **The village museum.**
Jana Negoiţa, translated into English by Irina Bojin. Bucharest: Meridiane Publishing House, 1986. 67p. bibliog.
One of the most interesting tourist attractions in Romania is the Village Museum which sits on the shore of Lake Herăstrău in the northern suburbs of Bucharest. Established in 1936, the museum contains a fascinating collection of rural buildings gathered from all four corners of Romania. Besides houses and farm buildings, there are also mills, richly carved wooden gateways and even churches. This book is a guide to the museum which in the words of the author was founded 'to present the traditional cultural patrimony of our rural world . . . and to illustrate better than any other [museum] the richness and variety of peasant life'. Another multilingual guide to the museum, with an introduction by the same author, is *Muzeul satului şi de artă populară, Bucureşti − Romania/Le musée du village et d'art populaire, Bucurest − Roumanie/The village museum and folk art museum, Bucharest − Romania* (Bucharest, 1983. 261p.).

882 **The research libraries of Romania.**
William O. Oldson. *International Library Review*, vol. 11, no. 3 (July 1979), p. 373-85.
The author intended this article to serve as an aid for the inexperienced Western scholar entering Romania's arcane library system for the first time. In particular, it was meant to be used to fill the gap resulting from the absence of reference books and

introductions to the research libraries. In examining specifically the libraries of
Bucharest, Cluj and Iaşi, Oldson discusses problems relating to the unearthing of
source material, consulting archives, using special collections, gaining admittance to
the libraries and securing borrowing rights. Although somewhat out-of-date, this
article still retains some relevance.

883 **Transylvanian libraries and archives in contemporary Romania.**
Martyn Rady. *Journal of the Society of Archivists*, vol. 12, no. 2
(Autumn 1991), p. 123-26.

A survey of the fate of Transylvanian archives under the Ceauşescu régime. The
author reveals that many suffered grievously at a time when local public and private
archives were forcibly amalgamated into government controlled regional and national
collections.

884 **Library resources in Britain for the study of Eastern Europe and
the former USSR.**
Compiled by Gregory Walker, Jackie Johnson. Oxford: Gregory
Walker, 1992. 92p.

This directory, which is an updated version of *Resources for Soviet, Eastern European
and Slavonic studies in British libraries* (Birmingham, England: Centre for Russian
and East European Studies, University of Birmingham, 1981), lists ninety-five
libraries in Britain containing material on Russia, the Soviet Union and the countries
of Eastern Europe. Entries are arranged alphabetically by town and give information
on the facilities available, the scope of the collection and a contact name and address.
National, academic and specialized collections are included.

885 **The book in Romania: a bibliographical mini-overview 1508-1985.**
Vladimir F. Wertsman. In: *Books, libraries and information in Slavic
and East European studies: proceedings of the second international
conference of Slavic librarians and information specialists.* Edited by
Marianna Tax Choldin. New York: Russica, 1986, p. 54-66.
bibliog. ('Russiac' Bibliography Series, no. 8).

This informative history of book printing and production in Romania since the Middle
Ages also contains a short exposition on the development of libraries and bibliographical organization systems within the country.

Mass Media

886 **From big lie to small lies – state mass-media dominance in postcommunist Romania.**
Henry F. Carey. *East European Politics and Societies*, vol. 10, no. 1 (Winter 1996), p. 16-45.

In a scathing attack on the shortcomings of the Romanian media in the years immediately after the Revolution, the author argues that the 'state-controlled media consolidate authoritarianism with a democratic face'. His ire is mostly directed at the state television stations and their reluctance to tackle key issues such as the continuing influence of the security agencies. However, considerable side swipes are also aimed at the new 'independent' television station, Tele 7abc, and the 'weak' print media.

887 **Mass media in revolution and national development: the Romanian laboratory.**
Peter Gross. Ames, Iowa: Iowa State University Press, 1996. 206p. bibliog.

In this full-length study, the author examines the various attempts to restructure the Romanian print and broadcast media at a time when it is expected to play a crucial role in the transition from communism. An overview of the communist and pre-communist legacy are followed by an analysis of the role of the media in the 1989 Revolution and the years immediately afterwards, before the author concludes by offering some of the lessons to be learnt from the 'Romanian laboratory'. Highlighting the ease with which the media has been abused in post-communist Romania, Gross calls not only for the better training of journalists – as he rightly notes technological improvements do not necessarily lead to a raising of standards – but also for more discernment amongst the consumers of this journalism.

888 **Restricting the free press in Romania.**
Peter Gross. *Orbis,* vol. 35, no. 3 (Summer 1991), p. 365-75.
Offers an analysis of the reasons for the National Salvation Front's resounding victory in Romania's first post-communist elections in May 1990. Rejecting the two most commonly voiced theories, that the Front won because Romania's electorate was politically immature or because it engaged in vote rigging, as being too simplistic, Gross instead suggests that the roots of its victory were grounded in the inability of the 'free' media to 'educate' society in the habits of democracy. He then proceeds to survey the media, noting its weaknesses and suggesting possible remedies.

889 **Trials, tribulations, and contributions: a brief history of the Romanian press.**
Peter Gross. *East European Quarterly,* vol. 22, no. 1 (March 1988), p. 1-22.
This chronologically ordered sketch of the development of the Romanian-language press, from its origins with the newspapers *Curierul Românesc* and *Albina Românească* in 1829 until the advent of communist rule in 1947, contains a useful listing of titles and bibliographical sources in the notes.

890 **The USA as seen through the eyes of the Romanian press: a study of images created by the Romanian Communist Party's *Scinteia*.**
Peter Gross. *East European Quarterly,* vol. 24, no. 3 (Sept. 1990), p. 373-92.
The author surveys images of the United States as portrayed in the chief Party daily, *Scînteia,* during the first six months of 1988. The methodology employed is a statistical examination of the types of items (news/commentary/analysis), the topic(s) covered, and the manner in which they were presented to the Romanian reader. The greatest concentration was on foreign affairs. These articles were mostly neutral in tone, although often the choice of issues and topics seems to have been designed to paint as negative impression as possible with, for instance, many items concerning US domestic affairs dwelling on homelessness. A brief history of Romanian news-gathering stresses the importance of the *Agerpres* agency (now *Rompres*), although after an *Agerpres* journalist had defected to France in 1976, all Romanian foreign correspondents had been withdrawn from overseas postings. During the 1960s *Agence France-Presse,* rather than the Russian press agency, TASS, had supplied the bulk of foreign news reports but by the late 1970s no one news agency dominated.

891 **The dynamics of media independence in post-Ceauşescu Romania.**
R. A. Hall. *Journal of Communist Studies and Transition Politics,* vol. 12, no. 4 (Dec. 1996), p. 102-23.
Although a range of public opinion exists in post-communist Romania, the author argues that the legacy of the communist past has ensured a continuing high level of media control. He supports his argument through an analysis of the portrayal of the 1989 Revolution in the state controlled media, where, despite the many questions raised both inside and outside Romania, only the 'official' version of the events is propagated.

892 **Journalistic activities of Romanian women, 1875-1926.**
Cornelia Mâță. *Romanian Civilization*, vol. 3, no. 2 (Fall-Winter 1994), p. 104-15.
A survey of the role of female journalists in the development of the Romanian press. Approximately fifty journals were edited and directed by women between the years 1875 and 1926, the year in which the Society of Romanian Women Writers was founded, with Adela Xenopol as its first president.

893 **The Romanian language press in America.**
G. James Patterson, Paul Petrescu. *East European Quarterly*, vol. 27, no. 2 (June 1993), p. 261-70.
Adopting an anthropological approach and placing particular emphasis on the milieu in which it developed, the authors trace the history of the Romanian-language press in the United States from *Romanul*, published by a Uniate Priest in Cleveland in 1905, to the more politically driven small circulation press of the 1980s produced by recent refugees. The Romanian émigré community in the United States was always small compared with other European emigrant groups but by 1920 they numbered approximately 80,000.

Professional Periodicals

894 **Country Profile: Romania.**
London: Economist Intelligence Unit, 1986- . annual.
This annual survey, part of a series covering most of the countries of the world, provides an invaluable summary of recent trends in the Romanian economy backed by useful statistical tables. There is also a short overview of the year's political developments. The Economist Intelligence Unit also produces two other useful publications. Quarterly it publishes a *Country Report: Romania* (1995-) and jointly with Business International, Geneva a weekly, *Business Eastern Europe*, which regularly contains information on developments in the Romanian economy.

895 **Dacia: Revue d'Archéologie et d'Histoire Ancienne.** (Dacia: Review of Archaeology and Ancient History.)
Bucharest: Editura Academiei Române, 1957- . biannual.
Contains articles on the archaeology and ancient history of Romania with papers appearing in French and English and, occasionally, German and Russian.

896 **Dacromania: Jahrbuch für Östliche Latinität.** (Yearbook for Eastern Latinity.)
Freiburg, Germany; Munich, Germany: Karl Alber, 1973- . annual.
This yearbook stresses the Latin origins and features of Romanian culture with contributions from Romania and elsewhere.

897 **Dialogue: Revue d'Études Roumaines.** (Dialogue: Review of Romanian Studies.)
Montpellier, France: Centre d'études et de recherches roumaines et de traditions orales Méditerranéennes, 1978- . biannual.
The emphasis in this scholarly review is on the literature, linguistics and cultural anthropology of Romania.

898 **East Europe Agriculture and Food.**
Tunbridge Wells, England: Agra Europe (London), 1987- . monthly.
This newsletter covers current developments in the food and agriculture industries of Eastern Europe. Entries are arranged by country with every issue usually having a section on Romania.

899 **Eastern Europe: the Fortnightly Political Briefing.**
London: East European Newsletter Ltd, 1987- . fortnightly.
This slim newsletter has provided informed coverage of the politics of the region since before the changes of 1989. It was formerly known as the *Eastern European Newsletter*.

900 **Emerging European Markets: Business, Finance and Investment in Central and Eastern Europe and the Former Soviet Union.**
London: Financial Times Finance, 1997- . monthly.
This country-by-country round-up of monthly business and economic news includes a section on Romania. Incorporated in this newsletter are two previous publications: *East European Markets* and *Finance East Europe*.

901 **Études et Documents Balkaniques et Méditerranéens.** (Balkan and Mediterranean studies and documents.)
Paris: Paul H. Stahl, 1979- . irregular/annual.
Until volume 5 (1982) this series was known as *Études et Documents Balkaniques* (Balkan studies and documents). Articles are mostly in French but also, occasionally, English. Issues are often devoted to the consideration of a single topic, such as the traditional costume of the Vlachs. Reflecting the origins and interests of the publisher, who is also the editor, articles regularly appear on Romania.

902 **Euresis: Cahiers Roumains d'Études Littéraires.** (Euresis: Romanian Journal of Literary Studies.)
Bucharest: Éditions Univers, 1973- . quarterly.
Known until 1993 as *Cahiers Roumains d'Études Littéraires* (Romanian Journal of Literary Studies), this journal contains articles on contemporary literary history and theory, together with criticism and essays. Many of the articles relate specifically to Romanian literature. Contributions are mostly in French but sometimes appear in English and, occasionally, in German, Italian and Spanish.

903 **Index on Censorship.**
London: Writers and Scholars International, 1972- . six times a year.
Over the years, in a number of informative articles, this journal has highlighted the plight of dissident intellectuals in Romania.

904   **International Journal of Romanian Sudies.**
      Amsterdam: Editions Rodopi, 1976-89. irregular.

Seven volumes of this irregularly produced scholarly journal appeared. Articles were written in French, English or German and were mostly concerned with literature, linguistics and philosophy, although history was also covered. Some editions were devoted to a single subject, such as the poetry of Mircea Dinescu. Early editions of the journal were published by Gunter Narr, Tübingen.

905   **Miorița.**
      Hamilton, New Zealand; Rochester, New York: Romanian Cultural Association and the Department for Foreign Languages, Literature and Linguistics, University of Rochester, 1973-90. biannual/annual.

Eleven volumes of this scholarly journal appeared. All articles were in English with the subject matter including the history, literature, anthropology and folklore of Romania. Some issues also included Romanian short stories and poems in translation.

906   **Problems of Post-communism.**
      Armonk, New York: M. E. Sharpe, 1992- . six times a year.

This journal continues the tradition of its venerable predecessor, *Problems of Communism* (Washington, DC: US Information Agency, 1952-92). All articles are in English and over the years both titles have included a number of interesting surveys of Romanian politics.

907   **Revista Romana de Proprietate Industrala/Romanian Journal for Industrial Property.**
      Bucharest: Oficiul de stat pentru invenții și marci, 1961- . quarterly.

Supersedes in part *Buletinul de invenții și inovații* (The Bulletin of Inventions and Innovations). The text is in Romanian with summaries in English, French and German.

908   **Revue des Études Roumaines.** (Review of Romanian Studies.)
      Paris; Iași, Romania: Association des amis de la RER, 1953- .
      irregular.

The last volume, number 17-18, of this irregularly produced series appeared in 1993 (volume 15 was dated 1975). Articles, which cover all aspects of Romanian culture from history, language and literature to social science and folklore, are mostly in French and, occasionally, English and German.

909   **Revue des Études Sud-Est Européennes: Civilisations – Mentalités.**
      (Review of South-East European Studies: Civilizations – Mentalities.)
      Bucharest: Institutul de Studii Sud–Est Europene, 1963- .
      quarterly/biannual.

As the subtitle suggests, this journal, which covers the wider South-Eastern European area, is largely concerned with cultural history. Articles are mostly in French but also English and, sometimes, German or Russian. Original texts and documents are also occasionally reproduced.

910 **Revue Roumaine de Géographie.** (Romanian Review of Geography.)
Bucharest: Editura Academiei Române, 1991- . annual.

Continues in part the *Revue Roumaine de Géologie, Géophysique et Géographie*
(Romanian Review of Geology, Geophysics and Geography) (1963-90) which, in turn,
superseded in part the *Revue de Géologie et de Géographie* (Review of Geology and
Geography) (1957-63). Articles on geography appear in English, French, German and
Russian.

911 **Revue Roumaine de Géologie.** (Romanian Review of Geology.)
Bucharest: Editura Academiei Române, 1991- . annual.

Continues in part the *Revue Roumaine de Géologie, Géophysique et Géographie*
(Romanian Review of Geology, Geophysics and Geography) (1963-90) which, in turn,
superseded in part the *Revue de Géologie et de Géographie* (Review of Geology and
Geography) (1957-63). Articles on geology appear in English, French, German and
Russian.

912 **Revue Roumaine de Géophysique.** (Romanian Review of
Geophysics.)
Bucharest: Editura Academiei Române, 1991- . annual.

Continues in part the *Revue Roumaine de Géologie, Géophysique et Géographie*
(Romanian Review of Geology, Geophysics and Geography) (1963-90) which, in turn,
superseded in part the *Revue de Géologie et de Géographie* (Review of Geology and
Geography) (1957-63). Articles on physical geography appear in English, French,
German and Russian.

913 **Revue Roumaine de Linguistique.** (Romanian Review of
Linguistics.)
Bucharest: Editura Academiei Române, 1964- . six times a year.

Continues the *Revue de Linguistique* (Review of Linguistics) (1956-64) and from
1974 contains the *Revue Roumaine de Linguistique: Cahiers de Linguistique
Théorique et Appliquée* (Romanian Review of Linguistics: Journal of Theoretical and
Applied Linguistics) (1962-74) either as part of a numbered sequence or in a separate
volume. Articles on all aspects of linguistics, including issues relating to the
Romanian language, appear in English, French, German, Italian and Russian.

914 **Revue Roumaine de Philosophie.** (Romanian Review of Philosophy.)
Bucharest: Editura Academiei Române, 1991- . quarterly.

Continues *Revue Roumaine de Philosophie et Logique* (Romanian Review of Philosophy and Logic) and *Revue Roumaine des Sciences Sociales: Série de Philosophie et
Logique* (Romanian Review of Social Sciences: Philosophy and Logic Series) which,
in turn, superseded in part *Revue de Sciences Sociales* (Review of Social Sciences).
The journal contains mostly theoretical articles in English and French or, occasionally,
German and Russian, on all aspects of philosophy. Contributors to the journal have
included philosophers of the stature of Constantin Noica.

915 **Revue Roumaine de Sciences Juridiques.** (Romanian Judicial Sciences Review.)
Bucharest: Editura Academiei Române, 1990- . biannual.

Prior to 1990, this journal was known as *Revue Roumaine des Sciences Sociales: Série de Sciences Juridiques* (Romanian Review of Social Sciences: Judicial Sciences Series). This, in turn, had in part superseded the earlier *Revue des Sciences Sociales* (Review of Social Sciences) (1957-1964).

916 **Revue Roumaine d'Études Internationales.** (Romanian Review of International Studies.)
Bucharest: Asociația de Drept International și Relații Internaționale 'N. Titulescu' with Editura Academiei Române, 1967- . every two months.

Articles on all aspects of international relations and related fields appear mostly in French but also in English and sometimes Russian. Publication of this journal has been uncertain since 1992. The same institution also produces, six times a year, the *Revista Romana de Studii Internationale/Romanian Journal of International Studies.*

917 **Revue Roumaine d'Histoire.** (Romanian Review of History.)
Bucharest: Editura Academiei Române, 1962- . quarterly/biannual.

The articles in this journal, which cover all aspects and periods of Romanian history, appear mostly in French and English.

918 **Revue Roumaine d'Histoire de l'Art: Série Beaux-Arts.** (Romanian Review of the History of Art: Fine Arts Series.)
Bucharest: Editura Academiei Române, in conjunction with Institutul de Istoria Artei 'G. Oprescu', 1970- . annual.

This journal continues *Revue Roumaine d'Histoire de l'Art: Série Arts Plastique*, which was published during the period 1963-69.

919 **Revue Roumaine d'Histoire de l'Art: Série Théâtre, Musique, Cinéma.** (Romanian Review of the History of Art: Theatre, Music and Cinema Series.)
Bucharest: Editura Academiei Române, in conjunction with Institutul de Istoria Artei 'G. Oprescu', 1970- . annual.

Articles, which are usually in French but also sometimes in English and German, cover various aspects of Romanian theatre, music and cinema, with issues occasionally being devoted to a single subject.

920 **Romania: Pages of History.**
Bucharest: Romanian News Agency 'Agerpres', Foreign Language Press Group 'Romania', 1976-89. quarterly.

This propaganda journal appeared in English, French, German, Russian and Spanish editions. Throughout the stress was on the role of the Romanian Communist Party in Romanian history, Romanian nationalism and the manifold wisdom of Comrade Nicolae Ceaușescu.

921 **Romanian Civilization.**
Bucharest: The Romanian Cultural Foundation with the Center of
European History and Civilization, 1992- . biannual.
This new journal carries a wide range of articles on Romanian history, literature and
culture in general. Articles appear mostly in English but also in German and French.

922 **Romanian Economic Review/Revue Roumaine des Sciences
Économiques.**
Bucharest: Editura Academiei Române, 1989- . biannual.
Between 1964 and 1989 this journal was known as *Revue Roumaine des Sciences
Sociales: Série de Sciences Économiques* (Romanian Review of Social Sciences:
Economic Sciences Series). This in turn superseded in part the earlier *Revue des
Sciences Sociales* (Review of Social Sciences) (1964-57). Articles on all aspects of the
Romanian economy appear in English, French and, occasionally, Russian.

923 **Romanian Journal of Geophysics.**
Bucharest: Institutul Geologic al Romaniei, 1933- . annual.
This journal has previously existed under a number of names. Prior to 1992 it was
known as *Institutul de geologie și geofizica: studii tehnice și economice geofizica* (The
Institute of Geology and Geophysics: Technical and Economic Geophysics Studies)
(1984-92). Before this it had been known as *Institutul de geologie și geofizica: studii
tehnice și economice: seria D, prospectiuni geofizice* (The Institute of Geology and
Geophysics: Technical and Economic Studies: Series D, Prospecting Geophysics)
(1974-84); and until 1974, *Institutul geologic: studii tehnice și economice: seria D,
prospectiuni geofizice* (The Institute of Geology: Technical and Economic Studies:
Series D, Prospecting Geophysics).

924 **Romanian Journal of Gerontology and Geriatrics.**
Bucharest: National Institute of Gerontology and Geriatrics, 1980- .
quarterly.
Articles appear in English and French.

925 **Romanian Journal of Meteorology.**
Bucharest: National Institute of Meteorology and Hydrology, 1994- .
biannual.
Articles appear in English and French.

926 **Romanian Journal of Mineral Deposits.**
Bucharest: Institutul Geologic al Romaniei, 1992- . annual.
Until 1992 this journal was known as *Institutul de geologie și geofizica. Dari de
seama ale sedintelor. 2. zacaminte, geochimie* (The Institute of Geology and Geo-
physics: Record of the Proceedings. 2. Ores, Geochemistry). Previously it had been
Institutul de geologie și geofizica. Dari de seama ale sedintelor. 2. zacaminte (The
Institute of Geology and Geophysics: Record of the Proceedings. 2. Ores) and
Institutul geologic. Dari de seama ale sedintelor. 2. zacaminte (The Institute of
Geology: Record of the Proceedings. 2. Ores).

927　**Romanian Journal of Mineralogy.**
Bucharest: Institutul Geologic al Romaniei 1907- . five times a year.

This supersedes in part the journal which, until 1992, was known as *Institutul de geologie și geofizica. Dari de seama ale sedintelor. 1. mineralogie, petrologie* (The Institute of Geology and Geophysics: Record of the Proceedings. 1. Mineralogy and Petrology). Previously it had appeared under a number of titles including *Institutul de geologie și geofizica. Dari de seama ale sedintelor. 1. mineralogie, petrologie, geochimie* (The Institute of Geology and Geophysics: Record of the Proceedings. 1. Mineralogy, Petrology, Geochemistry) and *Institutul geologic. Dari de seama ale sedintelor. 1. mineralogie, petrologie, geochimie* (The Institute of Geology: Record of the Proceedings. 1. Mineralogy, Petrology, Geochemistry). Articles are published in English, French and Romanian with summaries in English and French.

928　**Romanian Journal of Palaeontology.**
Bucharest: Institutul Geologic al Romaniei, 1949- . annual.

Until 1991 this journal was known as *Institutul de geologie și geofizica. Dari de seama ale sedintelor. 3. paleontologie* (The Institute of Geology and Geophysics: Record of the Proceedings. 3. Palaeontology). Previously it had been, amongst other names, *Institutul de geologie. Dari de seama ale sedintelor. 3. paleontologie* (The Institute of Geology: Record of the Proceedings. 3. Palaeontology).

929　**Romanian Journal of Petrology.**
Bucharest: Institutul Geologic al Romaniei, 1907- . annual.

Supersedes in part a journal which until 1992 was known as *Institutul de geologie și geofizica. Dari de seama ale sedintelor. 1. mineralogie, petrologie* (The Institute of Geology and Geophysics: Record of the Proceedings. 1. Mineralogy and Petrology). Previously it had been known by a number of titles including *Institutul de geologie și geofizica. Dari de seama ale sedintelor. 1. mineralogie, petrologie, geochimie* (The Institute of Geology and Geophysics: Record of the Proceedings. 1. Mineralogy, Petrology, Geochemistry) and *Institutul geologic. Dari de seama ale sedintelor. 1. mineralogie, petrologie, geochimie* (The Institute of Geology: Record of the Proceedings. 1. Mineralogy, Petrology, Geochemistry). Articles are published in English, French and Romanian with summaries in English and French.

930　**Romanian Journal of Sociology.**
Bucharest: Editura Academiei Române,1989- . biannual.

This journal continues *Revue Roumaine des Sciences Sociales: Série de Sociologie* (Romanian Journal of Social Sciences: Sociology Series). Articles are mostly in English but also in French and look at many aspects of Romanian society during the post-communist transition.

931　**Romanian Journal of Stratigraphy.**
Bucharest: Institutul Geologic al Romaniei, 1949- . annual.

Until 1992 this journal was known as *Institutul de geologie și geofizica. Dari de seama ale sedintelor. 4. stratigrafie* (The Institute of Geology and Geophysics: Record of the Proceedings. 4. Stratigraphy). Previously, amongst other names, it had been *Institutul geologic. Dari de seama ale sedintelor. 4. stratigrafie* (The Institute of Geology: Record of the Proceedings. 4. Stratigraphy).

932   **Romanian Journal of Tectonics and Regional Geology.**
Bucharest: Institutul Geologic al Romaniei, 1975- . annual.
Until 1992 this journal was known as *Institutul de geologie și geofizica. Dari de seama ale sedintelor. 5. tectonica și geologie regionala* (The Institute of Geology and Geophysics: Record of the Proceedings. 5. Tectonics and Regional Geology).

933   **Romanian Review.**
Bucharest: Foreign Language Press 'Romania', 1946- . monthly but currently irregular.
This general, cultural journal often contains a useful selection of items in translation. Recent issues have been concerned with Dracula, Romanian identity and the author Petru Dumitriu. French, German and Russian editions are also published.

934   **Romanian Sources.**
Pittsburgh, Pennsylvania: University of Pittsburg Libraries, American Romanian Institute for Research, 1975-80. biannual.
Six volumes of this journal appeared, the last being a joint issue of volumes 5-6. The articles, all in English, covered the history, literature and folklore of Romania and often contained a useful selection of translations of Romanian material into English.

935   **Rumanian Studies: an International Annual of the Humanities and Social Sciences.**
Leiden, Netherlands: E. J. Brill, 1970-86. irregular.
Edited by Keith Hitchins, this irregular academic yearbook contained many interesting articles on Romanian history and literature. Articles were in English and French and, occasionally, German. Five volumes were to appear.

936   **Short-term Economic Indicators: Transition Economies/ Indicateurs Économiques à Court Terme, Économies en Transition.**
Paris: Centre for Co-operation with the Economies in Transition, Organisation for Economic Co-operation and Development, 1993- quarterly.
Recent economic trends are reviewed country by country. This journal continues *Short-term Economic Indicators: Central and Eastern Europe.*

937   **Summary of World Broadcasts. Part 2: Central Europe, the Balkans: Third Series.**
Reading, England: BBC Monitoring, 1993- . daily
Provides an invaluable transcription of politically important Romanian radio and, occasionally, television broadcasts. The current series replaces the earlier *Summary of World Broadcasts: Part 2: Eastern Europe: Second Series.* A weekly economic report drawing on the same sources is also produced, and monthly indexes are published separately.

938 **Thraco-Dacia.**
Bucharest: Editura Academiei Române, 1976- . biannual.
Contains articles on archaeology, history, linguistics, ethnography and anthropology
in Romanian, French and also, occasionally, English.

939 **Transition: the Newsletter about Reforming Economies.**
Washington, DC: Macroeconomics and Growth Division, Policy
Research Department, The World Bank, 1990- . every two months.
Continuing *Socialist Economies in Transition*, this newsletter includes a number of
brief articles on current economic trends within the former communist countries.
Occasionally one of these is concerned with Romania.

940 **Transitions.**
Prague: Open Media Research Institute, 1994- . monthly.
In its latest incarnation this is a varied magazine covering all aspects of the transition
process in post-communist societies. Each issue is devoted to a single theme with
occasional articles featuring Romania. Until 1997, this journal, under the title
Transition, was the leading source for political analysis of Eastern Europe with
articles regularly appearing on Romania by Michael Shafir, Dan Ionescu and others.
Transition had, in turn, evolved out of the *RFE/RL Research Report* (1992-94) which
had superseded *Report on Eastern Europe* (1990-91). Prior to 1989, political analysis
had been contained in the *Radio Free Europe Research, Situation* and *Background
Reports*.

941 **Transylvanian Review.**
Cluj-Napoca, Romania: Romanian Cultural Foundation; Centre for
Transylvanian Studies, 1992- . quarterly.
This cultural review contains a broad range of articles on the history and literature of
Romania as well as profiles of leading Romanian scholars. Articles appear in English,
French, Italian, German and Romanian.

942 **Yearbook of Romanian Studies.**
Salinas, California: Romanian Studies Association of America, 1976- .
annual.
This annual publication is devoted largely to articles on Romanian language and
literature.

Directories and Encyclopaedias

943 **Directory of Eastern European film-makers and films.**
Compiled and edited by Grzegorz Balski. Trowbridge, England: Flicks Books, 1992. 546p. bibliog.

In recent years leading Romanian film-makers, such as Dan Piţa and Lucian Pintile, have begun to achieve international recognition – Piţa won an award at Cannes for his film *Hotel de Lux*. In this directory the author includes both these directors and eighteen other Romanian film-makers. In each case basic biographical details are followed by a brief appreciation of the film-makers' work, whether as a script-writer, director or producer. Each entry is completed by a list of works in both the language of production and English translation. This list is divided into shorts and features, and includes TV series as well as films.

944 **Eastern Europe and the Commonwealth of Independent States 1997.**
London: Europa Publications, 1997. 3rd ed. 926p. maps. bibliog. (Regional Surveys of the World).

Offers a comprehensive survey of Eastern Europe as it was in 1997. A series of introductory essays covering the whole region are followed by detailed surveys of each country. The section concerned with Romania (p. 572-609) is written by Tom Gallagher and Alan Smith. A brief outline of the geography of the country and a chronology largely focusing on events since 1989 is followed by a more lengthy exposition on Romania's history by Gallagher, in which the emphasis is again on the events after the Revolution and then one by Smith on the country's economy. The section is concluded by an extensive directory which provides addresses and other supporting details for a large number of organizations, including government bodies, political parties, the media, major companies, as well as cultural and educational institutions.

945 **Chronology of 20th-century Eastern European history.**
Edited by Gregory C. Ference with a foreword by Charles Jelavich,
Barbara Jelavich. Detroit, Michigan; Washington, DC; London: Gale
Research, 1994. 530p. maps. bibliog.

Each country is treated separately in this volume with the section dealing with
Romania on p. 301-36. After a page of introduction, which provides a sketch of the
country's history prior to 1900, the chronology runs from the beginning of this century
until the end of 1993. Attached to each date there is a brief description of the event
being marked. Following the chronology, a further section gives potted biographies of
some of the main political leaders of the period, including Marshal Antonescu,
Nicolae Ceauşescu, Gheorghe Gheorghiu-Dej and Ana Pauker.

946 **Dictionary of East European history since 1945.**
Joseph Held. London: Mansell, 1994. 509p. maps. bibliog.

Pages 374-436 of this volume cover Romania. General information about the country
and a chronology of events between 1945 and 1993 is followed by a dictionary of
prominent personalities, political parties, places and events. Amongst the entries, there
are subjects as diverse as Ceauşescu's aide Emil Bobu, the National Salvation Front,
the Danube-Black Sea Canal, de-Stalinization, the Timişoara revolt of 1989, national
minorities and oil production. Each entry is followed by a bibliography of works in
English, although the lack of specialist works means that in most cases a number of
more general books are merely cited several times.

947 **Who was who in twentieth century Romania.**
Şerban N. Ionescu. Boulder, Colorado: East European Monographs,
distributed by Columbia University Press, 1994. 318p. bibliog. (East
European Monographs, no. 395).

With almost 3,000 entries, this is a useful and comprehensive listing of Romanians
who have achieved prominence in the 20th century both at home and abroad, although
there are some notable omissions, such as the author Petru Dumitriu. The coverage
ranges from politicians to footballers, with each entry comprising biographical details
and a note on the person's achievements. In the case of cultural figures, this usually
involves a critical assessment of their work, the leading examples of which are noted.
The entries are informative, although they sometimes tend to reflect the author's
political preferences, for instance, the Democratic National Salvation Front, the
predecessor of the current Party of Social Democracy in Romania, is unambiguously
dubbed a 'neo-communist' party. A series of appendices carry lists of the rulers of
Romania, prime ministers, presidents of the Romanian Academy, political parties and
the century's most important dates.

948 **Romania directory: public institutions and organizations.**
Edited by Horia C. Matei, Nicolae Şteflea. Bucharest: Meronia
Publishing House/ Ecodata Publishing House, 1995. 127p. map.

After a short but informative introduction on Romania's current economic and social
position, this book offers the telephone numbers and addresses of most of Romania's
public institutions and organizations. It is arranged under nine broad categories:
central institutions and organizations (e.g. parliament, judiciary, etc.), local institutions (e.g. town halls, courts, etc.), foreign relations (e.g. embassies, consulates, etc.),

Directories and Encyclopaedias

trade and investment (e.g. banks, business centres, etc.), tourism (e.g. tourist agencies, hotels, etc.), transport and communications (e.g. Tarom offices, railway agencies, etc.), mass media (e.g. radio, television, publishing houses, etc.), science, culture and education (e.g. academies, museums, etc.) and entertainment (e.g. theatres, sports, etc.).

949 **The everyman companion to East European literature.**
Edited by Robert B. Pynsent, Sonia I Kanikova. London: J. M. Dent, 1993. 605p.

The first section of this work is an alphabetically arranged dictionary of East European writers. The twenty-three entries covering Romania, which were written by Dennis Deletant, include leading authors of the last three centuries from Vasile Alecsandri to Nichita Stănescu. Each entry contains biographical details of the author and an appreciation of their work, before closing with a list of any books available in English translation. The second part of the work focuses on Eastern Europe's rich tradition of anonymous, collective and oral texts and includes an extended piece on the history of bible translations in the region. This is followed by a brief history of the various national literatures, Romania being covered on pages 541-43. Three comprehensive indexes complete this useful work.

950 **Yearbook on international communist affairs 1991: parties and evolutionary movements.**
Edited by Richard F. Staar, managing editor Margit N. Grigory.
Stanford, California: Hoover Institution Press. 1991. 25th ed. 689p.

This, the 25th anniversary edition of this annual publication, was to prove to be the last as with the final collapse of communism in the USSR, the number of communist states were reduced to a number that made the volume superfluous. Prior to its demise, the *Yearbook on International Communism* provided an excellent annual outline of political developments in Romania. Although by 1991 Romania was no longer a communist state, this volume was to prove no exception to this rule with Robert R. King providing a comprehensive overview of political developments during the past year. Amongst other topics he traces the political evolution of both the National Salvation Front and the chief opposition parties, the progress of economic reforms, church-state relations, the rise of Romanian nationalism and its effect on ethnic relations.

951 **Who's who in the socialist countries of Europe.**
Juliusz Stroynowski. Munich; New York; London, Paris: K. G. Saur, 1989. 3 vols. 1,367p.

Published in the year of the demise of communism in Eastern Europe, this directory was instantly rendered somewhat out-of-date. However, with more than 12,600 entries covering the élite of communist Europe, it still remains an important reference work not only for the historian but also for those trying to trace the early careers of many of today's politicians. Treating the region as a whole, the directory is organized alphabetically but there is a useful listing of names by country at the beginning of the first volume. The work principally features politicians, but a number of cultural figures and scientists are also represented. Each entry contains biographical details, usually in terms of offices held, decorations received and, where relevant, works published.

952 **Political parties of Eastern Europe, Russia and the successor states.**
Edited by Bogdan Szajkowski. Harlow, England: Longman Information and Reference, 1994. 735p.

Since the Revolution large numbers of political parties have emerged in Romania. The majority have proved transitory, but many of the others, to complicate matters further, have frequently engaged in what has often seemed like an endless game of musical chairs, as they have formed and reformed in numerous shifting coalitions. In the section of this volume covering Romania (p. 343-406), Rasmas Bing and Bogdan Szajkowski valiantly try to catalogue this process. After a brief discussion of political developments, including recent election results, there follows a reasonably comprehensive listing of political parties. In each case both the Romanian name of the organization and an English translation is given, followed by details of the leadership, membership figure if revealed, date of foundation and location of the party headquarters, as well as a brief outline of the party's history and its programme. A previous edition of this book, also edited by Bogdan Szajkowski, appeared under the title *New political parties of Eastern Europe and the Soviet Union* (Harlow, England: Longman Current Affairs, 1991).

953 **Encyclopaedia of conflicts, disputes and flashpoints in Eastern Europe, Russia and the successor states.**
Bogdan Szajkowski with contributions by James Gow, Michael Anderson, Nicholas Bradshaw, George Christidis, et al. Harlow, England: Longman Current Affairs, 1993. 489p. bibliog.

The author states that this volume was directly inspired by the disorder produced by the fall of communism, although it was really the Yugoslav Wars that made many raise the spectre of further conflicts in South-Eastern Europe. Szajkowski argues that there are 70 potential ethno-territorial conflicts in Eastern Europe and a further 204 in the former Soviet Union. It is, therefore, a good omen that Romania does not feature large in this volume. Indeed, the listing throughout is rather idiosyncratic with there being, for instance, an entry for Bucovina and, of course, Transylvania but not one for Dobrogea, the southern part of which currently lies inside Bulgaria, but which formerly was part of Romania. Likewise the Romanian minority in the Ukraine warrants a separate entry, but those in the Federal Republic of Yugoslavia or Hungary do not. The entry on Romania includes details of the Romanian armed forces and further entries include one on relations between the Romanian and Russian Orthodox churches.

954 **Historical dictionary of Romania.**
Kurt W. Treptow, Marcel Popa. Lanham, Maryland; London: Scarecrow Press, 1996. 309p. maps. bibliog. (European Historical Dictionaries, no. 15).

This work begins with a chronology and a list of the rulers of Romania. This is followed by an introductory section which covers the geography, people, history, economy and political organizations of Romania before the start of the actual dictionary which makes up the bulk of this work. This covers people, places, events and even offices of state. The entries are informative and balanced but the breadth of the remit means that the selection is somewhat limited. The book concludes with a detailed and useful bibliography of works on history and literature, which is

295

accompanied by an apposite warning about the partiality of many of the books written under communism.

955 Handbook of reconstruction in Eastern Europe and the Soviet Union.
Edited by Stephen White, contributors John B. Allcock, John D. Bell, Marko Milivojević, Martin Myant, Daniel Nelson, et al. Harlow, England: Longman Current Affairs, 1991. 407p.

The section on Romania in this volume (p. 183-204) was written by Daniel Nelson. Covering the period from the Revolution until the incursion by the miners into Bucharest in June 1990, the author offers a brief overview of political and economic events. Sections deal with the policies of the National Salvation Front, foreign trade, the media, foreign relations and prominent personalities, although in the latter only three people are listed: Ion Iliescu, Petro (sic) Roman and General Stănculescu, who was prominent during the Revolution and later became Minister of Defence.

956 Dicţionarul scriitorilor Români A-C. (The dictionary of Romanian writers A-C.)
Coordinators Mircea Zaciu, Marian Papahagi, Aurel Sasu. Bucharest: Editura Fundaţiei Culturale Române, 1995. 812p. bibliog.

The first part of a monumental undertaking which will feature virtually every Romanian who has ever had a piece of work published. Aside from listing published works, each entry also includes a list of critical works written about the author in question.

Bibliographies

957 **Guide to the official publications of foreign countries.**
[Bethesda, Maryland]: American Library Association, Government
Documents Round Table, 1990. 359p.
Unfortunately the section concerning Romania (p. 265-68) in this useful publication is
now somewhat out-of-date, as it describes the situation in the country on 1 December
1989, that is before the collapse of communism. Compiled by Paul Michelson, each of
the Romanian entries notes the title of the official publication and the publisher as
well as details of publishing policy, which, especially towards the end of the
Ceauşescu régime, could be irregular.

958 **Bibliography of the Jews in Romania.**
Jean Ancel, Victor Eskenasy. Tel Aviv, Israel: The Goldstein-Goren
Centre of the History of the Jews in Romania, Diaspora Research
Institute, Tel Aviv University, 1991. 171p.
This detailed and practical bibliography is divided alphabetically into two sections
arranged according to the surname of author. The first contains 1,614 entries covering
works written in Romanian, French, English, German, Italian, Spanish, Polish,
Hungarian and Yiddish in Latin transcription. The second contains 576 items written
in Hebrew. Each list is accompanied by an index of names, places and subjects.

959 **Bibliographic guide to Slavic, Baltic and Eurasian States, 1994.**
New York: G. K. Hall; London, Mexico City, New Delhi, Singapore;
Sydney; Toronto: Prentice Hall International, 1994. 3 vols. 679p. 791p.
594p.
Formerly known as the *Bibliographic guide to Soviet and East European studies*, the
forty-one volumes of this series produced since 1978 serve in part as a supplement to
the *Dictionary Catalog of the Slavic Division of the New York Public Library*, the
second edition of which was published in 1972. Included are all items received by the
research libraries of the New York Public Library and the Library of Congress. The

criteria for selection are that the item has to be published in Romania or one of the other countries of the region, be a work written in Romanian or any Slavic, Baltic and non-western European languages from any country, and, regardless of the language and country of origins, has to be specifically concerned with a topic relating to Romania or one of the other countries of the region. Entry seems to depend on date of cataloguing in the two libraries, and so even this latest volume contains some works first published in the 1980s.

960   **COMECON: the rise and fall of an international socialist organization.**
Compiled by Jenny Brine.   Oxford: Clio Press, 1992. 225p. maps.
(International Organizations Series, no. 3).

Romania was a founder member of the Soviet bloc trading organization, Comecon (Council for Mutual Economic Assistance), when it was established in 1949. The 700 annotated entries in this volume cover all aspects of Comecon's activities. The section specifically concerned with Romania is located on p. 176-77, but many of the other works cited also contain passages or sections relating to the country. The author cites both books and articles related to the subject, and a chronological table listing the key dates in Comecon's history up until its demise at the time of the collapse of communism in Europe can be found at the front of the volume.

961   **Eastern Europe: a bibliographic guide to English language publications, 1986-1993.**
Robert H. Burger, Helen F. Sullivan with the assistance of Lisa
Radloff.   Englewood, Colorado: Libraries Unlimited, 1995. 254p.

This volume continues the series started by Stephan Horak and previously published under the title *Russia, the USSR and Eastern Europe: a bibliographic guide to English language publications* (q.v.). As before, each entry is accompanied by full bibliographical details and an annotation, which is usually a quotation drawn from the author's own description of the work. The titles listed are obtained from two sources: the *American bibliography of Slavic and East European Studies* (q.v). and *Books in print*. The fifty-six entries on Romania can be found on p. 190-202.

962   **Edgar Allan Poe in Romania, 1963-1983: an annotated bibliography.**
Thomas C. Carlson.   *Bulletin of Bibliography*, vol. 44, no. 2 (June 1987), p. 75-81.

This bibliography is divided into two major parts, the first offering a checklist of articles, theses, monographs, books and translations of Poe's works produced in Romanian, and the second covering articles, books and other publications which discuss Poe, the author, within a larger literary context. Its aim is to clarify the nature of Poe's reception in Romania. A previous study of the same subject can be found in Thomas C. Carlson, 'The reception of Edgar Allan Poe in Romania', *Mississippi Quarterly*, vol. 38, no. 4 (Fall 1985), p. 441-46.

963 **Romania.**
William E. Crowther.   In: *Handbook of political science research on the USSR and Eastern Europe: trends from the 1950s to the 1990s.* Edited by Raymond C. Taras.   Westport, Connecticut; London: Greenwood, 1992, p. 149-70.

A scholarly and critical review of the principal works published in English on the Romanian political system as it evolved between 1956 and 1989. The books cited are mostly drawn from the political sciences, but other relevant disciplines are also represented.

964 **European Bibliography of Soviet, East European and Slavonic Studies.**
Paris: Institut d'études slaves, 1975- . annual.

This series, which is an international undertaking involving institutions in Paris, London, Brussels, Amsterdam and Vienna, surveys books, articles and book reviews concerned with the countries of Eastern Europe published in Britain, Austria, Belgium, Finland, France, Germany, and the Netherlands. The emphasis throughout falls on the humanities and social sciences, and the entries are arranged first by country and then by subject, with a name index at the back. The latest volume in the series, number 18, covers publications from 1992.

965 **Eastern Europe bibliography.**
Compiled by Rebecca Gates-Coon.   Metuchen, New Jersey; London: Scarecrow Press, 1993. 174p. (Scarecrow Area Bibliographies, no. 2).

This book is largely intended for the historian or political scientist and is divided into two sections. The first, under the heading 'General works on East European History', provides bibliographical details but no annotations on the core history books for each country including Romania. The second section contains a subject bibliography with entries for figures such as Nicolae Ceauşescu and Nicolae Iorga. However, most books on Romania can be found under general headings such as 'foreign relations' or 'literature', although the only work cited under the latter reflects the somewhat eclectic choice of texts as it is the virtually unknown *Classical and contemporary Romanian writers: notes on their life and work* (Bucharest: Central Office of the Romanian Publishing Houses and Bookselling, 1969. 200p.).

966 **The human rights literature of eastern Europe.**
Richard Greenfield.   *Human Rights Quarterly*, vol. 3, no. 2 (Spring 1981), p. 136-48.

In this bibliographical review of professional international human rights literature on Eastern Europe, the author notes the paucity of such literature on Romania both inside the country and in the outside world.

967 **Soviet foreign relations and world communism. A selected, annotated bibliography of 7,000 books in 30 languages.**
Compiled and edited by Thomas T. Hammond. Princeton, New Jersey: Princeton University Press, 1965. 1,240p.

The section on Romania, which is edited by Stephen Fischer-Galaţi, can be found on p. 569-78. Chosen on a selective rather than a comprehensive basis, the cited works are divided into three categories: 'General works', 'Communist Party periodicals and newspapers' and 'The Bessarabian Question'. All entries are annotated and they include works in English as well as a number of other languages including Romanian and Russian.

968 **Eastern European national minorities, 1919-1980: a handbook.**
Stephan M. Horak, Richard Blanke, David Crowe, Keneth C. Farmer, Stephen Fischer-Galaţi (et al.). Littleton, Colorado: Libraries Unlimited, 1985. 353p.

After an introduction on Eastern Europe and national minorities, which contains a list of general works on the subject, the chapter 'National minorities in Romania, 1919-1980' by Stephen Fischer-Galaţi (p. 190-215) opens with a historical overview of the treatment of minorities in the country. This is followed by an annotated bibliographical guide of selected monographs on the German, Hungarian, Jewish and other minority populations in all languages, including those of the minorities themselves, but not Romanian.

969 **Russia, the USSR and Eastern Europe: a bibliographic guide to English language publications 1981-85.**
Stephan M. Horak. Littleton, Colorado: Libraries Unlimited, 1987. 273p.

This volume continues a series which began in 1978 with one volume covering publications from the years 1964-74 and a second following in 1982 dedicated to the years 1975-80. In each case full bibliographical details are given for each entry together with an annotation. The author aims to be fully inclusive, but in fact only sixteen books concerned with Romania are listed in this volume. This series has now been continued with the volume by Burger and Sullivan, *Eastern Europe: a bibliographic guide to English-language publications, 1986-1993* (q.v.).

970 **Balkan military history: a bibliography.**
John E. Jessup. New York; London: Garland, 1986. 478p. (Military History Bibliographies, no. 8; Garland Reference Library of Social Science, no. 234).

This volume is divided into nine chronologically ordered sections stretching from the late 14th and the 15th century until the period 1936-84. Each section begins with a historical and historiographical discussion in which the relative merits of key works on the subject are discussed. This is then followed by a listing of books and articles written in English and other languages, including Romanian. The author includes Romania in his remit and, stretching far beyond the bounds of purely military history, he also includes a great many works on general South-East European history.

971 **The American bibliography of Slavic and East European studies for 1993.**
Compiled, edited by Patt Leonard, Rebecca Routh. Armonk, New York: M. E. Sharpe, prepared at the University of Illinois at Urbana-Champaign for the American Association for the Advancement of Slavic Studies, 1996. 602p.

The most recent volume in a series which was first published in 1957. Appearing under the imprint of the *American bibliography series*, these annual volumes survey a plethora of books, articles and book reviews relating to all aspects of East European studies published in America. The works are all listed according to subject and then the country they represent, including Romania. Volumes published before 1967 were entitled *American bibliography of Russian and East European Studies*.

972 **Romania.**
Paul E. Michelson. In: *Nationalism in the Balkans: an annotated bibliography.* Edited by Gale Stokes. New York: Garland, 1984, p. 31-67. (Canadian Review of Studies in Nationalism, no. 3; Garland Reference Library of Social Sciences, no. 160).

In a short bibliographical essay the author first discusses nationalism and, in particular, the themes of unity and continuity in Romanian scholarship during the Ceauşescu era. In the second part of the work he provides an annotated review of selected works published since 1944, both in Romania and abroad, in a number of languages including English.

973 **Russia and Eastern Europe, 1789-1985: a bibliographic guide.**
Compiled by Raymond Pearson. Manchester, England; New York: Manchester University Press, 1989. 210p. (History and Related Disciplines Select Bibliographies).

Intended primarily for teachers and students, this volume lists 5,000 works, the majority of which display an emphasis on history, and some of which have a brief annotation. After a section listing general works, the book is divided into two sections, one covering the 19th and the other the 20th century. The books for Romania can be found on p. 32-33 and p. 102-104, although it is something of a puzzle as to why the works on the 19th century should be entered under the name 'Rumania' whilst those on the 20th century can be found under the more familiar 'Romania'.

974 **Ceauşescu's Romania: an annotated bibliography.**
Compiled by Opritsa D. Popa, Marguerite E. Horn. Westport, Connecticut; London: Greenwood, 1994. 153p. (Bibliographies and Indexes in World History, no. 36).

With over 1,000 entries this is a comprehensive and useful bibliography designed for students, teachers and researchers. The book is arranged by topic in twenty-one sections which after an 'Overview and bibliographies' are arranged alphabetically from 'Agriculture: economics, history and policy' until 'Urban and rural planning and development'. The articles and books listed, which are primarily in English, but also include works in French and German, are mostly drawn from the social sciences, although related disciplines are also covered.

Bibliographies

975   **The Romanian economic politics: a development strategy. Theses –
       bibliography – maps.**
       Viorel S. Roman.   Bremen, Germany: Falk, 1988. 200p. maps.
The first part of this book, which is reproduced in four languages, English, French,
German and Romanian, gives an overview of a periodization of Romanian
development policy, from the Phanariot era (1711-1829) to Nicolae Ceauşescu,
advanced by the author in previous works written in German. The following
bibliography, which contains citations to 2,500 books and articles mostly in Romanian
on economics and economic history, is then divided into these same chronological
categories. The chief drawback of this approach is that some works, such as Seton-
Watson, *A history of the Roumanians* (q.v.), enjoys a multiple representation in nearly
every category. After the bibliography, there is a selection of maps illustrating
Romanian economic and political development, the legends of which are mostly in
English or German depending on the source from which they are extracted.

976   **East European languages and literatures VI: a subject and a name
       index to articles in English-language journals, festschriften,
       conference proceedings and collected papers, 1991-1993.**
       Compiled by Garth M. Terry.   Nottingham, England: Astra Press,
       1994. 150p. (Astra Soviet and East European Bibliographies, no. 15).
An indispensable companion for researchers and students interested in the languages
and literature of East Europe. The current volume is the fourth supplement to the two
basic indexes in the series: *East European languages and literatures: a subject and
name index to English-language journals, 1900-1977* (Oxford; Santa Barbara,
California: Clio Press, 1978); and *East European languages and literatures: a subject
and name index to festschriften, conference proceedings, and collected papers in the
English language, 1900-1981, and including articles in journals, 1978-1981* (Notting-
ham, England: Astra, 1992). The three previous supplements covered the years
1982-84 (published 1985), 1985-87 (published 1988) and 1988-90 (published 1991).
Although the bibliographical entries do not carry annotations, these volumes, taken
together, form an invaluable aid to locating works written in English on Romanian
language and literature.

977   **Official publications of the Soviet Union and Eastern Europe:
       a select annotated bibliography.**
       Edited by Gregory Walker.   London: Mansell, 1982. 620p.
This volume offers an extensive and annotated guide to those documents of State
regulating life in the countries of Eastern Europe as well as publicizing and justifying
decisions and policies adopted by their leader. Brian Hunter is the compiler of the
Romanian section (p. 221-62), which consists of a brief historical introduction and
270 entries on constitutional documents, law codes, statistics, economic planning and
international relations.

Indexes

There follow three separate indexes: authors (personal and corporate); titles; and subjects. Title entries are italicized and refer either to the main titles, or to many of the other works cited in the annotations. The numbers refer to bibliographical entry rather than page numbers. Individual index entries are arranged in alphabetical sequence.

Index of Authors

L

Ladd, D. R. 146
Laird, B. A. 677
Laird, R. D. 677
Lajtha, G. 713
Lakey, C. K. 511
Lambert, A. 67
Lampe, J. R. 639
Lăncrănjan, I. 546
Landsberg, H. E. 698
Larrabee, F. S. 624
Larsen, S. Ugelvik 253
Lascu, D.-N. 571
Laufer, P. 35
Lauter, G. P. 646
Laux, J. K. 473
Law, J. M. 762
Lawson, C. W. 625
Lederer, G. 419
Lederer, I. J. 129
Lee, A. Gould 337
Leo, P. 377
Leonard, P. 971
Lepper, F. 170
Leschber, C. 418
Lesley, F. 627
Leuner, J. D. 511
Levițchi, L. 463, 742, 748
Levy, R. 311-12
Light, D. 46, 84
Linden, R. H. 531, 564,
   626, 648
Lippmann, H. 698
Livezeanu, I. 266, 795
Łobodzińska, B. 500
Longley, M. 816
Longworth, I. 106
Łos, M. 644
Lortat-Jacob, B. 855
Love, J. L. 640
Lowe, S. 68
Ludanyi, A. 374, 378, 381
Lukács, L. 383
Lumans, V. O. 297
Lungu, D. B. 267-68
Lupușoru, I. 793
Luttwak, E. N. 315

M

Mâță, C. 892
McArthur, M. 389, 486

Macaulay, R. 36
McCauley, M. 321, 539
Macedonski, A. 464
MacGregor-Hastie, R. 749
McIntosh, M. E. 379
McIntyre, R. J. 502
Mackendrick, P. 113
Mackenzie, A. 114, 139,
   144
Maclean, R. 36
McNally, R. T. 182, 188,
   192-94
Magocsi, P. R. 81
Magris, C. 37
Makkai, L. 123
Malcomson, S. L. 38
Mallinson, G. 440
Manea, N. 796-97, 800
Mango, C. 236
Manoilescu, M. 640
Manolescu, F. 747
Manolescu, N. 753
Manoliu-Manea, M. 441
Manuilă, S. 407
Marcea, P. 798
Marcus, G. E. 412
Marer, P. 646
Marga, A. 558
Margul-Sperber, A. 748
Marie, Queen 341
Marinescu-Bîlcu, S. 116
Marinkov, D. 760
Marinov, M. 98
Mark, E. 313
Marrant, J. 365
Matei, H. C. 948
Matley, I. M. 47, 56
Matras, Y. 418
Matthews, G. J. 81
Mayo, S. K. 61
Mehedinți, S. 47
Meirion-Jones, G. I. 874
Mertens, S. B. 117
Metes, R. J. 218
Meurs, van W. 314
Meyer, A. G. 502, 518
Michelson, P. E. 140, 237,
   287, 958, 972
Miclea, I. 111
Mihailescu, I. 559, 707,
   709
Mihăilescu, V. 49
Mihut, L. 560

Milivojević, M. 955
Miller, S. 841
Miller, W. 154
Miloș, J. 799
Miroiu, M. 465
Miskolczy, A. 123
Mitrea, B. 162
Miu, D. 238
Montalbetti, M. 445
Montias, J. M. 490, 647,
   651
Morariu, A. 103
Moraru, C. 732
Morris, L. 515
Motapanyane, V. 432, 442
Motyl, A. J. 694
Movileanu, G. S. 842
Muica, C. 57, 97, 493, 681
Muldoon, P. 816
Müller, H. 801-02
Mungiu, A. 561-62
Munteanu, D. 98
Murdock, G. 469
Murgescu, B. 469
Murgescu, M. L. 469
Murphy, D. 39
Murray, D. J. 599
Mușat, M. 141, 147
Musetescu, A. 660
Myant, M. 955
Myhill, J. 442
Myklbust, J. P. 253
Mykura, W. 52

N

Nadaban, F. 757
Nagelbach, M. 388
Nagy, K. 733
Nagy, O. 734
Nandriș, G. 195
Nandris, J. 118
Napoli, D. J. 436
Naum, G. 803
Neagoe, P. 756, 804
Necula, M. 872
Neeman, R. 424
Negoiță, J. 885
Negoșanu, P. 817
Negrescu, D. 667
Nelson, D. 502, 530-32,
   563-64, 587, 608, 955

Nemeș, E. 103
Nemoianu, V. 269, 490, 735-36
Neuberger, E. 646
Neugroschel, J. 832
Neumann, V. 238
Newsom, D. D. 613
Nicholas, P. K. 511
Nicolae, I. 46
Nicolae-Valeanu, I. 661
Nicolson, A. 124
Niculescu, A. 443
Niculescu, M. 781
Nielsen, E. 737
Niessen, J. P. 142
Nofi, A. A. 235
Noguchi, I. 834
Nolle, D. B. 379
Notholt, A. J. G. 52
Nouzille, J. 143, 271
Noyes, J. O. 6
Nydon, J. A. 498

O

Obolensky, D. 196
O'Brien, P. 7
O'Connor, P. 40
Ognean, T. 702
Oișteanu, A. 159
Oldson, W. 131, 239, 270, 703, 880
O'Leary, S. 61
O'Loughlin, J. 377
Ophir, E. 408
Oprișan, H. Barbu 863
Orescu, S. 525
Ormsby, H. 44
O'Shea, J. M. 119
O'Sullivan, J. 657
Otetea, A. 144
Owen, T. M. 685
Ozanne, J. W. 8

P

Pabisch, P. 738
Pacepa, I. M. 340
Paffen, K. H. 698
Paget, J. 9
Paikert, G. C. 390

Painter, K. 106
Paki, A. 103
Pakula, H. 341
Palm, C. G. 877
Pálmai, E. 210
Palotás, E. 251
Panaea, I. Grigorescu 740
Panduru, F. 695
Panovf, I. 466
Pantazzi, E. Greening 10
Papacostea, Ș. 145, 197
Papahaghi, T. 460
Papahagi, M. 285, 956
Papp, D. S. 605
Parkinson, M. 11
Parrott, B. 573
Pârvan, V. 171
Pârvu, S. 739
Pascovschi, S. 94
Pascu, I. M. 564, 627
Pascu, S. 123, 146-47
Paskaleva, V. 251
Pasti, V. 566
Pastor, P. 271
Patterson, G. J. 425, 893
Patterson, W. C. 673
Paul, Prince of Hohenzollern 338
Payne, S. G. 257
Pearson, R. 973
Pearton, M. 126, 272, 641
Pelham, R. A. 44
Pepper, R. 650
Percival, M. 126, 628
Perkowski, J.-L. 444
Perrie, W. 41
Péter, L. 147
Peters, C. R. 469
Petersen, P. 644
Petrescu, D. 736
Petrescu, E. 844
Petrescu, P. 893
Petrina, E. 682
Petrucci, P. R. 445
Pfeiffer, P. C. 737
Philip, F. 329
Philippi, P. 475
Phillimore, L. 12
Phinnemore, D. 46
Phinney, M. 445
Pietro, J. R. Di 426
Pilon, J. G. 567
Pippidi, A. 562

Pippidi, A. Mungiu 586
Pittman, R. 571
Platek, R. 695
Pleshoyano, D. V. 240
Pleșu, A. 533, 565, 567
Ploaie, G. 85
Podea, T. 148
Poenaru, V. 822
Poirot, C. 662
Pompilu, T. 134
Pop, C. 103
Pop, E. 99
Pop, I. 803, 851
Pop, I.-A. 198
Pop, L. 455
Popa, C. 459
Popa, M. 954
Popa, O. D. 974
Pope, E. A. 476
Popescu, A. 477
Popescu, C. 690
Popescu, C. M. 787
Popescu, D. R. 805
Popescu, F. D. 450
Popescu, H. F. 786
Popova-Cucu, A. 97
Popovici, F. 506
Popovici, V. 567
Porter, I. 126, 298, 348
Poruciuc, A. 730
Poulton, H. 384
Pourchot, G. 571
Pravda, A. 532
Preda, M. 724, 772
Price, G. W. 606
Prins, G. 522
Prodan, D. 149
Pullar, V. 512
Puwak, H. 509
Pynsent, R. B. 949

Q

Quinlan, P. D. 273-74, 299, 342, 629

R

Rabenhorst, C. 61
Raceanu, M. 623
Radloff, L. 962

309

Index of Titles

317

F

322

325

Index of Subjects

Balkans *contd.*
relations with other
Balkan states 232
Russian interest in 230
Ballads 719, 748, 850
Ballmann, Magdalene
(author) 738
Balotă, N. 269
Baltoz, Cezar (poet) 746
Banat 23
history 242
minorities 421
Band (village) 734
Banking 649, 675
Baptist Church 470, 476
Barbu, Ion (poet) 721, 742
Báthory, Elizabeth
(Hungarian countess)
192, 203
BBC 482
Bean goose 98
Bellow, Saul 324
Benn, Tony 323
Bernea, Horia (artist)
839
Berthelot, General Henri
271
memoirs 349
Berwanger, Nikolaus
(intellectual) 738, 745
Bessarabia 127, 211, 247,
266, 302, 314
Jews 395, 407-08
occupation of during
First World War 250
see also Moldova
Bessarabian Question
bibliographies 967
Bethlen, Istvan (Premier
of Hungary, 1921-31)
260
Bibliographies 957-77
Bessarabian Question 967
birds 94
Ceauşescu régime 974
COMECON 960
communism 967
constitutional
documents 977
demography 351
economic planning 977
economy 975
Edgar Allan Poe 962

English-language
publications 961, 963,
969, 976
foreign relations 965,
967, 977
German minority 968
history 965, 973
human rights 966
humanities 964
Hungarian minority 968
Jews 958, 968
languages 976
law 591, 977
literature 965, 976
military history 970
minorities 968
nationalism 972
social sciences 964, 974
state publications 977
statistics 977
Bibliography 885
Biographies 323, 325-26,
330, 337-38, 341-43,
347
Birds 95-96
bibliographies 94
see also individual
species by name, i.e.
Red-breasted goose
Birth patterns 353
Black Sea 634
Blaga, Lucian
(intellectual) 269,
721, 728, 742
Blandiana, Ana (poet)
743-44, 746-47, 750
Bobu, Emil (communist
politician) 946
Bodnăraş, Emil
(Romanian Minister
of Defence) 304
Bogdan, Ştefan 183
Border disputes 621, 953
Bossert, Rolf (poet) 730
Bota, Petru 370
Bourdieu, Pierre 547
Boyar class 8
18th century 220
Bracelets 846
Brăiloiu, Constantin 728
Brâncuşi, Constantin
(sculptor) 834, 840-
41, 845, 847

Brandy distilling 57
Braşov 18
housing 61
local politics 530
urbanization 64
Brătianu, Gheorghe
(historian) 134
Brătianu, Ion (Prime
Minister) 212,
249-50, 252
Brauner, Harry
(intellectual) 329
Brauner, Victor (artist)
715
Brazil
development 640
Breban, Nicolae (author)
729
Brîncoveneşti (village)
734
British Foreign Office
documents 284, 299
British Museum exhibition
106
British Public Record
Office
documents 321
Britz, Helmut (poet) 730
Bronze Age 119-20
Brooches 105
Brucan, Silviu
(intellectual) 327,
543
Bucharest 23, 25, 32, 34,
37, 64
19th century 8, 18
destruction of city
centre 30, 62, 72,
323
development of 72
First World War 10, 13
prisons 492
transport 690
Bucovina 32, 215, 266,
350
Jews 395, 407
monasteries 14
poetry 722
Budapest School 543
Budgets 649
Buildings
conservation 874
Bukovina *see* Bucovina

337

Periodicals *contd.*
  history 905, 908, 917,
    920-21, 934-35, 938,
    941
  industry 907
  judicial science 915
  language 908, 942
  linguistics 897, 904, 913
  literature 897, 902, 904-
    05, 908, 921, 934-35,
    938, 941-42
  meteorology 925
  minerals 926-27
  music 919
  palaeontology 928
  petrology 929
  philosophy 904, 914
  politics 899, 906, 940
  radio broadcasts 937
  social sciences 908
  sociology 930
  stratigraphy 931
  tectonics 932
  theatre 919
  Transylvania 941
Personality cults *see*
  Ceauşescu, Nicolae:
  cult of
Petraşcu, Gheorghe (artist)
  837, 877
Petrochemical industry
  675
Petroleum refining 675
Petrology
  periodicals 929
Petropavlosk monastery
  14
Phanariots 17, 19, 220,
  236, 246, 469
PHARE programme 632
Philhellenism 246
Philiki Etaireia 205
Philosophy 735
  periodicals 904, 914
Phonetics 427
Phonology 428
Phrasebooks 454
Pietroasa treasure 105,
  112
Pintile, Lucian (film-
  maker) 943
Piracy
  Roman period 166

Piţa, Dan (film-maker)
  943
Piteşti 40
Plămădeala, Antonie
  (Metropolitan of
  Ardeal) 481
Place-names 78-79
Planning 366, 650
Plays 758, 789, 818-19
Pleşoianu, Nicolae
  (patriot) 240
Ploieşti, air battle (1943)
  294
Pluralism *see*
  Democratization
Poetry 502, 714, 720, 740,
  753-55, 759-60, 763-
  65, 768, 773-74, 776,
  786-87, 793, 800,
  806, 814-17, 820,
  822-25, 828-30
  anthologies 742-46,
  749-52
  eroticism 720
  German-language
  745
  see also individual poets
  by name, i.e. Celan,
  Paul
Pogroms
  Bucharest (1941) 264
  Iaşi (1941) 296
Poineşti (cilivization) *see*
  Carpi
Poland
  housing 61, 71
  Jews 406
  law 588
  social structure 488
  women 502
Policy
  defence 532
  economic 531
  foreign 531
  military 531
Polish people
  mediaeval period 201
Political economy 486,
  519
  communist period 316
Political parties 552, 659,
  946, 952
  system 569

Politics 29, 34, 42, 955
  communist period 517-
  47
  local 502, 520, 532, 594
  periodicals 899, 906,
  940
  post-communist period
  548-77
  right-wing 288, 570
  see also Fascism; Iron
  Guard
  women's role 502
  see also Elections
Pollution 700
  air 702, 704
  noise 704
  soil 702, 704
  water 702, 704
Polytechnics 711
'Popeluc' (musical group)
  851
Popescu, Dumitriu Radu
  (author) 723, 729, 747
Poporanists (intellectual
  group) 135
'Popular war' doctrine
  601
Population 76, 91
  control 354
  growth 70
  statistics 696
  see also Demography
Posteucă, Vasile (poet)
  714
Praxis group 543
Prebisch, Raúl 640
Preda, Marin (author) 724,
  729, 772
Prehistory 108-10, 116-17,
  119
Press 888-89
  laws 583
  Romanian-language in
  the United States 893
  view of the United
  States 890
Prezan, Constantin 287
Pricolici (werewolves)
  367
Primo de Rivera, José
  Antonio 257
Printing
  history 127, 885

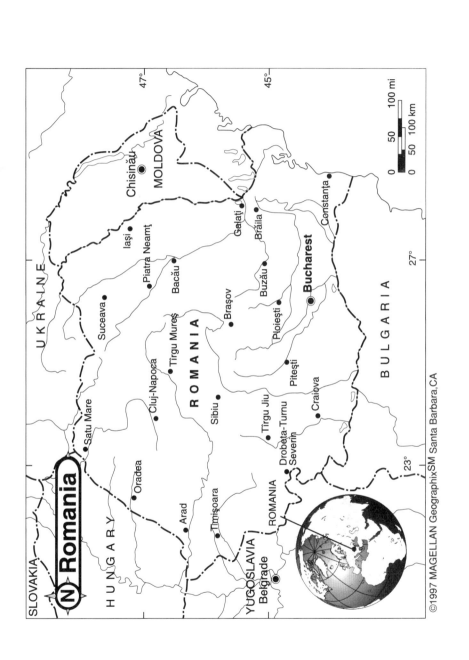

SLOVAKIA

N Romania

©1997 MAGELLAN GeographixSM Santa Barbara,CA

ALSO FROM CLIO PRESS

INTERNATIONAL ORGANIZATIONS SERIES

Each volume in the International Organizations Series is either devoted to one specific organization, or to a number of different organizations operating in a particular region, or engaged in a specific field of activity. The scope of the series is wide-ranging and includes intergovernmental organizations, international non-governmental organizations, and national bodies dealing with international issues. The series is aimed mainly at the English-speaker and each volume provides a selective, annotated, critical bibliography of the organization, or organizations, concerned. The bibliographies cover books, articles, pamphlets, directories, databases and theses and, wherever possible, attention is focused on material about the organizations rather than on the organizations' own publications. Notwithstanding this, the most important official publications, and guides to those publications, will be included. The views expressed in individual volumes, however, are not necessarily those of the publishers.

VOLUMES IN THE SERIES